6.61 P. Smith 9-68 (Gruffin)

America's Colonial Experiment ~ ~

AMERICA'S COLONIAL EXPERIMENT

How the United States Gained, Governed, and In Part Gave Away a Colonial Empire

by

JULIUS W. PRATT

Professor of American History
The University of Buffalo

GLOUCESTER, MASS.
PETER SMITH
1964

Preface ~ ~

It is the purpose of this volume to present a new synthesis of facts more or less familiar. Every diplomatic history of the United States tells the story of the acquisition of island possessions beginning with the Spanish-American War of 1898; though few such histories give as much analysis of motive as is here attempted. Every such history tells something of the establishment and subsequent surrender of protectorates in the Caribbean. Every book on American government has a chapter on the government of territories, including under that head such insular possessions as the Virgin Islands, Guam, and American Samoa; few such books, if any, have space for so much description of the evolution of those governments as is here presented. At least one volume, of some years ago, gave a brief account of the geography, ethnography, and economy of the American possessions. Much has changed since that volume was published. Numerous monographs tell separately the story of American policy and its achievements in the individual territories and possessions. No writer, so far as I am aware, has undertaken to bring together in a single volume the story of the rise and decline of imperialist sentiment in the United States, of the acquisition of America's overseas possessions, their government, their economic development and problems, and their political aspirations (achieved in the Philippines, current elsewhere). Yet all

v

those segments of history really form a whole—the story of an American experiment in colonialism, or imperialism —its motives, its methods, its achievements, and its present status. It is that story that I have attempted to tell in the present volume. I hope it may have some value to students of diplomatic, constitutional, and economic history, to political scientists interested in colonial government, to economists interested in the economics of empire, to laymen who are amateurs in one or more of these fields of knowledge·

I am happy to acknowledge my indebtedness for facilities placed at my disposal by the Library of Congress, Widener Library of Harvard University, the Grosvenor Library and Lockwood Memorial Library of Buffalo and for documents and other information supplied by the Division of Territories and Island Possessions, Department of the Interior, the Office of Island Governments, Navy Department, and Mr. George H. McLane of the Hawaii Statehood Commission, Washington. To Professor Rupert Emerson of Harvard University I am under obligation for information derived from his service in, and long acquaintance with, the Division of Territories and Island Possessions. Various chapters of the volume were read and helpfully criticized by Mr. Barnet Nover of the Washington Bureau of the *Denver Post* and by my colleagues at the University of Buffalo, Professors John Clarke Adams, Selig Adler, John T. Horton, and John D. Sumner. Miss Elizabeth R. Seymour and Mrs. Mabel S. Munschauer gave valuable assistance in preparing the manuscript and in checking footnotes and bibliography, and my wife assisted me in typing, editing, and countless other ways.

Julius W. Pratt

Table of Contents ~ ~

Table of Maps ~ ~

America's Colonial Experiment ～ ～

CHAPTER ONE

Pause at the Water's Edge ~ ~

Two Kinds of Expansion

Two related characteristics marked the territorial growth
of the United States during its first century of independence. First, that growth consisted of the acquisition,
step by step, of contiguous mainland territory; secondly,
each bit of territory so acquired was destined, by law
and in fact, to become an integral part of the United
States, to be admitted to the union of states with all the
rights and privileges of the original members. This was
true in law because each treaty of acquisition from the
Louisiana purchase in 1803 to the Gadsden purchase 50
years later promised both citizenship for the inhabitants
and incorporation for the territory. It could be made true
in fact because the areas thus acquired were so sparsely
settled that they presented no serious problem of assimilation of alien cultures. Their empty spaces invited migration from the growing population of the older states,
and the migrants quickly introduced into each new area
the habits, values, and institutions of their own civilization. Until population was sufficient to warrant statehood, the new areas were placed under a unique species
of temporary colonial government known as the territorial system. Expansion of this kind was not imperialism.

1

Imperialism began when American sovereignty was extended over lands already thickly settled, whose populations were so different from Americans in political institutions and habits, and even in language, that their assimilation into the American state system was impossible or of dubious feasibility. After the Spanish-American War of 1898, there was a distinction between ruled and rulers under the American flag; for although the people of the new possessions were given as much local self-government as they seemed capable of using, they had no share in shaping national policy, no votes in Congress, no voice, unless Congress chose to give it to them, in determining what their own future status should be. The territorial status, which for others had been temporary, for them seemed likely to be permanent. They were colonials, and the United States had become an empire.

The United States followed its acquisition of colonies (though that term was never officially used) by extending various kinds and degrees of control over certain of its small neighbors, which remained nominally independent. This establishment of protectorates (another term not in the official vocabulary) was a second phase of imperialism—a passing phase only.

To say that the United States became an empire in 1898 is not to condemn or even to criticize the course it followed. "Imperialism" has often been used as a term of reproach. It was so used by the critics of American expansionist policy in the 1890's, and even earlier. Today it has become a stock expression in the Marxist vocabulary, connoting, to the leftist mind, both the wickedness and the decay of capitalism. There is no reason why Americans should feel ashamed of their experiment in imperialism. They entered upon it from a variety of motives—economic, strategic, and benevolent. Rudyard Kipling's poem, "The White Man's Burden"—written to welcome the United States into the circle of imperial powers—expressed a concept sincerely held by many expansionists, both British and American. Only the naïve assume that a relationship of ruled and rulers is necessarily and always bad. Peoples of primitive or retarded cultures, thrust into the currents of advanced international politics and economics, may need guardians to guide and direct their development and to give them government and protection while they learn to care for themselves in the modern world. Those who have fallen under the guardianship of the United States have fared well in the main. No one would claim perfection for American colonial policy; yet it is true that that policy, although often haphazard and occasionally inconsistent in implementation, has aimed steadily at the material and educational advancement of the colonial peoples and the development of their capacity for self-government. American imperialism has, on the whole, been benevolent, and it has been so accepted by those living under it. The Filipinos resisted at first; but then acquiesced with good grace in temporary rule by the United States. Later they were given independence, even against the better judgment of some of their wiser leaders. For the terms on which that independence was granted Americans may properly feel some twinges of conscience. No other people living under the American flag have (since the days of Jefferson Davis) seriously demanded independence. Some of them have grumbled at American rule, but always with a realization that its benefits outweigh its burdens. Meanwhile they have attained steadily expanding shares in their own government.

That imperialism came only when island possessions were acquired was an accident. In reality, the extension of American rule over Indian tribes and their lands was imperialism—not recognized as such only because the Indians were so few in numbers as to be virtually swallowed up in the growing white population. Conversely, the annexation of Hawaii, where American culture was already predominant, was not an authentic instance of imperialism. Full statehood for Hawaii was always a possibility. Imperialism, as generally recognized, began with the acquisition of Puerto Rico and the Philippines, whose people were of alien culture and wholly unacquainted with American political ideals and techniques. It might have begun much earlier, with the acquisition of other islands (or continental territories like Central America) of non-Anglo-Saxon culture. Why it did not begin earlier, why it did begin in the 1890's—these are the themes of this chapter.

MANIFEST DESTINY HESITATES

Except for Alaska,[1] the continental growth of the United States was completed by the Gadsden purchase treaty of 1853. The United States now stretched from sea to sea. Its northern and southern boundaries, despite occasional covetous glances toward Canada and Mexico, were to prove stable. Further territorial expansion, if any there was to be, must bridge the waters of the Gulf of Mexico or the Pacific Ocean.

Why did American expansion, hitherto enthusiastic
and almost continuous, falter for half a century at the
water's edge? Certainly it was not because of fear of the
water, for Americans were well accustomed to going to
sea. It was not for lack of leaders—Manifest Destiny
statesmen—who urged the importance of island possessions. Presidents Polk, Pierce, and Buchanan sought in
vain to purchase Cuba. Narciso Lopez thrice organized
on American soil filibustering expeditions against that
island, and three American diplomats abroad declared,
in the "Ostend Manifesto," that the United States would
be justified in wresting Cuba from Spain if Spain refused
to sell it and if, in Spanish hands, it menaced the peace
and tranquillity of the United States. William Walker,
"the gray-eyed man of destiny," set up a short-lived filibustering régime in Nicaragua. President Buchanan
vainly asked Congress for authority to establish a protectorate over Central America. Commodore Matthew
Calbraith Perry, the opener of Japan, and Dr. Peter
Parker, missionary and United States commissioner to
China, both urged that the United States acquire island
footholds in the Far East—the Bonins, the Ryukyus, Formosa—to match England's newly won base at Hong
Kong. Responsible statesmen were not ready to go so far
afield as Perry and Parker proposed. Secretary of State
Lewis Cass, who had once boasted in the Senate that he
had "a capacious swallow for territory," informed
Parker's successor in China (1857) that the United
States had no "motives either for territorial aggrandizement or the acquisition of political power in that distant
region." But nearer American shores President Pierce
permitted his agent in Hawaii to negotiate a treaty of

annexation (not ratified by the Hawaiian government), and President Buchanan authorized an informal proposal for the purchase of Alaska from Russia.

These pre-Civil War expansionists—the politicians named were all Democrats—had their emulators among Republican leaders of the postwar decade. William H. Seward, Secretary of State from 1861 to 1869, had long believed that the United States was destined to play a great rôle in the Pacific. In harmony with that belief, Seward negotiated the purchase of Alaska from Russia when the opportunity was presented (1867), informed the United States minister in Hawaii that annexation of the Hawaiian Islands was "deemed desirable by this Government," collaborated with European powers in the advancement of commercial intercourse with China and Japan, and proposed a joint American-French military demonstration against Korea to open the "Hermit Kingdom" to western trade.

Seward was equally convinced that American interests in the Isthmian and Caribbean area demanded an aggressive policy. He negotiated canal treaties with Nicaragua and Colombia (the latter never ratified). He arranged with Denmark for the purchase of the two Danish West Indian islands of St. Thomas and St. John, the former embracing the beautiful and capacious harbor of Charlotte Amalie, only to see his treaty pigeon-holed in the Senate. He then turned to dicker with dictator-presidents of Santo Domingo for either the purchase of a naval base, Samana Bay, on the coast of that island or the outright annexation of the republic by the United States. The conditions of the moment, whether in Santo Domingo or in the American Congress, were adverse to the success of this enterprise, but Seward left as a monument to his zeal for expansion a passage in Andrew Johnson's annual message to Congress of December 9, 1868.

> Comprehensive national policy [the message declared] would seem to sanction the acquisition and incorporation into our Federal Union of *the several adjacent continental and insular communities* as speedily as it can be done peacefully, lawfully, and without any violation of national justice, faith, or honor.[2]

Ulysses S. Grant, who assumed the Presidency as Seward relinquished the State Department, took up the Santo Domingo scheme where Seward had left it. Influenced by unscrupulous American speculators in the island, and against the better judgment of his able Secretary of State, Hamilton Fish, Grant gave his approval to the negotiation of a treaty of annexation and attempted with characteristic persistence to drive it through the Senate. He was apparently sincere in his contention that the poverty-stricken republic would flourish mightily under the blessings of American sovereignty and would be of great economic and strategic importance to the United States. But his arguments failed to convince a recalcitrant Senate and the treaty died, in spite of the report of a reputable commission which investigated conditions in Santo Domingo and endorsed Grant's view.

Grant's susceptibility to the pressures of businessmen and speculators was responsible also for his interest in the distant Samoan Islands. In this case it was the head of a steamship company running steamers between San Francisco and Australia and New Zealand who drew the President's attention to the fine qualities of Pago Pago harbor in the Samoan isle of Tutuila. An American naval officer negotiated with the native chief of Tutuila a treaty giving the United States exclusive rights in Pago Pago harbor in return for assumption by the United States of a protectorate over the native government. Sent to the Senate with Grant's qualified endorsement, the Samoan treaty was never brought to a vote.

Grant was also desirous of seeing Canada annexed to the United States and was at least sympathetic to the proposal of Senator Charles Sumner of Massachusetts that Great Britain make amends for alleged unneutral behavior during the Civil War by ceding to the United States her North American provinces. The principal obstacle in the path of this and other postwar schemes for the annexation of Canada was the reluctance of the Canadian people themselves to submit to such a union. The creation of the Dominion of Canada by the British North America Act of 1867 brought new strength to the rising sentiment of Canadian nationalism and removed whatever chance there may previously have been for voluntary union with the United States. /

Projects of overseas expansion were almost continually held before Congress and the public during the two decades immediately preceding and following the Civil War. The failure of some of them may be explained partly by the unwillingness of foreign governments to cooperate. Spain was certainly not willing to part with Cuba, nor was Hawaii yet ready to surrender its independence. But with few exceptions, when favorable action was requested from the Senate or Congress—the approval of a treaty, the appropriation of funds (for instance, to support the Executive in attempts to purchase Cuba), or authority to establish a protectorate—such action was refused in no uncertain terms; and the general public, to all appearances, supported its representatives in their refusal. (

(Why was the country not willing to follow its expansionist leaders in adventures in the Pacific, Central America, or the Caribbean? In the prewar years the answer is clear. Most of the expansionist schemes proposed by Pierce and Buchanan pointed southward—to Cuba, Mexico, or Central America. This fact was enough to damn them, in the eyes of antislavery men of the North, as devices for the extension of slave territory; and although this charge had little truth except in relation to Cuba, the entire Pierce-Buchanan program of expansion was opposed almost unanimously by the Republican party, whose major tenet was resistance to the extension of slavery. (

(The reasons for the failure of the plans of Seward and Grant are more complicated. The treaty with Denmark was sent to the Senate before Congress had appropriated the funds required to compensate Russia for Alaska. The $7,500,000 that Seward proposed to pay for two diminutive Caribbean islands, coming on the heels of the $7,200-000 to be paid for Alaska, struck many congressmen as a rank piece of extravagance, especially at a time when the United States was burdened with a large war debt. While the treaty was pending, furthermore, the islands were devastated in the course of a few days by a hurricane, an earthquake, and a tidal wave. Legislators already accustomed to thinking of Alaska as a dreary waste of glaciers and icebergs were naturally skeptical of the value of tropical islands subject to even more uncomfortable natural phenomena.

President Grant's Santo Domingo project was less extravagant in terms of money—the price of annexation was to be merely assumption of the Dominican debt to a maximum figure of $1,500,000—but it had other objectionable features. The whole scheme exuded an odor of corruption, of connivance with an unprincipled native dictator, of high-handed use of United States naval forces to intimidate opposition in Santo Domingo itself and in the neighboring republic of Haiti. The plan was also denounced as "imperialism" (the first use of that term, so far as is known, by opponents of American expansionist policy). Thus Senator Thomas F. Bayard of Delaware warned that to adopt the policy proposed by President Grant would be to

> embark the Government of the United States upon the vast and trackless sea of imperialism, to change it into an imperial Government of outlying and distant dependencies with a foreign population, strangers to us in race, in blood, in customs, political, social, moral, and religious.

And Carl Schurz, at this time a senator from Missouri, argued that to govern tropical islands as dependencies—"satrapies"—would "demoralize and corrupt our political life beyond any degree yet conceived of"; to incorporate them as states, on the other hand, would be to admit into Congress "people who . . . have neither language, nor traditions, nor habits, nor political institutions, nor morals in common with us; . . . does not your imagination [he asked] recoil from the picture?"[3]

It may be guessed, however, that such active antagonism as appeared in these arguments had less to do with the discomfiture of Seward and Grant than simple popular apathy toward overseas adventures. The country was absorbed in its political and economic domestic problems. The earlier enthusiasm for Manifest Destiny had abated. Congress and the public simply could not see the need for islands far off in the Pacific Ocean or even nearer at hand in the Caribbean. Seward confessed as much. Public attention, he wrote in 1868,

> continues to be fastened upon the domestic questions which have grown out of the late civil war. The public mind refuses to dismiss these questions even so far as to entertain the higher but more remote questions of national extension and aggrandizement. . . .[4]

The only tangible fruits, accordingly, of the expansionist diplomacy of two decades were the strip of arid territory purchased by Gadsden in 1853, Alaska, bought by Seward in 1867, and Midway Island, occupied and claimed for the United States by the navy in the same year. To these should be added some dozens of tiny islands, most of them in the Pacific, claimed as "appurtenances" of the United States, under authority of a statute of 1856, by reason of valuable deposits of guano discovered thereon by American sea captains.

Certain rights of use in transit routes in the Isthmian region the United States had also acquired. By a treaty with New Granada (later Colombia) signed in 1846, the United States secured for its citizens and government equality of treatment with the citizens and government of New Granada in any means of transit across the Isthmus of Panama. In return the United States undertook to guarantee peaceful use of the transit route and the sovereignty of Colombia in the Isthmus. Similar rights, with less comprehensive guarantees, were obtained from Nicaragua in 1867. By the Gadsden treaty with Mexico of 1853 the United States secured special rights of use in a proposed "plank and rail road" across the Isthmus of Tehuantepec and the right to extend its protection to the route when "warranted by the public or international law."

From asserting any exclusive rights in or control over the various Isthmian canal routes the United States was estopped by the Clayton-Bulwer Treaty with Great Britain. This instrument, signed in 1850, settled a conflict of British and American interests in Central America by an agreement that neither power would seek exclusive control of any canal route and that any canal that might be constructed should be neutralized and receive their joint protection.

On the whole, the course of American expansion seemed to have reached an end by the middle 1870's. The Alaska treaty had been accepted with misgivings, but all subsequent attempts by the Executive to secure further accessions of territory had been firmly rejected by the Senate. The American people were apparently satisfied with the continental area already in their possession and quite uninterested in joining in the international competition for island colonies. Only a radical change in national thought and feeling could give adequate support to a new program of expansion. The change was not to be conspicuous until the 1890's, but in the interval the public was never allowed to forget completely that the United States did, after all, have a stake in certain strategic spots beyond its borders. The questions of who should build and control an Isthmian canal, of what great power should make a colony of Samoa, of what should be the future status of Hawaii were never for long kept out of the pages of American newspapers.

THE ISTHMIAN CANAL QUESTION

In 1881 a French corporation headed by Ferdinand de Lesseps, builder of the Suez Canal, operating under a concession from the government of Colombia, began the digging of a canal through the Isthmus of Panama. The prospect of a canal at Panama under European auspices was not relished in the United States. It was denounced as being in violation of the Monroe Doctrine. It brought from President Rutherford B. Hayes, certainly no chauvinist, a declaration that "The policy of this country is a canal under American control." An Isthmian canal, he continued, would be "virtually a part of the coast line of the United States," and it was "the right and duty of the United States to assert and maintain such supervision and authority over any interoceanic canal . . . as will protect our national interests."[5] Hayes had voiced what was to become accepted American opinion—that sound national policy called for a canal controlled exclusively by the United States.

No attempt was made, however, to interfere with the operations of the French company. Instead, Congress chartered an American corporation, the Maritime Canal Company of Nicaragua, to exploit the rival Nicaraguan route, while American Secretaries of State strove in vain to induce Great Britain to abrogate or amend the Clayton-Bulwer Treaty and thus open the way for a canal nationally owned or controlled. By the early 1890's the French company had gone bankrupt with only a minor portion of its work completed, and the Maritime Canal Company had failed to raise funds for its enterprise. It was evident that the United States government alone possessed the resources and the ability to do the work. The barrier to such a course was the Clayton-Bulwer Treaty.

INTERNATIONAL RIVALRY IN SAMOA

In Samoa, a colorful American, Colonel A. B. Steinberger, first sent to the islands by President Grant on a tour of investigation, had ingratiated himself with the natives, stopped their civil wars, supplied them with a constitution, and been made their "prime minister." For reasons not altogether clear, his activities became so objectionable to the consular agents of the United States and Great Britain that they joined forces to deport him on a British cruiser. His departure in 1876 left native politics in confusion. The government that he had set up continued to look to the United States for aid, and in 1878 a Samoan delegation visited Washington in quest of a treaty of protection or annexation. The Samoans were told that such a treaty could not pass the Senate. They accepted instead a treaty by which the United States agreed merely to use its "good offices" for the adjustment of differences that might arise between Samoa and any other government "in amity with the United States." In return the United States received the right to establish a coaling station in Pago Pago harbor.

The right thus acquired was evidently the source of the almost neurotic intensity with which the United States henceforth prosecuted its rivalry with German and British interests in Samoa. American economic interests in the islands were insignificant. The Samoan economy was dominated by Germany. A Hamburg firm, Godeffroy and Son, had acquired much valuable plantation property, and it and its successor conducted most of the export business of the islands from the port of Apia, island of Upolu. The new German Empire, after Bismarck's conversion to colonialism in 1884, supported German interests so aggressively that British and Americans were in danger of being squeezed out. The British were ready to concede Germany a *quid* in Samoa for a *quo* elsewhere. Not so the Americans. A three-power conference in Washington in 1887 failed to settle the controversy. When Germany thereafter deported one Samoan "king" and set up his rival under German protection, the United States espoused the native faction that forcibly resisted German domination. Though there had been no clear violation by Germany of American treaty rights, there was much reckless war talk in the United States. American naval vessels were ordered to Samoa, and William C. Whitney, Secretary of the Navy, opined that the United States would be "disgraced" by submission to German aggression.

It is barely possible that shooting might have started in Samoan waters in March, 1889 had not a timely hurricane strewn the American and German cruisers as wrecks on the reefs and beaches of Apia harbor. It is unlikely that such shooting would have led to war, however, for already the three governments concerned had agreed to a new conference to be held in Berlin. Here at last compromise proved possible. The Treaty of Berlin, signed June 14, 1889, paid lip-service to Samoan "independence" but in reality set up a three-power protectorate or condominium. Germany restored the deported king—Malietoa Laupepa—to his Samoan throne, and the Samoan natives were given the privilege of choosing his successors; but real power thereafter resided in a foreign chief justice, named by the three governments, a foreign land commission, and a municipal council for Apia with a president likewise chosen by the three powers. The arrangement, though a clumsy one, was a victory for American policy. It prevented German political domination and preserved American rights in Pago Pago. Though it did not work without friction, it did prevent serious international controversy during the ten years of its operation.

TOWARD HAWAIIAN ANNEXATION

A glance at a map of the Pacific Ocean will show that Hawaii is as naturally an appurtenance of North America as Samoa is of Australia or New Zealand. American interest in Hawaii was geographically as natural and legitimate as that in Samoa was fortuitous and artificial. Historically as well as geographically the interest of the United States in Hawaii was predominant. Though the discoverer of the Hawaiian—or, as they were then called, the Sandwich—Islands was the English explorer, Captain James Cook, American commercial interests were uppermost from the 1790's. In 1820 American traders were followed by American missionaries, who rapidly converted the native Polynesian population to Christianity and in other respects did much to mold local culture, politics, and government.

The special relation of Hawaii to the United States was recognized as early as 1842, when President John Tyler and Secretary of State Daniel Webster asserted that although the United States had no intention of annexing the islands, it could not consent to their annexation by any other power. The expansionist administration of Franklin Pierce, as previously mentioned, encouraged the negotiation of a treaty of annexation, which was never ratified, and Secretary Seward did not conceal his desire for annexation. Proposed treaties of commercial reciprocity failed of ratification in 1855 and 1867, partly, on the latter occasion, because certain senators feared that reciprocity might stand in the way of annexation. In 1875, however, a third attempt at reciprocity succeeded. A warning that Hawaiian sugar planters, if they failed to obtain a free market in the United States, might divert both their trade and their political attachments to the British Empire, proved efficacious in securing American consent to the treaty.

The reciprocity treaty of 1875 was terminable by either party after seven years. A renewal treaty was negotiated in 1884, but the United States Senate, before approving it in 1887, attached an amendment by which the United States was to enjoy the exclusive right to the use of Pearl River Harbor in the island of Oahu as a coaling and repair station for its naval vessels. The reciprocity arrangement was thus extended to 1894 at least, and the United States was free during the same period to develop and use Pearl Harbor—a privilege of which it made no use.

The free American market provided by the reciprocity treaty gave a great stimulus to Hawaiian sugar production, which multiplied tenfold in the next 20 years. It also made Hawaiian prosperity so dependent upon the American market that a change in American tariff policy in 1890—admitting other foreign sugar on equal terms with Hawaiian and giving a bounty to American domestic producers—brought about an economic crisis, and contributed to a political crisis, in the Hawaiian kingdom.

The imperfect integration of two cultures in Hawaii had resulted in the existence side by side of a modern system of economy and a monarchical government which retained primitive features. The dissolute and corrupt behavior of the last-but-one of the native monarchs— King Kalakaua, 1874-1891—invited revolution. In a bloodless coup in 1887, leaders of the white business community forced on Kalakaua a new constitution, which effectually clipped his wings, making his ministers (without whose consent he could perform no official act) responsible to the legislature and so restricting the suffrage as to make the legislature appear securely under the control of the propertied classes.

Kalakaua was succeeded in 1891 by his sister, Liliuokalani. Educated in the mission schools, active in local philanthropies, a composer of musical lyrics of some merit, "Queen Lil" was not endowed with political sagacity. She made no secret of her ambition to recover for herself and her native subjects the prerogatives and rights that her brother had signed away. In laying such plans, she underestimated the ability and determination of the white élite who had compelled Kalakaua to accept the reforms of 1887. Filled with apprehension at the course the queen might follow, and suffering from the economic depression induced by the change in American tariff policy, many white businessmen and lawyers in the islands came to look upon annexation by the United States as a guarantee of both stable government and economic prosperity. They therefore planned to persuade or compel Liliuokalani to abdicate and then to offer the islands to the United States. One of their leaders, Lorrin A. Thurston, visited Washington in the spring of 1892 and received definite encouragement from members of President Benjamin Harrison's cabinet and from leaders in Congress.

Not until January, 1893 did the revolutionists find a suitable occasion to carry out their plan. Their cue came in an announcement from the queen that she proposed to proclaim a new constitution—an act which itself would have been unconstitutional and revolutionary. The annexationists immediately formed a committee of safety, set up a provisional government, and demanded the queen's abdication. Their course had the sympathetic support of United States Minister John L. Stevens, who landed troops from the cruiser *Boston* and so disposed them as to give the impression that they would, if necessary, defend the provisional government, to which Stevens also granted precipitate *de facto* recognition. In this situation there was no course for the queen but to yield her authority, as she said, "to the superior force of the United States of America," until such time as the United States government should "undo the action of its representative" and reinstate her "as the constitutional sovereign of the Hawaiian Islands."

The provisional government at once dispatched a commission to Washington to negotiate a treaty of annexation. In the negotiation they met with no serious difficulty, and on February 15 President Harrison sent to the Senate a treaty providing for the annexation of the Hawaiian Islands as "an integral part of the territory of the United States" and for the payment to the deposed queen of a life annuity of $20,000. The treaty might well have received Senate approval had not the President-elect, Grover Cleveland, let it be known that he preferred to have it left for him to deal with after the fourth of March. One of Cleveland's first acts as President was to withdraw the Hawaiian treaty from the Senate "for the purpose of re-examination." A few days later he appointed a former Democratic congressman, James H. Blount of Georgia, a special commissioner to the Hawaiian Islands to investigate the character of the annexation movement and especially to report to the President whether Minister Stevens had played an improper part in the revolution and whether annexation was desired by any large proportion of the natives or only by the ruling clique of whites.

Blount's investigation convinced both him and President Cleveland, first, that the revolution would not have been attempted and could not have been carried out without the encouragement and support of Minister Stevens; second, that the great majority of the native people were supporters of the queen and opposed to annexation. Cleveland, therefore, not only declined to return the annexation treaty to the Senate, but concluded, somewhat quixotically, that he was under a moral obligation to undo "the great wrong done to a feeble but independent State" by restoring the queen to her throne. But when Cleveland's minister, Albert S. Willis, sent to Honolulu for this purpose, had secured from Liliuokalani a reluctant promise of amnesty for the revolutionists, he received from the provisional government an unqualified refusal of his demand that they step down and make way for restoration of the ex-queen. Only the superior armed force of the United States, said Hawaiian President Sanford B. Dole, could compel the provisional government (which the United States had formally recognized) to give up its authority.

Unprepared to make war on the provisional government—to right one wrong by committing another—Cleveland referred the whole matter to Congress, which resolved that nothing be done. In Hawaii a constitutional convention, held in 1894, provided the body politic with a regular republican constitution that perpetuated the power of the white minority who had overthrown the queen. The new instrument worked smoothly; a small royalist uprising in 1895 was easily suppressed; a new United States tariff in 1894 restored Hawaiian sugar to its favored position in the American market. The Hawaiian republic enjoyed several years of peace and prosperity, but its leaders never lost sight of their chief desire—annexation by the United States. They could only wait patiently until a turn in the political wheel should bring into power in Washington an administration willing to reverse the policy of Grover Cleveland.

New Prophets of Expansion

It was suggested earlier in this chapter that a prerequisite to the adoption of any program of colonial expansion would be a radical change in the attitude of

the American people. So long as public opinion displayed
that apathy to "questions of national extension and aggrandizement" of which Seward had complained, no
expansionist President or Secretary of State could hope
to see his plans fare well at the hands of Congress or the
Senate. When Cleveland declined the opportunity to
annex the Hawaiian Islands, such a change had actually
come about—so much so that Cleveland's "little America" policy was widely denounced in Congress and the
press by Republicans generally and even by some Democrats. Expansion had again become popular; a new phase
of Manifest Destiny had begun; the Republican party
had revived that very phrase in 1892 and in 1896 was to
write a specific expansionist program into its platform.
The same party, after fighting a war with Spain and
acquiring a colonial empire, was to win easily at the polls
in 1900. The opinion of the majority appeared to support the expansionists.

The reasons for this change in popular psychology are
not susceptible of precise definition or measurement. It
is possible, however, to point to certain intellectual currents and certain material facts that help to account
for the change.[6]

Of considerable importance in this shift in American
public opinion was the popularization in the United
States of the evolutionary philosophy of Charles Darwin,
the English naturalist. Darwin had published in 1859 his
epoch-making volume, *The Origin of Species*, and had
followed it 12 years later with *The Descent of Man*. Although Darwin was concerned primarily with biology,
his hypothesis of the evolution of higher life-forms
through natural selection—the "survival of the fittest" in

the "struggle for existence"—was easily adaptable to sociological theorizing, and his American interpreters made the most of it.[7] If a ruthless struggle for existence among individuals resulted in the survival and predominance of the "fittest," or biologically "best," a similar struggle among races or nations might be expected to produce similar results. Thus ruthless international competition was justified in the name of "progress." This was uncomfortable doctrine for the weak and "unfit," but gratifying to a nation like the United States, which felt no doubt of its superior virtues and capabilities.

Prominent among Americans who made this application of Darwinian theory were two popular writers, John Fiske, the historian, and Josiah Strong, a Congregational clergyman. Fiske, in an essay entitled "Manifest Destiny," published in *Harper's Magazine* in 1885 and in book form in the same year, wrote glowingly of the superior quality of Anglo-Saxon institutions and of the growing numbers and power of the Anglo-Saxon race. The work begun when the English race first colonized America, he wrote,

> is destined to go on until every land on the earth's surface that is not already the seat of an old civilization shall become English in its language, in its religion, in its political habits and traditions, and to a predominant extent in the blood of its people. . . . The race thus spread over both hemispheres, and from the rising to the setting sun, will not fail to keep that sovereignty of the sea and that commercial supremacy which it began to acquire when England first stretched its arm across the Atlantic to the shores of Virginia and Massachusetts.

Josiah Strong, in a widely circulated volume entitled *Our Country: Its Possible Future and Its Present Crisis,* also published in 1885, preached a similar doctrine, invoking Darwinian biology and the divine will in the same breath. The Anglo-Saxon, he declared, "divinely commissioned to be . . . his brother's keeper," was being prepared by God for the final competition of races.

> Then this race of unequaled energy . . . will spread itself over the earth. If I read not amiss, this powerful race will move down upon Mexico, down upon Central and South America, out upon the islands of the sea, over upon Africa and beyond. And can anyone doubt that the result of this competition of races will be the "survival of the fittest"?

Five years after Fiske and Strong gave their half-baked ideas to the world, America's leading political scientist, Professor John W. Burgess of Columbia University, published a pretentious work in which, from a different approach, he reached conclusions equally flattering to Anglo-Saxons, though other "Teutonic" peoples were included in his formula.[8] From two years of study in German universities, Burgess had returned to the United States with the conviction that the Teutonic races, Germans and Anglo-Saxons, excelled all other peoples, past and present, in their talent for government. As architects of the national state, they had, so Burgess asserted, found "the most modern and the most complete solution of the whole problem of political organization which the world has as yet produced." Such abilities were too valuable to be kept at home. Since "by far the larger part of the surface of the globe is inhabited by populations which have not succeeded in establishing civilized states," and since "there is no human right to the status of barbarism," the Teutonic nations were "called to carry the political civilization of the modern world into those parts of the world inhabited by unpolitical and barbaric races; *i.e.,* they must have a colonial policy." This was a matter not only of right but of duty. Thus the expansion of the United States into backward and misgoverned areas, which Fiske and Strong had seen as destiny, took on, in Burgess's teaching, the character of an obligation to civilization.[9]

The writings of all these men were widely read, and it may fairly be assumed that they did much to shape public opinion in the United States. Theodore Roosevelt, leading expansionist of a few years later, attended Burgess's lectures at Columbia, and it is not difficult to detect the Burgess influence in certain of his later pronouncements, as well as in those of another enthusiastic expansionist, Senator Albert J. Beveridge.[10]

A fourth writer, about whose influence on public opinion and public men there cannot be the slightest doubt, was Captain (later Rear Admiral) Alfred Thayer Mahan of the navy. In the year of Burgess's treatise (1890) Mahan published his own masterpiece, *The Influence of Sea Power upon History, 1660-1783.* The simple thesis of this work was that a wise cultivation of sea power had raised England in a century and a quarter from a second-rate power to the world's most powerful state. From this, Mahan went on to the generalization that without sea power no nation could attain a position of first importance in the world. Being an intensely patriotic American, he was naturally anxious to see his own nation profit by the British example. Not only in his original book, but in essays published in various magazines throughout the 1890's,[11] he urged his fellow countrymen to build up their sea power in order that the United States might be enduringly prosperous and influential. Widely read and respected at home and abroad, friend and confidant of Theodore Roosevelt and Senator Henry Cabot Lodge, Mahan exerted a potent influence upon the current of affairs.

What was the nature of the "sea power" whose possession Mahan thought indispensable to national greatness? Broadly he defined it as "all that tends to make a people great upon the sea or by the sea." Thus it included commerce, merchant marine, navy, naval bases at strategic points, and overseas colonies. All of these England had. The United States had a growing commerce—most of it carried in ships under other flags; it had, when Mahan first wrote, only the rudimentary beginnings of a modern navy. Of colonies and outlying naval bases it had none at all. Without these, the ships of war of the United States, when it had built them, would

> be like land birds, unable to fly far from their own shores. To provide resting-places for them, where they can coal and repair, would be one of the first duties of a government proposing to itself the development of the power of the nation at sea.[12]

Specifically, in addition to the upbuilding of her navy, Mahan urged upon the United States the importance of acquiring bases in the Caribbean and the Pacific. Without American control of the Caribbean and the Isthmian region, the piercing of the isthmus by a canal would be "nothing but a disaster to the United States." Bases in the Caribbean, now in the hands of other powers, the United States must not obtain "by means other than righteous; but," he declared, with an obvious fling at the rejection of Seward's and Grant's annexation projects,

> a distinct advance will have been made when public opinion is convinced that we need them, and should not exert our utmost ingenuity to dodge them when flung at our head.[13]

Like Seward, Mahan foresaw a great commercial future in the Pacific. But he went further than Seward in his prophecy that that ocean would be the theater of a gigantic struggle between Western and Oriental civilizations—a struggle in which the United States would be in a front-line position. Hence the possession of outposts in the Pacific was of crucial importance. The issue of such a contest might well be determined by "a firm hold of the Sandwich [Hawaiian] Islands by a great, civilized, maritime power," and the United States was "naturally indicated as the proper guardian for this most important position."

Such were some of the prominent men of thought and letters who contributed to the rise of a new philosophy of Manifest Destiny in the 1880's and 1890's. Material events also played their part in producing the same result. The foreign trade of the United States doubled in the 30 years from 1870 to 1900, and the proportion of manufactured goods among its exports increased from 15 per cent to nearly 32 per cent in the same period. This meant competition with other industrial countries in world markets and eventually supplied an argument for the possession of colonies that would help to absorb the surplus; though not until 1898 did many businessmen become interested in solving their export problem in this manner. From the 1870's onward, moreover, the great powers of Europe were engaged in a new race for colonial possessions in Asia, in Africa, and among the islands of the Pacific—a race brought home to the United States by the triangular quarrel over Samoa. If there was, indeed, any virtue in colonies, the United States would need to act quickly in order to get its share. "The great nations," wrote Henry Cabot Lodge in 1895, "are rapidly absorbing for their future expansion and their present defence all the waste places of the earth. It is a movement which makes for civilization and the advancement of the race. As one of the great nations of the world, the United States must not fall out of the line of march."[14]

EXPANSION BECOMES A PARTY ISSUE

The administration of Benjamin Harrison (1889-1893) was the first to show substantial evidence that it had been influenced by the ideas and tendencies just described. Harrison's Secretary of the Navy, Benjamin F. Tracy, had either read the manuscript of Mahan's first great book or been otherwise indoctrinated with that author's sea power philosophy. He was the first naval secretary since the Civil War to propose the building of an up-to-date fighting fleet. His *Annual Report* of 1889 called for a fleet of 20 battleships, 12 for the Atlantic and 8 for the Pacific, equal to the best in armor, armament, and speed; and a Policy Board that he had appointed went further yet, proposing a navy of some 200 ships to be built at a cost of $350,000,000. Congress was not to be stampeded into such an ambitious program but did, in 1890, authorize the building of three first-class battleships, the *Indiana, Massachusetts,* and *Oregon,* which, with the *Iowa,* were to form the backbone of the fleet in the war with Spain in 1898.[15]

Harrison's first Secretary of State, James G. Blaine, emulated Seward and Grant in attempts to secure naval bases in Santo Domingo and Haiti. He failed because of political complications in the two island republics. Harrison himself urged Congress repeatedly but unavailingly to assist in the building of a Nicaragua canal by guaranteeing the bond issues of the Maritime Canal Company and acquiring in return, for the United States, ownership of all or a majority of the company's stock. Harrison, Tracy, and John W. Foster, Blaine's successor in the State Department, were all sympathetic to the proposal for annexation of Hawaii. They would probably have succeeded in accomplishing it by treaty if the opportunity had occurred before the Democratic victory of November, 1892.

When Cleveland's scruples resulted in the defeat of annexation, expansionist sentiment was strong enough to produce a prolonged and heated debate in Congress and the press. Although much of the argument dealt with subsidiary issues—the propriety of Stevens's behavior, the morals of the Hawaiian queen, the quixotism of Cleveland's attempt to reseat her upon her throne—the advocates and opponents of expansion as a national policy found opportunity to air their views. The fact, moreover, that the annexation treaty had been negotiated under a Republican President and repudiated by his

Democratic successor created a definite party alignment, and the Republicans emerged from the struggle as the avowed advocates of territorial expansion.[16]

The most persuasive argument for annexing the islands derived from their value as a naval station and a defensive outpost for the West Coast and the future Isthmian canal. Hawaii was widely spoken of as the "key to the Pacific." It was only natural that Captain Mahan and his disciples should put in their word on this point. Mahan himself greeted the proposal for annexation with an article on "Hawaii and Our Future Sea Power" in *The Forum* for March, 1893. The Hawaiian Islands, he wrote, were important "as a position powerfully influencing the commercial and military control of the Pacific, and especially of the Northern Pacific, in which the United States, geographically, has the strongest right to assert herself." Our possession of them would have, also, a negative importance in that it would prevent a potential enemy from gaining a base within striking distance of our Pacific Coast.

Among those who seconded Mahan's arguments were Senator Henry Cabot Lodge and Representative William F. Draper, of Massachusetts. Both had obviously acquainted themselves with *The Influence of Sea Power upon History.*

> Without sea power [said Lodge] no nation has been really great. Sea power consists, in the first place, of a proper navy and a proper fleet; but in order to sustain a navy we must have suitable ports for naval stations, strong places where a navy can be protected and refurnished.

Draper, like Mahan, pointed to the dependence of trade

upon the protection of navies and naval bases. The trade
of the Pacific, he predicted, was entering upon an era of
great activity, "and this trade belongs to the United
States, if we are wise enough to secure it." Other nations
—Great Britain, Germany, France—had been busily appropriating islands in the South Pacific, "and the United
States is the only great power interested in the Pacific
trade which has not had the wisdom to acquire territory
in localities where the great trade of the future will need
guarding and supplying."[17]

To all these men the annexation of Hawaii appeared
as but an important first step in a comprehensive program of expansion.

> This is no mere question of a particular act
> [wrote Mahan], . . . but of a principle, a policy,
> fruitful of many future acts, to enter upon which,
> in the fulness of our national progress, the time has
> now arrived.

In more specific terms, Draper called for the acquisition
of bases not only in Hawaii but in Samoa and the Straits
of Magellan; with these and with a proper fleet, he said,
the United States would "hold the Pacific as an American
ocean, dominated by American commercial enterprise
for all time." Lodge said nothing of the Straits of Magellan but added to Draper's other items the control of a
Nicaraguan canal and secure bases in the Caribbean.
Another Republican senator, J. N. Dolph of Oregon, re-
minded his colleagues of Grant's effort to secure Santo
Domingo. In all Grant's brilliant career, he asserted, the
Santo Domingo treaty "was the act which reflected more
credit upon his foresight, sagacity, ability, and patriot-

ism than any other." The time had come, added the Oregon senator, to accept Grant's ideas. "We must abandon the doctrine that our national boundaries and jurisdiction should be confined to the shores of the continent."[18]

Such ideas, expressed by leading Republicans in Congress and widely endorsed in the party press, clearly indicated the Republican "party line" on foreign policy in the presidential campaign of 1896. On the Democratic side, though western and southern sections of the party had quarreled with Cleveland over his stand on the silver question, his foreign policy had, except in his effort to restore the Hawaiian monarchy, received general support. Cleveland's anti-expansionist position was by now well defined. A staunch defender of the Monroe Doctrine, a supporter of moderate increases in the navy and of governmental backing for the proposed Nicaragua canal, Cleveland had stood firm against any reopening of the Hawaiian question and had proposed that the United States withdraw from the tripartite administration of Samoa. The proposed annexation of Hawaii he regarded (as he wrote in 1898) "as not only opposed to our national policy, but as a perversion of our national mission. The mission of our nation is to build up and make a greater country out of what we have, instead of annexing islands."[19] A similar faith had been avowed by certain Democratic senators, who had denounced the proposed incorporation into the Union of Hawaii, "that heterogeneous mixture of all the nations of the earth," and had denied that "a career of colonial aggrandizement" was in keeping with the past history or the existing necessities of the nation.[20]

Party lines were, therefore, rather clearly drawn in

relation to the issue of colonial expansion even before the formal opening of the presidential campaign of 1896. They were drawn yet more clearly in the planks on foreign policy in the party platforms of that year. Whereas the Democrats offered only an endorsement of the Monroe Doctrine, the Republicans called for a "firm, vigorous, and dignified" foreign policy, "a naval power commensurate with [the nation's] position and responsibility," control of the Hawaiian Islands, a Nicaragua canal "built, owned, and operated by the United States," and "a proper and much-needed naval station in the West Indies." They looked forward, furthermore, "to the eventual withdrawal of the European powers from this hemisphere, and to the ultimate union of all English-speaking parts of the continent by the free consent of its inhabitants." Though questions of foreign policy attracted little attention in the campaign, which was concerned chiefly with the demand of Democrats and Populists for the free and unlimited coinage of silver, the Republican victory in November gave assurance that the party of expansionist principles would control all branches of the government in Washington after March 4, 1897.

CHAPTER TWO

Dominion Beyond the Seas ~ ~

UNLIKE James K. Polk, who deliberately led the United States into a war for territorial expansion, William McKinley, elected to the presidency in November, 1896, became an expansionist by force of circumstance. As a member of Congress (1877-1891) he had made the tariff his principal preoccupation, and as governor of Ohio (1891-1895) he had had no occasion to take a stand on foreign policy. As the Republican candidate for the presidency against William Jennings Bryan, he had devoted most of his remarks to combating Democratic heresies with respect to money and the tariff. Taking office in the midst of a serious business depression, he hoped, like his friend and political sponsor, Mark Hanna, that his administration could be signalized by a "policy of domestic economic amelioration."[1] Foreign complications were the last thing that he desired. To Carl Schurz he gave verbal assurance that under his administration there would be "no jingo nonsense," no scheming for the annexation of Hawaii. The aging John Sherman, his first Secretary of State, was of like mind, "opposed to all acquisitions of territory not on the main land."[2]

Yet McKinley was soon to yield to the expansionist forces within the Republican party, and before he had been in the White House 14 months, the United States was involved in a war from which it emerged with a colonial empire in the Pacific and the Caribbean. What those expansionist forces were has been in part indicated in the preceding chapter. Important contributions had been made by the new Darwinian philosophy and by the sea power doctrines of Captain Mahan. A new spirit of self-assertiveness gripped a large section of the American public—a spirit which, as a discerning British observer remarked, was "preparing [in the United States] as much of a change as we saw in Japan the other day, and perhaps as sudden."[3] Men imbued with the new outlook had written into the Republican platform of 1896 planks calling for naval bases in the Caribbean and the Pacific. Henry Cabot Lodge was their leading spokesman in the Senate, and in the new administration Lodge's friend, young Theodore Roosevelt, Assistant Secretary of the Navy, applied his abundant energy and enthusiasm to the same objects.

The fact should be emphasized that the influences responsible for the new expansionism were as yet chiefly intellectual and emotional, not economic. Despite the growing importance of foreign markets for the surplus of America's industrial production, most businessmen were still unconvinced of the need for colonies. Colonies, in the eyes of the average businessman, were not only difficult and expensive to administer; they meant foreign complications, perhaps war. Rather than engage in risky colonial ventures, he preferred to rely on the high quality and low prices of American products to insure their entry into the world's markets. Not until the spring and summer of 1898 did changes in the international picture convince the American businessman that colonial possessions might be economically advantageous.[4]

HAWAIIAN ANNEXATION REVIVED

McKinley's first surrender to the expansionists was on the Hawaiian question.[5] The men who had organized and who governed the Hawaiian Republic had never abandoned the hope of annexation. While Cleveland sat in the White House, they could do nothing. Encouraged by the Hawaiian plank in the Republican platform and by indirect assurances of McKinley's friendliness, two Hawaiian commissioners called upon the new President on March 25, 1897 and reported to their government that the difference between the new administration and its predecessor was "the difference between daylight and darkness." Forgetful, apparently, of his promise to Carl Schurz, McKinley gave his consent to the negotiation of a new treaty of annexation, and such a treaty—providing for the annexation of Hawaii as a territory—was signed on June 16, 1897 and sent to the Senate on the same day.[6] The Senate took no action, however, prior to the adjournment of the special session of Congress.

Former opponents of annexation, Democrats and domestic sugar men, rallied to oppose the new treaty. "Did you ever see such a preposterous thing as the Hawaiian business?" wrote Grover Cleveland in a private letter. Liliuokalani, the ex-queen, lodged a protest with the State Department, as well she might, for the new treaty, unlike that of 1893, made no provision for annuities for former Hawaiian royalty. More startling was a protest from Japan, which had expressed satisfaction with the earlier proposal for annexation. Japan had now fought her first successful foreign war, with China in 1894-1895, and was launched upon her career as a world power. She had, furthermore, a special interest in the Hawaiian Islands, for Japanese were now the largest single racial group in the republic, outnumbering the native Hawaiians two to one and the whites six to one. Such "peaceful penetration," if allowed to continue, might easily convert Hawaii into a Japanese dependency; and at the moment when the annexation treaty was being negotiated in Washington, a sharp controversy had arisen between the Japanese and Hawaiian governments over an attempt of the latter to restrict Japanese immigration. "It is the white race against the yellow, . . ." declared a Honolulu newspaper. "Nothing but annexation can save the islands."

The Japanese government, averse to seeing such attractive islands "saved" for the white race, complained through its minister in Washington that annexation would disturb the international balance in the Pacific and would endanger certain rights of Japanese subjects in Hawaii. The response in Washington was prompt. Theodore Roosevelt, alarmed by the Hawaiian-Japanese controversy, had already declared to Mahan: "If I had my way we would annex those islands tomorrow. . . . I would . . . hoist our flag over the island leaving all details for after action." Now, while the State Department assured the Japanese minister that annexation would not jeopardize vested Japanese rights, secret instructions were sent to the commanding officer of the United States naval forces in Honolulu to raise the United States flag

and declare a provisional protectorate over the islands at
the first indication of a resort to force on the part of the
Japanese, and preparations were made to dispatch the
new battleship *Oregon* to Hawaii in case of need. The
United States stood ready to fight Japan, if necessary, to
protect Pearl Harbor. Whether these secret warlike preparations "leaked" to Tokyo is not known. At any rate,
the Japanese government professed itself satisfied with
the assurances given by the State Department, and in
December, 1897 its protest was withdrawn.[7]

The "yellow peril" in Hawaii, though it stimulated the
friends of annexation in the United States, failed to convert its opponents. By March, 1898 it was evident that
the treaty could never command a two-thirds majority
in the Senate. The alternative of a joint resolution had
already been considered, and on March 16 such a resolution was introduced in the Senate—only to languish there
until the war with Spain and the victory at Manila Bay
provided a new argument for the need of Pacific naval
bases.[8]

Civil War in Cuba

The war with Spain was itself not the product of an
expansionist urge in the United States, but of a distressing situation in Cuba which became intolerable to American sentiment. Spain's misgovernment of its Cuban colony had been notorious for many decades, and Cubans
had periodically risen in armed revolt to demand independence or at least autonomy. Reforms promised by the
Spanish government at the close of the Ten Years' War
(1868-1878) had ended slavery in Cuba but otherwise
had brought little relief to the Cuban people. The cost

of the war had been saddled upon the population of the unhappy island. Ninety per cent of the revenues collected in Cuba went either into service on the debt or into the pockets of Spanish officialdom and military in the island. Cuba continued under the autocratic rule of a Spanish captain general, and a benighted commercial policy hampered Cuba's trade with its neighbors, like the United States, and even laid heavy taxes on exports to Spain itself.[9]

An already bad situation was made worse by the world-wide economic depression that began in 1893, and by the United States tariff law of 1894, which reimposed a duty upon raw sugar from abroad. Tariff policy is legally and traditionally a matter of purely domestic concern, but it is noteworthy that the American tariffs of 1890 and 1894 contributed, respectively, to revolution in Hawaii and in Cuba. In the latter island, economic distress now combined with political discontent to produce an armed revolt against Spanish rule, which opened in February, 1895, and raged unabated until the United States intervened in April, 1898. A so-called republican government was set up in eastern Cuba where large sections fell under insurgent control, and a Cuban *junta* in New York dispensed propaganda and tried desperately to secure money and other aid from sympathetic Americans.

In Cuba the war was waged with ruthless ferocity on both sides. The insurgents made it their policy to destroy cane fields, sugar mills, and other property in the hope of thus rendering the island worthless to Spain. In February, 1896 the newly appointed captain general, Valeriano Weyler, inaugurated a "reconcentration" policy, ordering the entire population of large districts of central and western Cuba into the cities and towns, which were surrounded with *trochas* or trenches, fortified with barbed wire, and guarded by blockhouses at frequent intervals. Cubans who disobeyed the order were regarded as insurgents and were shot on sight. For the many thousands of women, children, and old men herded in the concentration camps, no pretense was made of providing either food or sanitation. Famine and disease were rife, and by the spring of 1898 it was estimated that at least 200,000 of the *reconcentrados* had died out of a total population of only 1,600,000.

The Cuban war intimately affected American economic interests and American humanitarian sentiment. American capital to the amount of $40,000,000 to $50,000,000 was invested in Cuba—in sugar and tobacco plantations, sugar mills, manganese and iron mines, and other properties. Trade between Cuba and the United States, in good years, amounted to as much as $100,000,000. The effect of the war upon many of these enterprises was disastrous. The sugar crop dropped from 1,050,000 tons in 1894 to 200,000 in 1896; tobacco from 450,000 to 50,000 bales. Exports fell from $60,000,000 in 1895 to $15,000,000 in 1896.[10] American businessmen who made their living from investments in Cuba or trade with Cuba had an obvious reason for desiring a termination of the war. Much more important, probably, was the reaction of humanitarian and religious sentiment in the United States to the barbarities attendant upon the Cuban conflict, especially to the suffering and death inflicted upon innocent noncombatants in the concentration camps.

Of these barbarities the American public was supplied with vivid and frequently exaggerated accounts by the "yellow press," led by William R. Hearst's New York *Journal* and Joseph Pulitzer's New York *World*.[11] These and other papers sent talented reporters and artists to Cuba, and their descriptions of conditions in the island were widely published through the news services of the metropolitan papers that employed them. In view of the traditional American sympathy with a people struggling for liberty, it is not surprising that Spanish atrocities were played up to the virtual exclusion of insurgent ruthlessness. A wave of sympathy for the *reconcentrados* swept the United States. Americans contributed with customary generosity for the relief of suffering, and the venerable Clara Barton went to Cuba in person to direct the work of the Red Cross in the concentration camps. But as months lengthened into years, as Cuban conditions showed no improvement, and as neither party in the war showed promise of gaining a clear-cut victory, there was a rising demand that the United States intervene to terminate the struggle and to secure independence for Cuba.

The demand for intervention, which would almost inevitably involve war with Spain, arose plainly from humanitarian rather than from economic considerations. Although much of the Protestant religious press and numerous daily newspapers, both Democratic and Republican, clamored for intervention in behalf of the Cubans, mouthpieces of business—trade journals and resolutions of boards of trade and chambers of commerce—with few exceptions advocated a hands-off policy.[12] American business in general, which by the fall of 1897 was rapidly recovering from a prolonged economic depression, was fearful that a war with Spain would interrupt its upward march to prosperity. There were exaggerated fears of the losses that the Spanish navy might inflict upon American commerce, and in Wall Street and allied quarters there was apprehension lest the governmental expenditures necessitated by war might produce the very inflation against which the Northeast had successfully fought in the 1896 battle against Bryan and Free Silver. Practically the only business interests that agitated for intervention were seaboard firms normally engaged in trade with Cuba. In May, 1897 over 300 such firms signed a memorial to the State Department calling attention to their losses from the disturbance in Cuba and asking that the United States government take measures to bring about an honorable reconciliation between Spanish and insurgents. A similar petition, signed by many of the same firms, 174 in all, was presented to President McKinley in the following February. Neither petition advocated Cuban independence or proposed armed intervention. Both voiced a simple desire for the restoration of peace in order that trade might flourish. Nor is there any evidence that Americans with investments in Cuba worked for or desired intervention by the United States. There is proof, on the contrary, that a number of such persons or companies warned the State Department that they would suffer more heavily from a war between Spain and the United States than from the existing civil war.[13]

Intervention on humanitarian grounds ought to be divorced from any motive of profit for the intervening power, and it is notable in this case that the advocates of intervention usually said nothing of annexing Cuba or, if they mentioned that possibility at all, did so only to disclaim it. Senator Lodge, who in 1895 had spoken of Cuba as a "necessity" to the United States, indicated a year later that he would be satisfied if it were "in friendly hands, in the hands of its own people." Other senators, speaking for intervention, either declared themselves opposed to annexation or professed a willingness to wait until the hand of destiny and the desire of the Cuban people should bring about union in some indefinite future.[14] Most of the prominent newspapers also disclaimed all selfish designs on Cuba. The New York *Tribune* preferred to leave the question open, but the *Journal, World, Sun, Herald, Times,* and *Journal of Commerce,* of the same city, denounced any suggestion of annexation. "No annexation talk so far as Cuba is concerned!" declared the *Sun*. ". . . For human lives and the liberty of human beings, for Cuba Libre; not for an extension of United States territory!" And the *World* concurred: "We are not going to filibuster under the guise of honor or philanthropy."[15] When the United States minister in Madrid, in the spring of 1898, hinted that Spain might be induced to sell the island, he was told emphatically by the State Department: "We do not want Cuba."

THE ROAD TO INTERVENTION

The situation in Cuba was one of which the United States government could not avoid taking official cognizance. American citizens, usually naturalized Cubans, were frequently arrested by the Spanish authorities, and official interposition was necessary to secure their release, which was effected in every instance. It was also necessary to patrol the coasts of the United States, at the cost of millions of dollars, to prevent or break up attempts at "gun-running" by Cuban sympathizers. In the spring of 1896 both houses of Congress passed a concurrent resolution declaring that belligerent rights should be accorded the insurgents, but this declaration, being merely a statement of opinion on the part of Congress, was ignored by President Cleveland and Secretary of State Richard Olney. Both Cleveland and McKinley were anxious to avoid intervention, though both vainly tendered their good offices to Spain for a settlement of the difficulty. Cleveland at length found his patience very near the breaking-point and in his final annual message to Congress in December, 1896 intimated that unless the Cuban war were soon terminated, the dictates of humanity might compel the United States to take steps to end it.[16]

Some six months after McKinley's inauguration the prospects for peace in Cuba brightened perceptibly. The assassination of Canovas, the Spanish prime minister who was responsible for Weyler's presence and methods in Cuba, led to the formation of a new Liberal ministry under Sagasta, pledged to a more generous and humane colonial policy. Weyler was recalled, and the government announced that the Cuban people would be permitted to elect their own legislature, which would be empowered to exercise a large degree of autonomy in local affairs.

In view of this change of atmosphere, McKinley struck a hopeful note in his annual message to Congress on December 6, 1897. He deplored the inhumanities of the

Cuban war and the injuries to American interests in the island. He reviewed recent diplomatic exchanges with Spain and listed the possible courses of action open to the United States. Recognition of Cuban independence or belligerency he discarded as unwarranted by the existing situation of the insurgent government. There remained the possibility of intervention—either neutral intervention to impose a settlement on both sides, or intervention in favor of one of the parties. Against intervention in any form, for the present, the President cited the apparent good faith of the Sagasta ministry in its program of reform, and he urged further patience while the result of that program was awaited.[17]

The grant of limited autonomy to Cuba was, as it turned out, doomed to failure. It was not acceptable to the insurgent leaders, who now declared they would accept nothing short of complete independence, nor was it acceptable to the many peninsular Spaniards in Cuba, who resented the prospect of being ruled by a native Cuban legislature. It is barely possible, nevertheless, that Cuba might have been pacified along this line had not a series of unfortunate accidents suddenly inflamed relations between Spain and the United States.

On February 9, 1898 the New York *Journal* printed, with a photographic facsimile, a private letter from Dupuy de Lome, Spanish minister in Washington, which had been stolen from his correspondent by an insurgent sympathizer in Havana. The indiscreet minister had described President McKinley in unflattering terms and had gone on to intimate that Spain was merely stalling for time in certain commercial negotiations with the United States then under way. De Lome's immediate resignation and an apology from the Spanish government ended the episode but left an increment of ill will.

Six days later the United States battleship *Maine* was destroyed by an explosion at her anchorage in the harbor of Havana, whither she had been sent on a "courtesy call" following some rioting in that city early in January. Some 260 American seamen lost their lives. The cause of the catastrophe was never determined. The *Maine's* forward magazines had exploded, but a board of American naval officers, examining the wreck with divers, found that plates from the ship's bottom had been blown inward and upward to the height of the upper deck. They concluded that the initial explosion had been that of a submarine mine, which had in turn set off the magazines. A second investigation made by the navy 13 years later, when the hull was raised, reached the same conclusion, though there was at least one member of the board who believed the same results could have been caused by an internal explosion alone. A Spanish board of investigation, meeting just after the disaster, concluded that the only explosion had been an internal one.

The report of the navy board was not made public until March 28, when the President sent it to Congress, but in the meantime many of the American people, guided by the sensational newspapers, had adjudged Spain guilty of the act of destruction. "The readers of *The Journal*," boasted that New York paper in March, "knew immediately after the destruction of the *Maine* that she had been blown up by a Spanish mine."[18] "Remember the *Maine!*" became the popular watchword.

Although Congress, for the most part, refrained from recrimination over the *Maine* tragedy until after the naval experts had reported, there was, after the middle of March, an intensified denunciation in the Senate of Spanish atrocities in Cuba. On March 17 Senator Redfield Proctor of Vermont described to the Senate what he had seen and heard during a recent unofficial visit to Cuba, in the course of which he had toured the four central and western provinces. Outside of Havana, where conditions seemed almost normal, the situation, he said, "is not peace nor is it war. It is desolation and distress, misery and starvation." Of about 400,000 persons who had been driven into the concentration camps, "one-half have died and one-quarter of the living are so diseased that they cannot be saved." Outside the camps there was only desolation—no crops, no domestic animals; everything of value was destroyed. Captain General Blanco, Weyler's successor, he described as an "amiable gentleman" with good intentions but without capacity to relieve the situation or put down the rebellion. Of more than 200,000 Spanish troops sent to Cuba, only some 60,000 remained fit for duty, and they had little or no equipment for a field campaign. Virtually all Cubans, though many of the upper class had opposed the insurrection, now considered continuance of Spanish rule impossible; autonomy had been granted too late. Of Cuban businessmen, some were for annexation to the United States, some for a protectorate, some for complete independence. Proctor himself made no recommendation beyond remarking that he was opposed to annexation. He merely reported his observations, in calm and unimpassioned language.[19]

Senator Proctor's speech was highly significant. The New England senator had a reputation for accuracy and sound judgment. He was no sensationalist, and his report of the deplorable conditions in Cuba convinced many who had been skeptical of the revelations of the yellow press. Even the business interests that had hitherto opposed intervention now began to concede that something must be done and that business could stand the shock of war without disaster. The *Wall Street Journal* reported on March 19 that the speech had "converted a great many people in Wall Street." Senator Proctor's statements, "as many of them expressed it, . . . made the blood boil."

Under pressure from the public, the press, and virtually all Democrats and a large proportion of his own party in House and Senate, the peace-loving President on March 27 sent to Madrid his final proposal for a peaceful settlement of the Cuban question. Let Spain, he said, through a note signed by Assistant Secretary of State William R. Day, abandon at once the reconcentration policy, grant an armistice until October 1, and enter, through McKinley, into peace negotiations with the insurgents. Day added, as an admonition to haste, that the report of the navy board on the *Maine* could probably "be held in Congress for a short time without action." A telegram from Day on March 28 informed the American minister in Madrid that the President regarded Cuban independence as the only satisfactory outcome of the proposed peace negotiations.[20]

In Madrid the Sagasta ministry were caught on the horns of a dilemma. If they refused McKinley's demands, a disastrous war with the United States appeared certain. If they conceded those demands in full, popular indignation in Spain might overthrow the ministry and even the

reigning dynasty. The only hope of salvation lay in securing support from the European powers against intervention by the United States. Such support the Spanish
government had already sought from all the major courts
and cabinets of Europe, and in every capital except London it had received expressions of willingness to participate in a joint demonstration against the United States—
if someone else would take the lead. Such was the attitude in Paris, Berlin, St. Petersburg, Vienna, and Rome.
The crowned heads of continental Europe, and the government of the French Republic as well, desired the
preservation of the shaky Spanish Empire and dynasty;
none was willing to assume leadership in such an undertaking. "You are isolated," said the German foreign minister to the Spanish ambassador, "because everybody
wants to be pleasant to the United States, or at any rate,
nobody wants to arouse America's anger." In England
Queen Victoria was sympathetic to the Spanish queen
regent, but ministry and public were in this crisis incur-
ably pro-United States. The only result of the Spanish
supplications, aside from a hazy suggestion for mediation by the Pope, was a visit to President McKinley by
the ambassadors of the six powers on April 6, in which
they begged him, in the interest of humanity, to refrain
from armed intervention in Cuba. McKinley, who had
been apprised of the protest in advance by the friendly
British ambassador, Sir Julian Pauncefote, replied in
effect that intervention, if it came, would be in the
interest of humanity.[21]

Without hope of substantial support from Europe, the
Spanish government went as far as it dared toward
meeting McKinley's proposals. In its reply (cabled to

Washington on March 31) it announced that reconcentration was being abandoned and that an armistice would be granted upon application by the insurgents. Instead of accepting McKinley's proposal of mediation, the note stated that the Cuban parliament, provided for by the autonomy arrangement, was to meet in May and should be the instrument of pacification—an evident rejection of the demand for independence. Spain was willing to submit to arbitration the question of responsibility for the destruction of the *Maine*.[22]

A few days later, April 9, the Spanish government declared an armistice on its own initiative. On the following day Minister Stewart L. Woodford cabled from Madrid that he believed a solution satisfactory to all parties was obtainable.

Paying slight heed to these last-minute concessions and assurances, McKinley sent to a warlike Congress on April 11 a message in which he described the outcome of the recent negotiations as unsatisfactory, declared that

> In the name of humanity, in the name of civilization, in behalf of endangered American interests which give us the right and the duty to speak and to act, the war in Cuba must stop,

and asked authority to use the military and naval forces of the United States "to secure a full and final termination of hostilities between the Government of Spain and the people of Cuba."[23]

For thus leading the country into intervention and war at a time when Spain was showing evident signs of yielding and under conditions which gave little legal warrant for intervention, McKinley has been severely blamed by numerous historians.[24] We may well believe, however, that aside from being under tremendous political pressure for intervention, McKinley was convinced that the existing Spanish government, however good its intentions, was not physically, mentally, or morally capable of bringing about a tolerable situation in Cuba.

Congress, which had been champing at the bit for weeks, seized upon the President's message with eagerness but not with unqualified enthusiasm. Certain passages in the message were quickly pounced upon and denounced by Democratic senators. McKinley had spoken of "the forcible intervention of the United States as a neutral to stop the war" as justified by historical precedent and "on rational grounds," but had added:

> It involves, however, hostile constraint upon both
> the parties to the contest, as well to enforce a truce
> as to guide the eventual settlement.

This language evidently meant, said some Democrats, that we were to fight the insurgent forces of Maximo Gomez as well as the Spanish, that McKinley had abandoned the idea of Cuban independence and was intent upon enforcing some sort of compromise solution upon Spanish and insurgents alike.[25] Though the President's supporters denied emphatically that his language had this significance, the idea persisted and was presumably one reason why a combination of Democrats and Republicans in the Senate insisted that the resolutions responding to the President's message should contain not only a recognition of the independence of the Cuban people but also a recognition of the existing but insubstantial republican government of Cuba. The administration,

evidently feeling that it was unsafe to entrust the future
of Cuba to the existing government and that temporary
American tutelage might be necessary, held out against
recognition, and after a threatened deadlock its majority in the House compelled the Senate to recede, though
the latter secured a declaration that the people of Cuba
not only "of right ought to be," but "are" free and independent.

The ironing out of such differences required a week,
and not until between one and three A.M. on April 20
(though officially on the 19th) did Congress adopt the
resolutions, the final vote being 42 to 35 in the Senate,
311 to 6 in the House.[26]

The resolutions as adopted and approved by the President on April 20 declared that "the people of Cuba are,
and of right ought to be, free and independent," demanded that Spain "at once relinquish its authority and
government in the Island of Cuba and withdraw its land
and naval forces from Cuba and Cuban waters," and
empowered the President to use the armed forces of the
United States to enforce this demand. Without a record
vote or any expression of dissent the Senate had adopted,
and the House had accepted, a fourth resolution prepared by Senator Henry M. Teller of Colorado, declaring:

> That the United States hereby disclaims any dis-
> position or intention to exercise sovereignty, juris-
> diction, or control over said Island except for the
> pacification thereof, and asserts its determination,
> when that is accomplished, to leave the govern-
> ment and control of the Island to its people.

The Colorado senator had remarked that he wished to

make it impossible for any European government to say, "when we go out to make battle for the liberty and freedom of Cuban patriots, that we are doing it for the purpose of aggrandizement for ourselves or the increasing of our territorial holdings." He wished this point made clear in regard to Cuba, "whatever," he added, "we may do as to some other islands."[27]

Thus with a specific renunciation of annexationist designs in Cuba but with freedom of action with respect to Spain's other colonies—Puerto Rico, the Philippines, the Carolines and Marianas—the United States entered the conflict with Spain. Upon being informed of the approval of the Cuban resolutions, the Spanish government at once severed diplomatic relations and on April 24 declared war. Congress responded with a declaration of war the next day, making it retroactive to April 21. On the 22nd the President had instituted a blockade of portions of the coast of Cuba.

A Short War and an Easy Victory

The military and naval details of the war need not detain us long. The conflict was pathetically one-sided from the beginning. Although on paper the Spanish navy appeared something like the equivalent of the American fleet, it really had nothing to match the four new United States battleships, the *Massachusetts, Indiana, Iowa,* and *Oregon*—the last of which had joined the Atlantic Fleet after a two months' voyage around the Horn from San Francisco. Spanish ships and crews, moreover, were in a wretched state of inefficiency, and the officers were imbued with a defeatist spirit, whereas the United States navy, thanks to the energetic efforts of Assistant Secretary Roosevelt, was well prepared and spoiling for a fight. The Spanish army in Cuba outnumbered the American expeditionary force but was ill-equipped for war, and though Spanish soldiers fought bravely and stubbornly, the severance of their supply line from Spain made their case hopeless.[28]

Though Cuba had furnished the sole cause of the war, the first important blow fell in the Far East. Sensing the approach of war and knowing of the presence of a Spanish naval squadron at Manila in the Philippines, Theodore Roosevelt (who virtually took matters out of the hands of his conservative chief, Secretary of the Navy John D. Long) had secured the appointment of Commodore George Dewey to command the American Asiatic Squadron and on February 25, 1898 had cabled him to begin "offensive operations in the Philippines" as soon as he should be informed of a declaration of war. Nor had Roosevelt neglected to supply Dewey with the necessary ships and ammunition.

Dewey received the news of war at Hong Kong. Putting his ships into war trim at neighboring Mirs Bay on the Chinese coast, he steamed south to the Philippines and in the early morning hours of May 1 led his little squadron of light cruisers past the forts and through the rumored mine fields guarding the entrance to Manila Bay. At dawn he spied the Spanish ships, equal in number to his own but hopelessly antiquated, anchored in line off the naval station of Cavite. Circling repeatedly past the enemy squadron, the American cruisers poured in a destructive fire to which the Spaniards could make no effective reply, and before noon the entire Spanish naval force lay sunk or burning, at the cost, to the American squadron, of eight men slightly wounded. Dewey occupied Cavite and held control of Manila Bay, while the War Department prepared to send an army to take possession of the city of Manila, the Philippine capital. By the end of July some 11,000 United States troops under General Wesley Merritt had arrived in the Philippines, and on August 13 they entered Manila against little more than "token" resistance by the Spanish. As an incident of their expedition to the Orient, the American forces had occupied the little island of Guam in the Spanish Marianas. Unconnected with the outside world by cable, the Spanish officials in Guam knew nothing of the war until the cruiser _Charleston_ entered Apra harbor and tossed a few shells into a deserted fort. Unable to return the fire, which they had at first mistaken for a salute, they surrendered without resistance.[29]

Meanwhile, the main Spanish fleet, four armored cruisers and three destroyers, commanded by Admiral Cervera, had left the Azores for Cuban waters. Dodging American patrols, it slipped into Santiago harbor on the south coast of Cuba. Capture or destruction of this fleet now became the prime objective of the war in this theater, since without a fleet Spain could not possibly defend Cuba for any extended period. The Atlantic Fleet, under Commodores William T. Sampson and Winfield Scott Schley, closed in around the narrow entrance to Santiago Bay, while an army of 16,000 regulars and volunteers, commanded by Major General W. R. Shafter, landed on the Cuban coast a few miles east of Santiago and fought its way toward that city. On July 1, in the hard-fought engagements of El Caney and San Juan Hill, the Americans pierced the outer defenses of Santiago and reached high ground, whence they could look down on the city and harbor. Cervera was caught between the army and navy of the United States. On the morning of July 3, under orders from the captain general in Havana, he led his squadron out of the harbor in a dash for a safer haven farther west. In a running fight westward along the coast, all his ships were sunk or run ashore in a burning condition. American losses were one man killed and one wounded. On July 16 the city of Santiago was surrendered to the Americans.

The war was now virtually over, and on July 18 the Spanish government requested the good offices of France in arranging for a termination of hostilities. Before the fighting ended, however, another American expeditionary force, led by General Nelson A. Miles, landed in Puerto Rico and proceeded, against feeble Spanish resistance, to take possession of that island.

THE EXPANSIONISTS TAKE CHARGE

With the Spanish application for peace terms before them, President McKinley and his advisers had some difficult decisions to make. The independence of Cuba was a foregone conclusion; obviously it must be detached from Spain, and the Teller Amendment to the resolutions of intervention eliminated the possibility of annexation. But what of Spain's other islands—Puerto Rico, Guam, and above all the Philippines, an extensive and populous area where Spanish misrule had brought about native rebellion only less formidable than that in Cuba? The Teller Amendment said nothing of these, and its author had expressly excluded "some other islands" from his ban on the annexation of Cuba.[30]

It seems clear that McKinley entered the war with no thought of utilizing it for the territorial aggrandizement of the United States. Speaking of Cuba, in his message of December, 1897, he had remarked: "Forcible annexation ... cannot be thought of. That by our code of morality would be criminal aggression." To Senator Hoar of Massachusetts he had expressed an "emphatic disapproval of the acquisition of dependencies or Oriental Empire by military strength."[31] Far from having designs upon the Philippines, he was reported to have had only a vague idea even of their location when he was informed of Dewey's victory at Manila. Neither Secretary of State John Sherman nor William R. Day, who succeeded Sherman on April 28, 1898, had motives different from McKinley's in undertaking to expel Spain from Cuba. But the war, with its easy victories over Spain's decaying empire in the Pacific and the Caribbean, opened the door of a colonial career to the United States and so played directly into the hands of the group of Republicans who had been urging expansion ever since Hawaii had invited annexation in 1893. As McKinley had yielded to the advocates of Hawaiian annexation at the beginning of his administration, so he was now to yield to the men who urged the taking over of Spain's colonial empire.

The leaders of the expansionist group in Washington are easily identified. Theodore Roosevelt had resigned from the Navy Department to go to Cuba as lieutenant colonel of the "Rough Riders" regiment, but he kept in close touch by letter with his friend Henry Cabot

Lodge.[32] Upon the senator's willing mind he urged the
importance of securing and retaining possession of Puerto
Rico and the Philippines. Lodge himself, three days
after the battle of Manila Bay, had written another
friend: "We hold the other side of the Pacific, and the
value to this country is almost beyond recognition." On
no account, he said, must we "let the islands go . . . they
must be ours under the treaty of peace."[33] An influential
ally of Lodge and Roosevelt was Captain Mahan, who
had been recalled from inactive duty to help guide the
strategy of the war as a member of the Naval War Board.
Mahan's views on the importance of naval bases and
colonies being what they were, it was inevitable that he
should join forces with his young friends and disciples,
Lodge and Roosevelt. To Roosevelt, in Cuba, Lodge reported that he and Mahan had "talked the Philippines
with [Secretary Day] for two hours" and convinced him
that "we could not escape our destiny there." "Unless I
am utterly and profoundly mistaken," he assured Roosevelt in another letter, "the Administration is now fully
committed to the large policy that we both desire." Other
influential senators who shared the views of Lodge,
Roosevelt, and Mahan were William P. Frye of Maine
and Cushman K. Davis of Minnesota, chairman of the
Foreign Relations Committee. Outside of Washington
they received valiant support from Whitelaw Reid, pro-
prietor and editor of the New York *Tribune.*

This little group of expansionists, however, could
hardly have dictated the terms of the peace treaty to a
reluctant President if they had not had influential support in public opinion, and this they did have. The attitude of American newspapers in general toward the re-

tention of the Philippines and other Spanish possessions has never been adequately studied, but there is no doubt that large sections of the press that spoke for organized business and religion were heartily in favor of expansion.

American businessmen, who had generally opposed intervention in Cuba and had seen no need for colonies, underwent a sudden conversion on the latter point in the spring of 1898.[34] Dewey's dramatic victory at Manila, which offered an American foothold in the Far East, came just at the moment when American business for the first time was feeling the need for such a foothold. American exporters had long looked to China, with its 400,000,000 people, as offering a great future market for the surplus manufactures of the United States. Shipments to China were still small—less than 2 per cent of total American exports in 1897—but the Chinese market was regarded as capable of indefinite expansion, and the United States, under most-favored-nation clauses in its treaties with China, might reasonably expect to capture the lion's share of that trade. Such were American expectations when, beginning in the fall of 1897, a group of European powers initiated a process that threatened to partition China into European "spheres of influence" from which American trade would be excluded or in which, at best, it would suffer adverse discrimination. First Germany, then Russia, Great Britain, and France demanded and secured from China long-term leases on Chinese ports—Kiaochow, Port Arthur, Wei-hai-wei, and Kwang-chou Bay, respectively—and special rights of exploitation in the neighboring territory. If something were not done to halt this "break-up of China," the Chinese market for American goods might vanish into thin air.[35]

In February and March, 1898 chambers of commerce and boards of trade in cities on both the east and west coasts of the United States were urging the State Department, which, under John Sherman, displayed a very placid attitude toward the partition of China,[36] to take energetic measures for the protection of American interests. An American Asiatic Association was formed in New York to agitate for the preservation of American rights and interests in the Orient. The New York *Journal of Commerce,* which had hitherto scoffed at colonies, Isthmian canal schemes, and big-navy programs, now declared itself in favor of an Isthmian canal, the annexation of Hawaii, and an increased navy—all for the purpose of strengthening the United States in the Pacific and safeguarding its rights in China.

Dewey's victory at Manila found the Chinese situation unimproved but seemed to many to offer an effective remedy. With a naval base in the Philippines, way-stations in Hawaii and perhaps in Guam, with a growing navy and the prospect of an Isthmian canal through which the fleet could slip easily into the Pacific, might not the United States become at last a great Pacific power, quite capable of defending its interests in the Orient against aggressions from Europe? The *Journal of Commerce,* the *Wall Street Journal,* the *American Banker,* and other trade journals, east and west, raised a clamor for the retention of the Philippines. To give up those islands now, said the *Journal of Commerce,* "would be an act of inconceivable folly in the face of our imperative future necessities for a basis of naval and military force on the Western shores of the Pacific."

Converted to a belief in colonialism by the special situation in the Far East, American businessmen found it easy to apply the same philosophy to the Caribbean. The erstwhile anti-imperialist *Journal of Commerce* insisted that Puerto Rico be retained and suggested that it might be necessary to keep control over Cuba in spite of the Teller Amendment, and it and other papers hinted that the British and Danish flags would do well to follow that of Spain out of the Caribbean. The Chicago *Inter-Ocean,* after interviewing merchants and manufacturers in a number of cities, reported them "very generally waking up to the opportunities which the war has brought at a moment when the immense increase of our manufacturing capacity has rendered foreign outlets absolutely necessary to us." Opportunities for investment in the former Spanish islands—in banks, railroads, lumbering, sugar and tobacco growing—were also viewed with optimism by American business interests. It seemed that the war for humanity might be made to pay dividends in hard cash.

But the war might also pay dividends in the salvation of human souls. Of this the larger Protestant churches were as firmly convinced as were businessmen of its material advantages.[37] Religious groups that had favored the war as a humanitarian crusade regarded the quick and easy victory as a sure sign of divine approval and as a divine command to continue the good work in islands freed from Spanish tyranny. Although there were some dissenting voices, in general, Methodists, Baptists, Presbyterians, Congregationalists, and Episcopalians, together with several of the minor sects, united in urging that the United States accept the civilizing and Christianizing mission that Providence had placed before it;

and just as businessmen prepared to take advantage of the opportunities for trade and investment in the former possessions of Spain, so the churches began laying plans for new missionary enterprise. The parallel can be carried a bit further. As businessmen viewed the Philippines as a door to the trade with China, so some churchmen viewed them as a gateway to missionary work in China.

> We have been morally compelled to become an Asiatic power [wrote a Presbyterian clergyman]. . . . Every American missionary in Asia from whom I have heard in recent months, has thanked God that the American flag has entered the Far East. . . . America and Great Britain will see to it that China is not Russianized.

If the new career upon which the United States was about to enter was to be tinged with economic imperialism, it was also to be, as one religious writer remarked, "the imperialism of righteousness."

Politicians were by no means oblivious of the prevalence of religious sentiment in favor of keeping the Spanish islands. Senator O. H. Platt of Connecticut reported to McKinley in August, 1898 that probably nine-tenths of the people of his state felt intensely that the United States should insist upon the cession of the entire Philippine archipelago.

> Those who believe in Providence [he wrote] see, or think they see, that God has placed upon this Government the solemn duty of providing for the people of these islands a government based upon the principle of liberty no matter how many diffi-

culties the problem may present. They feel that it
is our duty to attempt its solution. . . . If in the
negotiations for peace Spain is permitted to retain
any portion of the Philippines it will be regarded
as a failure on the part of this nation to discharge
the greatest moral obligation which could be conceived.[38]

The ideas so freely expressed by the spokesmen of
business and of religion must certainly have aided President McKinley in deciding what disposition to make of
the Philippines, Guam, and Puerto Rico. McKinley was,
as is well known, devoted to the interests of American
business. He was also a religious man, and the missionary
spirit was present in his own household. A caller at the
White House found Mrs. McKinley evincing great enthusiasm for "converting the Igorrotes"—one of the "wild
tribes" of the Philippines. Months after the decision had
been reached to hold the Philippines, the President told
a Methodist delegation at the White House that in answer to his earnest prayers for guidance the revelation
had one night come to him that "there was nothing left
for us to do but to take them all, and to educate the
Filipinos, and uplift and civilize and Christianize them,
and by God's grace do the very best we could by them
as our fellow-men for whom Christ also died."[39]

Spain Surrenders Her Colonial Empire

The decision to demand from Spain the cession of the
Philippines was not reached, however, until after months
of uncertainty. Secretary Day had at first expected that
the islands would be returned to Spain, but by July 26,

when the French ambassador in Washington presented Spain's request for peace terms, the "imperial party" in Washington had so far prevailed that even Day proposed to demand the retention of a harbor in the Philippines for a naval base. Other members of the cabinet, however, wished to keep all the islands for commercial and humanitarian purposes. It was decided, for the present, to leave the question open. The reply to the Spanish note offered an immediate cessation of hostilities on condition that Spain relinquish all authority over Cuba, cede to the United States Puerto Rico and an island in the Ladrones (Marianas), and consent to American occupation of the city and harbor of Manila pending the conclusion of a definitive peace treaty which should determine the future of the Philippines. On this basis an armistice protocol was signed on August 12. American and Spanish peace commissioners were to meet in Paris not later than October 1.[40] Thus several months would be allowed for discussion and the testing of public opinion before the final decision on the Philippines would need to be made.

As peace commissioners to represent the United States the President selected William R. Day, who resigned as Secretary of State to become chairman of the commission, Senators Davis and Frye, Republicans, and George Gray, Democrat, and editor Whitelaw Reid of the New York *Tribune*. A majority of the commission—Davis, Frye, and Reid—were expansionists; all three favored retention of the entire Philippine archipelago. Gray, formerly a strong supporter of Cleveland's Hawaiian policy, was still an "anti," and Day occupied a middle ground.

Instructions to the peace commissioners were dated

September 16. By this time the desires of American business and religion had had ample opportunity to be
heard, and McKinley had also received from abroad significant hints that the United States would do well to
retain the Philippines. John Hay, formerly ambassador
to Great Britain, who now succeeded Day as Secretary
of State, had previously sent word that England would
be glad to see the United States keep the islands. Japan
expressed a similar preference, though adding that Japan
herself would be willing to join with the United States
and a third power in a joint administration. These
friendly gestures were presumably designed to forestall
the possibility that the Philippines might fall into German possession. Germany was still hungry for Pacific
islands, and the Philippines were a far richer prize than
any that she had yet acquired. The American ambassador in Berlin, Andrew D. White, had dropped an un-
authorized hint, after Dewey's victory, that the United
States did not wish the islands, and the Germans had
sent a naval squadron to Manila, where its untactful
commander, Admiral von Diederichs, made things difficult for Dewey by his disregard of the latter's rules of
blockade. Should the United States decide to abandon
the Philippines, the Germans were on hand to promote
their own interests.[41] To British and Japanese it seemed
better that the islands be held by the United States than
that they should pass to Germany or become a bone of
contention under weak Spanish or native rule.

By the instructions of September 16 the American
commissioners were told that the United States could not
accept less than full sovereignty over the principal island
of Luzon. The victory of Manila, said the President, had

"brought us new duties and responsibilities which we must meet and discharge as becomes a great nation on whose growth and career from the beginning the Ruler of Nations has plainly written the high command and pledge of civilization." There was also, he added, "the commercial opportunity to which American statesmanship cannot be indifferent." Thus the claims of business and religion were acknowledged in the same breath. The commissioners in Paris were advised by Americans who had been in the Philippines that division of the islands was undesirable. The archipelago formed an economic unit with Manila as its commercial center. Davis, Frye, and Reid, accordingly, cabled to the President a strongly worded argument for the retention of the entire group. McKinley, who had just sounded public opinion during a tour of the Midwest, had apparently reached a similar conclusion. On October 26 Secretary Hay cabled the commissioners that the United States must retain all the Philippines. Small heed was paid to the group of Filipino natives, led by Emilio Aguinaldo, who demanded independence and had set up a government of their own near Manila. It was generally agreed, by whites who knew the Philippines, that the natives were not prepared for self-government.

Spain, reluctant to surrender the last remnants of her once great colonial empire, held out as long as possible for retention of all or part of the Philippines, but in the end could do nothing but accept the American terms. The blow was softened by an agreement to pay her $20,000,000 for public works and improvements in the islands. The American commissioners were unsuccessful, however, in an attempt to purchase the island of Kusaie in the Carolines, which was of considerable interest to American missionaries and was also desired as a cable station by capitalists planning to lay a cable from Hawaii to Manila. The German government, disappointed in the Philippines, had exacted from Spain a secret promise not to cede the Carolines to the United States. They were subsequently sold to Germany, and with them went also the Pelew Islands and the Marianas with the exception of Guam.[42]

By the treaty of peace signed in Paris on December 10, 1898 Spain relinquished "all claim of sovereignty over and title to Cuba," ceded to the United States the Philippine Islands, Guam in the Marianas or Ladrones, Puerto Rico, "and other islands now under Spanish sovereignty in the West Indies." The inhabitants of the ceded islands were promised "the free exercise of their religion," but it was stipulated that their "civil rights and political status" should "be determined by the Congress." For the first time, in a treaty acquiring territory for the United States, there was no promise of citizenship. As in the case of Alaska, there was no promise, actual or implied, of statehood. The United States thereby acquired not "territories" but possessions or "dependencies" and became, in that sense, an "imperial" power.[43]

THE SENATE DEBATES IMPERIALISM

The treaty, however, still had to run the gauntlet of the Senate, and there it encountered determined opposition. Few senators appear to have objected seriously to the annexation of tiny Guam or of Puerto Rico, which was nearby and peopled chiefly by the white race, though of alien tongue. But annexation of the Philippines was a much greater break with American tradition. Their distance, 6,000 miles from San Francisco, their population of 7,000,000 Malays, including a minority of pagans and Mohammedans, the existence of a vigorous independence movement whose leaders were as hostile to American as to Spanish sovereignty—all these factors made their acquisition seem to many, in and out of the Senate, a dangerous venture in imperialism and a violation of time-honored American principles. An Anti-Imperialist League was organized to combat annexation, and in the Senate many Democrats and a few Republicans made clear their purpose to vote against ratification of the treaty.

Debate on the treaty was in executive session, but weeks before the treaty was sent to the Senate (January 4, 1899) senators found opportunity for public expression of their views in debating a number of resolutions dealing with the acquisition of colonial territory. The most important of these, introduced by Senator Vest of Missouri, declared:

> That under the Constitution of the United States no power is given to the Federal Government to acquire territory to be held and governed permanently as colonies.[44]

Democratic senators, ably supported by Republican George F. Hoar of Massachusetts, argued that under the Constitution there was no place for a colonial system like that of the European powers—a system based "upon the fundamental idea that the people of immense areas of territory can be held as subjects, never to become citizens." It was against that very system that Americans had rebelled in 1776. If the Philippine Islands were taken under American sovereignty, therefore, their inhabitants must become citizens with all the rights of citizens. They could not be governed as subjects, nor could they and their products be excluded from the United States by restrictions on immigration and importation. American agriculture and American labor would thus be subjected to unchecked competition from the Filipinos. It was foolish to suppose, furthermore, that American free institutions would operate successfully among a people so widely different in race, language, religion, and customs from the people of the United States.

But even if it were granted that the United States might constitutionally annex the Philippines and govern them as a colony, was it expedient to do so? No, answered opponents of the treaty. Departure from the spirit of our republican institutions in the government of colonies would spell the destruction of those institutions at home. Possession of the Philippines, moreover, would embroil the United States in the international politics of the Far East and would put an end to the Monroe Doctrine. How could we forbid Europe to interfere in the western hemisphere when we were interfering in the eastern? "The Monroe Doctrine is gone!" lamented Senator Hoar. Opposition senators also minimized the trade advantages to be expected from annexation and ridiculed the religious argument. "Some of our worthy clergymen," said Senator Hoar, were "of late preaching from their pulpits the new commandment to do evil that good may come." "In order to Christianize these savage people," said another senator, "we must put the yoke of despotism upon their necks; . . . Christianity cannot be advanced by force."

All of these arguments were answered by the supporters of the treaty. Of special interest is the constitutional argument advanced by Senator Orville H. Platt of Connecticut, since it anticipated subsequent decisions of the Supreme Court.[45] The right to acquire and the right to govern territory, said Platt, were sovereign rights, which the United States enjoyed in common with other sovereign nations, and the right to govern implied the right to establish whatever form of government was suitable to the condition of the territory and the character of its inhabitants—be they savages, barbarians, or civilized folk. We must, he said,

> provide for the people of any territory that we may acquire the most liberal, just, and beneficent government which they may be capable of enjoying, always with reference to their development and welfare and in the hope that they may be finally fitted for independent self-government. . . . To hold that we should legislate otherwise is to hold that we are bound to perpetuate folly and invite disaster.

Platt denied that there would be any obligation to admit the Philippines as a state or to confer citizenship upon the Filipinos. He denied that either the people or the products of the islands could be admitted to the United States without the consent of Congress.

Senator Platt affirmed, in brief, precisely what his opponents denied—that the United States had all the powers necessary to establish and maintain a full-fledged colonial system.

Other senators on the Republican side made light of any danger to the liberties or welfare of the Filipinos— "We come as ministering angels, not as despots"—or to the democratic institutions of the United States. On the contrary, the liberties of the English people had broadened since England became a colonial power. Indeed, new economic outlets might be just what was needed to preserve the integrity of American free institutions. Henry Cabot Lodge mentioned, though he preferred not to discuss, "the enormous material benefits to our trade, our industries, and our labor dependent upon a right settlement of this question" and "the far greater question of the markets of China, of which we must have our share for the benefit of our working-men." But duty and destiny were also invoked, as they had been in the religious press. To Senator Platt it seemed that the same force that had once guided Pilgrim sails to Plymouth Rock had impelled American ships at Manila and Santiago. Upon America rested the duty of extending Christian civilization, crushing despotism, and making the rights of man prevail. "Providence has put it upon us," said Platt. "We propose to execute it."

The debate continued from early December until February 6, 1899, the date set for a vote on the treaty. Wavering senators, both Republican and Democratic, were subjected to various forms of pressure from the administration, since Democratic votes were essential for ratification. Senator Gray of Delaware, a leading Democrat, had been a member of the peace commission, and though he had at first opposed taking the Philippines, he now defended the treaty in the Senate. William Jennings Bryan, titular head of the Democratic party, came to Washington to urge Democratic support of the treaty, arguing that peace should be made as soon as possible and that the question of freeing the Philippines could be disposed of later. He was also reported to have argued, in effect: "Let the Republicans have their way now with the treaty. We can attack them for it in the political campaign of 1900."[46] On February 6, 1899 the Senate approved the treaty by a vote of 57 to 27—a single vote above the necessary two-thirds majority. Fifteen Democratic, Populist, or Independent senators voted with the Republican majority, and two Republicans, Hoar of Massachusetts and Hale of Maine, voted in the negative.[47]

Having approved the treaty of peace, the Senate sought to clarify its intentions with regard to the Philippines. A resolution adopted on February 14 declared that it was "not intended to incorporate the inhabitants of the Philippine Islands into citizenship of the United States" nor "to permanently annex said islands as an integral part of the territory of the United States"; it was intended, rather, to give the islands and their people a suitable form of government, "to prepare them for local self-government, and in due time to make such disposition of said islands as will best promote the interests of the citizens of the United States and the inhabitants of said islands." Passed in the Senate by the small vote of 26 to 22 and never acted upon by the House, this resolution had no legal standing. It was merely an expression of opinion on the part of 26 senators.

Meanwhile, on February 4, two days before the Senate approved the treaty, hostilities had broken out between American troops at Manila and Filipino insurgents led by Aguinaldo, who were ready to fight for their independence against Americans as they had fought against Spaniards. In annexing an empire, the United States had also annexed a war that was to prove much longer and more troublesome than that with Spain.

HAWAII, WAKE, AND TUTUILA

The war with Spain, which gave the United States Puerto Rico, the Philippines, and Guam, also furnished the impetus necessary to effect the long-delayed annexation of Hawaii. The annexation was followed within a year by the partition of the Samoan group, in which the United States received the island of Tutuila, where since 1878 it had possessed rights for a coaling station in Pago Pago harbor.

In March, 1898, as previously noted, the advocates of Hawaiian annexation abandoned hope of accomplishing their object by treaty and brought into the Senate a joint resolution of annexation. The resolution, however, made no headway until June.[48] Dewey's victory at Manila turned American eyes to the Pacific as never before. If the American flag was to remain in the Philippines, if the United States, from the Philippines as a base, was to defend its rights in China, Hawaii, it was argued, was essential as a naval base and coaling station *en route* to the Far East.[49] The Hawaiian government, on advice from its minister in Washington, instead of proclaiming its neutrality in the war, placed all the facilities of Honolulu harbor at the disposal of the United States and even offered to make an alliance. The alliance offer was not accepted, but the friendly attitude of Hawaii and the fact that by aiding the United States it was subjecting itself to possible Spanish reprisals, enabled the annexationists to argue that Hawaii should be brought under the American flag as a reward for friendly aid and for its own protection. Thus the war situation greatly strengthened the case for annexation.[50]

Much was also said of the "yellow peril" in Hawaii— the rapid growth of its Japanese population and the danger that Hawaii might be absorbed in Japan's waxing empire. The Senate Foreign Relations Committee predicted a great struggle in the Pacific between the West and the East, America and Asia, and announced:

> The issue is whether, in that inevitable struggle, Asia or America shall have the vantage ground of the naval "Key of the Pacific," the commercial "Crossroads of the Pacific."

The testimony of Captain Mahan and other naval and military experts was brought forward to demonstrate that the possession of Hawaii was essential to the defense of the Pacific coast.

These arguments proved adequate, in the end, to secure a victory for the annexationists. A new joint resolution was introduced in the House of Representatives on May 4, three days after Manila Bay. Though blocked for some time by Speaker Thomas B. Reed, an implacable opponent of expansion, it passed the House by a large majority on June 15. Senate opponents brought out all the time-worn arguments—the sins of Minister John L. Stevens, the rights and wishes of the native Hawaiians, the perils of expansion into the tropics. As long before, in connection with Texas and Santo Domingo, opposition senators made the constitutional point that territories, as distinguished from states, could not be acquired by joint resolution but only by treaty.[51] Senators supporting the resolution made little effort to answer the arguments of the opposition. Senator Hoar, however, who was to be a bitter opponent of annexing the Philippines, justified his support of the Hawaiian resolution by pointing out that the people of Hawaii, unlike the Filipinos and West Indians, were "willing and capable . . . to share with us our freedom, our self-government, our equality, our education, and the transcendent sweets of civil and religious liberty." They would, he said, "in due time and on suitable conditions, be annexed to the United States as an equal part of a self-governing Republic."

The joint resolution annexing Hawaii "as a part of the territory of the United States" passed the Senate on July 6, 1898 by a vote of 42 to 21, and received the President's signature on the following day. On the following August 12, the date of the signature of the armistice protocol with Spain, Hawaii passed formally under the jurisdiction of the United States.

The Hawaiian Islands, their outpost at Midway, acquired by the United States in 1867,[52] and Guam provided stepping stones to the Philippines and the Far East in general. The wide gap between Midway and Guam was presently filled in by the annexation of Wake Island, 2,130 miles west of Honolulu and 1,034 miles from Midway. The naval explorer, Commander Charles Wilkes, had asserted title to Wake for the United States in 1841, but for nearly 60 years no effort had been made to enforce the claim. On January 17, 1899 Commander E. D. Taussig, commanding the gunboat *Bennington*, landed at Wake and took formal possession in the name of the United States.[53]

The year of the Spanish-American War witnessed a new outbreak of trouble in Samoa, which was solved the following year by a partition of the islands, the United States receiving Tutuila, and Upolu and Savaii passing to Germany.[54] The tripartite condominium set up in 1889 worked passably until the death of King Malietoa Laupepa, August 22, 1898. Thereupon rival native factions once more espoused rival candidates for the throne, and again the local representatives of the great powers found themselves at odds, with the Americans and British supporting Malietoa Tanu, whose election had been upheld by the local chief justice, an American, and the Germans now friendly to Mataafa, who had been their enemy in the earlier controversy. American and British cruisers shelled native villages, as German cruisers had done in the 1880's, and a three-man commission visited Samoa to seek a solution of the difficulty. The commissioners restored order, abolished the kingship altogether, and though submitting a plan for a modified condominium, expressed the opinion that joint administration would never work satisfactorily.

Meanwhile the German government was taking advantage of British difficulties elsewhere (the Boer War began in 1899) to press for a partition of the islands, insisting upon Upolu as the German share and offering England the less important Savaii. Neither Germans nor British, apparently, questioned the primacy of American rights in Tutuila. The British government was not interested in taking Savaii if Germany held Upolu, and despite the continuing interest of New Zealand and Australia in Samoa, it was finally agreed between Germany and Great Britain that the British should leave Samoa altogether, receiving as compensation the surrender of German rights in the Tonga and part of the Solomon Islands and territorial concessions in Africa. To this arrangement the United States made no objection, provided it obtain title to Tutuila. On December 2, 1899 a treaty of partition was signed in Washington. Great Britain renounced all rights and claims in Samoa. Germany renounced in favor of the United States all claim to Tutuila and other islands east of the meridian of 171 degrees west longitude, and the United States renounced in favor of Germany all claim to Upolu, Savaii, and other islands west of that line. Each of the three powers should continue to enjoy, in Samoan ports open to commerce, privileges and conditions equal to those of the power exercising sovereignty—the "open door" in other words.[55]

By the Samoan treaty of 1899 the United States obtained no title to Tutuila (subsequently, with the small neighboring islands, known as American Samoa), but merely a renunciation in its favor of German and British claims. All three powers had hitherto maintained the fiction of Samoan sovereignty and independence. The native chiefs of Tutuila, however, formally ceded their island to the United States in 1900, and those of the nearby Manu'a group followed suit in 1904. These cessions were accepted by President Theodore Roosevelt without submission to the Senate or to Congress. The American title seems not to have been questioned, but, to remove all doubt, Congress, by a joint resolution of

February 20, 1929, accepted, ratified, and confirmed the cessions of 1900 and 1904.[56]

IMPERIALISM APPROVED?

The expansionist policies growing out of the war with Spain had, in general, been sponsored by Republicans and opposed by Democrats, though with many exceptions in both parties. Under the circumstances it was perhaps inevitable that "imperialism" should become an issue in the presidential campaign of 1900 and that the Democrats should attack their opponents for holding the Philippines by armed force against the will and despite the resistance of the most vocal native faction. Accordingly, whereas the Republican platform of that year sought to justify the establishment of American sovereignty in the Philippines as a necessary consequence of the breakdown of Spanish rule and promised to confer upon the Filipinos "the largest measure of self-government consistent with their welfare and our duties," the Democrats officially denounced "the Philippine policy of the present Administration" and "the greedy commercialism" that had dictated it. "We are unalterably opposed," said the Democratic platform, "to the seizing or purchasing of distant islands to be governed outside the Constitution and whose people can never become citizens."

> . . . we favor [the platform continued] an immediate declaration of the Nation's purpose to give to the Filipinos, first,_a stable form of government; second, independence; and third, protection from

outside interference such as has been given for
nearly a century to the republics of Central and
South America—

the last reference being obviously to the Monroe Doctrine. "Imperialism," said the Democrats, "is the paramount issue" in the campaign.[57]

Mr. Bryan, the Democratic candidate, fully endorsed
(probably had dictated) the party's platform declarations with regard to the Philippines, and Theodore
Roosevelt, the Republican selection for the vice presidency, bore the brunt of defending his party's expansionist policy.

The attack upon imperialism, however, was not confined to the Democrats. Many prominent men of both
parties joined hands in the Anti-Imperialist League,
which conducted a vigorous campaign of propaganda
based upon the principle of "government by the consent
of the governed."[58] It included in its ranks two ex-Presi-
dents, Cleveland and Benjamin Harrison, perhaps a
dozen senators of both parties, eight former members of
Cleveland's cabinets, and, outside political circles, such
prominent figures as Andrew Carnegie, Charles Francis
Adams, Jr., Carl Schurz, William Graham Sumner, Mark
Twain, William Dean Howells, Moorfield Storey, and
Gamaliel Bradford. Before the end of 1899 national
headquarters had been established in Chicago, and
branches existed in a dozen cities from Boston to Los
Angeles and Portland, Oregon. Opposed, from the beginning, to annexation of the Philippines, the League joined
the Democratic party in denouncing the war of subjuga-
tion against the Filipino insurgents and in demanding

that they be given independence. After some discussion
of the formation of a third party, the League's leaders
resolved instead to support Bryan for the Presidency.

Thus, on the surface, the political issue for 1900
seemed clear-cut, but, as usual in presidential campaigns,
the "paramount issue" did not stand alone.[59] Bryan had
insisted upon incorporating, as in 1896, a "free-silver"
plank in the Democratic platform. "Bryan would rather
be wrong than President," commented Thomas B. Reed,
Republican speaker of the House. Many Republican
anti-imperialists, like Senators Hoar and Hale, discovered that they preferred McKinley, with the gold standard and a little imperialism, to Bryan and free silver.
Bryan himself, as the campaign progressed, found that
his diatribes against imperialism excited little popular
enthusiasm and shifted his emphasis to an attack on the
trusts, the plutocracy, and special privilege. But even if
attention had been concentrated on the single issue,
there was no black and white difference between the
Democratic and Republican positions on the Philippines.
Republicans promised "self-government" and had never
expressed a determination to hold the Philippines as a
permanent possession. The Democrats made no proposal
to surrender to Aguinaldo and his insurgents. They
promised to "give" the Filipinos "a stable form of government" and independence, but under "protection from
outside interference"—a "protectorate" of undefined
duration. Who could say whether Filipino liberties would
be safer under Republican or Democratic auspices, or
under which the United States would run less risk of
being involved in Far Eastern politics? From that angle

a protectorate might be more dangerous than full possession of the islands, since it would involve responsibility without complete authority.

Thus, when American voters went to the polls in November, 1900 to cast their ballots for McKinley or Bryan, it is none too clear what their votes meant with respect to policy in the Philippines or colonial expansion in general. Certainly those who wished to vote for McKinley and the gold standard or for McKinley and a continuation of the prosperity which had come in with his administration, could persuade themselves that they were voting for little more "imperialism" than was implicit in the Democratic proposals. But there must have been very many, influenced by the propaganda of business and the churches, who were anxious to vote for a profitable imperialism that was at the same time an "imperialism of righteousness."

At any rate, when McKinley and Roosevelt won the election by a handy popular plurality of nearly 900,000 votes, the Republicans could be pardoned for assuming that the nation had accepted and approved their "large policy" of territorial expansion.

CHAPTER THREE

The Oceans United ～ ～

THE WAR with Spain and the events that followed it marked the enthronement in American policy of the principles of Captain Mahan. Mahan himself and such disciples of his as Lodge and Roosevelt had had much to do with shaping the terms of peace imposed on defeated Spain—terms that gave the United States bases in the Pacific and the Caribbean. The battles of Manila Bay and Santiago had been the best possible advertisement for the young American navy. Henceforth public opinion supported its rapid growth until within a decade the sea power of the United States was competing with that of Germany for the position of runner-up to the British. An assassin's bullet, fired in Buffalo, was presently to elevate to the Presidency Mahan's most apt and energetic pupil. Even before Theodore Roosevelt grasped the helm of state, President McKinley and his Secretary of State, John Hay, were well on the way to an enlargement and consolidation of American power in the Caribbean which should embrace an Isthmian canal owned and controlled by the United States, a protectorate over Cuba with the privilege of establishing naval bases in Cuban waters, and the acquisition of the Danish West Indies as an additional strong point commanding the routes to the Isthmus. The Caribbean policy of McKin-

ley and Hay resembled that of Seward 35 years earlier.
In fact, it is the opinion of Hay's most competent biographer that Hay thought with satisfaction of his policy
as being a continuation of that of Lincoln's Secretary of
State.[1] In every feature this policy was in harmony with
the teachings of the author of *The Influence of Sea
Power upon History.* It was to continue under subsequent administrations until by 1917 the Caribbean had
become virtually an "American lake."

This chapter will tell the story of the acquisition of the
Panama Canal Zone and the Danish West Indies. That
which follows will show how, by establishing protectorates in Central America and the Caribbean islands,
the United States made still more secure its position on
the approaches to the canal.

THE ISTHMIAN CANAL QUESTION

The focal point of American interest in the Caribbean
region was at the site, whether in Nicaragua or Panama,
of the future Isthmian canal. Here was the key to the
naval strategy and national security of the future—a boon
to the United States if firmly held in American hands, a
menace if controlled by potential enemies. Chapter I of
this volume described the initial failure of French efforts
at Panama, the attempt by American private capital to
construct a canal through Nicaragua, and the growing
belief in the United States that only a canal under American control was admissible. This belief, the events of
the war with Spain—the voyage of the *Oregon,* the acquisition of new possessions and new interests in the
Pacific—had hardened into a national conviction that

was voiced by President McKinley when he remarked in his annual message of December 5, 1898 that "the construction of such a maritime highway is now more than ever indispensable" and that "our national policy now more imperatively than ever calls for its control by this Government."[2]

To the successful pursuit of such a "national policy" the situation in 1898 presented both encouragement and obstacles. After the failure of the original French company at Panama, its rights and assets had been taken over by the New Panama Canal Company, another French corporation, which had secured from Colombia an extension to 1904 (subsequently by executive decree to 1910) of the concession that originally was to expire in 1894. The New Panama Canal Company had resumed work on the Isthmus on a reduced scale but had been unable to raise adequate capital and, by the close of 1898, was in a mood to dispose of its rights to the government of the United States if the consent of Colombia could be obtained.[3]

In Nicaragua, meanwhile, the Maritime Canal Company of Nicaragua, unable to raise the necessary funds from the public or to secure the coveted support from Congress, was forced to see its concession cancelled by the Nicaraguan government because of nonfulfillment of its contract. Thereafter the governments of both Nicaragua and Costa Rica were ready to dicker with the United States for the rights necessary for the construction of a national canal by that route. It seemed, then, that the United States might have its choice of Nicaragua or Panama for the "indispensable" canal under governmental control.

But before such a canal could be built by either route, a serious political obstacle must be either removed or by-passed. The Clayton-Bulwer Treaty of 1850 with Great Britain still stood, debarring either Great Britain or the United States from exclusive control of an Isthmian canal and requiring that such a canal, if built, must be neutralized under international auspices. Congress now showed a disposition to legislate for the construction, control, and protection of a Nicaraguan canal by the United States government in disregard of the old restrictions. Such a course would have entailed a clash with Great Britain that John Hay was particularly anxious to avoid. Under his urging and moved by a new need for American friendship, the British government was at last willing to consent to some modification of the terms of the treaty—preferably at a price. The price, it was hoped, might be paid in the northwest. The discovery of gold in the Klondike and the ensuing "gold rush" had produced an acute controversy over the boundary between the Alaska "panhandle" and British Columbia. Sovereignty over the headwaters of the Lynn Canal and the boom towns of Dyea and Skagway was at stake. The American claim was without doubt legally superior to that of Canada, but it seemed to Canadians and Englishmen that the United States might properly yield something here, where her case was strong, in return for British concessions at the Isthmus, where the United States had no legal case at all.[4] The United States, however, refused to make any concessions on the Alaska boundary or to admit any connection between that question and the question of the canal. Canal negotiations were stalled, therefore, until agreement on a temporary *modus vivendi* in the boundary dispute in the fall of 1899 enabled Lord Salisbury, British foreign minister, to proceed with them without too much loss of face.[5]

THE HAY-PAUNCEFOTE TREATIES

On February 5, 1900 Secretary Hay and Lord Pauncefote, the British ambassador, signed in Washington a treaty which Hay mistakenly believed would free the United States from all burdensome restrictions upon its proposed canal enterprise. The treaty permitted the United States government, eitherly directly or through a corporation, to construct, regulate, and manage a ship canal to connect the Atlantic and Pacific Oceans. So far so good; but the treaty also stipulated that the canal should be neutralized in accordance with the "general principle" of the treaty of 1850; it set up seven rules for neutralization, of which the first made the canal "free and open, in time of war as in time of peace, to the vessels of commerce and of war of all nations," and the last prohibited the erection of fortifications "commanding the canal or the waters adjacent," and provided that "the other Powers" should be invited to adhere.[6]

The text of the treaty was soon made public, and to Hay's profound disgust, its terms were assailed within and without the Senate. The press divided sharply in opinion. Such influential New York papers as the *Tribune, Times, Herald,* and *Journal of Commerce* favored the treaty. Many others denounced the ban on fortifications. The New York *Sun* proposed to annex Nicaragua as a state in order that the proposed canal might lie within domestic jurisdiction.[7] The same paper presently printed an attack on the treaty from Theodore Roosevelt, now Governor of New York. To his friend the Secretary of State, Roosevelt explained his two objections to the treaty:

> First as to naval policy. . . . If the canal is open to the war ships of an enemy it is a menace for us in time of war; . . . If fortified by us, it becomes one of the most potent sources of our possible sea strength. Unless it is fortified it strengthens against us every nation whose fleet is larger than ours. . . .
>
> Secondly as to the Monroe Doctrine. . . . To my mind, we should consistently refuse to all European powers the right to control, in any shape, any territory in the Western Hemisphere which they do not already hold.

He wished Hay and the President "would drop the treaty and push through a bill to build *and fortify* our own canal!"[8] In similar spirit Senator Lodge was writing:

> The American people will never consent to building a canal at their own expense, which they shall guard and protect for the benefit of the world's commerce, unless they have virtually complete control. . . . The American people mean to have the canal and they mean to control it.[9]

The Senate undertook to meet such criticisms by attaching three amendments to the treaty before approving it on December 20, 1900. The first amendment declared the Clayton-Bulwer Treaty superseded. The second stated that certain of the rules for neutralization should not apply "to measures which the United States may find it necessary to take for securing by its own forces the defense of the United States and the maintenance of public order." The third eliminated the provision for the adherence of other powers.[10]

These amendments the British government declined to accept. Lord Lansdowne, the new foreign minister, objected to the attempt by the Senate, without ascertaining the views of Great Britain, to set aside the Clayton-Bulwer Treaty. With more weight he complained that the effect of the second and third amendments together was to leave Great Britain bound by the rules of neutralization from which the United States was partially released by the second amendment and by which other powers would not be bound because of the third. Lansdowne was, however, ready to start afresh on the negotiation of a new treaty, and such a treaty was actually signed by Hay and Pauncefote on November 18, 1901.

By the second Hay-Pauncefote Treaty Great Britain yielded to virtually all the desires of the United States with reference to the canal controversy. The Clayton-Bulwer Treaty was expressly superseded. The provision for the adherence of other powers was omitted. The prohibition of fortification was dropped. Although the other rules for neutralization were retained, the first was modified by the omission of the phrase "in time of war as in time of peace," and whereas in the first treaty the rules were declared adopted by "the High Contracting Parties," in the second they were adopted by the United States alone. Thus Great Britain was released from special responsibility for their observance or enforcement and put, in this respect, on an equality with third powers. The United States was at liberty "to maintain such military police along the canal as may be necessary to protect it against lawlessness and disorder." The omission of the nonfortification clause and the accompanying correspondence made it clear that Great Britain would not take exception to the fortification of the canal.

The setting aside of the Clayton-Bulwer Treaty removed the 1850 pledge by the two powers against acquisition of territory or establishment of protectorates in the Isthmian region. The British were clearly apprehensive lest the United States might annex the area in which it proposed to build the canal and thereupon feel itself released from the pledge of equal treatment of the ships of all nations. To meet this apprehension a new article was embodied in the second treaty, declaring:

> It is agreed that no change in territorial sovereignty or of international relations of the country or countries traversed by the beforementioned canal shall affect the general principle of neutralization or the obligation of the High Contracting Parties under the present Treaty.[11]

Thus the United States secured a free hand in the construction and the defense of an Isthmian canal. It agreed to the equal treatment of the shipping of all nations in the use of the canal and to the neutralization of the canal in time of war; though, as Secretary Hay explained to the Senate, if the United States itself were at war, it would have "the clear right to close the canal against the other belligerent, and to protect it and defend itself by whatever means might be necessary." The exclusion of other powers from adherence to the treaty meant that the United States was answerable to Great Britain alone for the fulfillment of its engagements.

Other powers, as a German newspaper lamented, had neither responsibilities nor rights. "As long as England interposes no objection, the United States may use the canal against a third Power in any way it pleases."[12] England, in return for her concessions, gained the certainty that a canal would be completed and the assurance that it would be open to her vast commerce upon the same terms as to the commerce of the United States.[13]

The new treaty was sent to the Senate on December 4, 1901 and approved 12 days later by a vote of 72 to 6.

NICARAGUA OR PANAMA?

With the obstruction of the Clayton-Bulwer Treaty removed, the United States had next to choose a site for the proposed canal. The choice lay between Nicaragua, where lake and river provided a partial water communication between the oceans, and Panama, where the French had done a substantial amount of excavation and were now prepared to dispose of their rights and properties to the United States. Nicaragua had long been the preferred route for an American canal. A commission appointed by President Grant had recommended it in 1876. The Maritime Canal Company had endeavored to exploit the Nicaragua route, and strenuous efforts had been made in Congress to secure governmental backing for that company. These efforts had resulted in the appointment of two official bodies to investigate the Nicaragua route—the Nicaragua Canal Board of 1895 and the Nicaragua Canal Commission (often called the first Walker Commission from the name of its chairman, Rear Admiral J. G. Walker) of 1897-1899—both of which, without examining other routes, reported that the Nicaragua project was feasible.

The leading champion in Congress of the Nicaragua route was the gray-haired Senator John T. Morgan of Alabama. Morgan's motives have never been certainly determined, but it is probable he regarded the Nicaraguan site as most advantageous to the South, since it lay much nearer than Panama to ports on the Gulf of Mexico. Whatever the reason, the superiority of Nicaragua became with him an obsession, and he could not listen dispassionately to the advocacy of any other route. Without waiting for the final report of the Nicaragua Canal Commission or for the completion of negotiations with Great Britain, Morgan introduced and pushed through the Senate early in 1899 a bill providing for the construction, operation, and fortification by the United States government of a canal through Nicaragua.

At this point, however, the Panama route entered the picture as a serious rival of Nicaragua. Adoption by the United States of the Nicaraguan route would seal the doom of a Panama canal, and the only chance for the New Panama Canal Company to realize anything on its investment was in the sale of its holdings to the United States. Aside from its physical advantages—shorter length, less curvature, excavation perhaps two-fifths completed, and so on—the Panama route had two redoubtable champions, "super-salesmen," in William Nelson Cromwell and Philippe Bunau-Varilla. Cromwell, a member of the New York law firm of Sullivan and Cromwell, was American counsel for the New Panama Canal Company and a master hand at pulling political wires. Bunau-Varilla, a former chief engineer of the original French company and a stockholder in the new company, no doubt had a material interest in bringing about a sale of that company's rights. In addition, he seems to have been as unreasoning an enthusiast for the Panama route as Senator Morgan was for Nicaragua. He was as adept and as tireless at propaganda as Cromwell was at wire-pulling. Thoroughly disliking each other, the two men worked in their separate ways to the same end.[14]

In part through Cromwell's influence—or at least so he claimed—the Morgan Nicaragua Canal Bill was defeated in the House of Representatives. In its stead there finally emerged, as part of the Rivers and Harbors Appropriation Bill of March 3, 1899, a provision for a new investigation "of any and all practicable routes for a canal," particularly "the two routes known respectively as the Nicaragua route and the Panama route." The investigation was to be made by a new commission—the Isthmian Canal Commission, or second Walker Commission— which was to be appointed by the President and was to determine "the most practicable and feasible route for such a canal."[15] Thus Panama gained a position of equality with Nicaragua as a possible canal site.

Before going to Nicaragua and Panama, the Isthmian Canal Commission visited Paris, where both Cromwell and Bunau-Varilla exercised their persuasive powers upon its members. The Commission found satisfactory evidence that the New Panama Canal Company had the legal right, if the consent of Colombia were secured, to dispose of its holdings to the United States; but the company proved so very "cagey" in stating its terms and finally set such a high valuation upon its rights and properties, that the Commission, in both a preliminary and a supposedly final report (November, 1900 and November, 1901), recommended the Nicaragua route. A Panama canal would be shorter and have less curvature than one at Nicaragua. The average time of passage of a ship through the canal was estimated at 12 hours for Panama and 33 hours for Nicaragua. The actual cost of construction at Panama was estimated as less than at Nicaragua by $45,630,704, and the annual cost of maintenance as less by $1,300,000. Against all these advantages stood the fact that the New Panama Canal Company had valued its holdings at over $109,000,000—a figure which the Commission thought prohibitive. A fair valuation, said the Commission, would be $40,000,000. In view of all these facts, the Commission, in its report of November 16, 1901, recommended the Nicaragua route as "the most practicable and feasible."[16]

The New Panama Canal Company now faced the choice of seeing the Nicaragua route adopted or meeting the terms suggested by the Commission. It chose the latter alternative. On January 4, 1902 the president of the company cabled from Paris that the company would sell all its rights and properties for $40,000,000. Thereupon President Roosevelt reconvened the Commission, and the latter, on January 18, submitted a supplementary report favoring the Panama route on condition that suitable arrangements could be made with Colombia.[17]

The choice of routes now lay with Congress. On the basis of the Commission's November report, the House of Representatives had already passed (January 9, 1902) the Hepburn Bill, authorizing the President to secure the necessary rights at Nicaragua and appropriating $180,-000,000 for the construction of a canal by that route. In the Senate, on January 28, Senator Spooner of Wisconsin offered an amendment to the Hepburn Bill, giving preference to Panama, authorizing the President to pay $40,000,000 for the rights of the New Panama Canal Company, to acquire from Colombia perpetual control of a zone six miles in width across the Isthmus of Panama, and to construct a canal by that route; or, if satisfactory arrangements could not be made with either the company or Colombia, to proceed via Nicaragua. Thus the Senate became the battleground between the respective advocates of the Nicaragua and Panama routes. The Senate's Committee on Interoceanic Canals divided 7 to 4. The majority, led by Senator Morgan, the chairman,[18] preferred the original Hepburn Bill for the Nicaragua route and reported to that effect to the Senate on March 13.[19]

In the meantime, however, the sponsors of the Panama route had been very active. Bunau-Varilla had visited the United States in January, 1901, had lectured on Panama before groups of businessmen in many cities, published a pamphlet, carried on propaganda in the press, and won the ear of important politicians. Cromwell had been equally active, though in a less showy fashion. As early as September, 1901 Senator Lodge had informed the President that he was "strongly inclined to think that Panama is best."[20] By January, 1902 Panama had more supporters in the press than Nicaragua.[21]

Among politicians the most important convert to the cause of Panama was the powerful Republican senator from Ohio, Mark Hanna. Both Cromwell and Bunau-Varilla had been in touch with Hanna, and both claimed credit for his conversion. The subject was congenial to him. "The operation of canals," he told the Senate, "was one of the few subjects with which in my business life I had become acquainted from experience in all directions." To what extent Hanna himself studied the merits of the rival routes is uncertain. Herbert Croly, his biographer, claims that Hanna initiated a survey of the opinions of 80-odd ship captains, all of whom, as it turned out, preferred Panama to Nicaragua. Cromwell, on the other hand, asserts that this survey was made by his law firm after being authorized by Hanna "at our suggestion." At any rate, as a member of Morgan's Senate Committee, Hanna became the leader of the minority of four which, on May 31, 1902, submitted an impressive report in support of the Panama route—a report that laid much stress upon the fact that all members of the Isthmian Canal Commission, a body of experts, considered the Panama route superior to that via Nicaragua. In the ensuing Senate debate, Hanna led, with skill and with a superb array of facts, the fight for Panama.[22]

Against Hanna's array of facts, Morgan and the other Nicaragua senators had to rely largely on an emotional appeal. They made much of the scandal that had attended the Panama enterprise from the first and deplored the prospect that the United States should expose itself to such contamination. They shed tears, figuratively at least, over the fate of the shareholders of the original French company, ignoring the fact that the choice for these shareholders was either a portion of the $40,000,-000 sale price or nothing at all. But the Nicaragua forces were still powerful, and they might perhaps have won their fight had not nature dealt them a telling blow. The fact that Nicaragua had volcanoes and Panama had none

had counted for little with the Isthmian Commission.
Early in Máy, 1902, however, the volcano of Mt. Pelée
in the Caribbean island of Martinique burst forth in a
terrific eruption, destroying the town of St. Pierre and
pouring out a volume of lava and ash sufficient, it was
claimed, to fill up every cubic yard of the proposed
excavation in Nicaragua. The champions of Panama
made the most of this opportune explosion. The minority of the Senate Committee pointed out that Nicaragua
excelled Panama both in the possession of volcanoes and
in the frequency of earthquake shocks. Bunau-Varilla, in
a famous gesture, placed on the desk of every senator a
Nicaraguan postage stamp featuring a smoking volcano
in the middle of Lake Nicaragua. Obligingly, Mount
Momotombo in Nicaragua produced an eruption—so it
was reported in the press—and an accompanying earthquake destroyed the wharves at a neighboring town.
Bad omen for the fate of a Nicaragua canal! The American press ascribed much importance to these events in
determining the outcome of the senatorial battle.[23] On
June 19, 1902 the Senate adopted the Spooner Amendment by a vote of 42 to 34 and passed the amended bill,
67 to 6. The House concurred, and on June 28 the Isthmian Canal Act became law. "We consider it," said the
New York *Evening Post*, "one of the most gratifying tri-
umphs of reason over prejudice that this country has
ever seen."[24]

Colombian Dilemma

It was now for the executive branch of the government to determine, first, whether a clear title to the
rights and property of the New Panama Canal Company

could be obtained, and second, whether the Colombian government would grant the rights that the United States thought essential to the construction and operation of a canal at Panama. On the first point the Attorney General's office satisfied itself during the summer and fall of 1902. The second problem was much more complicated.

From 1899 to late in 1902 the Republic of Colombia was torn by a destructive civil war. Its President, José Manuel Marroquín, an aging and well-intentioned intellectual, held office by a precarious tenure. The canal situation presented not the least of his difficulties. If he secured the canal for Panama by making the necessary concessions to the United States, he would run the risk of impairing his nation's sovereignty and promoting "Yankee imperialism." If not, either the adoption of the Nicaragua route by the United States, or a possible revolt of the Department of Panama, would deprive Colombia forever of the advantages expected to accrue from a canal located in Colombian territory. In either event, Marroquín would be held responsible by his political enemies.[25] It is not surprising that he vacillated. Alarmed at the progress in Washington of the Nicaragua project, in 1900 he sent Martinez Silva, his foreign minister, to negotiate with the United States but failed to give him adequate instructions and eventually recalled him. Silva's successor, Concha, proved so suspicious of American intentions that John Hay could make no progress with him. He was in turn recalled and the work of negotiation devolved upon Dr. Tomás Herrán, previously secretary of legation in Washington. Herrán took charge in November, 1902. By this time the Isthmian Canal Act had passed Congress, the Attorney General had found the New Panama Canal Company competent to confer legal title, and the choice of route depended solely on the issue of negotiations with Colombia. Herrán was instructed to agree to a treaty with the United States on the best terms obtainable. He and Secretary Hay signed a treaty on January 22, 1903. Three days later Herrán received a cable from Bogotá instructing him not to sign. He did not revoke his signature, and the treaty was sent to the United States Senate, which approved it on March 17, 1903.

The Hay-Herrán treaty provided that the New Panama Canal Company might sell or transfer to the United States all its rights and privileges on the Isthmus, including its stock in the Panama Railroad; that the United States should have for 100 years (renewable for similar periods at its discretion) exclusive rights to construct, operate, and control a canal and to use and control a zone across the Isthmus five kilometers (about three miles) wide on either side of the canal, excluding the cities of Colon and Panama. A system of mixed courts was to administer justice in the zone. The canal was to be neutralized according to the terms of the Hay-Pauncefote Treaty. The United States was to furnish armed forces to protect it if Colombia was unable to do so. The sovereignty of Colombia in the zone was affirmed and safeguarded. Finally, the United States was to pay to Colombia $10,000,000 in gold upon exchange of ratifications of the treaty and an annuity of $250,000 beginning 9 years thereafter.[26]

Peaceful conditions had now been restored in Colombia, and in June President Marroquín submitted the treaty to a newly elected Senate, which, like the Senate of the United States, had the constitutional right to approve or reject treaties. Weeks before the Senate met it was apparent that there would be strong opposition to the treaty. Colombian opinion objected to the monetary compensation as inadequate, to the perpetually renewable nature of the grant, and to the mixed courts as an infringement of Colombian sovereignty. Principle, avarice, and politics mingled in the opposition. There was a widespread belief that the United States was irrevocably committed to the Panama route and that, by holding out, Colombia could obtain better terms. Dr. Herrán was quoted as saying:

> The Colombian people believe that the consideration of the Nicaraguan Canal route by the United States Government was merely a ruse, a barefaced bluff, and they scoff at the idea that there was anything more in it than just that.[27]

It was characteristic of Marroquín's hesitant course that he now sought to shift responsibility for the treaty to the Senate, to which he submitted it without his signature and with a noncommittal letter. Senate opinion was adverse from the beginning. On July 9 General Reyes, a close friend of Marroquín, informed the United States minister that the treaty was not likely to win approval unless it could be modified to provide for a payment of $10,000,000 from the New Panama Canal Company and $15,000,000 from the United States—a total of $25,000,000 instead of the $10,000,000 specified by the treaty as it stood. Secretary Hay refused to consider any amendments to the treaty and warned Colombia that rejection or undue delay in ratification might result in action being "taken by the Congress next winter which every friend of Colombia would regret." This and other rather peremptory notes had the opposite effect from that intended. An infuriated Colombian Senate on August 12 voted down the treaty by 24 to 0, two senators not voting and one absent. A committee report subsequently submitted to the Senate argued that the extension by executive decree of the New Panama Canal Company's franchise to 1910 was illegal and that the company's rights would therefore expire October 31, 1904. The suggestion was plain that by delaying action until the last-mentioned date Colombia would be in a position to collect the $40,000,000 earmarked for the company. The Senate adjourned October 31, 1903, without further action on the treaty.[28]

ROOSEVELTIAN DILEMMA

What course should the United States follow? Two possible procedures were obvious and of unquestionable correctness. It might try further negotiations with Colombia, or it might abandon the Panama route altogether and proceed by way of Nicaragua. But neither of these courses appealed to the impetuous President Roosevelt. He was determined to have the Panama route[29] and equally determined not to be "held up" by the Colombian politicians, whom he described as "jack rabbits," "contemptible little creatures," and "foolish and homicidal corruptionists." In his view, the hesitant and timid Marroquín was a ruthless dictator who had made a treaty and had now instructed his "puppets" to repudiate it in expectation of further gain, thus obstructing an enterprise of world-wide importance.

How could Colombian obstructionism be circumvented? A method much talked of in the press was the secession of Panama from Colombia and a treaty with an independent Panama government. "The simplest plan of coercing Colombia," said the Indianapolis *Sentinel* in August, "would be inciting a revolution in Panama . . . and supporting the insurrectionary government." Many other papers echoed the suggestion, and a Washington correspondent reported that "many public men of prominence" privately favored this course.[30] Senator Lodge wrote Roosevelt from Paris: "I am in strong hopes that either under the treaty of '46 or by the secession of the Province of Panama we can get control of what undoubtedly is the best route." Roosevelt admitted a private wish that Panama were independent, but added: "for me to say so publicly would amount to an instigation of a revolt, and therefore I cannot say it."[31]

If Panama should not secede, there was another expedient that was brought to Roosevelt's attention. By the treaty of 1846 New Granada (now Colombia) had promised that "the right of way or transit across the Isthmus of Panama" should be "free and open to the Government and citizens of the United States"; and the United States in turn, by the same treaty, had guaranteed the neutrality of the Isthmus in the interest of peaceful transit and also "the rights of sovereignty and property" of New Granada in the Isthmus. Professor John Bassett Moore of Columbia University, a leading American expert in international law, now sent to Roosevelt by way of the State Department a memorandum in which he argued that since for over 50 years the United States had faithfully fulfilled its obligations under the treaty—landing troops on various occasions to keep the transit open—it had every right to insist that Colombia fulfill its side of the bargain by permitting the United States to utilize its "right of way" for the construction of a canal. In fact, Professor Moore hinted that even without the treaty of 1846, the United States might be justified in forcing a recalcitrant Colombia to consent to the construction of this essential link in the highways of the world's commerce. He quoted a note written by Secretary of State Lewis Cass in 1858. Referring to the governments of Central America, Cass had said: "Sovereignty has its duties as well as its rights; and none of these local governments, . . . would be permitted in a spirit of Eastern isolation to close these gates of intercourse on the great highways of the world, . . ."[32]

Moore's memorandum resulted in his being summoned to Roosevelt's summer home at Oyster Bay. There is no record of their conversation, but it is plain that Roosevelt planned to act along the line that Moore had suggested. If Panama remained quiet, he wrote later, "I was prepared to recommend to Congress that we should at once occupy the Isthmus anyhow, and proceed to dig the canal"; and his statement is supported by a tentative draft of a message that he planned in that event to send to Congress.[33]

But Panama did not remain quiet, and the contemplated message was never sent to Congress. On November 3, 1903, three days after the adjournment of the Colombian Senate, Panama declared its independence. This stroke, widely predicted in the American press, had been in preparation at least since the preceding May. In that month a little group of conspirators at Panama City, closely allied with the Panama Railroad (a subsidiary of the New Panama Canal Company), had begun laying plans for the secession of Panama from Colombia if the latter should reject the treaty. Economic life or death for the Isthmus hung in the balance till the canal question was settled, and the motives of the local Panamanians are as obvious as those of the agents of the company. During the summer the conspirators had approached Cromwell in New York and had received assurance of his financial and political support, but when Dr. Amador, who had become their leader, came to New York in September to make final arrangements, he found himself barred from Cromwell's office. The Colombian legation in Washington had got wind of the plot, and the attorney feared that if he were implicated in it, Colombia would summarily cancel the company's concessions.[34]

"Disappointed" was the laconic message which Amador cabled to his associates in Panama, and he was on the point of returning home disheartened when, on September 23, the ever-alert Bunau-Varilla arrived in New York from Paris and once more imparted a rosy hue to the prospects of Panama. For one thing, he promised Amador $100,000 for the expenses of the revolution. More important, perhaps, he secured interviews with both President Roosevelt and Secretary Hay in which —if we may believe his own account—by discreetly leading the conversation to the subject of the canal and watching the reactions of the two men, he assured himself that the United States would act to prevent Colombia from suppressing a revolt on the Isthmus. No inconvenient questions were asked and no promises of any kind were given, but on the basis of these interviews Bunau-Varilla felt warranted in sending Dr. Amador back to Panama with assurances that if the Panamanians would make a revolution, the United States would protect it. By similar indirect methods he was able, after Amador's return, to predict accurately the arrival of United States naval vessels at Colon and Panama.

Roosevelt's later assertion—"No one connected with the American Government had any part in preparing, inciting, or encouraging the revolution"[35]—was probably technically correct, but the government was well informed, by army officers who had visited the Isthmus and otherwise, that revolution was brewing and that it was likely to occur early in November. In September Hay had written Roosevelt that if insurrection should occur in Panama, the United States must act "to keep the transit clear" and had added significantly: "Our intervention should not be at haphazard nor, this time should it be to the profit, as heretofore, of Bogotá."[36] Accordingly, as the time for the insurrection drew near, naval vessels were dispatched to both sides of the Isthmus, and orders of November 2 directed their commanding officers to "maintain free and uninterrupted transit" and to "prevent landing of any armed force, either government or insurgent, at any point within fifty miles of Panama."[37]

These orders did not reach Commander John Hubbard of the *Nashville* at Colon in time to prevent the disembarkation of 400 Colombian troops who arrived at that port November 3, but officials of the Panama Railroad found means of delaying their transportation to

Panama. The revolution had been scheduled for November 4, but the situation demanded haste, and the standard of independence was raised at Panama November 3. A judicious use of money—a part of the $100,000 advanced by Bunau-Varilla—secured the adherence of the Colombian officers and troops at Panama and the departure of the force that had landed at Colon. Thanks to the insistence of the United States upon maintaining "peaceful transit," the revolution succeeded almost without bloodshed. (One Chinese was killed at Panama when a Colombian gunboat threw a few shells into the city.)

The government at Bogotá had received ample warning that rejection of the canal treaty might provoke the secession of Panama. It had taken that danger too lightly. Now, too late, General Reyes approached the United States minister with the proposal that if the United States would assist Colombia in recovering control of the Isthmus, the Colombian government would declare martial law and, as authorized by the constitution "when public order is disturbed," would "approve by decree the ratification of the canal treaty as signed"; or if the United States preferred, would call an "extra session of Congress with new and friendly members next May to approve the treaty."[38] It has been argued that this offer proves that Marroquín was really a dictator, that, had he so wished, he could easily have procured the ratification of the treaty in the recent session of Congress. This reasoning is not sound. A real national emergency had now arisen. Under stress of it the Colombian President could, both constitutionally and politically, exercise powers that in the earlier months were beyond his reach.

The Reyes proposal was of course rejected in Washington. On the very day it was made (November 6) Secretary Hay had instructed the United States consul general in Panama to extend *de facto* recognition to the new government as soon as he was satisfied that it was "republican in form, and without substantial opposition from its own people." This step the consul general took on the following day. On November 13 President Roosevelt formally received Bunau-Varilla, who, by the terms of his bargain with Amador, became first minister of Panama to the United States. This act gave the new government *de jure* status. On November 18 Hay and Bunau-Varilla signed a treaty between the United States and Panama, which the new envoy had been in great haste to negotiate before more authentic Panamanian representatives could arrive on the scene.

The treaty was accepted with some reluctance by Panama and approved by the United States Senate February 23, 1904, despite a vigorous opposition led by Senator Morgan. It closely resembled the defunct Hay-Herrán treaty, but was more favorable to the United States and contained novel features that made Panama a "protectorate" of the United States. "The United States," said the first article, "guarantees and will maintain the independence of the Republic of Panama." The United States received "in perpetuity the use, occupation and control" of a zone ten miles wide instead of six, and within it might exercise all rights and authority that it would possess if its position were that of sovereign. The United States might employ its armed forces and build fortifications to defend the canal. It might take steps to ensure sanitation and to maintain public order in the cities of Colon and Panama. The compensation to be paid to Panama was the same as that previously offered to Colombia—$10,000,000 at once and $250,000 annually beginning after nine years.[39]

END OF A CONTROVERSY

The circumstances of the Panama revolution—the appearance of American collusion, the veto by the United States of Colombian attempts to suppress the uprising, the unusual haste with which recognition was extended and an advantageous treaty made—created bitter resentment in Colombia and divided opinion in the United States. A number of influential American papers denounced the President's policy. The *New York Times* called it "the path of scandal, disgrace, and dishonor," and the *Evening Post* declared that an American administration had made "the Jameson Raid look respectable" and the "Walker filibusters appear like Christian statesmen." There were other critics, but most of the Republican papers supported the President's policy, and they were joined by a surprisingly large proportion of the independent and Democratic press. Southern papers found a sly satisfaction in this endorsement of the right of secession by a statesman who had denounced Jefferson Davis as a traitor.[40]

The President himself energetically defended his course of action, and he was ably backed by John Hay and Elihu Root, his Secretaries of State and War. In his annual message of December 7, 1903 Roosevelt described the events leading to the revolution and declared:

Under these circumstances the Government of the United States would have been guilty of folly and weakness, amounting in their sum to a crime against the Nation, had it acted otherwise than it did when the Revolution of November 3 last took place in Panama. . . .[41]

To his dying day Roosevelt not only defended his handling of the Panama crisis, he took evident pride in it. "By far the most important action I took in foreign affairs," he said of it in his *Autobiography.* "I took the canal zone and let Congress debate," he boasted in a public address in 1911.[42] Recent scholars have not shared Roosevelt's confident assurance that he followed the only right procedure but are inclined to think his action unnecessarily precipitate and unjustified by treaty or precedent.

Colombia, naturally enough, believed that she had suffered a grievous wrong at the hands of the United States. Later attempts by Secretaries of State Root and Knox to mollify Colombia's resentment and secure, for a consideration, her recognition of Panama's independence were coolly received in Bogotá. Colombia's repeated proposals that the question whether the part played by the United States was in accord with its treaty obligations and with international law be submitted to arbitration were rejected by the United States. Secretary Bryan, in 1914, signed a treaty expressing the regret of the United States that anything had occurred to mar a beautiful international friendship and providing for a payment of $25,000,000 to Colombia. The treaty was denounced by Roosevelt as submission to blackmail and blocked by his friends in the Senate. In 1921, two years after Roosevelt's death, the Senate approved a treaty giving Colombia

$25,000,000 but containing no expression of regret or apology. Thus Colombia received the very sum, without interest, that she had presumably been willing to accept in 1903. The payment was a tacit admission of wrong-doing on the part of the United States. It was reported that senatorial approval was made easier by pressure from American capitalists who were to be rewarded with oil concessions in Colombia for bringing about a satis-factory settlement of the old quarrel over Panama.[43]

Transfer of the French property on the Isthmus to the United States took place on May 4, 1904. Construction of the canal, though attended with some bungling at the outset, went forward rapidly, and on August 15, 1914 the Panama Canal was opened to the traffic of the world.[44]

At Last—The Danish West Indies

The tiny islands of St. Thomas, St. John, and St. Croix owe their importance entirely to two factors: their stra-tegic location on the Anegada Passage, giving access from the Atlantic to the Caribbean and the Isthmian area, and the fact that one of them, St. Thomas, contains a fine harbor, which, in a day of relatively small war-ships, had potentialities as a naval base. As related in earlier pages, their possible value to the United States had impressed William H. Seward, who in 1867 had negotiated with Denmark a treaty for their purchase, only to see it pigeon-holed by the United States Senate. Nearly 30 years later Senator Henry Cabot Lodge had secured in the Republican party platform of 1896 a plank calling for their acquisition and had obtained the back-ing of the McKinley administration for their purchase.

Denmark, willing to dispose of a white elephant, had called off the transaction on the eve of the Spanish-American war, fearing that under those circumstances a transfer of the islands might constitute "a diplomatic discourtesy to Spain."[45]

The results of the War with Spain—the acquisition of Puerto Rico and the subsequent arrangement with Cuba giving the United States the use of Guantanamo Bay as a naval base—lessened the positive importance of the Danish islands to the United States but did not remove the possibility that they might pass into the hands of a rival naval power, such as Germany, and thus become a threat to American dominance of the Caribbean and the approaches to the future Isthmian canal. Since this menace could not be removed by sinking St. Thomas in the ocean, it still seemed the part of statesmanship for the United States to acquire the islands and thus eliminate the possibility of their falling into unfriendly hands. This, at least, was the chief line of argument for their acquisition employed after 1898. The fact that a Danish adventurer, Captain Walter Christmas von Dirckinck-Holmfeld, had attempted to arrange a sale of the islands to Germany before visiting the United States for a similar purpose pointed up the possibility of German acquisition. That he had failed in his scheme gave no assurance that similar attempts in the future might not succeed. In reality, though the German Navy would no doubt have been pleased to have the islands, the German Foreign Office was too well aware of American sensitiveness to any violation of the Monroe Doctrine to risk American displeasure by attempting a purchase.[46]

Secretary John Hay, in any event, became convinced

that the safest place for the Danish possessions was under the Stars and Stripes. On January 24, 1902 he signed with the Danish minister a treaty for the sale of the three islands to the United States for a price of $5,000,000. For a third time, however, the advocates of purchase were doomed to disappointment. The new treaty, approved by the United States Senate, was defeated by a tie vote in the Danish Landsthing or Upper House. The islands had no economic value to Denmark —they were a burden in fact—but a patriotic or sentimental objection to parting with national territory, combined with a hope that they might be traded to Germany for North Schleswig (torn from Denmark in 1864) prevented ratification. A belief, common in the United States though apparently without foundation, that German influence had blocked the treaty increased American distrust of German intentions and helped pave the way for the next and final purchase negotiation.

Maurice Francis Egan, appointed United States minister to Denmark in 1907, was from the first anxious to achieve the purchase of the islands but received no encouragement from Danish circles until after the outbreak of the war in Europe. Though he became more hopeful in 1915, it was not until Secretary of State Robert Lansing combined a threat with an offer of a lucrative price that the Danish government finally yielded. Lansing, fearful that a German victory in Europe might bring both Denmark and her colonial possessions under German control, warned the Danish minister that if such an event seemed likely, the United States would be forced to seize the West Indian islands for its own protection. To prevent such a possibility the United States

was ready to buy the islands at a price of $20,000,000—
four times the amount of its offer of 1902. From the
Danish point of view it was obviously better to sell the
islands for a good round sum than to risk losing them by
seizure. Denmark asked $27,000,000 but agreed to ac-
cept $25,000,000. A treaty on these terms was signed on
August 4, 1916. The United States Senate gave prompt
approval. In December, after submitting the proposal
to a popular vote in Denmark, the Danish Parliament
approved, and ratifications were exchanged on January
17, 1917.[47]

On March 31, 1917 the three islands with their 26,000
inhabitants, mostly English-speaking Negroes, were
transferred to the United States. Henceforth they were
to be known as the Virgin Islands of the United States.
A half-century of intermittent effort had at last achieved
a result that added something to American security in
the Caribbean. The original cost was high; the upkeep,
in both dollars and headaches, was destined to be far
higher.

CHAPTER FOUR

Caribbean Sphere of Influence ～ ～

CONTROL of the Caribbean did not rest solely upon out-right annexations of territory, as in Puerto Rico and the Virgin Islands, or upon perpetual leases, almost the equivalent of annexation, as in the Panama Canal Zone. Between 1901 and 1917 the United States devised a system of "protectorates" by which it gained sufficient control of a number of small republics rimming the Caribbean to bind them securely into an American "sphere of influence." The term "protectorate," however, like the word "colony," had no place in the American official vocabulary.

The principal recipients of American "protection" were Cuba, Panama, the Dominican Republic, Nicaragua, and Haiti. The special relations of the United States to these republics were embodied in treaties, no two of which were exactly alike. To only one such state, the Republic of Panama, did the United States actually promise "protection"—in the declaration that "the United States guarantees and will maintain the independence of the Republic of Panama." Other treaties, such as those with Cuba and Haiti, contained engagements on the part of the "protected" states not to impair their independence or cede any of their territory to a third party; and the same two treaties permitted intervention by the

United States for the maintenance of independence or of orderly government. Since careless public finance was likely to lead to foreign intervention and possible loss of independence, a number of the treaties—those with Cuba, Haiti, and the Dominican Republic—contained restrictions upon, or gave the United States oversight over, financial policy. By the treaties with Cuba and Nicaragua the United States gained the privilege of using naval bases within the territorial limits of the "protected" states, and by that with Nicaragua it obtained exclusive canal rights through Nicaraguan territory.

In all the countries of this Caribbean semicircle of protectorates American investments existed. These no doubt benefited from the increased stability and financial responsibility induced by governmental policy. In the Dominican Republic, Haiti, and Nicaragua that policy resulted in a transfer of the ownership of government obligations from European to American bankers. Yet in none of the five republics save Cuba were American financial interests large or important, and the charge that the Caribbean policy of the United States was primarily one of "financial imperialism" is not sustained by the facts. The dominant motive was clearly political and strategic rather than economic. The acquisition of the Canal Zone and the building of the Panama Canal made the Isthmian area a vital spot in the American defense system. It became, then, a matter of the utmost importance that the United States itself should control the bases requisite for the defense of the canal and that no rival great power should obtain a foothold in the vicinity of the canal or on the approaches to it. Hence the securing of base rights in Cuba and Nicaragua, and hence the exaction of nonalienation agreements from Cuba and Haiti and the control of the public finance of these and other Caribbean republics. The establishment of protectorates thus became a species of "preventive intervention," which Theodore Roosevelt, in his celebrated "corollary" message of December, 1904, sought to justify as merely an application of the Monroe Doctrine. Still another motive, which influenced different administrations in the United States to varying degrees, was a genuine desire to substitute orderly democratic processes for the chronic addiction to armed revolution that afflicted most of the Caribbean and Central American states.

Panama, whose special relations with the United States were described in the last chapter, was the second Caribbean republic to become a protectorate of the United States. Cuba had preceded it, and it was followed by the Dominican Republic, Nicaragua, and Haiti. The story of how these things came about can now be related in chronological order.

CUBA AND THE PLATT AMENDMENT

The end of the war with Spain had left Cuba occupied by the armed forces of the United States but with its future status not clearly defined. By the Treaty of Paris, Spain had merely relinquished "all claim of sovereignty over and title to Cuba," and the United States had agreed, for the period of its occupation of the island, to "assume and discharge the obligations that may under international law result from the fact of its occupation, for the protection of life and property." The United

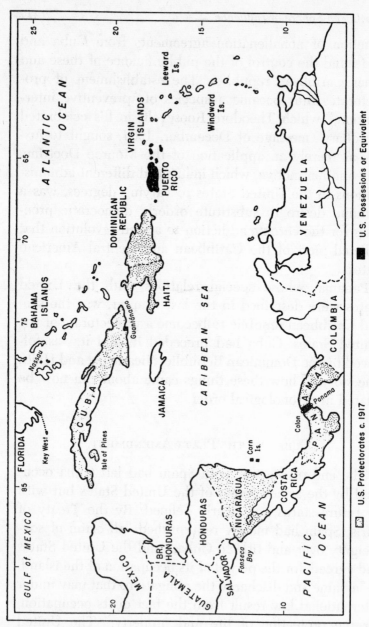

U. S. Possessions and Protectorates in the Caribbean

■ U. S. Possessions or Equivalent

▨ U. S. Protectorates c. 1917

States had never recognized the Cuban insurgent government but had, in the Teller Resolution embodied in its ultimatum to Spain, disclaimed all intention of annexing the island and declared its purpose, after pacification should have been accomplished, "to leave the government and control of the Island to its people." Did that mean that after pacification should be complete, the United States was to place Cuba in a condition of unfettered independence, washing its hands of the troublesome island? President McKinley evidently thought not. In his annual message of December 5, 1899 he remarked that the United States had "assumed before the world a grave responsibility for the future good government of Cuba." "The new Cuba," he continued, ". . . must needs be bound to us by ties of singular intimacy and strength if its enduring welfare is to be assured."[1]

The immediate problem, however, was to restore an island devastated by four years of war to a condition of economic, social, and political health, if that was possible. Direction of this task fell largely to General Leonard Wood, who served as military governor of Cuba from December 13, 1899 to May 20, 1902. The period was one of much beneficial achievement in the fields of sanitation, public works, education, court reform, separation of church and state, and preparation for self-government. Impatience with military rule among the people of Cuba as well as among anti-imperialists in the United States (with a presidential election impending in 1900!) led to the holding of municipal elections in June, 1900 and to the issuing by the governor on July 25, 1900 of an order for the election of delegates to a convention "to frame and adopt a Constitution for the people of Cuba." This was the normal American mode of procedure in setting up a government for a new political organism. That the Cuban government about to be formed was to bear a special relation to that of the United States was indicated when the order specified further that as a part of the Constitution, the convention should "provide for and agree with the Government of the United States upon the relations to exist between that Government and the Government of Cuba."[2]

The Cuban Constitutional Convention sat from November, 1900 to February, 1901, and on February 21 the delegates signed a constitution which in many respects resembled that of the United States. The delegates had paid no heed, however, to the second task that Wood had given them—the definition of relations between Cuba and the United States. What those relations should be Elihu Root, McKinley's Secretary of War, had undertaken to state in a letter to Wood of February 9, 1901.[3] Wood reported that there was opposition to some of Root's conditions and that, in any event, it would be easier for the Cuban delegates to accept them if they were presented as a demand than to yield to them voluntarily. Accordingly Root's proposals were introduced in the Senate by Senator Orville H. Platt of Connecticut as an amendment to the Army Appropriation Bill of March 2, 1901 and became law in that form.[4] The Platt Amendment, as it was henceforth called, authorized the President to terminate the military occupation of Cuba as soon as a Cuban government should have been established under a constitution that, "either as a part thereof or in an ordinance appended thereto," should "define the future relations of the United States and Cuba, substantially as follows." Then were stated, with minor changes, the points previously set forth by Secretary Root. These may be summarized as follows:

1. Cuba should never make any treaty with any foreign power that should impair its independence nor permit any foreign power to obtain "lodgement or control over any portion of said island."

2. Cuba should agree not to contract any debt beyond the capacity of its ordinary revenues to pay.

3. Cuba should consent that the United States might intervene "for the preservation of Cuban independence, the maintenance of a government adequate for the protection of life, property, and individual liberty," and for the discharging of the treaty obligations that would now devolve upon Cuba from the United States.

4. Cuba should ratify all the acts of the United States military government.

5. It should agree to execute the sanitary program instituted by the military government.

6. Title to the Isle of Pines (a small island south of the western end of Cuba) should be left to future adjustment by treaty with the United States.

7. "To enable the United States to maintain the independence of Cuba, and to protect the people thereof, as well as for its own defense, the Cuban Government will sell or lease to the United States the lands necessary for coaling or naval stations, at certain specified points, to be agreed upon with the President of the United States."

8. "The Government of Cuba will embody the foregoing provisions in a permanent treaty with the United States."

The terms of the Platt Amendment were objectionable to the members of the Cuban Convention, who at first rejected them by a vote of 24 to 2 and later accepted them by a close vote after a series of conferences with Secretary Root. Root gave assurance that the intervention contemplated in the third article was "not synonymous with intermeddling or interference with the affairs of the Cuban government" but would take place only in the event of foreign threat or domestic disturbance; otherwise Cuba would be left in entire control of her own affairs. He pointed out also that this article was "the Monroe Doctrine, but with international force. Because of it, European nations will not dispute the intervention of the United States in defense of the independence of Cuba."[5]

The new Cuban government was inaugurated on May 20, 1902. The Platt Amendment took its place as an Appendix to the Cuban Constitution and was embodied in the permanent treaty of 1903 between Cuba and the United States. It remained in force until 1934, when all of it except the naval base article was abrogated. Under that article the United States enjoyed the use of Guantanamo Bay, on the south coast near Santiago, as a naval station. Under Article 3 the United States exercised the right of intervention from time to time, notably in 1906-1909, following a breakdown of the Cuban government, but so frequently in subsequent years as to violate, in the opinion of many, Root's promise that the article would not result in "intermeddling or interference." Such intervention ceased after 1934 when the treaty basis for it ceased. In the meantime the United States had not only its naval base at Guantanamo, which it kept after 1934, but also the assurance that no rival power would secure a foothold in Cuba.[6]

THE ROOSEVELT COROLLARY OF THE MONROE DOCTRINE

Secretary Root had spoken of the Platt Amendment as supplying a basis in international law for intervention by the United States under the Monroe Doctrine to protect the independence of Cuba. But with how much justice or logic could the United States enforce the Monroe Doctrine against European intervention in turbulent American republics if it took no responsibility for the behavior of such republics or for the fulfillment of their obligations to Europe? The Platt Amendment, by restricting the debt-contracting power of Cuba and by permitting the United States to intervene for the preservation of orderly government, had hinted that the Monroe Doctrine involved certain policing responsibilities for the United States. That idea, though now for the first time written into law, was by no means novel. As early as 1858 Sam Houston had told the Senate that if the United States was to warn Europe to keep its hands off the Latin American countries, it must itself take some action "by which these nations may be made useful to the community of nations, and advantageous to the cause of commerce, social organization, and good government."[7] Several Secretaries of State had suggested that the United States might take over the collection of Venezuelan customs and apply the proceeds to payment of Venezuela's foreign debts. When President Cleveland and Secretary of State Olney in 1895 invoked the Monroe Doctrine to compel England to arbitrate her boundary dispute with Venezuela, the British foreign minister had complained of the disposition of the United States to use the Monroe Doctrine for the protection of "a number of independent states for whose conduct it assumes no responsibility," and the London *Chronicle* had remarked that if the United States proposed to enforce the Monroe Doctrine, it ought to take responsibility "for the foreign policy of all the petty, impetuous little states on the two continents."

In 1901, when the German and British governments were contemplating the use of force to collect debts from the Venezuelan dictator, Cipriano Castro, Roosevelt (as yet only Vice President) wrote to a German friend: "If any South American country misbehaves toward any European country, let the European country spank it"; and in his first annual message, a few months later, he declared that the Monroe Doctrine gave no guarantee to any American state against punishment for misconduct, provided that punishment did not take the form of acquisition of territory.[8] When, however, in the winter of 1902-1903, Germans and British actually undertook to bring Castro to terms by a "pacific blockade," anti-German sentiment flared up in the United States, and Roosevelt became alarmed over the possibility that such a situation might produce a serious quarrel between the United States and some European power. The Venezuelan crisis was settled when Castro agreed to submit the question of his debts to arbitration, but no one knew when Venezuela or one of its neighbors might present a new invitation to coercion. It seemed to Roosevelt desirable to find a formula by which all excuse for European intervention in the New World might be removed.[9]

The formula was announced by Roosevelt in 1904, first in May in a letter to Secretary Root, later, in almost identical language, in his annual message of December 6, 1904. As stated in the annual message it read as follows:

> Any country whose people conduct themselves well can count upon our hearty friendship. If a nation shows that it knows how to act with reasonable efficiency and decency in social and political matters, if it keeps order and pays its obligations, it need fear no interference from the United States. Chronic wrongdoing, or an impotence which results in a general loosening of the ties of civilized society, may in America, as elsewhere, ultimately require intervention by some civilized nation, and in the Western Hemisphere, the adherence of the United States to the Monroe Doctrine may force the United States, however reluctantly, in flagrant cases of such wrongdoing or impotence, to the exercise of an international police power.[10]

THE DOMINICAN RECEIVERSHIP

This "Roosevelt Corollary of the Monroe Doctrine"— so called because it was assumed to follow as a necessary consequence of the Monroe Doctrine—was to serve, whether expressly mentioned or not, as the theoretical basis for the subsequent establishment of protectorates in the Caribbean—in the Dominican Republic, Nicaragua, and Haiti. Uncle Sam now assumed the role of international policeman—kindly to the law-abiding, but apt to lay a stern hand upon little nations that fell into disorder or defaulted on their obligations, since disorder and default, if allowed to continue, might invite intervention from outside the hemisphere. The first application of the new doctrine was in the Dominican Republic. In fact, it was a threatening situation in the Dominican Republic that had led to Roosevelt's pronouncement.

The government of the Dominican Republic, or Santo Domingo, since that state won its independence from Haiti in 1844, had been a dictatorship generously tempered by revolution.[11] Ruling governments and revolutionists alike had borrowed money at home and abroad, and when revolution won, as it usually did, the debts of the revolutionists were superimposed upon those of the former government. By a repetition of this process, and in other ways, the Dominican debt had grown to a figure —some $32,000,000—that the national revenues, as administered by native collectors of taxes and customs, were incapable of servicing. The foreign debt was widely distributed. Portions of it were held in France, Belgium, Italy, and Germany. The largest single creditor, representing both American and British capital, was the San Domingo Improvement Company of New York. From time to time the Dominican government had pledged the customs duties at various ports as security for its debts, and the pledges sometimes conflicted. Intervention by the United States in behalf of the Improvement Company resulted, in 1903 and 1904, in that company's being placed in charge of the collection of customs at Puerto Plata and Monte Cristi on the north coast, bringing protests from the European creditors, who claimed that those same revenues had previously been pledged to them. An international scramble for control of the Dominican customhouses threatened, with the possible development of a situation resembling the one in Venezuela that had alarmed Roosevelt a scant two years earlier.[12]

It was under these circumstances that Roosevelt formulated his famous "Corollary," which was without doubt intended as a forecast of coming events. With the encouragement of Thomas C. Dawson, United States minister to the Dominican Republic, President Morales invited the United States to take charge of the nation's customhouses and administer the collection of import duties for the purpose of satisfying the creditors of the Republic and providing its government with revenue. An agreement to this effect was signed at Santo Domingo on January 20, 1905. It stipulated that the United States, "guaranteeing the complete integrity of the territory of the Dominican Republic," should undertake the adjustment of all its obligations, "foreign as well as domestic," should take charge of all customhouses and customhouse receipts, paying at least 45 per cent of these to the Dominican government and applying the balance (after expenses of collection) to the payment of interest and principal of the debt. The United States was also, at the request of the Dominican government, to "grant such other assistance as may be in its power to restore the credit, preserve the order, increase the efficiency of the civil administration, and advance to [the] material progress and the welfare of the Republic."[13]

The agreement contained no provision for its submission to either the United States Senate or the Dominican Congress, and as it was to go into effect on February 1, 12 days after its signature, it is evident that it was designed as an executive agreement. This was the wish of President Morales, who feared the effect on his fortunes of a possible rejection by the United States Senate, recalling that "Baez had been overthrown in 1873, when the American Senate rejected the annexation treaty."[14]

With a view, apparently, to bolstering the waning strength of his administration, Morales promptly published the agreement in Santo Domingo, whence it was as promptly cabled to the United States. This attempt by President Roosevelt to by-pass the Senate in the conclusion of what was essentially a treaty produced such an uproar in Congress and the press that the State Department was compelled to cable new instructions to Minister Dawson, and a new agreement, in the form of a treaty, subject to ratification in the constitutional manner, was signed on February 7. The new treaty, or "protocol," invoked the principles of the Monroe Doctrine as the justification for intervention, substituted a promise to "respect" for the promise to "guarantee" the territorial integrity of the Republic, and embodied a number of other changes designed to make it more acceptable to the Senate.[15] President Roosevelt sent it to the Senate February 15, with a message strongly urging its approval and assigning the Monroe Doctrine as its justification. The only means, he said, by which foreign creditors could enforce their claims against the Dominican Republic was acquisition of territory or the occupation of customhouses, which amounted to almost the same thing, and which, if effected by European governments, was repugnant to the principles of the Monroe Doctrine.

It has for some time been obvious [the President continued] that those who profit by the Monroe doctrine must accept certain responsibilities along with the rights which it confers; and that the same statement applies to those who uphold the doctrine. . . . The justification for the United States taking this burden and incurring this responsibility is to be found in the fact that it is incompatible with international equity for the United States to refuse to allow other powers to take the only means at their disposal of satisfying the claims of their creditors and yet to refuse, itself, to take any such steps.[16]

Despite the President's urgent plea and the unanimous support of Republican senators, Democratic opposition prevented Senate approval of the treaty, which was not brought to a vote. By an executive agreement of April 1, 1905, however, referred to as a *modus vivendi,* the essence of the proposed arrangement was put into effect. The Dominican government agreed to appoint as receiver of customs a citizen of the United States nominated by the American President. As in the proposed treaty, 45 per cent of the receipts were to be turned over to the Dominican government; the remainder, less costs of collection, was to be deposited in a New York bank, to be apportioned among the creditors of the Republic if the Senate approved the treaty, or returned to the Dominican government if the treaty was finally rejected.[17]

The *modus vivendi* remained operative for over two years. During that period the Morales government, and the like-minded government of Cáceres, who succeeded Morales in December, 1905, was supported by the presence of United States naval vessels in Dominican waters. At the same time the adjustment of the Dominican debt was undertaken by Professor Jacob H. Hollander of Johns Hopkins University, with the result that the debt of over $30,000,000 was reduced to $17,000,000. A new $20,000,000 bond issue was floated in the United States, and the proceeds were applied to paying off the adjusted debt and to the execution of needful public works in the island. In February, 1907 a new treaty was signed, which the Senate promptly approved through the switch of a few Democratic votes to its support. By the new treaty, proclaimed July 25, 1907, it was agreed that the President of the United States should appoint a general receiver of Dominican customs and such subordinates as might be necessary, who should have full control of the collection of customs duties until the $20,000,000 bond issue should have been liquidated. All revenues not required for expenses of collection (limited to 5 per cent) and for interest, amortization, and cancellation of the bonded debt were to be turned over to the Dominican government, which agreed not to increase its public debt without prior consent of the United States until the existing bonded debt should be discharged. The Dominican government promised protection, "to the extent of its powers," to the general receiver and his assistants; the United States promised to give them "such protection as it may find to be requisite." The treaty made no mention of the Monroe Doctrine, and the United States assumed no obligation other than the administration and protection of the receivership.[18]

The Dominican receivership, under both the *modus vivendi* and the subsequent treaty, produced gratifying results. Not only was the old adjusted debt paid off and satisfactory service on the new debt established, but such was the improved efficiency and honesty of the customs collection that the sums paid over to the Dominican government after service on the debt exceeded the total customs revenues that had found their way into the treasury under the earlier régime. For some four years after the conclusion of the treaty it appeared that the receivership had produced not only financial solvency but political stability as well. Then began a new series of revolutionary disturbances which led to a more drastic form of intervention by the United States.[19]

INTERVENTION IN NICARAGUA

The next Caribbean country to receive the "protection" of the United States was Nicaragua. Intervention in Nicaragua, initiated under William H. Taft as President and Philander C. Knox as Secretary of State, was a prominent example of the "dollar diplomacy" usually associated with that administration. Dollar diplomacy had a dual character. On one side, it was the use of diplomacy to advance and protect American business abroad; on the other side, it was the use of dollars abroad to promote the ends of American diplomacy. In the first sense, as Professor J. Fred Rippy has remarked, it was practiced by many an administration before Taft and after.[20] The employment of American dollars to advance the political and strategic aims of diplomacy was a less familiar technique. There was a hint of it in the Platt Amendment. It was plainly seen in the refunding of the debt and the instituting of the receivership in the Dominican Republic under Theodore Roosevelt. Invoking, as Roosevelt had done, the Monroe Doctrine as their justification, Taft and Knox made a similar arrangement with Nicaragua and sought unsucessfully to do the same with Honduras and Guatemala.[21]

The setting up of the Nicaragua customs receivership was preceded by the ousting of the dictator José Santos Zelaya, who had ruled the little republic with an iron hand since 1893. The United States gave both moral and material support to the revolutionists who overthrew Zelaya in 1909. How far the revolution, and the official American support of it, stemmed from the dislike of American business interests for Zelaya is problematical. The undisputed facts are that Zelaya had threatened to cancel certain American concessions in Nicaragua, that Adolfo Diaz, who eventually emerged as the pro-American President of Nicaragua, had been secretary of an American mining company at Bluefields, and that Philander C. Knox, in the days of his private law practice, had been an attorney for Pittsburgh capitalists with Nicaraguan investments. Beyond that, we have little but hearsay evidence for the influence of American business in the Nicaraguan intervention,[22] and American investments in that little country were then, and have since remained, of minor consequence, amounting to only about $2,500,000 in 1912 and $17,000,000 in 1928—less than in any other Latin American country except Paraguay.[23] They simply do not explain the intense interest in Nicaragua shown by the Taft administration.

That interest is easily explicable on grounds of national

policy. Nicaragua not only lay close to the Panama Canal —in the "danger zone"—it was the possessor of the only alternative canal route. The dictator Zelaya had made himself quite as objectionable to the American government as to American business by keeping Central America in international turmoil; by paying slight heed to the Central American peace treaties, negotiated in 1907 in Washington under the sponsorship of the United States and Mexico; by contracting sizable loans in Europe; and by rumors, at least, that he was willing to dispose of canal rights to Great Britain or Japan. The American interest in this situation was clearly expressed by Secretary Knox in an address in 1912.

> The logic of political geography and of strategy [he stated], and now our tremendous national interest created by the Panama Canal, make the safety, the peace, and the prosperity of Central America and the zone of the Caribbean of paramount interest to the Government of the United States. Thus the malady of revolutions and financial collapse is most acute precisely in the region where it is most dangerous to us. It is here that we seek to apply a remedy.[24]

The remedy that Taft and Knox sought to apply was precisely that which Roosevelt had applied in the Dominican Republic—an adjustment of the claims against Nicaragua through the good offices of the United States, the refinancing of the Nicaraguan debt through loans from American banks, and a guarantee of the services on that debt through the appointment of a United States expert as receiver of customs. By these means it was hoped that Nicaragua might attain both financial and political stability, the peace of all Central America might be made more secure, and all peril of European intervention in that quarter might be removed. American banks and other forms of business would presumably profit in the process, but the evidence seems more than adequate that such profits were a minor consideration with the administration; that its main motive was peace and security in the area surrounding the canal. American dollars were to serve the ends of American diplomacy rather than *vice versa*.

It is not necessary to recount all the details of the American intervention in Nicaragua. After the ousting of Zelaya and his adherent, Madriz, General Juan J. Estrada served briefly as President and was succeeded in May, 1911 by Adolfo Diaz. Almost alone among Nicaraguan politicians Diaz was no "general." A businessman, formerly secretary of the American-owned La Luz and Los Angeles Mining Company, he despised militarism, craved order and good government, and to that end was willing to compromise his country's independence by granting to the United States broad powers of intervention. It is not surprising that before he had been long in office he was faced with a military revolt headed by General Mena, his secretary of war. At the request of Diaz, the United States landed over 2,000 marines in Nicaragua, suppressed the rebellion, deported Mena to Panama, and left at Managua, the capital, a "legation guard" of marines, which, for the next 13 years (1912-1925), "stabilized" the Nicaraguan government under Diaz and his successors.

Before the accession of Diaz, however, Thomas C. Dawson (the same diplomat who had negotiated the

Dominican customs controls) had arranged with Estrada for the creation of a claims commission consisting of one Nicaraguan and two Americans, which went to work in May, 1911 and eventually scaled down claims of $13,-750,000 against the Nicaraguan government to a mere $1,750,000.[25] In Washington, on June 6, 1911, Secretary Knox and Nicaraguan Minister Castrillo signed a convention providing for a customs receivership. Nicaragua was to arrange with American banks for a loan for the purpose of refunding its internal and external debt, settling claims, and placing its finances on a stable basis. The new loan was to be secured by the Nicaraguan customs, and these were to be administered, during the life of the loan, by a collector general of customs, appointed by the Nicaraguan government from a list submitted by the bankers and approved by the President of the United States. The collector general was to enjoy the full protection of Nicaragua and, if necessary, that of the United States.[26]

Accepted by the Nicaraguan Congress and warmly endorsed by President Taft, the Knox-Castrillo convention was never brought to a vote in the Senate of the United States. The bankers, Brown Brothers and J. and W. Seligman, who had agreed to a refunding loan of $15,000,000 if the convention was approved, reduced the amount to a paltry $1,500,000, to be followed later by other hand-to-mouth loans. The receivership, however, was not dependent upon the ratification of the treaty. It was instituted by simple agreement between Nicaragua, the bankers, and the State Department, and in December, 1911 Colonel Clifford D. Ham, formerly surveyor of the port of Manila, began 17 years of efficient service as collector general of customs. The British bond-holders, the principal European creditors of Nicaragua, agreed the next year to permit the collector general to provide for service on their bonds. By another agreement of 1917, a new High Commission—one Nicaraguan appointee, one named by the Secretary of State, and, if necessary, an umpire also named by the Secretary of State—was given limited control over Nicaragua's spending policy, and the collector general might, under certain circumstances, take over the control of internal revenue as well as customs.[27]

The Senate's failure to approve the Knox-Castrillo convention and the resulting failure of the proposed $15,000,000 loan left the Nicaraguan treasury in a necessitous condition. Diaz needed money. The United States was willing to pay a moderate sum for a long-term option on Nicaragua's canal route. Which side took the initiative in this matter is not clear, but on February 8, 1913, just before Knox left office, a treaty was signed by which the United States was to pay $3,000,000 for the canal option and certain other privileges. This treaty reposed in the Senate until after the advent of Woodrow Wilson as President and William Jennings Bryan as Secretary of State, and then negotiations were begun anew. President Diaz, who had previously expressed a desire to permit the United States "to intervene in our internal affairs in order to maintain peace and the existence of a lawful government," now proposed that the substance of the Platt Amendment be embodied in the canal treaty,

> so that my countrymen may see Nicaragua's credit improved, her natural resources developed, and peace assured throughout the land. I believe [he

continued] that revolutions will cease if your Government can see its way clear to grant the addition of the Amendment as requested.[28]

Secretary Bryan and his chief, anti-imperialists and critics of dollar diplomacy though they had been, saw merit in these suggestions from Diaz, and a treaty was prepared which, in addition to the canal clauses, contained provisions by which Nicaragua undertook not to declare war without the consent of the United States and not to make any treaty that would impair its independence or its territorial integrity, with provision that the United States might intervene in Nicaragua to preserve its independence or to protect life and property. Consultation with members of the Senate Foreign Relations Committee, however, convinced Bryan that these clauses had no chance of Senate approval. They were therefore deleted, and a canal treaty without them was signed by Bryan and Emiliano Chamorro, Nicaraguan minister, on August 5, 1914. Even so, it was not approved for nearly two years. It was finally proclaimed on June 24, 1916.[29]

By the Bryan-Chamorro Treaty the United States obtained a perpetual and exclusive right to construct a canal through Nicaragua, a 99-year lease of the Great and Little Corn Islands in the Caribbean, and a 99-year right to establish a naval base in Nicaraguan territory on the Gulf of Fonseca, both lease and right renewable for another 99-year period. In return the United States paid Nicaragua $3,000,000 to be applied on the payment of its indebtedness or for other purposes approved by the Secretary of State of the United States.

Three of Nicaragua's neighbors—Costa Rica, El Salvador, and Honduras—filed protests against the canal treaty, Costa Rica on the ground that she had equal rights with Nicaragua in the San Juan River segment of the canal route; the others asserting that their rights were violated by the grant of privileges in the Gulf of Fonseca. The United States Senate amended the treaty by adding a proviso that nothing therein should impair the existing rights of the protesting states. Not satisfied with this declaration, Costa Rica, El Salvador, and Honduras carried their case before the Central American Court of Justice, where they won a verdict against Nicaragua. Neither Nicaragua nor the United States accepted the decision. The Court, hopefully created by treaties negotiated in Washington in 1907 with the blessing of the United States, went out of business in 1918 as a consequence of this defiance of its authority. This unfortunate result might have been avoided if the State Department had shown more regard for the sensibilities of the states concerned and more tact in consulting them before and during the negotiations with Nicaragua.[30]

By 1916 the United States had secured from Nicaragua at trifling cost a perpetual monopoly of the canal route through that country and the privilege of setting up naval bases, if they should be needed, at each end of the route. It had also succeeded, not by treaty but by informal agreement with Nicaragua and the bankers, in reducing and simplifying the Nicaraguan debt and in setting up a customs receivership which would see to it that a suitable portion of the national revenue was applied on the debt. Application of the Roosevelt Corollary, implemented by dollar diplomacy and the landing of a few marines, had made Nicaragua secure against any violation of the Monroe Doctrine.

WILSONIAN INTERVENTION

That the treaty that consummated the success of dollar diplomacy in Nicaragua bore the name of William Jennings Bryan was ironical, for Bryan, out of office, had been a severe critic of dollar diplomacy. Equally ironical was the circumstance that Bryan, the arch-anti-imperialist of other days, who had denounced the Platt Amendment as destroying Cuban independence, had tried earnestly to incorporate the main provisions of the Platt Amendment in the treaty with Nicaragua. Still more surprising developments were to come, however. The anti-imperialist Wilson administration, with first Bryan and later Robert Lansing as Secretary of State, while promoting independence for the Philippines and self-government for Puerto Rico, was to force at gunpoint upon Haiti a protectorate treaty of unprecedented severity and to set up in the Dominican Republic, when its demand for new reforms was rejected, a régime of naked force.

There is perhaps less of contradiction than at first appears between the new administration's policy in the Philippines and Puerto Rico and its policy toward the independent republics of the Caribbean. The Philippines and Puerto Rico, under American tutelage, had been learning the lessons of democracy and conducting orderly elections in which ballots, not bullets, determined the outcome. Perhaps a few years of American tutelage would suffice to complete the political education of the natives of Haiti and the Dominican Republic, who hitherto had found the bullet a more congenial instrument. Wilson had been in the White House but a week when he read to his Cabinet, and subsequently gave to the press, a statement on his proposed Latin American policy in which he stressed the importance of orderly government and democratic processes. The desired friendship and cooperation with the "sister republics" of Latin America, he said, would be possible

> only when supported at every turn by the orderly processes of just government based upon law, not upon arbitrary or irregular force. . . . We can have no sympathy with those who seek to seize the power of government to advance their own personal interests or ambition.

To his Cabinet Wilson remarked, as one of them reported, that "the agitators in certain countries wanted revolutions and were inclined to try it on with the new administration. . . . he was not going to let them have one [revolution] if he could prevent it."[31] To an official British visitor he later asserted: "I am going to teach the South American republics to elect good men!"[32]

These declarations, though called forth primarily by disturbed conditions in Mexico, were equally applicable in the Caribbean republics. They foreshadowed a new turn in American interventionist policy, in which the promotion of democracy would take its place as an objective beside the preservation of the Monroe Doctrine and the protection of the economic and strategic interests of the United States. Unfortunately, although the new measures were effective in restoring order and preventing revolutions by force, they did little or nothing toward providing a substitute for revolutions in the form of free and fair elections. Whether because of the absorption of effort in World War I or for other reasons, the Washington schoolmaster quite neglected to "teach the . . . republics to elect good men," or to elect any men at all by democratic methods.

Bryan, who had been a more outspoken anti-imperialist than Wilson, now surpassed his chief in the degree of his conversion. Influenced by the permanent staff of the State Department, alarmed at the possibility of violations of the Monroe Doctrine, and susceptible to arguments based on the needs of military security, he became the advocate of a new corollary by which the United States government should itself become banker to the republics of the "Caribbean Danger Zone," supplying on easy terms the funds needed to liquidate their European debts and to promote essential economic development and social services. This variation of dollar diplomacy was never accepted by Wilson, and Bryan, like his predecessor, had to rely upon American bankers as sources for the funds needed to promote his policy. His policy embraced the establishment of customs and financial control in Haiti, the strengthening of that in the Dominican Republic, and the supervision of elections in both. He was urging such measures at the time of his resignation (June, 1915). Under his successor, Robert Lansing, forcible intervention came about in both republics.[33]

HAITI—THE FIFTH PROTECTORATE

The "black republic" of Haiti, unlike its eastern neighbor the Dominican Republic, had maintained its independence continuously since the time of Toussaint l'Ouverture. It had also been more successful than its neighbor in meeting the interest payments on its rather large foreign debt; but in the prevalence of corrupt tyranny complicated by frequent revolution it surpassed its rival on the island. In the early twentieth century corruption grew more flagrant and revolution more frequent, and bankruptcy, default, and the menace of European intervention loomed on the horizon. Here seemed an obvious point for an application of the Roosevelt Corollary. Albert Shaw, editor of the *Review of Reviews,* inquired of Secretary Root in 1908 whether, having established American control over Cuba, Panama, and Santo Domingo, he could not "invent a way to put Haiti under bonds" before leaving the State Department. The cautious Secretary replied that "for any positive step . . . we must wait for the 'psychological moment.'" President Roosevelt would willingly have established some sort of control over Haiti if public opinion, as he wrote, would "back a reasonable and intelligent foreign policy."[34] Secretary Knox, in his turn, secured for American bankers a 20 per cent share in the French-dominated Banque Nationale d'Haiti when it was reorganized in 1910 (German interests at the same time obtaining entry to the extent of 6 per cent), but the "psychological moment" for intervention was delayed until after the advent of Wilson and Bryan.[35]

Revolution in Haiti assumed a regular cyclical pattern. For years every occupant of the president's palace at Port au Prince owed his position to successful revolution (followed, of course, by a "regular constitutional election" by the Haitian Congress) and lost it in similar manner. Any would-be president hied to the north coast, where he gathered an army of "*cacos*"—a species half bandit, half mercenary soldier, always ready to follow a revolutionary leader for pay or generous promises. He proceeded along the coast, via Gonaives and St. Marc, to Port au Prince, where he won an easy victory over a predecessor who had lost the support of the fickle populace of the capital. The new president installed himself in the palace, while a leading rival or a dissatisfied lieutenant departed for the north coast to repeat the process.

Thus in the summer of 1911 Cincinnatus Leconte overthrew Antoine Simon. A year later, in a minor variation of the cycle, he was blown up with the palace. His successor, Tancrède Auguste, died within less than a year, presumably by poison. Michel Oreste then ruled for nine months and in January, 1914, was turned out by Oreste Zamor. In October of the same year Zamor was driven into exile by Davilmar Théodore, whose term was cut short the following February by Vilbrun Guillaume Sam. As Sam assumed office, a Dr. Rosalvo Bobo, friend of Théodore, headed for the *caco* country, but the next cycle was destined to be interrupted by an external force.

Conditions in Haiti approximated those which Roosevelt had described as calling for "the exercise of an international police power." "Chronic wrongdoing," he had said ten years before, "or an impotence which results in a general loosening of the ties of civilized society, may . . . ultimately require intervention by some civilized nation." "Chronic wrongdoing" and governmental "impotence" certainly characterized Haiti in these years. The national finances were falling into chaos. At the request of the Banque Nationale, American marines in 1914 had removed to New York $500,000 pledged for redemption of the currency, lest it be seized by the government for current expenses. Subsequently the Banque, as fiscal agent, found it necessary to suspend payments to the government, since all funds in hand were required for service on the debt. It is possible that the Banque was seeking to bring about intervention. An American-owned railroad company was threatened with cancellation of its concession and appealed to the State Department. French and German creditors were restive. The German government had earlier shown special vigor in pressing the claims of its subjects against the Haitian government and now demanded to have a part in any plan for the control of Haitian finances—a demand that Wilson and Bryan rejected as incompatible with the Monroe Doctrine. Lansing later told a mysterious tale of German sailors having been secretly landed at Port au Prince and suddenly withdrawn on the eve of the outbreak of war in Europe in 1914.[36]

Under these circumstances it is not surprising that the United States began urging upon Haitian presidents measures designed to bring some order out of the chaos into which the country had fallen and to guard against European intervention. Thus Mr. Bryan asked for the United States the right to appoint a customs receiver, as in Santo Domingo, and a financial adviser. He asked the right to supervise Haitian elections, and he asked a non-alienation pledge as to Mole St. Nicholas—potential naval base at the northwest corner of the island. Negotiations along these lines proceeded, but so kaleidoscopic were the changes in Haitian administrations that no results had been achieved by July, 1915, when Mr. Guillaume

Sam met an end even less peaceful than was customary with presidents of Haiti.

As was previously stated, Dr. Bobo had gone to the *caco* country to inaugurate a revolution. President Sam retaliated by seizing some 170 supposed partisans of Bobo in and around Port au Prince. An attack on the palace on the night of July 26 served as a signal for the cold-blooded massacre of almost all these political prisoners. Sam sought asylum in the French legation. Two days later an infuriated mob invaded the legation, threw Sam into the street, and hacked his corpse to bits as if for souvenirs. On the same afternoon (July 28) the U.S.S. *Washington*, flagship of Rear Admiral Caperton, dropped anchor in Port au Prince harbor, and before nightfall the marines had occupied the town. The "psychological moment" had arrived.

Marines, American and of various other nationalities, had landed before on Haitian soil, to protect life and property or to enforce claims, and had departed, leaving the Haitian government intact. The 1915 occupation was to be different. Exasperated at the long reign of anarchy in Haiti and at the failure of treaty negotiations, the United States was resolved to use the new crisis to enforce its demands upon the Haitian government. The first step toward that end was to secure, as successor to Sam, a president who would be amenable to American wishes. Had nature been permitted to take its course, the National Assembly would have elected Dr. Bobo to the presidency, for his candidacy was backed by the persuasive force of his *caco* army.[37] But Dr. Bobo was not acceptable to the United States, and it fell to Admiral

Caperton to select a rival candidate. The man eventually chosen was Philippe Sudre Dartiguenave, president of the Haitian Senate and inclined to be friendly to the United States. High Washington officials were outspoken about their preferences and about what they would expect of the successful candidate. The State Department instructed the United States minister to make clear to the Haitian Congress that the United States could not recognize "action which does not establish in charge of Haitian affairs those whose abilities and dispositions give assurances of putting an end to factional disorders." The Secretary of the Navy was still more explicit. "The United States prefers election of Dartiguenave," he cabled Admiral Caperton. The United States, Caperton was further informed, would "insist that the Haitian government will grant no territorial concessions to any foreign governments" and would take up the question of the cession of Mole St. Nicholas with other matters to be settled after the reorganization of the Haitian government. The State Department, meanwhile, instructed the United States minister to make clear to the presidential candidates in advance of the election "that the United States expects to be entrusted with the practical control of the customs, and such financial control over the affairs of the Republic of Haiti as the United States may deem necessary for efficient administration."[38]

Dartiguenave apparently agreed to meet these conditions.[39] What was the real preference of the members of the National Assembly between the rival candidates can only be guessed, but with Bobo backed by a tatterde-malion *caco* army and Dartiguenave supported by the United States Marine Corps, the expedient choice was plain. On August 12, 1915 Dartiguenave was elected to the presidency by 94 votes out of 116.

A few days after the election President Dartiguenave was presented with a project of a treaty drafted under the direction of Secretary of State Lansing and was virtually requested to sign on the dotted line. The proposed treaty combined the principal features of the Platt Amendment and the Dominican Receivership and added such improvements as the nomination by the President of the United States of a financial adviser to the Haitian government, the organization under American command and direction of a national constabulary, and the appointment, upon American nomination, of an engineer, or engineers, to supervise measures of sanitation and public improvements which the United States was to decide upon and Haiti was to carry out. This was more than Dartiguenave had bargained for; he objected and threatened to resign. Lansing conceded a few minor modifications in phraseology, and the treaty, so modified, was signed on September 16, 1915. Meanwhile, on instructions from Washington, Admiral Caperton had seized the Haitian customhouses and impounded the revenue, using a part thereof for the organization of a national constabulary to war on the *cacos;* on his own initiative he had taken over the municipal administration of the coastal towns and had put the entire republic under virtual martial law. These high-handed measures antagonized such conservative Haitians as had looked with favor upon a limited protectorate; they increased the opposition in the National Assembly to the ratification of the treaty. Only when it was made plain that the choice was between accepting the treaty and submitting to military government by the United States did the legislative houses yield. The Chamber of Deputies gave its consent on October 6, the Senate on November 11. The United States Senate approved the treaty in February, 1916 without public debate. Ratifications were not exchanged until May, 1916, but by executive agreement the terms of the treaty had been put in effect on the preceding November 29.

THE HAITIAN TREATY OF 1915

The Treaty of 1915 with Haiti went further in establishing American control and supervision than the Platt Amendment treaty with Cuba or the Dominican treaty of 1907, or than both combined. It provided that the following officials should be appointed by the President of Haiti upon nomination by the President of the United States:

> A general receiver of customs, to collect all duties on imports and exports.
>
> A financial adviser, to devise a system of accounting, inquire into the status of the national debt, and make recommendations to the minister of finance.
>
> An engineer, or engineers, to supervise measures of sanitation and public works.
>
> Officers of the newly organized native constabulary, who might, however, be replaced by Haitian officers as the latter became qualified.

All Haitian governmental debts were to be classified

and arranged, and Haiti was not to increase its debt without the consent of the United States. Revenues collected by the general receiver were to be applied (1) to the expenses of the offices of general receiver and financial adviser, (2) to interest and sinking fund on the debt, (3) to payment of the constabulary, and (4) to other expenses of the government. Haiti agreed to do nothing to alienate any of its territory or impair its independence (the United States made no demand for the cession of Mole St. Nicholas). Finally, as in the case of Cuba, the United States might take any necessary measures to preserve Haitian independence or to maintain "a government adequate for the protection of life, property, and individual liberty."[40] The treaty was to remain in force for ten years, but a clause permitting its extension for another ten-year period upon either party's showing sufficient cause was invoked by the United States in 1917, thus prolonging to 1936 the prospective life of the treaty.

Aside from the immediate restoration of order and the elimination of all excuse for European intervention, it was presumably hoped that tying up the revenues and organizing an efficient constabulary would remove at once the chief motive for revolution and the chance of its succeeding. Unfortunately neither at this time nor in the new constitution, drafted with American aid in 1918, were any steps taken to complement these reforms with the introduction of democratic political processes. The result was a reasonably efficient dictatorship dominated by the United States treaty officials with the support of the navy and Marine Corps.

THE NAVY GOVERNS THE DOMINICAN REPUBLIC

Interest in the Caribbean area now shifted eastward to the Dominican Republic. Here, until 1911, the customs receivership of 1905 and 1907 had worked admirably. Under the presidency of Ramón Cáceres (1906-1911) stable government and orderly finance had been the rule; constitutional reforms had been adopted, and surplus revenues had been applied to port improvements, highway and railroad construction, and education.[41] Such a novel employment of the powers and resources of government was displeasing to many Dominican politicians, and on November 19, 1911 Cáceres fell victim to an assassin's bullet. At once the Republic reverted to its seemingly normal condition of factional turmoil and civil war, and the necessities incident to the conducting and suppressing of revolutions resulted in the contraction of a large floating debt, contrary to the spirit if not to the letter of the 1907 treaty with the United States. Secretary of State Knox, by an application of financial pressure, brought about the resignation of one president and the election of a successor, Archbishop Nouel of Santo Domingo. It was hoped that he might reconcile the factions and restore order. For this he proved entirely incompetent and finally fled to Europe.

Thus the Wilson administration found in the Dominican Republic a situation as difficult as that in Haiti. In July, 1914 Wilson himself drafted a plan under which factional hostilities were to cease, the leaders were to agree upon a temporary provisional president, and elections were to be held with American observers at the polls to insure their fairness. The United States would recognize a president and congress so chosen and would thereafter feel free to insist that all future changes in government be accomplished by peaceful and constitutional processes.[42] The plan was accepted and elections were held in October, 1914. Of the new president, Jiménez, the United States now demanded a new treaty providing for the appointment of a financial adviser with control over disbursements, for the extension of the authority of the general receiver to cover internal revenue as well as customs, and for the organization of a constabulary. These demands were rejected as violative of Dominican sovereignty, and in the spring of 1916 the situation went from bad to worse when the Dominican secretary of war, Desiderio Arias, an open opponent of the United States, launched a new revolution and seized Santo Domingo, the capital. On May 15 United States marines were landed in Santo Domingo, and the occupation was gradually extended to other ports and to the interior of the island. Jiménez resigned the presidency. To his successor, chosen by the legislature, the United States refused both recognition and—through its control of the receivership—funds, until he should agree to accept the proposed treaty. When this was refused, Secretary Lansing proposed to President Wilson that the Dominican Republic be placed under military government, such action to be based "on the interpretation which the United States has given to the Dominican Convention of 1907 and also upon the present unsettled conditions in the Republic." Wilson reluctantly gave his consent to this course, "convinced [he wrote] that it is the least of the evils in sight in this very perplexing situation."[43]

Accordingly, on November 29, 1916 Captain H. S. Knapp, the naval officer commanding at the capital, proclaimed the establishment of a military government by the forces of the United States in Santo Domingo. Cabinet posts were taken over by Marine Corps officers, the legislature was suspended, and for the next six years the government of the Dominican Republic was administered by the United States Navy Department. The situation differed from that in Haiti in that the weak Haitian government, by consenting to the protectorate treaty demanded by the United States, had preserved some vestiges of its independence, whereas the Dominican government, by refusing less drastic demands, had seen all its functions taken over by officers of a foreign power. Had Haiti similarly refused, there is little doubt that it also would have been subjected to military government. In both republics, though in slightly different ways, the Wilson Administration had carried to its logical conclusion the "international police power" doctrine of Theodore Roosevelt.

CHAPTER FIVE

The Government of Overseas Possessions: Central Administration and General Policy ~ ~

WHILE engaged in setting up protectorates in the Caribbean, the United States had also been experimenting with colonial administration and colonial policy in its new possessions. Long before the navy took charge of the Dominican Republic, the larger insular colonies acquired in 1898 and 1899 were all under civilian rule. All of them enjoyed large measures of self-government, and one—the Philippines—was being encouraged to expect early independence. The American government, on the whole, seemed disposed to apply generally to its colonial possessions the promise made to the Philippines in the Republican platform of 1900: "The largest measure of self-government consistent with their welfare and our duties shall be secured to them by law."

ADMINISTRATIVE MACHINERY

The United States had taken up its colonial responsibilities without machinery for colonial administration and amid grave doubts as to whether the government had the constitutional power to hold and govern its new possessions as colonies. The necessary administrative machinery was improvised, a bit here and a bit there.

153

The Territory of Hawaii was treated in much the same fashion as earlier territories on the continent. For it, and in part for Alaska, administrative responsibility lay in the Department of the Interior. Guam and Tutuila (or American Samoa) were made naval stations and administered by the Navy Department. The Virgin Islands, though not made a naval station, were under naval officers as governors until 1931, when they were transferred to the Department of the Interior. The Panama Canal Zone was from its beginning under the control of the War Department. The Philippines, too, were placed under the War Department, in which a Bureau of Insular Affairs (originally the Division of Customs and Insular Affairs) was created as an agency to deal with them and with other new responsibilities. Puerto Rico, at first under the divided authority of several departments, was in 1909 handed over to the Bureau of Insular Affairs, which likewise assumed responsibilities in connection with the customs receivership in the Dominican Republic and the provisional government in Cuba (1906-1909). The Bureau was for many years the nearest approach to a colonial office to be found in the American system.[1]

The varieties of administrative work that the Bureau handled were described in a report by its chief to the Secretary of War in 1901. The Bureau served at that time as the repository for all civil records of the governments of Cuba and the Philippines except those remaining in the island capitals. It prepared and transmitted to the Secretary of War any information in regard to the insular possessions required of him by Congress. It handled the correspondence between the Secretary of War and the insular governments and the correspondence of those governments through the Secretary of War with other departments in Washington and through the State Department with foreign governments. It acted for the insular governments "in the procurement and transportation of personnel, supplies, and equipment that have to be obtained in the United States." As a bureau of information, it distributed thousands of printed documents and conducted a voluminous correspondence "covering all manner of inquiries ranging from applications for positions, . . . to questions of land titles, Chinese immigration, Spanish baptismal certificates, customs regulations, etc." "It may be truly said," remarked the chief, "that every question involved in the conduct of governmental affairs lies within the possible scope of examination by this division."[2] It may be added, on the basis of later experience, that the Bureau became an effective lobbying agency, working with Congress for legislation beneficial to the insular possessions and against laws likely to affect them adversely.

Proposals were made from time to time for the creation of a single department to handle all colonial affairs, or if not that, for the bringing together of all colonial responsibilities into a single existing department in order to permit a pooling of experience and of trained personnel. Nothing was accomplished in this direction, however, until 1934, when President Franklin D. Roosevelt set up in the Department of the Interior a new Division of Territories and Island Possessions. Under the general supervision of the new Division were placed Puerto Rico (transferred from the War Department), Alaska, Hawaii, and the Virgin Islands. The five Pacific "equatorial islands" of Howland, Baker, Jarvis, Canton, and

Enderbury, of which the United States took formal possession between 1935 and 1938, were placed under the authority of the Division—Canton and Enderbury under joint control with Great Britain. In 1939 the Bureau of Insular Affairs—with such responsibility as it still held for the Philippines, now in the Commonwealth stage—was transferred to the Division. As of 1941, therefore, the Division of Territories and Island Possessions had become responsible for all the inhabited outlying possessions of the United States except Guam* and Samoa, which remained under the navy, supervised by the Chief of Naval Operations through an Office of Island Governments,[3] and the Canal Zone (technically not a possession), which continued under army rule, supervised by a special administrative assistant to the Secretary of War.

The Division, with three geographic branches (Alaska, Caribbean, and Pacific) and two functional branches (administrative and legal), was given a wide variety of responsibilities. It advised the President and Congress in regard to policy and legislation affecting the territories and assisted the several territorial governments in making plans for both economic and political development. It acted as a liaison office between the territorial governments on the one hand and all branches of the federal government and the general public on the other. It represented the territories in cases appealed to the higher federal courts and in proceedings before federal regulatory agencies. It assisted in preparing the annual territorial budgets. It attempted, though not very suc-

---

* On August 1, 1950 Guam was transferred from the Navy Department to the Department of the Interior. See page 232-233.

cessfully, to coordinate the activities of other federal agencies functioning in the territories. It supervised the operations of such federally sponsored agencies as the Alaska Railroad, the Alaska Road Commission, the Alaska Rural Rehabilitation Corporation, the Puerto Rico Reconstruction Administration, and the Virgin Islands Company. Strangest, perhaps, of the Division's operational functions was the care of the Alaska insane— a responsibility that Congress had handed to the Secretary of the Interior in 1909. When the United States, as a member of the United Nations, assumed the obligation (under Article 73 (e) of the Charter) to make annual reports to the U.N. on the administration of its non-self-governing territories, the preparation of those reports for Alaska, Hawaii, Puerto Rico, and the Virgin Islands devolved upon the Division of Territories and Island Possessions, working in cooperation with the territorial governments. Members of the Division also represented the United States in numerous international conferences dealing with matters related to American policy in the territories.[4] The Division is an active and useful body, whose usefulness is restricted by small personnel and lack of funds. It is not a powerful body, since most of its powers are advisory only.

Did the Constitution Follow the Flag?

But before the United States government could go very far in administering its new possessions or in providing local governments for them, it had to face the question of the constitutional limits of its authority. Had the United States really any power to hold and govern colonies? Did all the constitutional guarantees, such as the right of trial by jury, the right to bear arms, and equality in respect to the tariff extend automatically to every new acquisition? Did the people of the new possessions become United States citizens with all the rights implied in that term, including the right to immigrate to the United States? In a word, did the Constitution follow the flag? If so, the problem of governing the Philippines, for example, might prove insoluble, for no one would maintain that the Filipinos were ready for government on the American model.

This question had been earnestly debated in the Senate during its consideration of the treaty with Spain (see pages 68-71), and the debate continued thereafter. Both sides could cite Supreme Court decisions of some authority. Anti-imperialists found their views forcibly expressed in Chief Justice Taney's opinion in the Dred Scott decision (1857). Wrote Taney:

> There is certainly no power given by the Constitution to the Federal Government to establish or maintain colonies bordering on the United States or at a distance, to be ruled and governed at its own pleasure; nor to enlarge its territorial limits in any way, except by the admission of new States. . . .

Territory might indeed be acquired "not fit for admission at the time, but to be admitted as soon as its population and situation would entitle it to admission." While the territory remained a territory, the federal government could exercise no power there not granted in the Constitution. "Nor can congress deny to the people [of a territory] the right to keep and bear arms, not the right to trial by jury. . . ."[5]

Quite different was the opinion of the Court as expounded by Mr. Justice Bradley in *Mormon Church* v. *United States* (1890). "The power of Congress over the Territories of the United States," wrote Bradley, "is general and plenary." The territories formerly acquired from France and Mexico "became the absolute property and domain of the United States," subject to conditions embodied in the treaties of cession relative to the rights of the inhabitants and subject also "to those *fundamental* limitations in favor of personal rights which are formulated in the Constitution and its amendments; . . ."[6]

The term "fundamental" as here used, and likewise the emphasis on the provisions in the treaties of cession, were significant for future developments. The whole question was examined by A. Lawrence Lowell, then lecturer in government at Harvard, in an article in the *Harvard Law Review* for November, 1899. Acknowledging that prevalent judicial opinion had held the Constitution applicable in the territories (except that Congress had a free hand in organizing the territorial courts), Lowell suggested that this was true not because of anything in the Constitution but because of provisions in the treaties by which the territories had been acquired. All such treaties before 1898 had promised the incorporation of the territory in the United States or the granting of citizenship to the inhabitants, or both. The treaty with Spain promised neither. Lowell concluded

> that territory may be so annexed as to make it a part of the United States, and that if so all the general restrictions in the Constitution apply to it . . .; but that possessions may also be so acquired as not to form part of the United States, and in that

case constitutional limitations, such as those requiring uniformity of taxation and trial by jury, do not
apply. It may well be that some provisions have a
universal bearing because they are in form restrictions upon the power of Congress rather than reservation of rights.

It follows [said Lowell in another paragraph]
that the incorporation of a territory in the Union,
like the acquisition of territory at all, is a matter
solely for the legislative or the treaty-making authorities.[7]

Lowell had said in a few lucid sentences very much
what the Supreme Court was to say, more diffusely but
more authoritatively, a year and a half later in the well
known case of *Downes* v. *Bidwell*.[8] The issue in that case
was whether, in view of the constitutional requirement
that all duties be uniform throughout the United States,
Congress had the right to impose a tariff on goods imported into continental United States from Puerto Rico.
The answer to this question depended upon whether
Puerto Rico was or was not in the full sense a part of the
United States. In another case (*De Lima* v. *Bidwell*)
decided the same day, the Court held, five to four, that
Puerto Rico was not a foreign country.[9] In the Downes
case, Mr. Justice Henry Billings Brown, one of the five who
had just voted that Puerto Rico was not foreign, joined
with those who had been in the minority in the De Lima
case, thus producing another five-to-four decision which,
in effect, held that Puerto Rico was not in the full sense
domestic territory and that therefore the tariff was
constitutionally imposed.

Mr. Justice Brown delivered the official opinion of the

Court, but the reasoning that was to become the Court's established doctrine was found in the concurring opinion of Mr. Justice (later Chief Justice) Edward Douglas White. Brown held the Constitution (except for certain sweeping prohibitions) not applicable to any territories unless expressly extended to them by Congress. White, on the other hand, distinguished between two kinds of territories—unincorporated and incorporated. The mere annexation of territory did not incorporate it. Incorporation could be accomplished only (here he differed from Lowell) with the express or implied consent of Congress, not by the treaty-making power alone. Once incorporated, a territory became, like a state, subject to all provisions of the Constitution not obviously meant only for states. In an unincorporated territory only certain "fundamental" provisions of the Constitution would apply.

> Undoubtedly, there are general prohibitions in the Constitution in favor of the liberty and property of the citizen which are not mere regulations as to the form and manner in which a conceded power may be exercised, but which are an absolute denial of all authority under any circumstances or conditions to do particular acts. In the nature of things, limitations of this character cannot be under any circumstances transcended because of the complete absence of power.[10]

Such restrictions as that requiring uniformity of duties, on the other hand, were "mere regulations as to the form and manner in which a conceded power may be exercised." They did not bind Congress in legislating for an unincorporated territory. Puerto Rico, since the treaty of cession reserved to Congress the right to determine the "civil rights and political *status* of the native inhabitants," and since Congress had passed no act of incorporation, was such a territory—not a foreign country in an international sense, since it was under the sovereignty of the United States, but "foreign to the United States in a domestic sense, because the island had not been incorporated into the United States, but was merely appurtenant thereto as a possession." The act providing for collection of duties on imports from Puerto Rico was therefore constitutional.[11]

Thus Justice White, in an opinion concurred in by Justices Shiras and McKenna,[12] laid down those distinctions that were later accepted by the whole Court—between incorporated and unincorporated territories, between what came to be called "formal" and "fundamental" provisions of the Constitution. The fundamental provisions, it was held, were applicable in all territories; the formal provisions only in incorporated territories. The Court has never produced a full list of the formal and the fundamental provisions. *Obiter dicta* it has mentioned as fundamental: freedom of religion, freedom of speech and the press, immunity from unreasonable searches and seizures and from cruel and unusual punishments, free access to the courts, and the protection against deprivation of life, liberty, or property without due process of law.[13] Uniformity of customs duties and trial by jury it has expressly held to be formal provisions only.[14]

Congress, prior to May, 1901, had been unaware of the distinction between incorporated and unincorporated territories and of its own prerogative in determining which type of territory any given acquisition should be.

It became necessary, therefore, for the Supreme Court to decide in case after case whether Congress had, unawares, given incorporated status to any of the more recently acquired territories. Only two of these did the judges find to have been incorporated: Alaska, by the treaty of cession, promising the rights of citizenship to the non-Indian inhabitants, and by subsequent legislation extending to Alaska the customs and revenue laws of the United States, and so on;[15] and Hawaii, by the organic act of 1900, formally extending the Constitution of the United States to the islands.[16] The Philippines were unincorporated,[17] and Puerto Rico remained so even after Congress had conferred blanket United States citizenship upon its inhabitants in 1917.[18] The Virgin Islands (though their inhabitants likewise were made United States citizens in 1927) have been held to be unincorporated by opinions of successive Attorneys General.[19] Guam, Samoa, and the other minor possessions seem never to have been even threatened with incorporation.

In devising the "doctrine of territorial incorporation," as it has been called, Mr. Justice White hit upon a clever plan for enabling the United States to acquire and govern colonial possessions without the necessity of at once extending citizenship, jury trial, and free trade with the United States to populations unprepared for those privileges. In other words, he pointed the way by which this country could become a colonial power without violating the Constitution. Although this was probably one of his purposes, another almost certainly was to leave Congress free to surrender new possessions like the Philippines if they should prove burdensome and unprofitable. Had the Supreme Court held that the Filipinos, for example, had once been incorporated in the United States, there might have been constitutional barriers to giving them up.[20]

SELF-GOVERNMENT IN THE NEW POSSESSIONS

The power to determine the forms of territorial governments had always been exercised by Congress, which might provide as much or as little self-government for any given territory as conditions seemed to justify. In practice, Congress had customarily been liberal in extending democratic privileges to the territories, and it did not depart from that practice in dealing with the more populous and more advanced of the new possessions, though caution properly dictated an experimental and gradual procedure.[21] In all except Hawaii (which prior to annexation had set up its own government on the Anglo-Saxon pattern) self-government came by a series of steps; but by 1917 Alaska, Puerto Rico, and the Philippines had joined Hawaii as largely self-governing territories or possessions. Each of the four had an appointive governor, an elective bicameral legislature, and a delegate or resident commissioner (the Philippines had two resident commissioners) enjoying either by right or by courtesy a seat and a voice, but not a vote, in the House of Representatives in Washington. Each legislature was empowered to make laws on most matters of local concern (though in Alaska the authority of the legislature was greatly circumscribed by the powers reserved to Congress and by the presence and operation of numerous federal bureaus). The appointed governor could veto bills passed by the legislature; bills passed over such a veto by a two-thirds vote could, in Puerto Rico and the Philippines, be killed by a presidential veto. In the Philippines, bills on certain subjects (tariff, public lands, immigration, and the like) must in every case be submitted to the President. Congress, having supreme power over the territories, could (but rarely if ever did) annul any enactment of a territorial legislature that it found objectionable.

The Virgin Islands, from 1917 to 1936, might be described as semi-self-governing. In lieu of a legislature, they had two municipal councils, in part elected (upon a narrowly restricted suffrage), in part appointed. The power of these councils to enact ordinances, pass the annual budgets, and so on was subject to the approval in some cases of the governor, in others, of the President. This was the system inherited from Danish rule. It was not changed in essentials until 1936, when Congress broadened the suffrage, made the municipal councils wholly elective, combined them for certain purposes into a unicameral legislative assembly, and empowered councils and assembly to override gubernatorial vetoes. After 1936 the Virgin Islands enjoyed approximately the same degree of self-government as the four territories and possessions[22] mentioned above. They did not, however, have either a delegate or a resident commissioner in Washington.

The Philippines, Hawaii, and Puerto Rico had each its system of courts with a supreme court at the top and lesser courts in appropriate numbers and grades. Hawaii and Puerto Rico had each, in addition, a United States district court (statutory) to try cases under the Constitution or laws of the United States. In Alaska and the

Virgin Islands similar United States courts (the Alaska court having four branches) handled both federal and local cases. There was no United States court in the Philippines; Philippine courts enforced applicable federal laws. Cases involving United States law and major cases of other kinds could be appealed from the highest local courts to federal circuit courts of appeals in the United States or to the United States Supreme Court, depending upon circumstances.

Citizens of Alaska and Hawaii, incorporated territories, were citizens of the United States. Citizens of the unincorporated territories and possessions did not enjoy that status unless it was extended to them by Congress, as it was to the Puerto Ricans (1917), the Virgin Islanders (1927), and the Guamanians (1950). Before attaining United States citizenship these people, and the Filipinos, were "nationals" of the United States,[23] entitled to its protection abroad, but at home only to such rights as could be claimed under acts of Congress or the "fundamental" provisions of the Constitution. Nor did the attainment of citizenship, without incorporation, entitle the people of the Virgin Islands or Puerto Rico, so long as they stayed at home, to rights embodied in the "formal" provisions of the Constitution, such as trial by jury. Upon coming to the United States they enjoyed, of course, the same rights as other citizens. With the exception, however, of the rights of trial by jury and indictment by grand jury and of the right to bear arms, all the customary Anglo-Saxon freedoms were assured to the islanders in bills of rights enacted by Congress—for the Philippines in 1902, Puerto Rico in 1917, the Virgin Islands in 1936, Guam in 1950. Pending such legislation, the island people could claim most if not all of such freedoms as guaranteed to them by the "fundamental" provisions of the Constitution.

Guam, till 1950, and American Samoa were in a different class from the territories and possessions just considered. For them Congress passed no organic laws till 1950. Executive orders made them naval stations, and as such they were governed. The naval governor made the laws and also enforced them. He consulted, it is true, native councils or assemblies, but their function was purely advisory. The governor also either served as chief judge or appointed that official, and there were no appeals to mainland courts. The naval governor, in other words, was the executive, the legislature, and the judiciary all in one.*

The Canal Zone, though not a possession, had to have a government nonetheless. That government was to the army much as the governments of Samoa and Guam were to the navy. The governor, an army officer, and his subordinates performed all nonjudicial duties connected with civil government. The Zone had its statutory United States district court with two branches and with appeals to a circuit court of appeals in the United States. Minor cases were tried in magistrates' courts; the magistrates, appointed by the governor prior to 1933, were thereafter appointed "by the President or by his authority."

The Tariff in the New Possessions

One of the chief mercantilist arguments for the possession of colonies had been the opportunity of monopolizing their trade enjoyed by the home country. This

---

* For the Guam organic act see page 232.

selfish motive President McKinley had repudiated on
behalf of the United States, at least so far as the Philippines were concerned. In his instructions to the peace
commissioners, September 16, 1898 he had written:

> we seek no advantages in the Orient which are not
> common to all. Asking only the open door for our-
> selves, we are ready to accord the open door to
> others.[24]

This expression of liberality could not, of course, bind
either the Congress or McKinley's successors in the
presidency, nor did it do so for long. Article IV of the
peace treaty with Spain, it is true, provided that for a
period of ten years Spanish ships and merchandise
should be admitted to the Philippines upon the same
terms as those of the United States. The letter of this
treaty the United States observed, but from 1901 onward
import duties in the Philippines were so adjusted as in
reality to favor the United States while maintaining a
nominal equality. Upon the expiration of the ten-year
period all pretense of maintaining the open door in the
Philippines was abandoned. The Payne-Aldrich tariff
act of 1909 established, subject to quotas in a few commodities, reciprocal free trade in native products between the United States and the Philippines, whereas
imports from foreign countries into the Philippines paid
duties fixed by the Philippine government, subject to
the higher authority of Congress.

Elsewhere, with one exception, there were no treaties
to restrict the right of the United States to establish a
preferential system. The exception was American Samoa,
where the tripartite treaty of 1899 contained a stipula-

tion for equality of treatment among the partitioning powers.[25] In Samoa alone, after 1909, a duty was collected on imports from the United States—the same duty paid by imports from foreign shores. In the remaining territories and possessions a preferential system prevailed. Alaska and Hawaii, as incorporated territories, were parts of the United States for tariff purposes. Puerto Rico, by the Foraker Act of 1900 (the first organic act for Puerto Rico), was also brought within the United States tariff wall. From 1900 to 1902, as a temporary measure to provide funds for the Puerto Rican government, duties to the extent of 15 per cent of the regular tariff rates were collected on imports from Puerto Rico into the United States and from the United States into Puerto Rico. After 1902 there was complete free trade in native products between the island and the mainland.

Free trade with the Virgin Islands in native products was provided for on March 3, 1917, immediately upon their acquisition, though this freedom of trade was qualified by the continuance of the Danish practice of imposing export taxes on sugar and certain other island products. Those taxes were paid upon commodities shipped to the United States as well as upon those shipped abroad. The organic act of 1936 gave the municipal councils authority to abolish the export taxes. That on sugar from St. Croix was repealed in 1942. Imports from foreign countries were taxed at low rates inherited from the Danish régime and left in effect by Congress.

As the Panama Canal Zone is technically not a United States possession, it is treated as foreign soil in respect to the tariff. Goods imported into the United States from the Zone pay the regular tariff rates. Imports into the

Canal Zone for the use of the administration and its employees pay no duty regardless of their origin.

To summarize, products of all the territories and possessions (the Canal Zone excepted) commanded, after 1909, a free market in the United States. Products of the United States went freely into every territory and possession except Samoa, where they paid the regular duties. Imports from abroad paid duties everywhere except in the Canal Zone. In Alaska, Hawaii, and Puerto Rico these were the regular metropolitan duties. In the Virgin Islands they were left by Congress as they had been under Denmark; in the Philippines they were fixed by the Philippine government; in Guam and Samoa by the naval administrations. The Virgin Islands alone collected a tax on exports.[26]

This chapter has described the development of an American colonial policy from the center and as a whole. The next will outline the evolution of government in the territories and possessions one by one. Chapter Seven will examine economic conditions and causes of discontent in the same dependencies, and the remedies adopted or proposed, ranging from independence for the Philippines to proposed statehood for Alaska and Hawaii.

CHAPTER SIX

The Government of Overseas Possessions: The Evolution of Territorial Self-Government ⁓ ⁓

THE GOVERNMENTS of the larger overseas territories and dependencies of the United States in the twentieth century approached a common pattern, which found precedents in the earlier governments devised for continental territories and, still further back, in the governments of British colonies before the American Revolution. In each of the new possessions, however, governmental evolution followed a course dictated by local peculiarities of geography, ethnography, and historical background. It is necessary, therefore, in following the story of such development, to devote some attention to the physical and human characteristics of the individual dependencies. Such factors will be considered not only in the larger dependencies, which attained a high degree of self-government, but also in the minor possessions of Guam and Samoa and in the Canal Zone, which remained under the authoritarian rule of naval or military officers.

ALASKA

Alaska, purchased from Russia in 1867, has an area of 586,400 square miles, about one-fifth that of the United States proper. A land of rich natural resources—mineral,

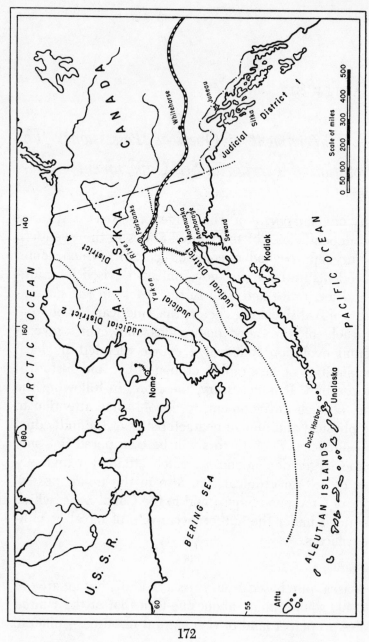

TERRITORY OF ALASKA

forest, and animal—it had at the time of acquisition an estimated population of only 29,097, of whom nearly 27,000 were Indians and Eskimos. Of the remainder only 150 were Americans. About half of the white inhabitants resided at Sitka in the "panhandle"; the remainder dwelt mostly on far-off Kodiak and Unalaska islands. The population grew slowly. The Indian and Eskimo portion remained nearly stationary. The white population reached a figure of over 30,000 in 1900 and 36,000 in 1910, but declined again to less than 28,000 in 1920.[1]

The sparsity of the civilized population and the disparity between the scanty population on the one hand and the large area and rich resources on the other help to account for several characteristics of Alaska's governmental history, for instance, the neglect of Congress during many years to provide Alaska with a civil government and the retention by the various departments in Washington of control over Alaskan resources instead of placing those resources at the disposal of the local authorities.

The treaty of cession promised that such of the civilized inhabitants as chose to remain in Alaska should be "admitted to the enjoyment of all the rights, advantages and immunities of the citizens of the United States." The promise implied, at least, that some form of civil government should be provided, but not for 17 years did Congress pass the first organic act for Alaska or make any provision for its government beyond extending to it the internal revenue and customs and navigation laws of the United States and constituting it a customs collection district.[2] At times the collector of customs at Sitka was the only federal official in Alaska. From 1867 to 1877, however, the army exercised authority there, and from 1879 to 1884 a naval officer stationed at Sitka performed a similar function.

A rush of goldseekers into the panhandle in the vicinity of modern Juneau and ensuing local agitation for a legal government helped persuade Congress to enact the organic act of May 17, 1884.[3] The act constituted Alaska "a civil and judicial district," with a governor, judge, attorney, marshal, clerk, four commissioners, and four deputies serving under the marshal and appointed by him. The other officers were appointed by the President. The judge was to preside over a district court and was to hold at least two terms a year, one at Sitka and one at Wrangell. The attorney, marshal, and clerk bore the usual relation of such officials to the court. The four commissioners (stationed at Sitka, Wrangell, Juneau, and Unalaska) were similar to justices of the peace with the functions also of notaries public, recorders, and probate judges. The deputy marshals served as constables and as executive officers of the commissioners' courts. The laws of Oregon, so far as applicable, were made the laws of the district.

Congress was careful to designate Alaska a "district," not a "territory," presumably because the latter term might suggest an intention to provide the usual form of territorial government. To dispel any possible doubt upon that question, the act expressly stated: "there shall be no legislative assembly in said district, nor shall any Delegate be sent to Congress therefrom." No taxation for local purposes was provided, and although a United States land office was opened at Sitka, it dealt only in mining rights. The general land laws of the United States, with their provisions for homesteads, preemption, and so forth, were not extended to Alaska. As a protection for the native races, the importation, manufacture, and sale of intoxicating beverages were prohibited.

Inadequate though it was, the organic act of 1884 served Alaska until the Klondike gold rush of 1896-1898 broke down its frail machinery. Parts of the district were then placed under temporary military rule. Prohibition, which had never been workable, was ended. Saloons as well as other businesses were licensed, the fees providing Alaska with its first local revenue. A criminal code designed specifically for the district replaced the Oregon code. An inadequate homestead act of 1898 was followed by a more satisfactory one in 1903. A civil code act of 1900 split the judicial district into three divisions with courts at Juneau in the panhandle, St. Michael on Norton Sound, and Eagle City on the Yukon. It made provision for municipal governments with limited taxing power and provided commissioners for all communities of suitable size. It made Juneau instead of Sitka the seat of government as soon as the necessary buildings could be erected at the new capital. The changes were all desirable, but they left Alaska, as before, a "civil and judicial district" without either legislature or delegate in Congress.[4]

The growing white population of Alaska and the importance of having someone in Washington to handle the district's relations with the federal government—a task that had often kept governors in Washington to the neglect of their duties at home—persuaded Congress in

1906 to give the people of Alaska the long-desired privilege of electing a delegate to the House of Representatives.[5] Other improvements followed quickly. In 1909 a fourth division was added to the district court. The locations and court seats of the four divisions were as follows: (1) southeast Alaska extending north and west to Yakutat, with seat at Juneau; (2) the Bering Sea coast area north of Bristol Bay and the western Arctic coast, with seat at Nome; (3) the south coast region from Yakutat to the end of the Aleutians, with seat at Valdez; (4) the interior and eastern Arctic region, with seat at Fairbanks. Finally, in 1912, Congress established a legislature for Alaska and advanced her to full territorial status.[6]

The Act of Congress of August 24, 1912 transformed the district into the Territory of Alaska. It directed that previous laws establishing the executive and judicial branches of the Alaskan government continue in effect. To those branches it added a legislature of two houses: a senate of 8 and a house of representatives of 16 members. Two senators and four representatives were to be chosen from each of the four judicial divisions, the senators for four years, the representatives for two. Candidates and electors must be citizens of the United States, 21 years of age, and must have resided in Alaska a year and (in the case of electors) in their respective voting precincts for 30 days prior to election. In 1927 Congress added the requirement that new voters be able to read the Constitution of the United States in English and to write in the same language. In 1942 the membership of the senate was raised to 16, 4 from each judicial division, that of the house to 24, with 8, 4, 7, and 5 members chosen respectively from the first, second, third, and fourth divisions.[7]*

The governor's veto power extended to individual items of appropriation bills. His vetoes could be overridden by a two-thirds vote of each house. All acts of the legislature must be transmitted to the President and the Secretary of State, and by the President to Congress. If disapproved by Congress, such laws were to be "null and of no effect."

The Alaska legislature was given authority over a wide variety of local matters. It could make laws with respect to health, sanitation, quarantine, relief of destitution, compulsory school attendance, the regulation of corporations, the protection of civil and religious liberty. It could amend or repeal any parts of the Alaska civil and criminal codes. It could impose road and poll taxes. But there was also a long list of things that the legislature could not do. It could not impose a property tax in excess of 1 per cent of assessed valuation; municipalities were limited to a 2 per cent property tax. The legislature might enact a general incorporation law, but it was forbidden to grant exclusive privileges to any corporation, and neither the territory nor any of its subdivisions could subscribe to stock in any corporation or issue bonds or undertake any indebtedness beyond the capacity of the current year's revenues to meet. This provision placed obstacles in the way of any community that might desire to establish a municipal light or power plant. The legislature might make no change in the United States game, fish, or fur-seal laws, or make any

---

* For proposals for further changes in the government of Alaska and the statehood movement see pages 252-253.

law "interfering with the primary disposal of the soil." The land and other natural resources of the territory continued to be held, in trust as it were, for the people of the United States as a whole. They were not placed at the disposal of the few thousand persons who made up the territorial electorate.

HAWAII

Hawaii, annexed to the United States by the joint resolution of July 7, 1898 and formally placed under American sovereignty on the 12th of the following August, comprises 8 principal islands strung out in a southeast-northwest line nearly 400 miles long, and hav-

ing a combined area of 6,433 square miles. The largest of the islands is Hawaii. The most important—seat of Honolulu city and of Pearl Harbor naval base—and today the most populous is Oahu. The others are Maui, Kahoolawe, Lanai, Molokai, Kauai, and Niihau. The distance from San Francisco to Honolulu is 2,100 miles. The population of 154,001, as shown by the census of 1900, was composed of the following racial groups: Japanese, 39.7 per cent; Hawaiian and part Hawaiian, 24.4 per cent; Caucasian, 18.7 per cent; Chinese, 16.7 per cent; all others, 0.5 per cent.[8]

Immediately prior to annexation Hawaii was a republic with a constitution adopted in 1894.[9] The joint resolution of annexation left the existing municipal legislation of Hawaii in effect so far as it was not inconsistent with the resolution itself or with the Constitution or treaties of the United States, and directed that, until Congress should provide otherwise, all civil, judicial, and military powers exercised by the officers of the existing government should be vested in such persons as the President of the United States might appoint and exercised in such manner as he might direct. It directed further that the President appoint five commissioners, at least two of them from Hawaii, who should recommend to Congress suitable legislation for the islands.[10]

For nearly two years the existing machinery of the republican government, with few changes in personnel, continued to function under the authority of the United States. On April 30, 1900, after study and report by the commissioners, Congress enacted an organic act for the Territory of Hawaii, to take effect 45 days after the date of approval.[11]

The effect of the organic act of 1900 was to make Hawaii an incorporated territory. The act declared the Constitution of the United States and, with a few exceptions, all United States laws not locally inapplicable to have the same force in Hawaii as elsewhere in the United

States. All persons who had been citizens of the Republic of Hawaii on August 12, 1898 were declared to be citizens of the United States and of the Territory of Hawaii; all citizens of the United States who resided in Hawaii on that date, or who had subsequently resided there for one year, were declared to be citizens of the territory. The right of suffrage was to be exercised by male citizens of the United States 21 years of age, who had resided in the territory for a year, were duly registered, and could speak, read, and write either the English or the Hawaiian language.

As in other territories, the governor was a presidential appointee, as was the secretary. But, contrary to the practice in other territories, both these appointees and the lesser administrative officers appointed by the governor must be citizens of the territory. Hawaii was to have no "carpet-bag" régime. Another peculiar feature of the Hawaiian act was a provision that territorial officials appointed by the governor with the consent of the territorial senate could be removed from office only with the senate's consent. The legislature comprised a senate of 15 members elected for 4-year terms and a house of representatives of 30 members elected for 2 years. Legislative sessions were biennial and limited to a duration of 60 days, though the governor might extend the period by 30 days and might convoke special sessions of the legislature or of the senate alone. Should the legislature adjourn without making the appropriations necessary for carrying on the government or meeting its legal obligations, the governor was directed to call a special session to repair the omission, and until this was done, "the sums appropriated in the last appropriation bills [should] be deemed to be reappropriated."[12] The governor was given the customary veto power, including the right to veto individual items in appropriation bills. The legislature could override his veto by a vote of two-thirds of the entire membership of each house. All laws must be transmitted by the secretary within 30 days of the end of the legislative session to the President of the United States, the president of the Senate, and the speaker of the House of Representatives. There was no express statement of the power of Congress to annul territorial enactments. The supreme authority of Congress over Hawaii, as over other territories, was of course understood.

Restrictions upon the power of the Hawaiian legislature resembled in some respects those found in Alaska's organic act. The legislature could not, without the consent of Congress, grant any special or exclusive privilege, immunity, or franchise. It could not grant divorce, appropriate money for the benefit of sectarian or private schools, or subscribe to stock in any corporation. Its borrowing power was limited, but not, as in Alaska, its taxing power. Unlike the legislature of Alaska, it was given control (under the supreme authority of Congress) over public lands in the territory, though actually these were the property of the United States. With the purpose, presumably, of checking the growth of great sugar plantations, the act forbade the leasing of government-owned agricultural land for a longer period than 5 years (later raised to 15 years) and provided that no corporation should acquire and hold more than 1,000 acres. This last provision, which did not affect existing property rights, proved ineffective and was repealed in 1921.

The territory was to be represented in the national

House of Representatives by a popularly elected delegate.

The act provided for a supreme court consisting of one chief justice and two associate justices, an unspecified number of circuit courts, and such inferior courts as the legislature might establish. The existing pattern of courts was to continue until modified by the legislature. In practice this meant 3 (later 4) circuit courts and 29 district courts, the latter being the equivalent of police courts. Justices of the supreme and circuit courts were appointed by the President, the former to serve until removed by him, the latter for four-year terms. The district judges were named by the chief justice of the territory. A United States district court with a judge (later two judges), marshal, attorney, and clerk completed the judicial machinery. Like a state, Hawaii had two distinct judicial systems, one for cases under territorial law, one for federal cases.[13]

Determination of the form and structure of local government was left to the legislature. No units of local government had existed under the monarchy or the republic. An act of the legislature of 1905 created county units, each county governed by a board of supervisors. Two years later the county of Oahu was transformed into the City and County of Honolulu with a municipal government having jurisdiction over the entire island of Oahu. In addition there are three regular counties and the special county of Kalawao, the small peninsula on the north coast of Molokai reserved for a leper colony, which is governed by the territorial board of health. As there are no incorporated towns or cities within the counties, county and territorial governments together perform many of the functions that on the mainland are assigned to municipalities and towns. Especially notable is the extent of authority reserved by the territorial government. In the words of Governor Ingram M. Stainback in 1947,*

> the most significant feature of the government of Hawaii is that the Territorial government, as a part of its historical heritage, still retains a centralized control rarely, if ever, encountered on the mainland, with the administration of all important functions under the direction of the executive branch.[14]

PUERTO RICO

Puerto Rico, acquired from Spain by the treaty of Paris in 1899, is an almost rectangular island 100 miles long and 35 miles wide with an area of 3,435 square miles. A mountainous interior is flanked by valleys and coastal plains well suited to tropical agriculture. The population in 1899 was 953,243.[15]

As a colony of Spain Puerto Rico had suffered less than had Cuba from maladministration. Discontent had occasionally flared into armed revolt, but there had been no such prolonged civil wars as in Cuba. Partly for this reason Puerto Rico had attracted little notice in the United States. General Nelson A. Miles, who commanded the invading army in July, 1898, assured the islanders by proclamation that the Americans came to bring protection to lives and property and "the guarantees and blessings of the liberal institutions of our government." The American troops occupied the island against small

---

* For the statehood movement in Hawaii see pages 261-265.

opposition. United States military government, formally installed on October 18, 1898 when the Spanish garrison departed, continued until May 1, 1900 when it was supplanted by civil government under the Foraker Act.

The military governors, of whom Brigadier General George W. Davis, a volunteer officer, was the most important in length of service and achievement, gave much of their attention to re-establishing order, suppressing

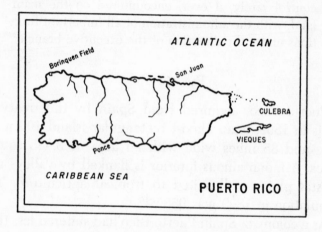

crime, and introducing American ideas of sanitation and preventive medicine (some 750,000 persons were vaccinated in the first six months of the occupation). They— or more accurately, Davis—also found time to reform the ancient tax system, reconstruct the island judiciary, introduce the writ of *habeas corpus* to a population that had never known it, hold municipal elections, and establish the suffrage requirements therefor. Most of these reforms were adopted by the ensuing civil government. Davis, the last of these military governors, believed that the Puerto Ricans (85 per cent of whom he reported to be illiterate) were not yet ready for democratic government. In a recommendation prepared at the request of the War Department, he proposed a government consisting of governor, executive council, and judiciary, all appointed. Only later, he thought, "when experience shall have shown that the people comprehend the gravity of the duties and obligations of self-government," should an elected legislative assembly be added. ". . . this island," he said, "is not now capable of carrying on such a government as Hawaii is able to maintain. . . ."[16]

Congress, disagreeing in part with General Davis, provided in the Foraker Act of April 12, 1900 a mixed system of government in which an elected house of delegates was checked by an appointed upper house, or executive council, as well as by an appointed governor wielding the usual veto power.[17] The 35 members of the house of delegates were elected biennially, 5 from each of 7 disdistricts. The executive council consisted of the secretary (who was also a vice governor), the auditor, the four heads of the executive departments (attorney general, treasurer, commissioners of interior and education), and five other persons, all appointed, like the governor, by the President of the United States (with the consent of the Senate) for four-year terms. Five of the eleven must be native inhabitants of Puerto Rico. The heads of departments were required to report annually through the governor to the appropriate federal officials—the Attorney General, Secretary of the Treasury, Secretary of Interior, and Commissioner of Education, respectively—until 1909, when Puerto Rico was placed under the Bureau of Insular Affairs in the War Department and all reports were ordered made to that department.[18]

The legislative assembly, as this bicameral body was called, was given wide legislative power. It could repeal or amend existing laws and ordinances, create, consolidate, or reorganize municipalities, and provide for the use or disposition of public property acquired by the United States from Spain. Its power to borrow money was limited by the provision that the public debt of Puerto Rico or of any municipality should not exceed 7 per cent of the assessed value of the taxable property therein. The right to grant franchises was reserved to the executive council with the approval of the governor and subject to the right of Congress to annul or modify such grants. By a separate act of Congress, approved May 1, 1900, no agricultural corporation thereafter chartered was to own or control more than 500 acres of land.[19]

The judiciary was to remain for the most part as it had been set up by the military government—a supreme court of 5 judges, 7 district courts, 24 municipal courts, and numerous justices of the peace.[20] The Foraker Act stipulated, however, that the judges of the supreme court should be appointed by the President and Senate, those of the district courts by the governor and executive council. A United States statutory district court replaced a "provisional court" created by the military government to try federal cases.

A resident commissioner, to represent Puerto Rico in Washington and "entitled to official recognition as such by all Departments," was to be chosen every two years by the qualified voters of the island. Subsequently the House of Representatives allowed him as a courtesy what territorial delegates enjoyed by right—a seat and a voice in the House.

The act did not prescribe in detail the qualifications for suffrage, specifying only that voters must be citizens of Puerto Rico who had been residents of the island for one year and possessed the other qualifications established under existing laws and military regulations. These regulations, slightly amended by the executive council before the first election, restricted the suffrage to male citizens 21 years of age who either could read and write or owned real property or personal property not less than $25 in value.[21]

The treaty of peace had left the status of the inhabitants of the ceded territories to be determined by Congress. The Foraker Act declared all inhabitants of the island who had resided there as Spanish subjects on April 11, 1899 (the date on which the treaty of peace had been proclaimed) and who had not elected to preserve their Spanish allegiance, and their children born since that date, to be citizens of Puerto Rico and entitled to the protection of the United States. They, together with such citizens of the United States as might reside in Puerto Rico, should constitute a body politic under the name of "The People of Porto Rico."[22]

The Puerto Ricans found little reason for rejoicing over their status under the Foraker Act. Under Spanish rule the island had been a province of Spain with representation in the Cortes, and the islanders had been like any other Spanish subjects. Now they were denied United States citizenship and in the American Congress their only representative was a single voteless resident commissioner who enjoyed a seat and a voice in the House of Representatives only by the courtesy of that body. They had, it is true, an elective house of delegates, but it could not legislate without the concurrence of the appointed executive council, a majority of whose members were Americans. United States citizenship and an elective upper house became the principal goals of Puerto Rican reformers.

Both objectives were attained in the Jones Act of 1917, but prior to that legislation the Wilson administration, which looked with favor upon more' autonomy for the possessions in general, had given the Puerto Ricans a majority in the executive council by appointing islanders to the posts of secretary and commissioner of the interior, hitherto held by Americans. The council so reconstituted consisted of seven natives and four Americans. Governor Arthur Yager, Wilson's appointee, cooperated further with the local politicos by filling the positions at his disposal chiefly from among members of the dominant Unionist party.[23]

The new organic act, or Jones Act, of March 2, 1917 granted collective United States citizenship to the citizens of Puerto Rico, though permitting avoidance of that honor to those who did not wish it. It contained a bill of rights, guaranteeing to Puerto Ricans the essential liberties—freedom of speech, press, religion, and so on—as well as such novelties as the eight-hour day in employment on public works and prohibition of child labor "in any occupation injurious to health or morals or dangerous to life or limb."[24] The only omissions from the list familiar in the United States were the right to bear arms and those peculiarly Anglo-Saxon privileges of indictment by grand and trial by petty jury.

The governor remained as before, a presidential appointee. Of the heads of the executive departments, now six in number, only the attorney general and the commissioner of education were to be named by the President. The treasurer and the commissioners of the interior, health, and agriculture and labor were appointed by the governor with the advice and consent of the Puerto Rican senate. At least one year's residence in the island was made a prerequisite to appointment to the headships of these four departments.[25] The six department heads made up an executive council, which, however, lost completely its former legislative functions. The auditor, still a presidential appointee, was no longer a member of the executive council. There was to be an executive secretary, appointed by the governor. The President was permitted to designate a head of department to act as governor in the event of a temporary vacancy.

The legislature under the new act consisted of a senate of 19 and a house of representatives of 39 members, all elected for 4-year terms. Voters must be American citizens over 21 years of age; the legislature might establish such other requirements as it saw fit, with the exception of property qualifications, which were prohibited. The power of the legislature remained substantially as before. Laws must receive the approval of a majority of all the members of each house. A bill passed over the governor's veto by a two-thirds vote in each house was referred to the President, who might approve or veto it. His veto was final. Congress reserved the power to annul or amend any enactment of the legislature. If the legislature should adjourn without making the appropriations essential for carrying on the government, the preceding year's appropriations were to continue operative.

The power to grant franchises, which the Foraker Act had assigned to the executive council, was now conferred upon a public service commission consisting of the heads of the executive departments, the auditor, and two elected commissioners. Franchises so granted must receive the governor's approval and might be annulled or modified by Congress.[26]

The courts remained unchanged, but the legislature was empowered "to organize, modify, or rearrange the courts and their jurisdiction and procedure." The status of the resident commissioner also continued as it had been, save that he was now elected, like the legislature, for a term of four years instead of two.

For most practical purposes the status of Puerto Rico now approximated closely that of the older territories. It had a resident commissioner instead of a delegate, but the difference was theoretical, not practical. It was not, as the Supreme Court was to hold (see page 163), an "incorporated territory" and was therefore subject only to the "fundamental" provisions of the Constitution, but this distinction was of little practical concern now that the people of Puerto Rico were United States citizens and enjoyed all the rights of self-government customarily allowed to territories.*

THE PHILIPPINES

Most distant, largest, and most populous of America's acquisitions from Spain were the Philippine Islands. Lying within the tropics just north of the equator, some 6,000 miles from San Francisco and 4,500 from Honolulu,

---

* For later governmental and political changes in Puerto Rico see pages 279-283.

the Philippines were a natural geographical outpost of East Asia. Largest of the group were the islands of Luzon and Mindanao; 9 or 10 others could be called large; of large and small islands and minute islets there were in all some 7,000 with a total area of 114,830 square miles—the area of Arizona or of New England and New York together, or three-fourths the area of Japan. Much of their surface was mountainous, but there were great unused reserves of potential agricultural land. Two-thirds of the area was forested. Mountains and heavy rainfall spelled abundant possibilities in water power. Gold, copper, iron, chrome, and manganese existed in considerable quantities, but the islands lacked coal and petroleum.[27]

The first comprehensive census of the Philippines, taken under American direction in 1903, showed a total population of 7,635,426, of whom nearly 7,000,000 were described as "civilized" and the remainder as "wild people."[28] Racially, the vast majority were Malays. There were a few thousands each of Negritos (pygmy negroid people found in several mountain localities), of Chinese, and of persons with both Malay and Chinese or Spanish blood. Fifteen years later, there were 10,314,310 people living in the Philippines, of whom, roughly speaking, 91 per cent were Christians, 4 per cent were Mohammedans ("Moros") and 5 per cent pagan "wild tribes." The pagans, descendants of early Malay invaders, occupied various mountain valleys in Mindanao and northern Luzon. Primitives in religion and addicted to such habits as head-hunting, still they had developed, on their terraced hillsides, a form of agricultural engineering of amazing skill and beauty. They and the Negritos were the only hold-outs against the two great proselytizing religions, Christianity and Mohammedanism. From their starting place in the Near East, these expansive faiths had gone half-way around the world in opposite directions to meet again in this distant archipelago. Islam had entered the southern Philippines probably from Malacca, Sumatra, or Borneo in the fifteenth century. Christianity had come with the Spaniards from Mexico after 1565 and had confined its rival for the most part to southwestern Mindanao and the Sulu islands. Christian Filipinos occupied most of Luzon, parts of Mindanao, and nearly all of the Visayan islands lying between them.

Of the same race and religion, the Christian Filipinos spoke differing dialects of the same mother tongue. Philologists could distinguish 80 or more such dialects. The most important were Tagalog, spoken by the politically conscious people of central Luzon, and Visayan, the speech of the middle islands.

Spain had governed the Philippines with her customary ineptitude. Underpaid officials had been dishonest officials, and to the exactions of officialdom had been added those of the Catholic religious orders, especially the Franciscans, Dominicans, Augustinians, and Recollects. Though strikingly successful in implanting Christianity and other aspects of European culture in the Philippines, the orders had not endeared themselves to the natives. As owners of great landed estates, they were reputed to be harsh landlords. They virtually monopolized education and exercised innumerable minor governmental functions. Important posts in both state and church were reserved for Spaniards. The Filipinos—"Indios" (Indians) as the Spanish called them—were consistently treated as inferiors.[29]

Misgovernment and racial discrimination bred sporadic local rebellions over the years—notably the Cavite revolt of 1872, in consequence of which three native priests were executed as rebels. Another outbreak, aimed at reform, not at independence, occurred in 1896 and was terminated the next year by the treaty of Biac-na-bató, in which the Filipino leaders agreed to turn over their arms and leave the country, accepting in return amnesty for their followers, money for themselves, and a vague promise from the Captain General, Primo de Rivera, to recommend reforms to the Spanish government.

Chief among the leaders who thus departed into voluntary exile was Emilio Aguinaldo, a young man of 27. At Singapore when the United States went to war with Spain, Aguinaldo received through the American consul general an invitation from Admiral Dewey to return to the Philippines. Here he organized a native military force which proved useful in breaking down Spanish authority in Luzon. Aguinaldo's later assertions that he had received promises of independence for his people were roundly denied by Consul General E. Spencer Pratt at Singapore and by Admiral Dewey. He proceeded, nevertheless, to set up a Filipino government at Malolos, north of Manila, and to appeal to foreign powers for recognition. As was noted in a previous chapter, hostilities between Aguinaldo's forces and those of the United States began on February 4, 1899, two days before the Senate approved the treaty of peace with Spain. Then followed a long and costly war. The insurgent armies, courageous but ill-equipped, were quickly driven out of the towns and plains of central Luzon into the mountains, whence they kept up a guerrilla warfare. Aguinaldo was captured March 23, 1901, and the next month took the oath of allegiance to the United States, advising those of his followers still in arms to do likewise. Peace was so far restored that on July 4, 1901 it was possible to substitute a civilian for an army officer as executive head of the Philippines government, and one year later the "Philippine Insurrection" was declared at an end. Not until 1913, however, was American authority firmly established among the Moros, who had never fully accepted Spanish sovereignty.

President McKinley, acting under his war powers,

sent two commissions to the Philippines—the first to investigate, the second to inaugurate civil government. The first, headed by President Jacob Gould Schurman of Cornell University and appointed in January, 1899, reached the islands after the beginning of hostilities between Filipinos and Americans and held some inconclusive conferences with spokesmen for Aguinaldo. The Filipinos, it reported in November, 1899, were not ready for independence.

> Their lack of education and political experience, combined with their racial and linguistic diversities, disqualify them, in spite of their mental gifts and domestic virtues, to undertake the task of governing the archipelago at the present time.

American withdrawal, under existing conditions, would lead to anarchy, the intervention of other powers, and the probable partition of the islands. Only continued American occupation could insure a united and eventually self-governing "Philippine commonwealth." Rejecting the idea of a protectorate and likewise the use of the emotionally charged term "colony," the commission proposed a territorial form of government with a legislature consisting of an elected lower house and an upper house half elected and half appointed, and an appointed governor. Congress should retain the right to veto any territorial legislation, and "for that very reason, in addition to other good grounds, the Filipinos should be represented by a delegate in Congress." This plan, said the commission, should be promptly put in effect in those parts of the islands where peace had been restored.[30]

President McKinley was not ready to go so far in the

direction of self-government as his commission recommended. Instead, he sent a new commission to the islands, to carry on the work, already begun, of establishing civil government at the municipal and provincial levels, and to take over on September 1, 1900 all legislative authority from the military government. This second Philippine commission was headed by William H. Taft as president and is often referred to as the Taft Commission. Its instructions, signed by President McKinley April 7, 1900, were written by Elihu Root, Secretary of War. They largely shaped the character of the Philippine government for the next 16 years.[31]

The commission was to bear in mind, wrote Secretary Root, that the government it was establishing was designed

> for the happiness, peace, and prosperity of the people of the Philippine Islands, and the measures adopted should be made to conform to their customs, their habits, and even their prejudices, to the fullest extent consistent with the accomplishment of the indispensable requisites of just and effective government.

But at the same time the natives were to be made acquainted with certain great principles of government that American experience had shown to be essential to the rule of law and the maintenance of individual freedom. These principles were embodied in a "bill of rights," which was to bind Philippine government at all levels. This "bill of rights," as drawn by Root, contained all the familiar Anglo-Saxon guarantees except trial by jury and the right to bear arms. All officers of local governments, the instructions continued, were to be selected by the people. In the designation of officers of larger units, natives of the islands were to be preferred. In the distribution of powers among the various governments, the presumption was always to be in favor of the smaller subdivisions. Whenever the commission believed that the central administration could be safely transferred from military to civil control, it was to report to that effect to the Secretary of War, with "recommendations as to the form of central government to be established for the purpose of taking over the control."

The commission was to investigate the titles to large tracts of land, especially those held by the friars, and to seek a just settlement of the controversies therewith connected. It was to promote and extend education, with special attention to primary education and to the teaching of English. It was to permit the uncivilized tribes to retain their tribal organization but should attempt, "without undue and petty interference, . . . to prevent barbarous practices [for instance, head-hunting] and introduce civilized customs."

The commission was coolly received by General Arthur MacArthur, who now headed the military government. After September 1, 1900, however, the commission held both the purse strings and the power of appointment to civil positions; and, as previously noted, on July 4, 1901 executive power passed from the army to Mr. Taft as first civil governor of the Philippines. The executive branch of the government was organized in four departments—Commerce and Police, Finance and Justice, Interior, and Public Instruction—with a commissioner at the head of each. In September, 1901 three Filipino members were added to the commission. They headed no departments but gave the American members useful advice in both legislative and executive matters.

Thus far, all provisions for government in the Philippines had been made under the authority of the President of the United States, acting at first under his war powers and, after March 2, 1901, under a blanket grant of authority by Congress.[32] On July 2, 1902 Congress passed the first organic act for the Philippines. This act ratified and approved all action previously taken by the President and the Philippine Commission, including the letter of instructions of April 7, 1900, written by Secretary Root. It declared the inhabitants of the islands who had been Spanish subjects on April 11, 1899 and who continued to reside there to be citizens of the Philippine Islands and entitled to the protection of the United States (except those who had elected to retain their Spanish allegiance). It embodied the bill of rights contained in Secretary Root's instructions. It continued the judicial machinery established by the commission—supreme court, courts of first instance, and municipal courts —with the proviso that justices of the supreme court should in future (like the governor and members of the commission) be appointed by the President with the consent of the Senate, the judges of the courts of first instance by the governor with the consent of the commission. Judgments of the supreme court of the Philippines might be appealed to the United States Supreme Court in cases involving the Constitution or statutes of the United States or in which the amount at issue exceeded $25,000. No United States court for the Philippines was provided.

An important feature of the organic act of 1902—a feature for which Governor Taft was primarily responsible [33]—was the provision for an elective assembly. It stipulated that within two years of the completion of a census of the islands (which was to be taken as soon as peace should have been restored), the President should direct the commission to call a general election for the choice of members of an assembly, which thereafter should constitute the lower house of the Philippine legislature, with the commission serving as the upper house. Areas inhabited by Moros and other non-Christian tribes were not to be represented in the assembly and were to continue under the authority of the commission. Suffrage qualifications were to be those already in effect in municipal elections.[34] Elections were to be biennial, sessions annual. As in Hawaii, and later in Puerto Rico, appropriations for the support of the government held over from one year to the next if the later legislature failed to provide them. The legislature was to choose biennially (the houses voting separately) two resident commissioners to represent the Philippines in Washington.

The property and rights acquired by the United States from Spain (excepting military or other reservations designated by the President of the United States) were placed under the control of the government of the Philippines to be administered for the benefit of the inhabitants. The act contained detailed regulations for the disposal of mineral lands and limited grants of agricultural land from the public domain to 16 hectares (about 40 acres) for an individual and 1,024 hectares (about 2,500 acres) for a corporation. The act empowered the government to purchase the lands of the religious orders and to dispose of such lands as part of the public domain; to permit municipalities to issue bonds for public improvements; and to grant franchises, subject to amendment or repeal by Congress. All laws passed by the legislature must be reported to Congress, which reserved the right to annul them.[35]

The first census of the Philippines was taken in 1903. The first assembly was elected in 1907, and from that year to the passage of the Jones Act in 1916 the legislative power in the Philippines was exercised by the bicameral legislature provided for by the act of 1902—elected assembly and appointed commission. In 1908 a fourth Filipino member was added to the commission, which from then till 1913 consisted of five Americans and four Filipinos. In 1905, meanwhile, the title of the chief executive had been changed from civil governor to governor general. Taft resigned as civil governor in November, 1903 to become Secretary of War. He was succeeded by Luke E. Wright (the first governor general) and he in turn by Henry C. Ide (*ad interim*), James F. Smith, and W. Cameron Forbes. Forbes was followed in 1913 by Woodrow Wilson's appointee, Francis Burton Harrison. Harrison's appointment and the reconstitution of the commission with a Filipino majority, marked a turning-point in American policy in the Philippines. The time had come, in the opinion of Harrison and Wilson, when much more responsibility could be placed in native hands in preparation for complete independence at no distant date.

It was in the years from 1901 to 1913 that American civilization made its strongest impact upon the Philippines. Volumes could well be devoted to the useful reforms and achievements of that period, which here can only be alluded to in a few sentences. A democratic system of local and provincial government was established, capped by the semi-democracy of the Philippine legislature. An excellent judicial system was organized, and for the first time the Filipino without money or influence could hope for justice in the courts. A civil service system based on merit was instituted. An impressive beginning was made in public education, with primary schools established in most communities, a high school in each province, vocational schools, normal schools, and a new University of the Philippines in Manila. Church and state were separated, religious freedom was guaranteed, and American Protestant churches engaged in missionary activities on a modest scale and with moderate success. The Friar Lands (some 400,000 acres) were purchased from the Church and sold in small units and on easy terms, for the most part to former tenants. The friars themselves, Spaniards who had been cordially hated by the Filipinos, were largely replaced by American and native clerics. Land titles were regularized and natives were encouraged to acquire homesteads from the public domain. Modern sanitation and medical techniques were introduced and a vigorous scientific attack was made upon diseases of man and beast. A Bureau of Agriculture promoted improved farming methods, and appropriate legislation fostered the development of forest and mineral resources. Transportation was greatly improved by both land and water; an efficient native constabulary was trained; the Moros and "wild tribes" were brought into a state of comparative industry and order. All of these reforms (except the few that involved activity by the army or navy of the United States) were paid for from Philippine revenues, but the Philippine tax rate remained but a small fraction of the federal tax rate in the United States, and the bonded indebtedness of the Philippine government in 1913 was only $16,000,000.[36]

In the meantime Filipinos had come to occupy an overwhelming majority of governmental positions. In October, 1913 they constituted 71 per cent of the employees in the classified civil service, 92 per cent of teachers, all justices of the peace and governors of the Christian provinces. Three of 5 land court judges were Filipinos, as were 12 of 24 judges of the courts of first instance and 3 of the 7 judges of the supreme court.[37] The assembly was solidly Filipino, and, before the coming of Harrison, four of the nine appointed members of the commission were Filipinos.

Relations between American administrators and Filipino leaders, between commission and assembly, were personally cordial, but in official relations tension developed. The assembly from the beginning was dominated by the Nationalist party, whose platform called for independence. A Federal party, which had been organized in 1900 and had originally advocated statehood, had changed its name to Progressive and its program to increasing autonomy and eventual independence. No native politician deemed it expedient to oppose independence, and politics in the assembly prescribed opposition to the administration. Opposition took the form of disagreement on appropriations. In the three consecutive years, 1911-1913, the two houses of the legislature failed to agree on the general appropriation bill.[38] No bill was passed for either of those years. Governmental paralysis was prevented only by invoking the clause in the organic act that made available the sums appropriated in the last bill passed. Thus the appropriations of 1910 were utilized for each of the three succeeding years. Philippine affairs were in this unhappy state of deadlock when on March 4, 1913 Woodrow Wilson entered the White House.

Since its anti-imperialist campaign of 1900 the Democratic party had continued to advocate independence for the Philippines. The platform of 1912 declared:

> We favor an immediate declaration of the Nation's purpose to recognize the independence of the Philippine Islands as soon as a stable government can be established, such independence to be guaranteed by us until the neutralization of the islands can be secured by treaty with other powers.

Wilson himself gave a hint of his future policy when he declared, a few weeks after his election: "The Philippines are at present our frontier but I hope we presently are to deprive ourselves of that frontier." The existing conflict between commission and assembly made the time opportune for a change in policy if a change was to come. It is not surprising, therefore, that Harrison, Wilson's appointee as governor general, bore to the Filipinos a message from the President containing these two significant paragraphs:

> Every step we take will be taken with a view to the ultimate independence of the islands and as a preparation for that independence. And we hope to move toward that end as rapidly as the safety and the permanent interests of the islands will permit. . . .

The administration will take one step at once and will give to the native citizens of the islands a majority in the appointive Commission and thus in the upper as well as the lower house of the legislature a majority representation will be secured to them.[39]

The reconstitution of the commission with a Filipino majority gave the natives a preponderance of power in Manila. The governor general, a member of the commission, had no separate power of veto, nor—as later experience showed—would Harrison have been disposed to use the veto if he had possessed it. Thus a long step toward Filipino autonomy had been taken. The next step came three years later with the passage of the new organic act of August 29, 1916, usually, like the law of 1917 for Puerto Rico, called the Jones Act.[40]

The most important features of the Jones Act were the declaration of policy contained in the preamble and the reorganization of the legislative branch of the Philippine government. The preamble declared that it was and had always been "the purpose of the people of the United States to withdraw their sovereignty over the Philippine Islands and to recognize their independence as soon as a stable government can be established therein." In the legislature, an elective senate replaced the commission. Senators were to serve for terms of six years, one-half the membership to be chosen at each triennial election. Members of the house of representatives were to serve for three-year terms. Two of the 24 senators and 9 of the 90 representatives were to be appointed by the governor general to represent the non-Christian provinces. The suffrage requirements were liberalized by lowering the voting age from 23 years to 21 and by accepting ability to read and write a native tongue as an alternative to English or Spanish as one road to the ballot.

The governor general and vice governor, who was also head of the Department of Public Instruction, continued to be appointed by the President with the advice and consent of the Senate of the United States. The auditor also was a presidential appointee. The heads of other executive departments were named by the governor general with the advice and consent of the Philippine senate. The governor general received the veto power, including the right to veto separate items in appropriation bills. Bills passed over the gubernatorial veto by a two-thirds vote were referred to the President, from whose veto there was no appeal. Bills dealing with public lands, immigration, coinage, currency, or tariff must, though approved by the governor general, be referred to the President for final approval or rejection. The regulation of trade between the Philippines and the United States was reserved exclusively to Congress. The act retained the provision for a carryover of appropriations if the legislature should fail to pass essential money bills.

Provisions for the judiciary, the resident commissioners, citizenship, and bill of rights remained substantially as under the act of 1902. For the protection of the non-Christian tribes, which hitherto had been under the legislative authority of the commission alone, the act created a Bureau of Non-Christian Tribes, to be placed in an executive department designated by the governor general and to exercise supervision over the public affairs of the territory occupied by such tribes.

On the assumption that the Philippines were to become independent at a very early date,[41] Governor General Harrison was perhaps justified in abetting the Filipino political leaders—notably Sergio Osmeña, speaker of the house of representatives, and Manuel Quezon, after 1917 president of the senate—in obtaining a share of power greater than that conferred by the Jones law. Having begun his administration with a speeding-up of the Filipinization of the public service, he continued it after 1916 by acquiescing in the transfer, whether by legislation or executive order, of much of the governor general's authority to Filipino department heads, or to a Council of State comprising the governor general, the department heads, and the president and speaker of senate and house, or to a Board of Control consisting of the governor general and the same president and speaker (Quezon and Osmeña). What the Filipino leaders were deliberately aiming at and largely achieving was the conversion of the insular government into one on the parliamentary pattern, with the governor general reduced to a figurehead and actual power wielded by the leaders of the majority, or Nationalist, party in the legislature.

Despite an increase in costs and a rather obvious decline in efficiency in some branches of the service, Philippine economy flourished and the Philippine government functioned harmoniously in the prosperous war years, 1916-1920. A "stable government"—specified by the Jones Act as the single prerequisite for independence—appeared to have been achieved. Accordingly, the governor general, in his report for 1920, urged that independence now be granted, and President Wilson endorsed the recommendation in his last annual message to Congress.

The Harding administration was more skeptical. President Harding sent to the Philippines a mission headed by Major General Leonard Wood and former Governor General W. Cameron Forbes. The purpose of the mission was, in the words of the Secretary of War, to investigate the claim, made by some and denied by others, "that the Philippine Government is now in a position to warrant its total separation from the United States Government and that the Filipino people are in a position to continue to operate the Philippine Government without aid of any kind from the United States. . . ." Messrs. Wood and Forbes reported the existence of a very general desire for independence among Christian Filipinos, but found that in the minds of all but a few the desire was qualified by a wish for continued American protection. The non-Christian groups hoped almost unanimously for retention of American sovereignty, as did Americans in the islands. The commissioners pointed to governmental extravagance and decline in efficiency during the Filipino-dominated Harrison régime, and to the unfortunate consequences of governmental ventures into business in the same period, as evidences of the incapacity of the Filipinos for complete self-government.

> We are convinced [they declared] that it would be a betrayal of the Philippine people, a misfortune to the American people, a distinct step backward in the path of progress, and a discreditable neglect of our national duty were we to withdraw from the islands and terminate our relationship there without giving the Filipinos the best possible chance to have an orderly and permanently stable government.

The mission recommended (1) that the existing general status of the islands continue "until the people have had time to absorb and master the powers already in their hands"; (2) that all powers surrendered by, or taken from, the governor general since the enactment of the Jones law be restored to him—by act of Congress if the Philippine legislature refused the necessary action; (3) that in the event of a deadlock over appointments between the governor general and the Philippine senate, the President of the United States be empowered to make the final decision; (4) that no situation be allowed to arise "which would leave the United States in a position of responsibility without authority."[42]

Congress took no action on the recommendations of the Wood-Forbes Commission, but it was tacitly understood that the report was approved by the President. Major General Wood remained in the Philippines as governor general. His efforts to recover the lost authority of the office—his abolition of the Board of Control and his attempts to control the action of department heads—soon produced a deadlock between him and the senate, a battle with Quezon and Osmeña, and a demand by the legislature for his recall. An investigator sent to the islands by President Coolidge in 1926, though no less opposed to immediate independence than Wood and Forbes had been, nevertheless laid the blame for the existing deadlock partly on General Wood's doorstep. He found the military atmosphere of the executive offices (Wood had surrounded himself with military aides) detrimental to good relations with the legislature. He opposed any drastic action by Congress. He believed restoration of cooperation between the governor general and the legislature possible on a basis of mutual accommodation.[43]

The crisis ended with the return of General Wood to the United States for an operation that resulted in his death, and with the appointment, early in 1928, of Henry L. Stimson as his successor. Stimson had visited the Philippines in 1926 at the request of Governor General Wood. While there he had held friendly conversations with Quezon and Osmeña and had outlined to them and to Wood the terms of a compromise arrangement by which he believed harmony could be restored. Such an arrangement had little chance of success while Wood remained. Though it involved concessions by the Filipino leaders, Quezon and Osmeña were both favorably impressed with the proposal and with the man who had made it. After Wood's death they both urged Stimson to accept President Coolidge's proffer of the governor generalship, and promised him their cooperation if he would do so.[44]

Stimson arrived in Manila March 1, 1928. He had already secured the confidence of the native leaders, and their trust in him grew during the year of his stay in the Philippines. Friendly relations with the legislature were promptly restored, and concessions were made on each side. The new governor general appointed department heads acceptable to the majority party and allowed them wide freedom of action. He reconstituted the Council of State, which had fallen into abeyance under Wood, with an enlarged membership but with advisory functions only. The legislature amended its rules to give department heads the privilege of the floor in both houses. It also provided salaries for civilian advisers to the governor general to replace General Wood's so-called "cavalry cabinet." Stimson had recovered much of the authority that Governor General Harrison had surrendered. At the same time he had conceded to the Filipinos a modified type of parliamentary government[45] and had stilled, for the time being, the agitation for independence.* What was most important was the restoration of good feeling between the American executive and the Filipino legislature, which continued under Stimson's successors until the establishment of the Commonwealth in 1935.[46]

THE VIRGIN ISLANDS

The Virgin Islands of the United States, formerly known as the Danish West Indies, were purchased from Denmark by the treaty of August 4, 1916 and transferred to American sovereignty on March 31, 1917. They comprise the islands of St. Thomas, 40 miles east of Puerto Rico, St. John, 3 miles east of St. Thomas, St. Croix, 40 miles south-southeast of St. Thomas, and some 50 islets and keys, mostly uninhabited. Tradition has it that Columbus, on his second voyage in 1493, sighting a galaxy of islands too numerous to name individually, called them the Virgin Islands in honor of the 11,000 martyred virgins of Saint Ursula.[47] St. Thomas attracted attention because of its fine harbor and St. Croix because of its agricultural possibilities. Spanish, French, Dutch, English, and Danes all took an interest in the islands, but eventually the three that were to become American possessions were acquired by Denmark—St. Thomas in

---

* For the revival of the independence movement and its eventual success see pages 291-310.

1672, St. John in 1717, St. Croix in 1733. Much of the
land and business in the islands, however, passed into
English and Irish hands, and the Negroes (slaves until
1848) who constituted the labor force and the bulk of

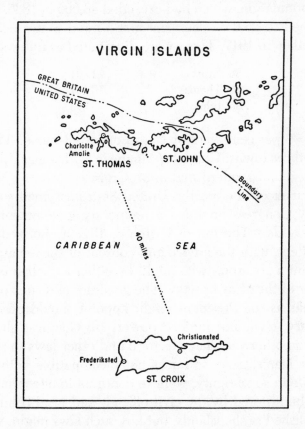

the population were for the most part drawn from the
British West Indies and were themselves English-
speaking—a circumstance that facilitated the transition
from Danish to United States sovereignty.[48]

The area of the three American islands is 132 square

miles. St. Thomas and St. John are mountainous. St. Croix has a range of hills along its northern margin; elsewhere it is nearly level, the soil is fertile, and only a deficient rainfall prevents it from being agriculturally prosperous. The population, which had exceeded 43,000 in 1835, had dropped to 26,051 when the first United States census was taken in 1917. These were distributed as follows:

St. Croix	14,901
St. Thomas	10,191
St. John	959

Over 90 per cent were of Negro or mixed blood. There were three towns: Charlotte Amalie in St. Thomas, Christiansted and Frederiksted in St. Croix.

Four weeks before the United States assumed sovereignty Congress provided a temporary government for the islands.[49] The Act of March 3, 1917 authorized the President, with the advice and consent of the Senate, to appoint a governor, who might be either a civilian or an officer of the army or navy. The governor and such other persons as the President might appoint should exercise military, civil, and judicial powers till Congress should provide otherwise. The electoral and other laws in force under Danish rule, so far as not incompatible with the change in sovereignty, were to continue in effect and to be administered by the civil officials and local tribunals established in the islands, but any such laws might, with the approval of the President, be repealed or amended by the insular legislative bodies. Judicial appeals that previously could have been taken to the courts of Denmark could now be taken to the Circuit Court of Appeals for the Third Circuit at Philadelphia. Existing customs laws remained in force, except that native products of the United States were admitted to the islands free of duty. Island products likewise found a free market in the United States, but all exported sugar was taxed at a rate of $8 per ton (later reduced to $6).

In effect, this legislation simply took over the Danish system of colonial government, substituting the higher authorities of the United States for those of Denmark. Locally, the governmental arrangements remained substantially as they had been fixed by the Colonial Law of April 6, 1906[50] and by Danish practice thereunder. The islands comprised two municipalities, St. Thomas and St. John in the north with the seat of government at Charlotte Amalie (called St. Thomas by the United States until 1937, when the old name was resumed), St. Croix in the south with seat of government at Christiansted. Each municipality had a colonial council. That of St. Thomas and St. John consisted of 11 elected and 4 appointed members; that of St. Croix of 13 elected and 5 appointed. All members were chosen for four-year terms. The right to vote for council members was vested in male citizens (or residents of 5 years' standing), 25 years of age, "of unblemished character," and possessed of property or income of moderate amount.[51] Such requirements restricted the suffrage to about 1 in 20 of the population. The secret ballot was employed in elections.

Under Danish rule the making of "laws" for the colonies was reserved to the Danish parliament, but the colonial councils might, with the consent of the King, pass "ordinances" affecting local matters. The distinction between laws and ordinances was retained under United States rule, but the President (though reserving a final veto power) delegated to the governor the authority to approve provisionally or to veto ordinances passed by the councils. A veto by the governor was final. In "extraordinary circumstances" the governor could issue provisional ordinances, which must be laid before the appropriate council at its next meeting. The governor might also, with presidential approval, dissolve either of the colonial councils, though not more than twice in any two-year period, and when such dissolution occurred, new elections must be promptly held.

Originally the municipal councils shared administrative authority with the governor, appointing members of commissions on schools, hospitals, quarantine, and other matters, but an early American governor persuaded the councils to supersede such commissions with department heads appointed by and responsible to him. In addition to the governor and such department heads, the executive branch included a government secretary, who served as the chief executive officer under the governor, "dispatching secretaries" in St. John and St. Croix, and certain assistants to these officials. All governors from 1917 to 1931 were naval officers, rear admirals or captains, and their assistants and department heads were also officers, generally from the supply, engineering, medical, or chaplain corps of the navy or the marine corps, with the exception of the directors of education and police, who were civilians. Since the salaries of navy personnel were paid by the United States government, the arrangement was financially advantageous to the islands.

The judicial branch consisted of one district court and three police courts for the three towns. The police court judges were appointed by the governor, as was the district judge until 1931; in that year his appointment was assigned to the Secretary of the Interior of the United States, and in 1933 it was given to the Attorney General. After 1925 any case in which the Constitution or a law or treaty of the United States was involved, or in which the amount in controversy exceeded $1,000 could be appealed to the Circuit Court of Appeals, Third Circuit. The Danish Colonial Law contained a liberal bill of rights. The list of protected rights was enlarged by codes adopted by the municipal councils in 1920 and 1921, based on those of Alaska. Thereafter jury trial might be had in felony cases upon the demand of the accused, and the district judge might prescribe it in either felony or misdemeanor cases or in civil suits.

For ten years after the acquisition of the islands, their inhabitants were denied United States citizenship. The treaty of cession had provided that Danish citizens who did not within one year make formal declaration of their wish to retain their Danish allegiance should be deemed to have renounced it and "to have accepted citizenship in the United States," but it had added that "the civil rights and the political status of the inhabitants shall be determined by the Congress." To the great chagrin of the islanders, Congress, in the act of March 3, 1917, neglected to confer the expected boon of citizenship, and the oversight was not remedied until February 25, 1927, when new legislation extended United States citizenship to most former Danish citizens or other Virgin Islanders who were not citizens or subjects of any foreign country. Subsequent legislation provided the same status for certain groups not covered in the 1927 law.[52]

Woodrow Wilson appointed a naval officer as first American governor of the Virgin Islands, and the precedent thus set was followed until 1931. Seven naval governors served in those 14 years. The average term of two years was, by general agreement, too short to produce the best results. The relation of the governor to the Navy Department was never clearly defined. After 1922 he made his annual reports via the Secretary of the Navy, and the Department sponsored the monetary needs of the Virgin Islands government before the Director of the Budget and Congress. But the governor was responsible to the President, not to the Secretary of the Navy, and he governed the islands not like the autocrat of a battleship but rather like a constitutional monarch with very limited powers. Although headed by a naval officer, therefore, the government was a civil, not a naval, government. Those who maintained otherwise and raised a demand for "civil government" appear to have been principally local aspirants for office who thought their chances would be improved if the naval governor and his naval aides were eliminated.[53]

This is not to say that naval officers made ideal governors. Although their defenders could point to admirable progress in such matters as roads, paved streets, water supply, education, sanitation and health (the annual death rate per thousand of population fell from 35.4 for 1911-1917 to 21.5 for 1923-1926), they were generally without political experience and sometimes pursued high-handed tactics that furnished ammunition for agitators against United States rule.[54] On the whole, however, there was much more occasion for pride than for apology in the period of rule by naval governors.

President Herbert Hoover's order of February 27, 1931, placing the administration of the Virgin Islands under the supervision of the Secretary of the Interior, was occasioned not by local criticism of the navy but by a quarrel between the governor, Captain Waldo Evans, and Herbert D. Brown, director of the Bureau of Efficiency, who had recommended a rehabilitation program that the governor deemed visionary.[55]

The first civilian governor of the Virgin Islands, appointed by President Hoover when he transferred the islands to the Interior Department, was Paul M. Pearson, a former professor of public speaking who had shown executive ability in organizing an extensive Chautauqua circuit. Pearson served until 1935, when President Roosevelt transferred him to another post. In the meantime the Division of Territories and Island Possessions had been created by executive order in the Interior Department and vested with the supervision of the governments of the Virgin Islands, Alaska, Hawaii, and Puerto Rico.

On June 22, 1936 the President signed a new organic act for the Virgin Islands. Agitation for revision of the system of government inherited from Denmark had begun soon after the acquisition of the islands. A joint congressional committee visited the new possession in February, 1920 but reported against a change at that time. Four years later a commission of American Negroes, appointed by the Secretary of Labor, after spending two weeks in the islands, recommended full American citizenship and criticized the restricted franchise, but made no other important proposals. From the middle 1920's on, proposals for new organic legislation, sponsored by native Virgin Islanders, by the American Civil

Liberties Union, and by other interested persons or groups, were periodically before Congress. Most such proposals contained provisions for a more democratic suffrage, for the elimination of the appointed element in the councils, and for some qualification of the governor's veto power. Suggestions that the islands, or at least St. Croix, be attached to Puerto Rico and placed under its government met with less favor, partly because of the difference in language. Because of the widely differing economies of St. Croix and St. Thomas, it was generally agreed that the separate municipal councils should be retained, though with provision for joint sessions to consider matters of common interest.[56]

Many of these suggestions were embodied in the organic act of June, 1936.[57] All members of the municipal councils—nine for St. Croix, seven for St. Thomas and St. John—are now elected for two-year terms. Members must be citizens of the United States, 25 years of age, qualified voters of their municipalities, must have resided in the Virgin Islands for at least 3 years, and must not have been convicted of a felony or a crime involving moral turpitude. Each council must meet every second month or more often at the call of the governor or the chairman of the council. At least once a year at the call of the governor, on other occasions either at the governor's call or in pursuance of resolutions passed by both councils, the two councils shall meet jointly at St. Thomas (Charlotte Amalie) as the "Legislative Assembly of the Virgin Islands." "The legislative assembly shall have power to enact legislation applicable to the Virgin Islands as a whole, but no legislation shall be considered other than that specified in the message by the Governor calling such a session, or in both of said resolutions."

The governor may veto bills passed by either municipal council or by the legislative assembly and may veto specific items in appropriation bills. A vetoed bill may be repassed by a vote of two-thirds of the entire membership of the body concerned. If the governor still disapproves the bill, he must send it to the President, who may either approve or veto it. If he fails to veto it within three months, it becomes law. All laws passed by the legislative bodies must be transmitted by the governor to the Secretary of the Interior and by him to Congress, which reserves the right to annul such legislation. If a municipal council fails to make appropriations necessary for the support of the municipal government in any fiscal year, the sums appropriated for the preceding fiscal year are deemed to have been reappropriated.

Each of the three legislative bodies is empowered to amend or repeal any law of the United States of purely local application when such amendment or repeal is not inconsistent with the organic act. Export duties in effect when the act was passed could be reduced, repealed, or restored by the municipal council having jurisdiction, but no new export duties could be imposed.

The organic act not only eliminated the appointive members of the councils; it also liberalized the suffrage requirements. Voters must now be citizens of the United States, 21 years of age, and able to read and write the English language. The legislative assembly may impose additional qualifications, but none based upon property, income, race, color, sex, or religious belief.

The governor and government secretary, who is also a vice governor, are appointed by the President, the former but not the latter with the advice and consent of the Senate. An administrator for St. Croix and other administrative officers of the central government are named by the Secretary of the Interior. Executive officers of the two municipalities are appointed by the governor with confirmation by the respective councils. All officers of the government of the Virgin Islands must be citizens of the United States.

The only important changes in the judicial branch were the provisions that the judge of the district court and the district attorney should be appointed by the President (with the consent of the Senate) for four-year terms, and that the district judge should hold court at least once in every two months in each municipality. The legislative assembly was authorized to create a superior court to relieve the district court of jurisdiction over nonfederal cases, but to 1950 this right had not been exercised. Jury trial in criminal cases was allowed upon the demand of either party, and the municipal councils were empowered to provide for six-member juries in misdemeanor cases. There was no provision for grand juries. A bill of rights embodied the usual guarantees with the exception of jury trial, indictment by grand jury, and the right to bear arms, and including a prohibition of the employment of children under 14 years of age "in any occupation injurious to health or morals or hazardous to life or limb."

With the exception of the division into two municipalities with separate legislative bodies and of the failure to provide for a delegate or resident commissioner to represent the islands in Washington, the organic act of 1936 gave to the Virgin Islands approximately the same governmental status as that of other territories considered in this chapter. They are officially described in the annual reports transmitted to the United Nations as "an organized but unincorporated territory of the United States."

If the organic act of 1936 was expected to produce harmony between the governor and the legislative bodies in the Virgin Islands, its sponsors must have been disappointed in its initial results. The legislative assembly convened for the first time on November 22, 1937 and at once began a quarrel with the governor over his assumed right to introduce bills. It adjourned without enacting any measure save one for the payment of the salaries of the members, and this the governor vetoed with a declaration that the assembly had performed no public service.[58] Subsequent relations were somewhat more amicable.*

GUAM AND AMERICAN SAMOA

If, as was suggested above, the naval governors of the Virgin Islands governed like constitutional monarchs, the reign of naval officers in Guam and American Samoa was more like that of enlightened despots. They were restrained by no constitution, no organic act, but only by their own moderation, their short terms of office (normally 18 months to 2 years), and, of course, the superior authority of the Navy Department and the President, which seldom interfered with their activities.

As related in Chapter Two, Guam, in the Marianas,

---

* For later proposals for changes in the government of the Virgin Islands see page 290.

was obtained from Spain by the Treaty of Paris of 1898; American Samoa lost its nominal independence by the American-British-German treaty of 1899 and the subsequent cession of the islands to the United States by their native chiefs.

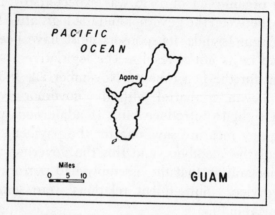

Guam, 3,400 miles west and slightly south of Honolulu, has an area of 225 square miles. Its population in 1901 was 9,630. Its people, known as Guamanians, were descendants of the aboriginal Chamorro stock, but so

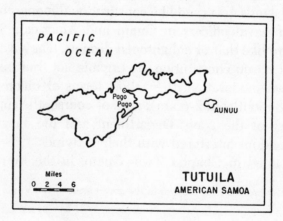

intermixed with Spanish, Mexican, Filipino and other strains that few, if any, pure-blooded Chamorros remained. The Chamorro language, however, still prevailed. Guam had been under Spanish rule since 1668. The population had been thoroughly Christianized (at the cost of much rebellion and bloodshed in the early years) and enjoyed a government with not a few liberal features, including elective local officials and appeals from its courts to those of Spain.

American Samoa, beside the principal island of Tutuila, comprises four small neighboring islands, Rose Island (an uninhabited coral atoll slightly to the southeast), and Swain's Island, 207 miles to the north, which was added in 1925. The total area is 76 square miles. Tutuila lies over 15 degrees south of the equator, 2,275 miles southwest of Honolulu. The population of American Samoa in 1900 was 5,679. Like the Hawaiians, the Samoans were of Polynesian stock; they had been converted to Christianity chiefly through the work of the London Missionary Society.[59]

Both Guam and American Samoa were made United States naval stations by executive order. The naval officer designated to command such a station governed it very much as he governed a battleship; the supreme executive, legislative, and judicial power was in his hands. As chief executive, he administered his dependency through a staff of naval officers with an occasional civilian member (in Samoa there was often a civilian secretary of native affairs, who might he a trained anthropologist). As the highest law-making authority, he issued orders that had the force of law. He might, of course, take advice as he chose, and in both dependencies governors availed themselves of the advice of native deliberative bodies—in Samoa, of the annual *fono*, or gathering of native officials and elected delegates; in Guam, of the Guam Congress, from 1917 to 1931 a body made up of the governor's appointees, after 1931 an elected body of two houses. But neither the *fono* nor the congress had legislative power. Each could advise the governor; he could give its advice as much or as little weight as he saw fit.

As head of the judiciary, the governor might sit in person on the bench of the highest court. In any event, he appointed the judges; he might review their decisions, and from his decisions there was no right of appeal to any higher tribunal. In Samoa there were a high court, 6 district courts, and 35 village courts. The village courts, under native magistrates, handled various minor cases. In the district courts, which had jurisdiction over more serious cases and cases involving non-natives, the district judge (an American, who usually also held the post of secretary of native affairs) sat jointly with a local native judge. If a difference of opinion arose between the two, that of the American judge prevailed. In the high court the governor himself, or someone designated by him, presided, with two associate judges—the American district judge and a native. In Guam there were a police court, a justice court, and an island court, each presided over by a Guamanian judge, and with jurisdiction shading upward from minor to major cases. Above all was the court of appeals, consisting of a presiding justice and four associate judges. The presiding justice and two of the associates were naval officers; the other two were Guamanians. "All five members of the court serve by virtue of appointment by the governor and may be removed by him at will without restriction from higher authority. The presiding justice is usually an attorney, but there is no requirement that any one of the five members of the court of appeals be an attorney or be qualified in the law."[60]*

The Samoan courts administer a code of civil and criminal law "based on American law but modified according to the special needs of the area" and with a proviso that Samoan customs not in conflict with such law shall be preserved. In Guam the old Spanish and Filipino codes remained in effect until 1933, when new civil and criminal codes based upon California law were adopted. Such codes were not of great importance, however, since they were put in effect by order of the governor and could be withdrawn or departed from at will by him or his successors. No bill of rights for the inhabitants of either possession existed till 1931, when the Samoans received such a bill—by gubernatorial fiat. A similar bill of rights proclaimed for Guam by the governor in 1930 was revoked by the Navy Department, but many of its features were incorporated in the codes of 1933. Samoans were not citizens of the United States, nor were Guamanians till August 1, 1950.

In local government, the policy in Samoa has been to adapt native tribal organization as far as possible to the needs of American rule; in Guam the system devised by the Spanish has been taken over with modifications. American Samoa is divided into three districts corresponding to early Samoan political divisions: East and

---

* But see pages 231-232 for recent changes in the judiciary of American Samoa and Guam.

West Tutuila and Manu'a, the latter embracing the islands of Tau, Olosega, and Ofu. Each district, in turn, is divided into counties, and each county comprises village units. There are village councils with some legislative power in local matters. Each village, however, is controlled by a chief, nominated annually by the village council and appointed by the governor if he approves the nomination. Counties are administered by hereditary chiefs who hold office during good behavior as determined by the governor, and each district has a district governor, named by the governor of Samoa from among the county chiefs in the district. To the annual *fono* go the district governors and judges, the county chiefs, and 30 *matais* (local chiefs or orators), 10 from each district, chosen by district councils. The system has, on the whole, worked satisfactorily for the maintenance of peace, order, and sanitation and has at the same time given the natives a wholesome degree of self-government.[61]

In Guam the first American administrators found four municipalities with native officials chosen by a joint system of election (or nomination) and appointment. The American authorities retained the general framework of local government but abolished its elective features. The local officials—a commissioner for each municipality, supported by deputy commissioners and assistant commissioners—were appointed by the governor, and the native policeman who had been the arm of the law in each municipality was supplanted by a marine patrolman. The number of municipalities increased gradually from 4 to 15. The government of Agaña, the most important municipality, was headed by a native chief commissioner who supervised the work of the commissioners of the other municipalities. Monthly mass meetings were held in each municipality, attended by the chief commissioner and the naval officer heading the executive department of the Guam government. At these meetings the people of the island were acquainted with government orders and policies and the reasons therefor.

A step in the direction of democracy was taken in 1931, when a liberal-minded governor of Guam revived the Spanish custom of giving the people a voice in choosing their commissioners and deputies; but another governor five years later abolished the practice and made these native officials again appointive. "Thus at one stroke," writes an American authority, "the people of Guam lost the only really effective measure of self-government they had gained during the American rule."[62]

Government policy in Guam seems, on the whole, to have been less consistent and less sympathetic to native customs and ambitions than that in Samoa.

Both Samoans and Guamanians have from time to time expressed their desires for American citizenship, for guaranteed bills of rights, and for real self-government under civilian control, but up to the end of World War II no such reforms had been adopted, though bills embodying one or another of them had several times passed one house of Congress. A bill designed to provide Guam with civil government was passed by the Senate in 1903 but was blocked in the House of Representatives, allegedly by navy influence. Bills to confer United States citizenship upon the Guamanians were introduced in both Senate and House in 1937 and in the Senate in 1939 but did not come to a vote.[63]

The 1920's brought serious manifestations of disaffection in American Samoa, where a native organization, the *Mau*, agitated for American citizenship and the elimination of naval government. In 1929 Congress created an American Samoan Commission consisting of two members each from the Senate and House of Representatives and two chiefs of American Samoa to recommend to Congress such legislation for Samoa as they should deem necessary or proper.[64] The commission, headed by Senator Hiram Bingham of Connecticut (born in Hawaii of American missionary parents), held hearings in Honolulu in September and in American Samoa in September and October, 1930 and submitted a report dated January 5, 1931.[65]

In a preliminary statement Senator Bingham had described the naval government as "the most unlimited autocracy the world has ever seen," but had then gone on to say (at a time of deep economic depression in the United States):

> There is no such thing as poverty in Samoa, . . . because everyone belongs to a group or clan with a chief at its head who is responsible for their welfare.[66]

This poverty-less condition apparently impressed the commissioners as an unfortunate anachronism, for their report recommended

> a form of government flexible in nature, which will allow them to develop themselves, should they so choose, away from their present communal system of social organization and property into one more completely in tune with American civilization, . . .

The report included a proposed organic act for American Samoa, of which the following were the most notable features:

1. A grant of United States citizenship to persons wholly or partly of Polynesian blood residing in American Samoa February 20, 1929 (the date on which Congress had formally accepted the Samoan cession and provided for the commission).

2. A bill of rights following the usual pattern for unincorporated possessions.

3. A grant of full legislative power to the *fono*, including the power to override the governor's veto by a two-thirds vote, with reference thereafter to the President.

4. Appointment of governor and attorney general by the President with the advice and consent of the Senate, the governor to be an active, retired, or reserve officer of the army or navy, or a civilian, at the discretion of the President.

5. A chief justice appointed by the President with the advice and consent of the Senate; appeals from the high court to the United States district court for Hawaii.

6. No person not a citizen of Samoa to be permitted to own land or to lease it for a period of more than 20 years—a provision designed to continue a policy of "Samoan land for the Samoans" consistently practiced by the navy.[67]

A bill embodying most of the features of the commission's report passed the Senate on January 26, 1931 but failed to pass the House. Another bill, with some modifications, passed the Senate in February, 1932 but was rejected by the House. No further serious attempt was made to provide Samoa with an organic act. Still the work of the commission was not entirely fruitless. As consequences of its report, the naval administration added a bill of rights to the Samoan code; to meet the criticism that the secretary of native affairs acted upon occasion as both judge and attorney for the government, it instituted the new office of attorney general and appointed a naval officer thereto.[68]

No further changes occurred in the governments of Guam and American Samoa until after World War II, during which Guam was captured and occupied for two and one-half years by the Japanese. In 1945 President Truman asked the Secretaries of State, War, Navy, and the Interior to make recommendations for the future administration of those two dependencies and of such other Pacific islands as might be placed under United States rule. The Secretaries recommended an early transfer of the islands to a civilian department and the passage of organic legislation providing United States citizenship, bills of rights, civil government, and legislative power for the insular assemblies.

Following this report, which was submitted in June, 1947, the Navy Department prepared organic legislation for Samoa and the Departments of the Navy and the Interior drafted similar legislation for Guam. These proposals were submitted to Congress, but that body showed little disposition to be guided by recommendations of the executive departments. Instead, it set up a joint committee to study all Pacific islands under the jurisdiction of the United States and to recommend to Congress whatever legislation might be necessary to establish civil government in those islands. The committee, however, failed to make the trip of inspection to the islands planned for November, 1948, and the whole matter went over to the next Congress.[69]

Without waiting for Congress to enact organic legislation, President Truman in May, 1949 directed the Secretaries of the Navy and the Interior to prepare for the transfer of both Guam and American Samoa from the Navy to the Department of the Interior—Guam within the ensuing year, American Samoa within the next two or three years.[70] The first step toward civilian rule in Guam was taken promptly. Although the Navy Department was not due to relinquish control until June 30, 1950, a civilian governor, designated by the Department of the Interior, was named in August, 1949 and was inaugurated at Agaña, the island capital, on September 27. The new governor faced the task of building up a civilian staff to replace naval personnel at the time of the formal transfer.[71]

Meanwhile, the naval administrations had instituted some reforms in the governments of both dependencies. In August, 1947 the Secretary of the Navy conferred legislative power upon the Guam Congress, including the right to override the governor's veto, but with reservation of a final veto power by the Secretary of the Navy.[72] In American Samoa in February, 1948 the annual *fono* was replaced by a bicameral body known as the Legislature of American Samoa. The legislature comprises an elective House of Representatives and a House of Alii—a sort of primitive House of Lords—composed of the holders of the 12 highest ranking titles in American Samoa. Since the legislature, like the *fono*, has only advisory powers, the change is not of great importance.[73]

It appears, however, to have satisfied the current aspirations of the Samoans for self-government. A petition adopted in November, 1948 by 300 clan leaders requested that the recently instituted form of government—including, presumably, administration by the Navy Department—"be continued forevermore." This attitude appeared to stem from fear that more self-government would lead to factional quarrels and would place an intolerable burden on the modest native economy.[74]

There were changes also in the judicial branches of both dependencies. In Samoa the post of chief justice, the official who presides over the high court, was filled by an American civilian with legal training. In Guam, likewise, there was a new chief justice, an American jurist selected by the Secretary of the Navy, who presided over the court of appeals and also over a newly created superior court. The new court handled cases in which the naval government was a party and criminal cases in which—because of the disturbed postwar situation and the presence of a large number of Americans—it might be thought inexpedient to have native judges participate. From the superior court appeals might be taken, not to mainland courts but to the Secretary of the Navy.[75]

For Guam all this was changed on August 1, 1950. On that date, President Truman signed the long-awaited organic act conferring United States citizenship and a bill of rights on the Guamanians, vesting legislative authority in an elective, unicameral legislature, and creating an independent judiciary with the possibility of appeals to the higher United States courts. On the same date (instead of on June 30 as first directed), the administrative supervision of Guam was transferred from the Navy Department to the Department of the Interior. It seemed probable that similar legislation and a similar change in administrative responsibility for American Samoa might follow in the near future.[76]

THE PANAMA CANAL ZONE

It remains to speak only of the Panama Canal Zone, the ten-mile-wide strip of territory running across the Isthmus of Panama, five miles on either side of the canal. Its combined land and water area, as newly computed in 1948 and including an "item of tidewater lying within the 3-mile boundary of the Atlantic and Pacific Oceans," was 648.01 square miles. Its estimated population in April, 1948, exclusive of United States military personnel, was 47,462, of whom slightly less than one-half were United States citizens. Most of the remainder were Negroes from the British West Indies. Virtually all the inhabitants were employees of the Panama Canal, the families of the employees, or families of the armed forces personnel stationed there. Private industry is nonexistent in the Canal Zone.[77]

The "use, occupation, and control" of the Canal Zone were granted in perpetuity to the United States by the Republic of Panama by the treaty of 1903, with the further provision that the United States should enjoy within the Zone "all the rights, power and authority . . . which the United States would possess and exercise if it were the sovereign of the territory." With such a sweeping grant of rights and authority in the Zone, it is perhaps rather technical to say that it is not a possession of the United States, but such is the official ruling, and for purposes of the application of the tariff and immigration laws, the Canal Zone is treated as foreign soil. Laws applicable to the United States and its possessions do not apply in the Zone unless there is express declaration to that effect. On the other hand, laws applicable to "the United States and all territory under its control and jurisdiction" obviously cover the Canal Zone. " . . . the provisions of the Constitution concerning civil and political rights do not apply in the Canal Zone unless and except in so far as they are extended by Congress."[78]

While the canal was under construction (1904-1914), the Zone was governed by the President through the Isthmian Canal Commission, but in 1912 Congress authorized the President, upon completion of the canal, to discontinue the Commission and to govern the Zone through a governor, to be appointed by him with the advice and consent of the Senate, and such other officials as he might deem necessary.[79]

The law provided that when the United States should be at war, or when, in the opinion of the President, war should be imminent, the Zone should be under army control;[80] at other times the President was left free to govern it through such agency as he saw fit. The President chose to delegate most of his wide powers to the Secretary of War; in the War Department there was an administrative assistant charged specifically with oversight of canal matters, and the governor—designated officially Governor of the Panama Canal and appointed for a four-year term—has always been, though he need not be, an army engineer officer.[81]

The government of the Canal Zone has its executive and judicial branches, but the power of legislation is reserved to Congress. The governor is directed by law to "perform all duties in connection with the civil government of the Canal Zone." Under him is a staff including army and navy officers and civilians. An executive secretary (who has usually been a civilian) heads the executive department, which is in charge of most of the governmental activities in the Zone. An army engineer officer, known as the engineer of maintenance, is virtually a vice governor and in every instance has been appointed to the governorship upon the transfer or retirement of his superior. The governor is also president of the Panama Railroad Company, a corporation chartered in New York and wholly owned by the United States through the Secretary of War (from 1947, Secretary of the Army), who appoints the directors. The engineer of maintenance is second vice president of the company, and the first vice president runs the New York office.

The law of 1912 made provision for the establishment of organized towns in the Zone. Only two towns—Balboa at the Pacific terminus of the canal and Cristobal at the Caribbean terminus—have been officially designated,[82] and these are "towns" only for administrative and judicial purposes; they have no such elective government as is generally implied by the term "town." The peculiar nature of Canal Zone government is described in a recent governor's report:

> The usual functions of government, such as schools, police and fire protection, quarantine, public health, immigration service, posts, customs, aids to navigation, steamboat inspection, hydrographic and meteorological work, water supply, sewers,

construction and maintenance of streets, and similar activities, which, in the United States are directed by various officers of the National, State, and municipal governments, are entrusted in the Canal Zone to the Governor, and are executed under his authority and responsibility. This centralization of all governmental activities under one head is essential to economical and efficient administration.[83]

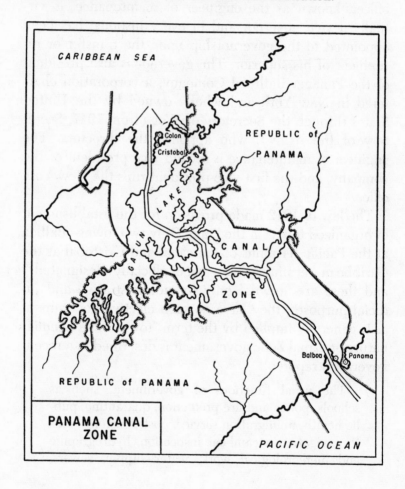

PANAMA CANAL ZONE

The judicial branch alone is not under the authority of the governor. In each town is a magistrate's court with jurisdiction over minor civil and criminal cases. The magistrates, in earlier years appointed by the governor, have since 1933 been appointed "by the President or by his authority" for four-year terms.[84] Above the magistrates' courts is a statutory United States district court with two divisions, one for Balboa and one for Cristobal. It has original jurisdiction in more serious civil and criminal cases, equity, probate, and divorce cases, certain admiralty cases, and cases involving the Constitution, laws, or treaties of the United States. It also hears appeals from the magistrates' courts, and appeals from the district court may be taken to the United States Circuit Court of Appeals for the Fifth Circuit at New Orleans. Jury trial may be had in any civil or criminal suit in the district court upon the demand of either party. The judge, marshal, and district attorney are appointed for four-year terms by the President with the advice and consent of the Senate, and the court is under the supervision of the Department of Justice.

It will be noted that of all populated areas under the jurisdiction of the United States (with the exception of the District of Columbia), the Canal Zone alone is without a single feature suggestive of popular self-government. It has not even such native advisory bodies as are found in Guam and American Samoa. The reasons for this distinction are not obscure. The Canal Zone exists solely for purposes of the operation and protection of the canal, which is a vital link in the defense system of the United States. Necessarily, therefore, the Canal Zone is governed in the interest of the 147,000,000 people of the United

States, not in that of its few thousand population. That it can be thus governed autocratically without serious protest is due to the absence of two possible sources of opposition—private business and an indigenous population. Private property, other than personal belongings, does not exist in the Zone; all land, industry, and business are the property of the United States. The population is composed exclusively of military personnel and civil employees of the United States and their families, virtually all imported either from the United States or the West Indies. There is no indigenous population, and hence there are no traditions or patterns of self-government that need to be respected.

That the Canal Zone has been well governed and the canal and its subsidiary enterprises efficiently administered is generally admitted, and this success can properly be attributed to the care exercised by successive Presidents and Secretaries of War in filling the position of engineer of maintenance—the post whose occupant after four years of experience has invariably been promoted to the governorship. In the words of a prominent authority on public administration:

> It is no exaggeration to say that freedom from partisan appointments and the experience which a Governor has when he comes into office have been largely responsible for the honesty and excellence of Panama Canal administration. The plan is miles ahead of the system of political appointments usually employed in the case of other American possessions.[85]

On February 1, 1950 President Truman proposed a sweeping set of changes in Panama Canal administration. He asked Congress to authorize a transfer of the administration of the canal to the Panama Railroad Company, with a change in the company's name to Panama Canal Company. He asked that the company's board of directors be empowered to establish toll rates, subject to the President's approval, that the company be permitted to retain all toll revenues, and that Congress authorize appropriations to cover losses suffered in the operation of the canal. Without waiting for action by Congress, the President delegated to the governor of the Panama Canal authority to make changes in the internal organization of the canal administration and transferred to the Panama Railroad Company a number of business operations previously carried on by the government. Among these were commissaries, docks, coal-handling facilities, oil storage tanks, gasoline service stations, and a printing plant. Transferred with the enterprises were the personnel, properties, and records connected with them. The President acted upon the recommendation of the Bureau of the Budget, whose director, Frank Pace, believed that the change would "promote the more effective administration of the Panama Canal enterprise."[86]

CHAPTER SEVEN

The Imperial Economy and Political By-Products ∼ ∼

THE ECONOMICS OF COLONIALISM

ANY realistic analysis of the policy of the United States in its outlying possessions must take account not only of the systems of government that it devised for those possessions, but also of the economic relationships that it established with them and of the effects of those relationships both upon the United States and upon the various dependencies.

Despite early professions of devotion to the principle of the open door, the United States lost little time in adopting a preferential system in trade with its new possessions. Free trade between the continent and the dependencies became the rule, with trifling exceptions only in American Samoa and the Canal Zone (see pages 167-170). Competing foreign products were admitted but were subject to import duties.

Thus the United States, like other colonial powers, found in its colonies a protected market for its own manufactures and a source of needed raw materials—precious metals, furs, and fish in Alaska; sugar, pineapples, copra, hemp, tobacco, and other tropical and subtropical products in the insular possessions. In further conformity to the classical analysis of economic imperialism,[1] "surplus capital" from the United States also found opportunities for investment in Alaska and the tropical islands. Such opportunities, however, were not unrestricted. Presumably with the object of preventing excessive or unhealthy "exploitation" of insular lands and populations, either Congress or the local governments placed a number of restrictions upon the acquisition or ownership of land. Thus in American Samoa no land might be acquired by persons not at least three-fourths Samoan in blood; in Guam, no land might be sold to "aliens"—a term that embraced citizens of the United States—though in both possessions lands might be leased to aliens with the approval of the respective governors.[2] In Hawaii and Puerto Rico Congress undertook to restrict corporate holdings to 1,000 acres and 500 acres respectively (the Hawaiian restriction was repealed in 1921), and in the Philippines it limited corporate acquisitions from the public domain to 2,500 acres. In the Philippines this restriction seems to have been generally observed. In Puerto Rico the 500-acre law was widely evaded or violated; in fact, no attempt was made to enforce it until 1935. In Guam and Samoa the prohibitions were effectively enforced, with the result that little if any land passed into alien private ownership.

Economic relations with the territories and possessions, attributable at least in part to the political connection, attained respectable magnitude but never assumed large proportions as compared with similar relations with foreign countries. Among customers of mainland United States in 1931, Hawaii ranked eighth, Puerto Rico tenth, and the Philippines eleventh. In that year the United

Kingdom, Canada, Germany, Japan, France, Russia, and China were all bigger buyers than Hawaii.[3] The relative importance of the territories and possessions and of foreign countries as markets for American products is indicated by the following tabulation for the years 1920, 1925, and 1930:[4]

DOLLAR VALUE OF EXPORTS FROM THE UNITED STATES
TO AREAS INDICATED

Destination	1920	1925	1930
Alaska	36,876,855	32,352,530	31,303,291
Hawaii	74,052,453	72,924,409	81,726,404
Puerto Rico	121,561,574	77,499,807	74,219,219
Virgin Islands	3,993,478	1,915,277	1,672,903
Philippines	92,289,778	69,297,583	78,183,028
Guam	234,960	324,619	375,276
American Samoa	126,185	92,514	142,393
Total Amer. Possessions	329,135,283	254,406,739	267,622,514
Foreign countries	8,228,016,000	4,909,848,000	3,843,181,000
Exports to possessions in percentages of total exports	3.8%	4.9%	6.5%

The expectation, so hopefully advanced in 1898, that possession of the Philippines would assure the expansion of American trade with China was not realized. Manila never became, as the prophets had predicted, a distribution center for American exports to the Far East in general, nor is there evidence to prove that the presence of the United States in the Philippines contributed to the preservation of China's territorial integrity or of the open door in Chinese markets.

In capital investments, too, the share absorbed by America's colonial possessions was small compared with that in foreign countries. Private capital from outside Puerto Rico invested in the island in 1928 was estimated at $176,294,000, of which we may surmise that four-fifths, or $140,000,000 was from the United States.[5] All American assets in the Philippines in 1943 were estimated at $167,100,000.[6] These figures may be compared with the sum total of American-owned assets in foreign countries, placed in 1943 at $13,542,200,000, or with assets in Mexico of $422,000,000, in Cuba of $590,500,000, in Canada of $4,419,200,000, in Europe as a whole of $4,418,000,000.[7] It will be seen that American investments in Puerto Rico and the Philippines together (assuming the above estimates to be reasonably accurate) amounted to little more than 2.5 per cent of all investments abroad. We must conclude that, as markets and fields for investment, the colonial posessions of the United States, though valuable, were by no means a major factor in its economic prosperity. The raw materials that they produced would presumably have been available for the American market had the possessions remained independent or under foreign ownership.

Whatever the results to the United States of free trade relations with its possessions and of the openings for capital that they afforded, the results to the possessions themselves varied widely from one to another. The economics of Guam and American Samoa were little affected by the new political relationship. The annexation of Hawaii merely assured the permanence of an economic connection that had existed on a treaty basis for a quarter of a century. Hawaiian development continued along familiar lines and for the most part with capital accumulated in the islands. In Alaska, only the extractive industries—mining, fishing, and fur-taking—were stimulated to any marked degree. The Virgin Islands and the Canal Zone were special cases. But in Puerto Rico and the Philippines the free American market, combined with the investment of considerable sums of American capital, induced economic changes of vital importance.

THE ECONOMY OF THE MINOR DEPENDENCIES: GUAM, AMERICAN SAMOA, THE CANAL ZONE

The small area and limited natural resources of Guam and American Samoa, combined with the previously mentioned policy of keeping land in the possession of natives, have effectually prevented any significant intrusion of private business interests from the United States or elsewhere. The only important effect of American sovereignty upon native economy, prior to World War II, was the employment given to natives by the naval station and the naval government in each island—employment that enticed numerous young men away from their normal agricultural pursuits and reduced the native populations to greater and greater dependence upon imported food and clothing. The public school systems fostered by the naval governments have also contributed to a diversion of native interest away from agriculture in the direction of white-collar jobs.[8]

Both islands have in recent years exhibited consistently unfavorable trade balances—the discrepancies presumably being made up in wages and salaries paid by the naval stations and naval governments. In American Samoa the figures for several fairly representative prewar years were as follows:

	Imports	Exports
1935	$136,753	$ 91,332
1937	215,820	115,072
1940	177,554	68,042

Comparable figures for Guam were:

	Imports	Exports
1935	$586,335	$ 87,104
1937	774,244	215,203
1940	642,935	102,574

The only commodity exported in significant quantities from either possession was copra. From Samoa, where efforts of the naval authorities to stimulate greater production availed little, most of the exported copra went to the United States or Hawaii. From Guam, where copra exports rose from 1,000,000 pounds in 1910 to nearly 6,000,000 pounds in 1929 and dropped again to 3,300,000 pounds in 1940, the largest amounts over the years were shipped to the United States and Manila, with Japan occasionally pushing from third to second place, and Honolulu usually coming fourth. The United States was far from enjoying a monopoly of the goods imported into Guam and Samoa. Japan, in the prewar years, was an important supplier of goods to Guam, and Australia and New Zealand performed a similar service for American Samoa. It will be seen from the figures that neither of these diminutive possessions had real commercial significance for the United States.

Both Samoans and Guamanians, under their native economy as modified by naval rule and with the benefits of naval medicine and sanitary science, whether or not they were happy, appeared to be healthy. At any rate, their numbers had increased substantially—the Samoans from 5,659 in 1900 to 17,077 in 1946; the Guamanians from 9,630 in 1901 to 25,168 in 1948. The numbers in both instances represent the indigenous population only.

The people of Guam suffered from the Japanese occupation and even more from the American reconquest, which resulted in the destruction of Agaña and other towns and villages. Plans for rehabilitation proceeded slowly because of delay in congressional appropriations, and as late as 1949 were still partly in the blueprint stage. Meanwhile, the elevation of Guam to the rank of a major naval and military base was threatening to alter drastically the economic and social patterns of native life.

In the Canal Zone, as previously indicated, there is neither indigenous population nor private enterprise in the ordinary sense. Hence one does not look for economic development as in other areas under United States sovereignty. Early in the history of the canal, however, the authorities recognized the waste involved in keeping potential grazing and farm lands idle while importing all the food consumed by canal employees. An early attempt to lease farm lands in the Zone to any person or persons who would engage in agriculture produced no results and was abandoned. Later, the supply department of the canal government undertook to do a part of the producing for its own commissaries, and "by 1918 domestic beef, pork, poultry, eggs, dairy products, fruits, and vegetables had replaced importations to a large extent."[9]

In 1921, in order to relieve seasonal unemployment in

canal work and at the same time enable the West Indian employees of the canal to become partly self-sustaining, arrangements were made to lease to such employees or former employees as desired them garden plots of not over 5 hectares (12½ acres) each. By July 1, 1922, 1,026 licenses had been issued for a total of 3,138 hectares of land. Subsequently model gardens or farms were established and an agronomist was employed to study and direct the introduction of new plants adapted to conditions of soil and climate in the Zone. Apparently the enterprise proved popular. In 1931 the governor reported 1,927 licenses in effect, covering 4,916 hectares (about 12,500 acres). But in 1935, as a health measure, the authorities decided to issue no more such licenses and to prohibit the sale or transfer of those then in effect. By 1948 the number of licenses had declined to 626, the area licensed to about 3,100 acres. In the same year, however, nearly 40 square miles were reported as in use for cattle pasture.[10]

Alaska—Empty Outpost

Not until Pearl Harbor, or shortly before, did the people of the United States recognize the importance of Alaska as a strategic spot in the age of air power. General William Mitchell, contemplating its relatively short air-line distance from the capitals and industrial centers of North America and Europe, had described it as "the most important strategic place in the world." In a war with Japan its Aleutian Islands appendage reached out to within easy striking distance of the Japanese Kuriles. For American offense Alaska's possession might be vital; for defense it was indispensable.

Preparations for holding and using Alaska were under way when the war began. The army was building major air bases at Fairbanks and Anchorage. The navy had an air and submarine base at Dutch Harbor on Unalaska Island and was building installations on Kodiak Island and elsewhere. There was a listening post at Kiska, near the end of the Aleutians—soon taken by the Japanese. Other bases were building or planned. But these bases must be manned, equipped, and supplied over long and tenuous communication lines, for they stood in an empty land.

Alaska was, in its way, a rich and productive area but it was still thinly peopled and slightly developed economically. Its products had repaid the purchase price several hundredfold. From 1880 to 1935 its salmon products alone had been valued at over $900,000,000. By 1937 minerals to the value of $750,000,000 had been taken from Alaska mines.[11] In the year ending June 30, 1947 Alaska exported to the United States fish products worth $62,000,000, fur skins valued at $5,500,000, gold to the amount of $4,800,000, with other commodities bringing the total to over $80,000,000. But its possibilities in the production of coal, petroleum, tin, lead, and platinum had not been explored; its great forests had hardly been touched; its swiftly flowing rivers drove no great hydroelectric plants; its farms numbered only 623, with but 11,332 acres in cropland; its total white population (1939) was only 39,170, with Indians, Eskimos, and others raising the aggregate to 72,524.[12]*

Why this neglect of the potentialities of "Uncle Sam's

---

* The 1950 census showed an increase in Alaska's population to 127,117 (*New York Times*, July 14, 1950, 23).

Attic"? Numerous answers have been given to that question. "Too much bureaucracy!" say some critics, pointing at the multiplicity of federal bureaus operating in the territory, their overlapping jurisdictions, and the miles of red tape that must be unwound in the process of obtaining land or timber or mining rights. One writer in the 1920's thus described the battle of the would-be Alaskan entrepreneur with the array of 38 bureaus, each with headquarters in Washington. A person desiring to acquire an island for a fox farm, he wrote, must apply, not to the General Land Office, Bureau of Animal Industry, or Forestry Service, but to the Bureau of Fisheries. For permission to drive piles for a fish trap he must go to the War Department.

> Having filed on a homestead, and addressed to that effect the General Land Office, he is dismayed by being informed that if he can persuade the Geological Survey that it doesn't want his "160" for coal or oil, the Bureau of Forestry that it hasn't preempted the land for timber, or the Bureau of Fisheries that it isn't entitled to a lien by virtue of a trout stream running through it, he may eventually be granted title to his claim, provided that tract has not been set aside for allotment to an Indian.[13]

If the evils of bureaucracy were exaggerated in this passage, they were real nevertheless. Congress in 1927 attempted to mitigate them by authorizing the President, with the concurrence of the Secretaries of the Interior, Agriculture, and Commerce (whose departments embraced most of the bureaus operating in Alaska), to centralize responsibility for Alaskan matters in the hands of one commissioner for each department, purposing that these three commissioners should reside in Alaska and make decisions on the spot instead of referring all questions to Washington.[14] The departments concerned appointed commissioners who looked into the possibilities of such coordination of federal responsibility in Alaska, but apparently the net result of such efforts was that the care of the reindeer herds was transferred from the Office of Education to the governor's office; the administration of native schools passed from the Office of Education to the Indian Service; and the duties of the army's board of road commissioners were taken over by the Interior Department.[15] The number of federal agencies operating in the territory, far from diminishing, had grown to 52 by 1939, and though many of these agencies had headquarters in Juneau, control of numerous matters of vital concern to Alaskans still centered in Washington.[16]

It is probable, however, that bureaucratic red tape has had less to do with Alaska's retarded development than climate, distance from population centers, inadequate and expensive transportation, and certain disadvantages arising from its territorial status. In most of the territory the growing season is so short as to limit strictly the crops that can be matured. American steamship lines serving Alaska are inadequate and high-priced, and coastal shipping laws exclude the superior Canadian steamers from the trade between United States and Alaskan ports. The only railroad of consequence is the government-owned Alaska Railroad from Seward to Fairbanks, which can make ends meet only by charging high rates. Automobile roads within the territory have an aggregate length of not over 2,500 miles and are likely to be closed in winter. The Alcan Highway, completed in 1942, provides Alaska with a tenuous overland connection with the United States; except from tourists, it is not likely to have much patronage while the water routes remain open. Air transportation for mail and passengers is good; for freight, its cost is excessive.

Inadequate and costly transportation resulted in scarcity and high prices of all imported commodities. An acute housing shortage, during and after World War II, was a serious obstacle to both the growth of civilian population and the expansion of military personnel.

Territorial status, with consequent want of political bargaining power in Washington, has denied to Alaska the full benefit of federal aid in such matters as roads, education, and agricultural research and has prevented the development of an efficient system of law enforcement outside the incorporated towns. The prohibition by Congress of municipal bond issues has stood in the way of some wholesome enterprises. Many of these handicaps, it is believed, would vanish if Alaska became a state, and this belief largely accounts for the statehood drive of 1945-1950.[17] A plebiscite of October, 1946, authorized by the legislature the preceding year, showed a majority of 9,630 for statehood to 6,822 opposed. An enabling bill, introduced by Delegate E. L. Bartlett and endorsed by the Secretary of the Interior and the President, languished for three years in the House of Representatives. A special message from President Truman May 21, 1948, urging statehood among other salutary measures for Alaska's development, brought no action until March 3, 1950, when the House of Representatives finally passed a statehood bill. This bill and a similar one for Hawaii were reported favorably to the Senate on June 28 by the Committee on Interior and Insular Affairs, but in mid-August the fate of both statehood bills remained in doubt. Congress had, however, authorized the expenditure of some $250,000,000 in Alaska—for military, naval, and air installations, housing, road construction, airports, renovation of the Alaska Railroad and other improvements.[18] Despite such expenditures as those that Congress had authorized, Alaska, whether state or territory, seemed destined for some time to come to remain thinly populated, poorly served in transportation, and weakly defended.

HAWAII—PRECARIOUS PARADISE

Annexation and incorporation by the United States assured Hawaii of protection against possible aggressors from abroad, of the preservation of domestic order, and of the permanence of the free market in the United States. With these encouragements, Hawaiian agriculture continued its rapid expansion. Sugar production, amounting to 289,000 tons in 1900, passed the million mark in 1932. Thereafter, in the face of world overproduction of sugar, expansion ceased. Almost all Hawaiian sugar had been marketed in continental United States, where it competed with domestic beet and cane sugar and with sugar imported from Puerto Rico, the Philippines, and Cuba. The Jones-Costigan Act of May 9, 1934 empowered the Secretary of Agriculture to set quotas for imports from the territories and from Cuba, and Hawaii's quota was fixed at 917,000 tons. Production thereafter stayed close to this figure.[19]

Sugar did not, however, maintain unchallenged the primacy that it had long held in Hawaiian economy. Its new rival was the pineapple industry. The Hawaiian Pineapple Company, founded in 1901 by James Drummond Dole—a nephew of Sanford B. Dole, only president of the Republic of Hawaii—began in a modest way, making its first shipment of 1,893 cases of canned pineapples in 1903. Production expanded rapidly, reaching 2,000,000 cases in 1907 and 4,000,000 the next year. A vigorous advertising campaign popularized the product in the United States. In 1924 the company acquired the island of Lanai, almost uninhabited and used previously only for cattle pasturage, and turned it into a huge pineapple plantation, watered by tunneling into the crater of the extinct volcano that formed the center of the island.[20] In all, seven corporations engaged in the commercial production of pineapples. In 1939 the exports of canned pineapples and pineapple juice were valued at over $50,000,000—only $5,000,000 less than the sugar exports for the year.[21]

Coffee, in third place as an exportable crop, followed far behind sugar and pineapples. Truck farming and stock-raising were also practiced to a considerable extent, but so large a proportion of the arable land was devoted to the two great export crops that Hawaii was far from self-sufficient in food production. So dependent was the population upon imported food that great concern was felt about the food supply should war or other emergency produce a state of blockade. Experiments in the 1930's suggested that in extreme emergency the population might be able to subsist on sugar alone, through the cultivation of yeast in sugar solutions.[22] Fortunately the shipping shortage in World War II was never so acute as to compel the Hawaiians to live on yeast. Though at the time of Pearl Harbor the food supply on hand was not adequate for more than six weeks, hunger never really threatened. The production of local food crops and the growing of hogs, poultry, and rabbits were drastically stepped up, and shipping was always adequate to supply the deficit.[23]

Situated as it was within the American tariff wall, Hawaii normally did more than 90 per cent of its buying and selling in the United States. The growth of its trade with the mainland is indicated by the following figures:

Year	Imports from U.S.	Exports to U.S.
1913	$29,943,000	$41,346,000
1925	72,924,000	98,261,000
1930	81,726,000	98,324,000
1935	78,925,000	98,696,000
1939	101,817,000	113,207,000

From 1929 to 1936 Hawaii ranked from fifth to eighth among the customers of mainland United States.[24]

Most of the business in Hawaii was, in the 1930's, under the general direction of the "Big Five"—commercial firms of long standing that had grown up with the island industries.[25] The Big Five were, as of 1941, the buying and selling agents for 36 of the 38 sugar plantations in the islands and for most of the pineapple companies. In addition they handled banking and insurance, supplied engineering and legal advice, negotiated for the purchase or lease of lands, and through their close affiliate, the Hawaiian Sugar Planters' Association, directed research and shaped labor policy. They received modest fees for their services but profited more as stockholders in the sugar and pineapple companies, which in turn held one another's stock and stock in the Big Five. All in all, there existed an elaborate system of interlocking stock ownership and interlocking directorates through which Hawaiian economy was controlled by about a dozen men.

The Hawaiian Sugar Planters' Association (H. S. P. A. for short) deserves a few additional words.[26] It was organized in 1895 as a successor to the Planters' Labor and Supply Company, a body formed by planters and their agents in 1882, which had been very successful in expanding the sugar area through irrigation and drainage and in importing suitable labor for the plantations. The H. S. P. A. took over these functions and also assumed responsibility for the promotion of legislation desired by business interests, for labor management, and for scientific research. Most notable have been its accomplishments in the field of research. It has maintained an experiment station with an annual budget of $500,000, "which has made a world-wide reputation for its achievements in developing new varieties of cane, in fighting off insect invasions and plant diseases, and in pioneering otherwise in scientific agriculture."[27] The H. S. P. A. has been governed by five trustees—none other than the heads of the Big Five, who serve in rotation as chairman.

The rapid expansion of the sugar industry called for an expanding supply of labor. This was a need that could not be met locally. The native race of "Kanakas" appeared to be dying off, and in any event they had never taken kindly to regular labor. Agents of the planters searched the world over. They tried other Pacific islanders (who proved no more adaptable than the Hawaiians to plantation labor), Portuguese, Puerto Ricans, Norwegians, Russians, and Koreans. The groups that proved most adaptable, however, were Chinese, Japanese, and Filipinos. From 1852 to 1898 some 33,000 Chinese were imported; between 1868 and 1907 some 80,000 Japanese. Chinese immigration was halted temporarily by the Hawaiian government in 1886 and permanently as a result of annexation by the United States; Japanese immigration (except "picture brides") was stopped by the Gentlemen's Agreement in 1907. As both groups tended strongly to drift away from the plantations into retailing or the skilled crafts, it was necessary constantly to replenish the supply, and after 1907 a source of replenishment was found in the Philippines. Filipino workers came chiefly from the Ilocano provinces of northwestern Luzon. They were carefully screened for bodily health by agents of the H. S. P. A., signed contracts upon arriving in Hawaii, were placed in well kept villages where they enjoyed free houses, gardens, fuel, recreation, and medical care under the paternalistic rule of the plantation owners and the H. S. P. A. They generally remained for three years. They were then, if they so desired, transported free of charge, with their families if any, back to the Philippines.[28] By 1930 there were over 63,000 Filipinos in Hawaii. Thereafter there was a net decrease, the result at first of depression in the sugar industry and the introduction of labor-saving machinery. After 1934, however, Filipino immigration was halted by the Tydings-McDuffie Act, which provided that upon the creation of the Commonwealth of the Philippines, Filipinos should have the status of aliens with an immigration quota of 50 annually.[29]

The result of this labor policy was a greatly enlarged and an extraordinarily diverse population. By 1939 the 154,000 of 1900 had grown to 414,991, distributed racially as follows:[30]

Japanese	155,042	37.36%
Hawaiian and Part-Hawaiian	63,858	15.39
Caucasian	107,381	25.88
Filipinos	52,430	12.63
Chinese	28,601	6.89
Koreans	6,738	1.62
All others	941	.23

The presence of so many Japanese in this vital military and naval stronghold of the United States was a cause of grave concern as relations between Japan and the United States grew strained. Who could foretell the behavior of Hawaiian Japanese in the event of war? Those born in Hawaii (over three-fourths of the Japanese population in 1940) were American citizens, but the parents of thousands of them had registered their children with the Japanese consul, thus making them also Japanese subjects—young men and women of dual allegiance. Thousands of them, too, had attended—in addition to the regular public schools—special Japanese language schools, which the Supreme Court had declared to be exempt from control or regulation by the territorial government, where they were taught the Japanese language and where it was suspected that they also learned loyalty to the Mikado. That their loyalty to the United States was doubted is not surprising. That when the test came the behavior of most of them was exemplary was a tribute to them and also to the freedom and tolerance of the society that had nourished them and won their loyalty.[31]

World War II brought about pronounced changes in the population and the balance of economic forces in Hawaii. Large-scale military construction led to the importation of an estimated 60,000 skilled workers from the mainland. Total population (exclusive of military and naval personnel) soared to 519,503 in 1946, with the Caucasian group now constituting 33.43 per cent against 32.4 per cent of Japanese.[32] Big Five domination of Hawaii's economic life, already threatened in a small way by the coming to Honolulu of Kress, Sears, Roebuck and Co., and a branch of the Mitsukoshi department store of Tokyo, now of necessity gave way to military authority for the duration—for the military had full control of shipping and of imports. Death and retirement, furthermore, were removing from the scene the individuals who had dominated the Big Five firms, and control of the enterprises was being spread among a wider group.[33]

The most significant change in the Hawaiian economic picture, however, was the rise of organized labor. Until the 1930's labor organization had made no headway in the islands, plantation labor had been managed under a régime of reasonably benevolent paternalism, and occasional strikes had been put down, in some instances with bloodshed. "Labor organizations in the Hawaiian Islands," said the *Monthly Labor Review* in 1931, "are few in number, small in membership, and, with the exception of the barbers' union, have no agreements with the employers."[34]

The New Deal in Washington gave the first real impetus to labor organization in Hawaii. The N. I. R. A. and the Wagner Act guaranteed the right of labor to organize and bargain collectively throughout the United States. Congressional committees that held hearings in Hawaii on the statehood question listened with disapproval to allegations of anti-union espionage on the sugar plantations and elsewhere. The Hawaiian legislature, sensing the new trend, established the territory's first labor department in 1939. Both the A.F. of L. and the C.I.O. sent organizers to Hawaii, and before Pearl Harbor urban and factory labor was pretty generally organized and at least one sugar plantation had signed a contract with its workers, organized in a C.I.O. union. During the war the military régime preferred to deal with unions and discouraged any tendency in local business to invoke the war emergency against labor. In 1945 the legislature passed a labor relations act ("Little Wagner Act") extending rights of collective bargaining to plantation labor. In the fall of 1946 a strike of 28,000 sugar plantation workers caused a loss of an estimated 180,000 tons of sugar but ended with the signing of new contracts under which wages were substantially raised but the free perquisites of an earlier day—rent, fuel, medical care, and the like—were abandoned. Unskilled plantation labor, which in 1931 had made an average wage of $1.72 for a ten-hour day with the addition of the perquisites mentioned, now received a minimum of $5.64 for an eight-hour day without perquisites.[35] When allowance is made for the higher prices of 1946 as well as for the loss of perquisites, the extent of the net gain in real income is less impressive than the figures suggest.

The plantation strike and other strikes that followed, notably a crippling longshoremen's strike in the summer of 1949, indicated that labor, unorganized and powerless 15 years before, now held as potent a grip as the Big Five upon Hawaii's economy.

Although Hawaii could not, like Alaska, declare that it needed statehood as a means of attracting population and fostering economic development, it had its own reasons for demanding to be the forty-ninth state.[36] Since 1903 statehood resolutions had been regularly introduced in each session of the legislature, but until the 1930's no one took these proposals seriously. Then the sugar planters and the Big Five, previously unfriendly to the idea, became its advocates. Their motives were clear enough. The Hawaiian sugar industry considered itself unfairly treated—put on a par with unincorporated Puerto Rico and the prospectively independent Philippines—in the quotas imposed under the Jones-Costigan Act. As a state, with two senators and several representatives, Hawaii would be better able to protect its interests. There was, furthermore, in the early 1930's, serious talk of placing the Territory of Hawaii under a less autonomous form of government than that in effect—of sending a governor from the mainland or even of creating a commission form of government in which the army and navy would be represented. Such proposals arose from the facts, first, that from the mainland point of view Hawaii was primarily a fortress whose function was defense of the West Coast; second, that a lax system of law enforcement in the islands seemed to threaten the security of this fortress. A more authoritarian government, in which they had a hand, would have been welcomed by the armed forces. Such a government, however, was feared by Hawaiian businessmen, who might find the military less amenable to their wishes than a resident governor and an elected legislature. The surest way to forestall the institution of such a government was to make Hawaii a state.

Beginning in 1935, therefore, through resolutions of the legislature and bills introduced in Congress by the Hawaiian delegate, Hawaii moved officially for statehood. At the same time it launched an elaborate publicity campaign aimed at the same goal. Hawaii, it was pointed out, had a larger area than three states and was more populous than four. The assessed value of its property was greater than that of nine, and it regularly paid more money in federal taxes than it got back in disbursements. It was more populous than any other territory had been when admitted to the Union as a state, with the single exception of Oklahoma.[37] That its people wanted statehood was demonstrated, so it was argued, in a plebiscite in 1940, when 46,000 citizens voted for the program to half that number against it.

Two congressional committees—one from the House of Representatives, one representing both House and Senate—held hearings in the islands in 1935 and 1937 but were not sufficiently impressed by the arguments for statehood. In view of the growing tension with Japan, the large Japanese group in the islands, and "the present disturbed condition of international affairs," it seemed to the senators and representatives unwise to surrender any degree of federal control over this Pacific defense bastion.[38]

The war, of course, interrupted the statehood movement, but Hawaii emerged from the war with the old arguments re-enforced and some of the earlier objections removed or mitigated. Hawaii's wartime experience with military government had not been happy. Military courts had taken jurisdiction over all kinds of penal offenses, and their decisions had been often arbitrary and always without appeal.[39] Hawaiians believed that statehood would guarantee them against similar infringements of their liberties in future. Hawaii's total population had grown by 25 per cent. Caucasians now outnumbered Japanese, and for that matter, the Japanese no longer constituted a hazard. Their loyalty as a group had been demonstrated, their dual allegiance and special schools had been eliminated,[40] and so had the Land of the Rising Sun as a military menace.

In view of the new situation, two successive Secretaries of the Interior, and President Truman as well, recommended the admission of Hawaii as a state. A House of Representatives subcommittee concurred. A statehood bill, introduced by Delegate Farrington, was passed by the House of Representatives June 30, 1947.[41] The Senate Committee on Interior and Insular Affairs, however, deferred action on the bill until its chairman, Senator Hugh Butler, could make another investigation on the spot. Senator Butler's report, not submitted until June 21, 1949, was adverse. He charged that Communists and their allies, chiefly in the International Longshoremen's and Warehousemen's Union (I.L.W.U.) had captured control of the Democratic party in Hawaii and were so firmly entrenched that their dominance might be permanent if Hawaii became a state with complete local autonomy—although "an overwhelming majority of the people of the Territory desire to see Hawaiian communism put down." Statehood, therefore, "should not be considered seriously . . . until the people of the islands demonstrate by positive steps a determination to put down the menace of lawless communism."[42] Though statehood for Hawaii (and Alaska) was endorsed in both major party platforms in 1948 and though the House Public Lands Committee made a favorable report in March, 1949, the Butler report and the disastrous I.L.W.U. strike, which began April 30, 1949 and lasted till October, appeared to have weakened Hawaii's case. The charges of Communism were probed further by the House of Representatives Un-American Activities Committee, which began an investigation in Honolulu on April 10, 1950. Undaunted by these obstacles, and without authorization from Congress, Hawaii proceeded with plans to hold a constitutional convention and draft a state constitution. The convention met April 4, 1950 and completed the drafting of the proposed constitution on July 15. Idaho, Wyoming, and several other territories had prepared constitutions and been admitted to statehood without the formality of enabling acts, and Hawaiians hoped for similarly generous treatment. They received encouragement when the House of Representatives, without awaiting its committee's report on Communism in Hawaii, passed a statehood bill on March 7, 1950. Hawaii's chances for statehood then rested with the Senate. Favorable action was urged upon the Senate Committee on Interior and Insular Affairs by the Departments of State, the Interior, and Defense, and by President Truman in a letter in which he argued that granting statehood to both Alaska and Hawaii would "not only promote the welfare and development of the two Territories but also greatly strengthen the security of our nation as a whole." The committee approved the House bill on June 28, but in mid-August, 1950, Senate action still appeared uncertain.[43]

PUERTO RICO—"THE STRICKEN LAND"

In its human problems as well as in geography and climate, Puerto Rico is the antithesis of Alaska. Alaska has too few people for its resources; Puerto Rico has too scanty resources for its population. Puerto Rican agricultural productivity and trade with the United States have expanded steadily since 1898, but an increase in population from 953,243 in 1899 to 2,113,058 in 1947 has prevented the increased production from resulting in any notable improvement in the average standard of living. The average population density in 1947 was nearly 620 persons per square mile; the figure for the rural areas was 385 per square mile.[44] For the United States as a whole the population density in 1940 was 44.2 per square mile. Only highly industrialized states like New Jersey or Rhode Island showed figures comparable to Puerto Rico's.

Free trade with the United States gave a great impetus to the production of sugar, which grew from 72,000 tons in 1897 to 856,109 in 1930 and over a million in 1940. Land planted in sugar cane increased from 72,000 acres in 1899 to 238,000 in 1929 and 318,000 in 1935. Tobacco lands and tobacco exports (especially cigars) also increased. Coffee, which under Spain had been the leading export, shrunk to insignificance, as depression wiped out its European markets and tropical hurricanes (especially those of 1928 and 1932) destroyed the coffee bushes. Though much of the hilly part of the island continued to be devoted to coffee culture, most of the product was consumed locally. The only important nonagricultural industry in the island before World War II (if rum manufacture is considered merely a branch of the sugar industry) was needlework, which gave employment to thousands of women and girls. The following table, showing averages of Puerto Rico's export trade for the five years 1935-1939, will give an idea of the relative importance of the various products in the prewar economy:

	Value	*Percentage*
Sugar and Molasses..........	$60,507,000	64.5%
Needlework	16,025,000	17.2
Tobacco	8,651,000	9.3
Rum	2,451,000	2.6
Fruits	1,627,000	1.7
Coffee	158,000	.2
Other	4,184,000	4.5
	$93,603,000	100.0%

The most notable change during the war years was the increase in production and export of rum, which in 1944 accounted for 23.6 per cent of all exports to the United States. In 1946 rum had dropped back to 8 per cent, whereas sugar and molasses, though up in quantity from the earlier period, amounted to only 51 per cent of the total. Needlework had maintained approximately its former relative position, and tobacco and "other" had increased.[45]

The growing of sugar cane and the production of

sugar are done most efficiently, it seems, in large units, and the expansion of sugar production in Puerto Rico has been accompanied by a concentration of ownership and control. In 1897 there were almost 500 little sugar mills, producing not over 125 tons annually per mill. In 1938 there were 41 sugar centrals with an average annual production of over 20,000 tons each. Eleven of the 41 mills were owned by four American companies, and these 11 American-owned mills produced slightly less than one-half of all Puerto Rican sugar. Of land in sugar cane farms, the mill companies owned or controlled 396,000 acres, or 51.4 per cent; the four American companies, 183,000 acres, or 23.7 per cent—this despite the congressional enactment of 1900 forbidding the ownership or control by any corporation of more than 500 acres of land. Of the remaining sugar cane farms, those of 25 acres or over, numbering about 2,200, accounted for 43.2 per cent of the cane lands, and 5,306 little farms of less than 25 acres occupied only 5.4 per cent of the lands.[46]

Sugar production, as pursued in Puerto Rico, involved three groups of people—the mill-owners, the independent farmers (*colonos*), and the wage-earners (*agregados*).

Of the *colonos* there were some 7,500 cultivating sugar farms large and small, but mostly small. Their only means of disposing of their cane was by sale to the mills, and this sale was regulated by contract, under which the *colono* received the New York price for a stated proportion of the estimated yield of his cane. This proportion was customarily seven-twelfths until 1937, when it was fixed by law at 65 per cent. The same law gave the *colono* the right to check, through a representative, the testing of his cane for sugar content. Normally he would receive the price of about 7 pounds of sugar for 100 pounds of cane. It was estimated in 1938 that about two-thirds of the *colonos* had to borrow from the mills to finance their crop production; for such loans they paid interest at rates ranging from 7 to 9 per cent.[47]

Of wage-earners, the mills and larger planters employed about 125,000 at the season's peak, 50,000 at its bottom, with a monthly average of some 80,000. Of these, about 90 per cent worked in the fields, 10 per cent in the mills. Wages were low, judged by continental standards. In 1924 the estimated average was 50 to 60 cents a day; in 1938, 75 cents to $1, though an attempt had been made in 1936 to establish a minimum wage of a dollar a day. Employment was so irregular, however, that daily or hourly rates had little significance. The average annual earnings of a sugar worker were estimated in 1931 at $169; in 1941, after substantial price rises on the one hand and various New Deal attempts at improvement on the other, at $269.[48]

In a tropical country like Puerto Rico, adequate housing and clothing are less costly than in more northerly climes, but it is obvious that even there a laborer with an annual income of $269 can afford only the most primitive kind of clothing and shelter. As for food, since Puerto Rico devotes most of its land to sugar and tobacco for export, much of its food must be imported, and since most of it comes from the United States, the Puerto Rican peasant must pay American food prices. The result is that the Puerto Rican worker must spend a very large percentage of his income for food. A survey in 1947 showed food accounting for 50.8 per cent of all expenditures of urban wage-earning families, 61.1 per cent for rural lowland families, and 68.5 per cent for rural highland families.[49] Even at that, the typical *agregado* suffered from chronic undernourishment and from diseases for which undernourishment and inadequate sanitation prepare the way—tuberculosis, diphtheria, typhoid fever, and hookworm. Since the sugar *agregado* was the best paid of Puerto Rican rural workers (with the possible exception of the few engaged in fruit-growing), and since large numbers of small *colonos* were little better off than wage-earners, we can form an estimate of what country life was like in Puerto Rico. And yet Puerto Rico is said to have the highest standard of living in the Caribbean.[50]

There has been a rather naïve tendency to hold the sugar industry, and especially the four big American companies, responsible for the plight of the Puerto Rican workers and *colonos*—to blame them for Puerto Rico's poverty.[51] The three American companies that were willing to open their books to American economists in the mid-1930's had done quite well but had not, it would seem, made excessive profits. They had made net earnings in every year since 1923, with the exception of two years "in the red" (hurricane years) for one company, and in the six years preceding the survey had earned on their net investments after income tax, returns averaging 7.1 per cent, 10.3 per cent, and 12.3 per cent respectively. Their combined net earnings since 1923 had averaged about $3,500,000 a year, of which about $2,750,000 annually had been paid to investors, mostly in the United States. Some payment of profits to absentees is the inevitable consequence of industrial development in a land that cannot supply its own capital. Not much could have been done for the *colono* and *agregado* without wiping out this profit. The addition of one dollar a week to the *agregado's* wages and one dollar a ton to the price of the *colono's* cane "would probably eat up almost the whole profit of good years and create large losses in poor years."[52]

Critics have also complained that the diversion of land from food crops to sugar has added to the Puerto Rican's food bill and that the illegal concentration of land under control of the sugar companies has deprived thousands of small farmers of a chance to make an independent living. These assertions are debatable. Some experts, at any rate, have concluded that Puerto Rico's lands are so well adapted to sugar culture that the Puerto Rican can live better on the food he buys with his sugar than he could on the food he might grow in place of sugar. He could, of course, buy some foods, such as rice, more cheaply if Puerto Rico were not within the United States tariff wall, but he could hardly expect to be permitted to buy his food freely in the world market and at the same time continue to sell his sugar and tobacco free of duty in the protected market of the United States.

The accumulation by corporations of landholdings over 500 acres in extent was admittedly illegal—though till 1935 no attempt was made to enforce the restriction— but the economist answered here that, apart from the question of legality, the efficiency of sugar production varied directly with the size of the acreage. If Puerto Rico could best live by sugar production therefore, it could live better from a few big farms than from many little farms.[53] But enforcement of the 500-acre law was to become a crucial point in New Deal policy in Puerto Rico.

Certain early New Deal measures, though well intended, had unforeseen and unfortunate effects in Puerto Rico. The National Industrial Recovery Act and the Agricultural Adjustment Act, by raising prices of food, clothing, and the like in the United States, added an estimated $18,000,000 to $21,000,000 annually to Puerto Rico's cost of living. Puerto Rico's sugar quota of 803,000 tons under the Jones-Costigan Act gave the industry a choice between a crop reduction and a surplus. The extension of minimum wage regulations to Puerto Rico, under the N.R.A. codes and subsequent legislation, closed down the needlework industry, or most of it, three times and large sections of the sugar industry at least once, throwing thousands of employees out of work on each occasion. Eventually, adjustments were made to the necessarily low wage levels of the island.

The most important New Deal agency in Puerto Rico was the Puerto Rico Reconstruction Administration (P.R.R.A.), set up in 1935 as successor to the Puerto Rico Federal Emergency Relief Administration (F.E.R.A.), which had been spending $1,000,000 a month for direct relief. The P.R.R.A., with Ernest Gruening as its first director and with an initial appropriation of $42,000,000, launched an ambitious program of public works, slum clearance, rural rehabilitation and electrification, and sponsorship of cooperatives in agriculture, handicrafts, and industry. Among other projects, it acquired areas of marginal lands, which it parceled out in small farms, built concrete houses to replace the palm shacks that disfigured the rural landscape, set up farm experiment stations, took measures to improve livestock, and experimented with new money crops, such as vanilla and perfumes, which might supplement the traditional staples. Among the cooperatives it sponsored, the most ambitious was the Lafayette Project—a sugar mill with 10,000 acres of land owned and 8,000 acres leased, which was taken over from its French owners in 1937 and placed in the hands of a group of cooperatives—one for the mill and 8 (later 12) for the land. The experiment appeared for several years to be prospering, but in 1940 first the land cooperatives, and later the mill, proved unable to meet their obligations and were liquidated. The lands, over and above some scores of small subsistence plots, were sold to individual farmers in lots ranging from 3 to 140 acres each. The mill was taken over and operated by the P.R.R.A. Another sugar cooperative, Los Caños, had a similar history.[54]

By 1942 the P.R.R.A. had spent about $70,000,000 and appropriations had stopped. It continued to operate, however, on a "revolving fund" consisting of income from housing or other projects. In 1944 it was operating, in addition to the Lafayette and Los Caños sugar mills, 1,210 urban dwelling units, 6,254 rural houses, and 4,891 three-acre subsistence plots without houses.[55]

One of the early proposals of the P.R.R.A. was to break up large plantations held by corporations in violation of the 500-acre restriction and to distribute the surplus among families on relief. The restrictive clause, originally in a joint resolution of 1900 and re-enacted in the Jones Act of 1917, contained no enforcement provision. In 1935 the legislature of Puerto Rico took the first step toward enforcement, giving the island supreme court exclusive original jurisdiction in *quo warranto* proceedings to be instituted by the insular government against violators of the 500-acre clause. Eventually, in 1940, the United States Supreme Court upheld the right of the government of Puerto Rico to enforce the law through its own supreme court.[56] Thereupon the legislature created a Land Authority, a board of seven members, empowered to acquire from corporations land holdings in excess of 500 acres, through expropriation, public sale, or agreement, and to redistribute such land in small parcels, to be paid for on easy terms by the recipients. By the end of 1947 the Land Authority had acquired, generally by agreement with the corporations, 67,763 acres of land—about 36 per cent of corporate holdings in excess of 500 acres—and had distributed it in three ways: (1) family-size farms, 5 to 25 acres, sold to selected farmers at the price paid by the Authority plus interest at 5 per cent, payable over a 40-year period; (2) proportional profit farms of 100 acres or more, each run by an experienced manager on a salary-plus-percentage basis, while workers receive the minimum legal wage plus a percentage of the profits and the Land Authority retains the title; (3) subsistence plots for day laborers, one-fourth acre to three acres in extent, given free or sold on easy terms depending upon circumstances.[57]

The Land Authority was one of the agencies of what may be called the second phase of Puerto Rico's New Deal. The first phase was dominated by an institution, the P.R.R.A.; the second, beginning in 1941, was dominated by two men—Rexford G. Tugwell, governor from 1941 to 1946, and Luis Muñoz Marin, founder and leader of the new Popular Democratic party (*Populares*) and president of the Puerto Rican senate, 1941-1948.

Muñoz Marin was the son of Luis Muñoz Rivera, who had negotiated an autonomy arrangement with Spain in 1897 and had later been a resident commissioner in Washington. Muñoz Marin had been expelled from the Liberal party in 1937 because of his insistence on a program of immediate independence for Puerto Rico. In organizing the new party and in campaigning for it in 1940, however, he had dropped the immediate independence plea and appealed to workers and small *colonos* with the slogan, "Bread, Land, Liberty" and promises of an economic and social New Deal for Puerto Ricans. In a close election his *Populares*, with minor allies, won control of both houses of the legislature from the hitherto dominant Coalition. The election was a victory of the masses over the classes.

Tugwell, an agricultural economist and a member of Roosevelt's original brain trust, had been interested in Puerto Rican land problems since 1934, and late in 1940 had been sent to the island by Secretary of the Interior Harold Ickes as chairman of a committee to report on that subject. He was appointed to the governorship in September, 1941. Like Muñoz, he was determined to promote the welfare of the Puerto Rican masses, at the cost, if need be, of antagonizing vested interests. He and Muñoz generally saw eye to eye.

In his inaugural address, September 19, 1941, Tugwell declared:

> To bettering the condition of the poor I shall bring every resource I am able to find in the governorship. I will be the friend of every man or

> woman who helps; I will be the opponent of every
> man or woman who hinders. Whatever needs chang-
> ing for this purpose must be changed; whatever is
> useful must be fully employed. . . . There must be
> no question in any mind of our resolve to use all
> the resources of government not only to insure
> freedom but to create plenty.[58]

In his opening message to the first regular session of the
legislature, February 10, 1942, he charged that private
enterprise had failed in its duty of developing adequately
the agricultural and industrial potentialities of Puerto
Rico, and that without some drastic change in existing
arrangements, "many Puerto Ricans must actually
starve."

> What is certainly indicated [he continued] is
> that government must intervene. It must gather up
> Puerto Rican capital and help to direct its uses,
> together with the energy of the people, into chan-
> nels which will yield livings for all of the two mil-
> lions on this Island.[59]

The basic objective of the Tugwell-Muñoz program
was provision of a better living for the Puerto Rican
masses. In part, it was hoped, this could be achieved
through improvements in agriculture and the expropriation of large corporate holdings. But since agricultural
employment had remained static for two decades and
showed no promise of expanding with the growing population, it was held essential to meet the employment
problem through such industrialization as the resources
of the island would support. The basic principle was
that government must direct private enterprise and must

itself do the needful things that private enterprise would
not or could not do. The means for such governmental
activity was a windfall of nearly $150,000,000 in a four-
year period, in the form of internal revenue taxes collected in the United States on Puerto Rican rum and returned to the insular treasury.[60]

In addition to the Land Authority, already noted, and
a Water Resources Authority, created just before the
advent of Governor Tugwell with the object of taking
over all the electric power systems in the island, the
legislature, under Tugwell-Muñoz leadership, set up the
following public bodies:

A Transportation Authority to take over the San
Juan bus line.

A Communications Authority to assume control
of the government-owned telegraph system and to
take over the properties of the Puerto Rico Tele-
phone Company.

An Agricultural Company charged especially
with developing new commercial crops and finding
markets for them.

The Puerto Rican Development Company to promote industrialization.

A Development Bank to give financial assistance
to the Development Company.

A Planning, Urbanizing, and Zoning Board, which
laid out a long-range development program of slum
clearance, rural housing, schools, hospitals, and
other improvements, to cost eventually some
$344,000,000.

These bodies were instituted despite the very vocal
objections of business groups and the opposition party

in Puerto Rico, the Puerto Rican resident commissioner in Washington, Bolívar Pagán, and conservative elements in Congress, who found in Governor Tugwell everything that they most detested in the New Deal. The program was supported by Tugwell's superiors, Secretary Ickes and President Roosevelt, and was overwhelmingly endorsed in 1944 by the Puerto Rican voters, who elected *Populares* candidates to nearly all the seats in the legislature and replaced Pagán in Washington with Muñoz's candidate, Jesus T. Piñero.

The program was popular. How successful it would be in the long run remained to be seen. The expropriation of corporate lands proceeded slowly. Sugar refineries, to prevent their sabotaging the land program by shutting down, were declared to be public utilities. Some progress was made in industrialization. In June, 1946 there were in operation, as subsidiaries of the Development Company, a cement factory (a pre-Tugwell enterprise initiated by the P.R.R.A.), a glass factory, designed to make bottles for rum, and a pulp and paper mill, making containers for the rum bottles. Partly completed were a ceramic works and a shoe and leather factory, and a cotton textile mill was in the planning stage.[61] For heavy industry Puerto Rico had no raw materials whatever. How inadequate the existing program was as a solution to the problem of surplus population and unemployment is suggested by the fact that four of the enterprises described above were expected to give employment, directly and indirectly, to less than 3,200 persons.[62]

After Tugwell's resignation in 1946 and the appointment of Jesus T. Piñero as the first native governor, a different approach to the problem of industrialization was tried—an attempt, through promises of twelve-year tax exemption, cheap labor, and aid from the Development Company in financing plants, to tempt industries from the United States to Puerto Rico. Dubbed by Muñoz Marin "Operation Bootstrap," the plan was getting results. In January, 1950 it was reported that more than 50 new industries, including flour mills, textile mills, furniture factories, household equipment plants, and hotels, were either in operation or preparing to sign up for lease or purchase of plants built partly with government funds. A survey of the programs of these plants indicated that their annual production would be worth more than $50,000,000 and that they would pay $8,000,000 annually in wages, but their anticipated employment—8,000 persons—would be far short of the goal of 360,000 jobs set by the planners for the year 1960.[63]

Puerto Rico's basic problem, overpopulation, was no nearer a solution than ever. A law passed by the legislature in 1937 permitting the establishment of birth control clinics had, in the opinion of Governor Tugwell, proved completely futile.[64] A committee of the House of Representatives had proposed emigration to Central and South America, but such emigration as took place was mostly to New York City. A sampling survey of the New York colony in 1948 indicated that it numbered between 160,000 and 200,000 persons. Though one commentator remarked that such migration "does little more . . . than transfer misery from a warm place to a cold one," the survey showed only 6 per cent of New York Puerto Ricans on relief.[65] Emigration was no solution.

Without some check upon population growth, any advance in Puerto Rico's economy seemed more likely to multiply the hungry mouths than to feed them.

Although no easy solution could be found for Puerto Rico's population problem, measures were at last taken to alleviate political discontent in the island. Few if any Puerto Ricans appear to have been satisfied with the extent of self-government they enjoyed under the Jones Act of 1917, but they disagreed widely as to the desired remedies. Puerto Rican culture, despite a prolonged attempt at "Americanization," remained essentially Spanish.[66] Many Puerto Rican intellectuals favored independence and cultural ties with Spain, and independence as a political slogan always had a popular vote-getting appeal. On the other hand, the whole Puerto Rican economy was built upon the free American market and would inevitably collapse if that market were lost, as it presumably would be if independence were achieved. Few practical politicians, therefore, advocated "immediate" independence, though at election time they might declare for it as an ultimate goal. Another group professed a desire for admission to the United States as a state, but it was recognized that statehood would be only less costly than independence, since as a state Puerto Rico would forfeit to the federal treasury the proceeds of the tariff and internal revenue duties that as a territory it was permitted to retain.[67] "Dominion status" was a third solution sometimes proposed, in the hope that it might combine complete self-government with the protection and the economic advantages derived from the existing connection with the United States. In default of all these solutions, Puerto Ricans might at least be permitted to elect some or all of the officials who, under the Jones Act, were appointed by the President.

Puerto Rican political parties divided, recombined, and assumed new titles with almost kaleidoscopic rapidity, but there was always a party that stood, at least nominally, for independence and one that stood for statehood. In the middle 1930's the dominant party was the Coalition, a union of so-called Republicans and Socialists, whose platform called for statehood. The Liberals, led by the veteran politician, Antonio Barcelo, were for independence, though not until a solution of the economic problem had been found. The Liberals took a bad beating at the polls in 1936. A small group calling themselves Nationalists were for immediate independence at all costs. They rejected all cooperation with the United States and resorted to terrorism and assassination. Their leader, Pedro Albizu Campos, and seven other members were sent to the federal penitentiary in Atlanta as a result of the assassination of the chief of the insular police in 1936. They represented an insignificant minority of the island's population.

Luis Muñoz Marin, whose new Popular Democratic party ousted the Coalition from power in 1940 and elected all but four members of the legislature in 1944, had, as a Liberal, shown more enthusiasm for independence than was pleasing to the party leadership. As head of the *Populares,* however, he played down the independence issue and emphasized the program of economic rehabilitation previously described. In conjunction with Tugwell—who declared at the beginning of his governorship that as an American he would favor independence if the Puerto Ricans wished it, but that as a Puerto Rican he would oppose it for obvious economic reasons[68]—he worked for a larger measure of self-government for Puerto Rico within the general framework of the existing relationship. With such a program Secretary Ickes and Presidents Roosevelt and Truman were sympathetic.

Various proposals were made in Congress. Senator Tydings of Maryland (chairman of the Committee on Interior and Insular Affairs), repeatedly introduced a bill for complete independence with gradual raising of tariff duties on imports from Puerto Rico and retention by the United States of naval bases in Puerto Rican waters.[69] This bill was never voted on. Another proposal, to permit the Puerto Ricans to choose by plebiscite between independence, statehood, dominion status, and the existing system, was dropped after Senator Tydings indicated that Congress was not likely to grant either statehood or dominion status, however the Puerto Ricans might vote.[70]

Previously, in March, 1943, President Roosevelt had recommended that Puerto Rico be permitted to elect its own governor. A committee of Puerto Ricans and Americans named by him had repeated the recommendation, along with other proposals, and a bill for the elective governorship had passed the Senate, February 15, 1944 but died in the House of Representatives. A similar bill finally became law on August 5, 1947. It provided that, beginning in the fall of 1948, the governor of Puerto Rico should be chosen for a four-year term by popular election. The governor should appoint, with the consent of the Puerto Rican senate, the heads of the executive departments, but not, as had at first been proposed, the justices of the supreme court, who, like the auditor, were to continue to be appointed by the President. The veto power of governor and President and the right of Congress to annul legislation remained unchanged. Since the governor would no longer be a representative of the federal government, the law created the position of Coordinator of Federal Agencies, to be filled by presidential appointment.[71]

In the meantime, following Governor Tugwell's resignation, President Truman had appointed, as the first native Puerto Rican governor, Jesus T. Piñero, since 1944 resident commissioner in Washington. He was inaugurated on September 3, 1946. The first election under the new law took place on November 3, 1948, and, as was generally expected, Luis Muñoz Marin swept the field. He took office January 2, 1949, the first governor in any United States territory or possession to be popularly elected.

A further step in the direction of complete self-government for Puerto Rico was taken on July 3, 1950, when President Truman signed a bill (Public Law 600, 81st Congress) empowering the people of Puerto Rico, if they should so determine by plebiscite, to elect a constitutional convention with authority to draw up a constitution to replace the organic act of 1917. Such a constitution, which must be republican in form and contain a bill of rights, would have to be approved by a vote of the Puerto Rican people and by Congress before becoming effective. It would not alter Puerto Rico's territorial status or economic relationship to the United States but might effect substantial changes in the internal government of the territory. It would almost certainly make elective the few officials still appointed by the President of the United States.

THE VIRGIN ISLANDS—"EFFECTIVE POORHOUSE"

Compared with Puerto Rico, the Virgin Islands are insignificant in area and population, in productivity and trade. Aside from their strategic importance the islands have no conceivable value to the United States. They have, in fact, been an economic liability, a "white elephant," to the United States as they had been for many years to Denmark. The United States treasury has not only borne the expenses of the central administration but has regularly made up deficits in the budgets of the two municipalities. These annual deficits for the two municipalities together averaged about $195,000 from 1918 to 1931. The average combined deficit during the last eight years of Danish rule had been less than $10,000. The cost of municipal government rose about 68 per cent under American rule; the increase was attributable chiefly to much greater outlays for public health, public works, and education.[72] Depression and relief measures added to the cost of maintaining the islands after 1931. When we add such expensive upkeep to the original cost, which at the price of $25,000,000 for 132 square miles came to $295 per acre, compared with 3 cents per acre for California, 4 cents for Louisiana, and $35.80 for the Canal Zone,[73] it is obvious that the purchase of the Virgin Islands was Uncle Sam's most extravagant investment in real estate.

Once, perhaps, a valuable possession, the Virgin Islands were economically in declining fortunes when the United States acquired them. Certain trends of the times and certain United States policies accentuated the decline. Charlotte Amalie, or St. Thomas as the Americans called it until 1937, had once been a busy port—a coaling and cable station for several steamship lines. The trend in steamship fuel from coal to oil and in communications from cable to wireless lessened its importance, and American methods of quarantine inspection, less elastic than the Danish, placed new inconveniences in the path of visiting steamers. American prohibition, also, put an end to what had been an important item of trade in St. Thomas. The number of transatlantic steamship lines making St. Thomas a port of call dwindled from eight in 1914 to one in 1924. The people of the island of St. Thomas, who had lived principally by the activities of the port, thus saw their means of livelihood diminishing. The decline of the port was inadequately compensated for by the establishment of a United States naval station at St. Thomas.[74]

St. Croix, an agricultural island whose chief exports were sugar and the well known St. Croix rum, was also injured, so far as the last item was concerned, by American prohibition, and in the export tax on sugar it suffered a disadvantage in competition with other American possessions. A land system under which 80 per cent of the island was owned by 20 families and one Danish corporation and a chronic state of antagonism between landowners and workers were not conducive to high productivity. But if all these man-made difficulties had been removed, St. Croix would still have been incapable of providing much more than a bare subsistence for its 15,000 people. Its basic difficulty was deficient rainfall.

In only one-half of the 80 years for which records had been kept had precipitation been adequate to produce a satisfactory sugar crop. Alternatives to sugar were cotton-growing and cattle-raising, but the cotton fields had been disastrously invaded by the pink bollworm, and cattle-raising, though it might utilize the land, could not give employment to more than a tiny fraction of the population.[75]

On top of these chronic difficulties came the world economic depression beginning in 1929. The markets for sugar and beef collapsed. Governor Pearson reported in 1931 that of three sugar mills in St. Croix only one remained in operation, that cotton exports had fallen from 31,000 pounds in 1921 to nothing, that most laborers in St. Croix were unemployed, and that the Red Cross was feeding one-quarter of the population of the island. St. Thomas was also suffering from unemployment and from apprehension at the expected closing of the naval station. In St. John, where the 735 inhabitants normally supported themselves through home gardens, cattle-raising, and charcoal-burning, drought had ruined the gardens and there was no market for cattle or charcoal.[76]

In view of the economic plight of most Virgin Islanders, it is not surprising that the decline in population, long apparent under Danish rule, continued in the American period. The first United States census in 1917 had shown a population of 26,051; the census takers of 1930 found only 22,012. The decline was evidently due to emigration, since the birth rate substantially exceeded the death rate.[77] President Herbert Hoover, after a brief visit to the poverty-stricken islands in March, 1931, declared that, "when we paid $25,000,000 for them, we acquired an effective poorhouse, comprising 90 per cent of the population."

> Viewed from every point except remote naval contingencies [the President added], it was unfortunate that we ever acquired these islands. Nevertheless, having assumed the responsibility, we must do our best to assist the inhabitants.

President Hoover explained the transfer from the navy to the Interior Department, which he had just ordered, as designed

> to see if we can develop some form of industry or agriculture which will relieve us of the present costs and liabilities in support of the population or the local government from the Federal Treasury or from private charity.[78]

The President's efficiency expert, Mr. Herbert D. Brown, chief of the Bureau of Efficiency, had already made several official visits to the islands and finally submitted a long typewritten report in which he expressed more optimism than the President had shown about the prospects of making the islanders self-supporting. His chief recommendations for economic rehabilitation were: (1) a homesteading plan for St. Croix, by which the large landholdings might be broken up into small farms; (2) improved harbor facilities and hotel accommodations in St. Thomas with the object, among other things, of cultivating the tourist trade; (3) improvement of the bay oil industry (the basis of bay rum production) for St. John; (4) improved roads for all the islands.[79]

Congress appropriated funds for the projects proposed by Mr. Brown, thus inaugurating a "new deal" in the

Virgin Islands before the New Deal began in the United States.[80] But this little "new deal" was presently merged in the big New Deal. Early in 1934 the Public Works Administration moved into the Virgin Islands and, at a cost of $2,700,000, acquired some 5,000 acres of land, 2 sugar mills, a distillery, warehouses, a short railroad, 12 old slave villages, shops, agricultural buildings, trucks, work animals, and so forth. To operate these properties (which in effect constituted the whole moribund St. Croix sugar and rum industry), the Department of the Interior secured from the municipal council of St. Thomas and St. John (the St. Croix council having refused) a charter for a government-owned corporation called the Virgin Islands Company. The purpose of the company was declared to be "to aid in effecting the economic rehabilitation of the Virgin Islands of the United States, and to promote the general welfare of the people."

The principal undertaking of the company was the production of sugar and—now that prohibition had ended—rum, the latter on the theory that the quondam popularity of St. Croix rum could be restored. By the end of 1945 the company had 3,000 acres of cane in cultivation and was also grinding the cane produced by over 500 independent growers. It had provided new dwellings and small subsistence plots for its employees and had rehabilitated old plantation houses and rented them at low cost to its officials. It had established an abattoir, a poultry farm. and an electric light plant, and had acquired a yacht for inter-island communication. Its rum production had been profitable, but it had taken a loss on sugar. Though making a net profit in the two years

1944 and 1945 (years of large rum sales), its books at the end of June, 1946 showed an accumulated loss of $456,325.[81] The company had a payroll varying from 500 to 1,500 persons depending on the season of the year. It was estimated in 1948 that one-fifth of the families in St. Croix were dependent directly on the company for a livelihood, and many more indirectly.

Meanwhile, under the homesteading plan, about 400 families had been settled in subsistence plots of 6 acres each. An appeal had been made to tourists through the opening of the government-owned Blue Beard's Castle Hotel in Charlotte Amalie. The Works Progress Administration, the National Youth Administration, and the Civilian Conservation Corps were all extended to the islands. The Virgin Islands also profited from the war— although the early war years brought a food shortage. Construction or enlargement of Marine Corps and submarine bases in St. Thomas and an army air base in St. Croix, and the demands incidental to their operation, helped the employment situation. The prosperity of the rum industry was beneficial, though Congress did not, as in Puerto Rico, permit the return to the insular treasury of internal revenue collected on the mainland. Congress did, however, extend to Virgin Island planters the benefits paid to domestic sugar growers. For three successive years (1942-1944) the municipality of St. Thomas and St. John balanced its budget without federal aid, and the St. Croix municipal council took advantage of the improved financial situation to repeal the export tax on sugar.[82]

In December, 1944 when withdrawal of W.P.A. from the islands was creating a new unemployment problem,

Congress authorized the appropriation of $10,028,420 for a long-range program of rehabilitation in the Virgin Islands. The projects contemplated, which were to be carried out by the Federal Works Administrator, included hospitals, water supply, sewer systems, fire protection, schools, harbor facilities, roads, street improvements, market facilities and many other items. The act provided that $2,028,420 of the sum authorized should be available during 1945 and $2,000,000 in each of the four succeeding years.[83]

The program got off to a slow start because of scarcity of critical materials and difficulty in securing satisfactory bids. Not before January, 1947 did any of the projects actually get under way. Meanwhile the islands had reverted to their normal state of depression. Employment was at a minimum, the governor stated in June, 1946. A year later he reported that rum sales were down about 60 per cent from the preceding year, that the cane crop was more than 23 per cent under 1946's and the sugar yield 40 per cent under. Though shipping at Charlotte Amalie exceeded that of the year before, the islands were suffering all the evils of a depression. Government expenses exceeded revenues by $400,000.[84]

By the middle of 1948 about half of the authorized $10,000,000 had been made available, but as yet there was not much to show for it. "Sewers, fire protection and road projects are in progress in both municipalities," said the 1948 report to the United Nations. "The development and improvement of a potable water supply system will shortly be undertaken. A modern abattoir will shortly be constructed in St. Thomas." The Virgin Islands Company, whose rights would otherwise have ceased

June 30, 1948, was rechartered by Congress first for one year and subsequently given a new lease on life as the Virgin Islands Corporation.[85] The Virgin Islands remained a substandard area. Median family incomes were $430 in St. Thomas and St. John, $339 in St. Croix. Malnutrition was general. Of over 9,000 dwellings, only 580 had inside running water, 560 had flush toilets, 575 had bathtubs or showers. Despite the millions of federal money poured into the islands, the phrase "effective poorhouse" seemed almost as applicable in 1948 as when President Hoover had used it in 1931.[86]

But at least the Virgin Islanders had less reason than they had had in the 1920's to complain that the United States had acquired and then forgotten them. They had been given most of the benefits of the New Deal and some special benefits of their own. They had been given a more liberal and democratic charter. They had been given a governor of the Negro race, to which the vast majority of the islanders belonged—Judge William H. Hastie, who was inaugurated May 17, 1946 and served until elevated to the bench of the United States Circuit Court of Appeals, Third Circuit, in October, 1949. Morris F. de Castro, who succeeded Hastie, was the first native Virgin Islander to hold the office. Proposals to make the governorship elective and to provide for a resident commissioner in Washington were under discussion. Whatever the effect of these measures, actual and proposed, the flight from the islands had been halted. The census of 1940 showed the first population increase in many decades—a population of 24,889 as compared with the 22,012 in 1930. A survey in 1947 estimated the population in that year as 30,000—16,200 in St. Thomas, 13,000 in St. Croix, and 800 in St. John.[87]

THE ECONOMICS AND ETHICS OF PHILIPPINE INDEPENDENCE

No chapter in the history of American policy toward its possessions was marked by such glaring contradictions and inconsistencies as that relating to the Philippines. Although political policy pointed steadily toward self-government and eventual independence, economic policy as steadily built up the Philippines as a source of raw materials for the American market and created an economy dependent upon continued free access to that market. The Democratic party, which from first to last insisted upon early political independence for the Philippines, by its policy of complete free trade with the islands gave the final twist to the bonds of economic dependence. The Independence Act of 1934, then and since advertised to the world as an exemplary deed of renunciation, found probably 90 per cent of its motivation in a cynical desire of American producers to close the American market to the Filipinos at whatever cost to the latter. Independence was granted when the wiser Filipino leaders had ceased to desire it and upon terms almost certain to produce economic disaster in the Philippines.[88]

The American market was opened to Philippine products early in the period of American sovereignty. Although the treaty with Spain prevented for ten years preferential treatment of American trade in the Philippine market, it contained nothing to prevent preferential treatment of Philippine products in the United States. In 1902 Congress prescribed that imports from the Philippines should pay only 75 per cent of the regular tariff rates, and that the proceeds should be returned to the Philippine treasury. The Payne-Aldrich tariff of 1909 established two-way free trade between the United States and the Philippines, except for generous quotas on Philippine sugar, cigars, and tobacco. The Underwood tariff of 1913 removed these quotas and also abolished the last of certain export taxes that had been inherited from the Spanish régime. Thereafter, trade in native products between the United States and the Philippines was entirely free.

The natural result of the free trade policy was to bind the Philippines by commercial ties to the United States and to give a great stimulus to the production in the Philippines of commodities that found a profitable protected market in America. Total trade with the United States, which from 1901 to 1905 averaged $14,425,000 annually, reached $45,395,000 in 1915, $178,342,000 in 1925, and over $183,000,000 in 1930. The growing trade with the United States was a steadily increasing share of the total foreign trade of the Philippines, as the following figures demonstrate:[89]

Year	Per Cent of Total Imports Coming from U.S.	Per Cent of Total Exports Going to U.S.
1901-05 (Average)	13%	35%
1915	50	45
1925	57	73
1930	63	79

Sugar, copra, coconut oil, tobacco, and abacá, or Manila hemp, were the commodities whose production expanded most rapidly under the influence of the American demand. Average sugar production in short tons by five-year periods was as follows:

1890-1894	196,000 tons
1900-1904	94,000
1905-1909	141,000
1910-1914	345,000
1915-1919	447,000
1920-1924	581,000
1925-1929	820,000

In 1932, exports alone exceeded 1,120,000 short tons.[90]

Without giving similar details, we may add that *exports* of copra rose from 15,000,000 kilos in 1899 to 174,000,000 in 1930; coconut oil from 2,852,000 kilos in 1908 to 147,364,000 in 1930; tobacco from 3,862,000 pesos in value in 1899 to 15,672,000 pesos in 1930; abacá from 70,000,000 kilos in 1899 to 169,000,000 in 1930. At the close of the period the United States was taking over 99 per cent of the sugar exported from the Philippines, 81 per cent of the copra, 99 per cent of the coconut oil, 43 per cent of the tobacco, and 34 per cent of the abacá.[91] The most important crops were those of which the United States took the largest share—sugar, copra, and coconut oil. Sugar alone accounted for 60 per cent in value of all Philippine exports and provided 30 per cent of the national income and 60 per cent of the government's revenues. It was estimated (in the middle 1930's) that 2,000,000 people derived their livelihood directly from the sugar industry and that 4,000,000 more depended on it indirectly. Another 4,000,000 Filipinos, it was estimated, were dependent upon the coconut industry—the source of copra and coconut oil. If these estimates are approximately correct, some 10,000,000 Filipinos out of the 16,000,000 living in the islands in 1940 would owe their livelihood largely to the two crops that were sold almost exclusively in the United States and that could be sold elsewhere, if at all, only at greatly reduced prices.[92]

The chief beneficiaries of the free American market (if we follow the customary practice of forgetting the American consumers, who got their sugar and coconut products at low cost) were the Filipinos themselves. Though the Filipinos had been fruitful and multiplied— 12,500,000 in 1930, 19,000,000 in 1948—they had not, like the Puerto Ricans, overpopulated their islands. Except for some of the central islands, indeed, the Philippines had a much sparser population than neighboring lands of the Far East. Population density for the archipelago as a whole in 1930 was 111 persons per square mile, compared with 392 for Japan, 454 for the coastal provinces of China, and 720 for Java. The rich but slightly developed island of Mindanao had only 16 persons per square mile. The Filipinos still had room; some 46,000 square miles were still public domain; and most agricultural land was owned and farmed by Filipinos, though the farmers were often not the owners. Of 3½ billion pesos invested in agriculture in 1939, 3 billion were Filipino capital. Though since 1918 there had been a trend toward larger farms and more farm tenancy, the small farm of about three acres was still the characteristic unit of Philippine agriculture.[93]

The limitation upon the acquisition of public lands—

355 acres to an individual, 2,500 to a corporation—had been respected here as the 500-acre law had not been in Puerto Rico. The Philippine legislature in the 1920's had resisted proposals to change the law for the benefit of the Firestone rubber interests.[94] The Philippines differed from other major sugar-producing areas in adhering to a small-farm rather than a plantation economy. Nor had foreign capital monopolized the refining of sugar. Of 45 sugar centrals in the Philippines in 1936, 22 were owned by Filipinos, 12 by Americans, and the remainder by Spaniards and others. Filipino capital invested in these mills almost equaled that of Americans and Spaniards together. In the processing of coconuts, fibers, and tobacco Filipino capital made a poorer showing.[95]

The purpose of citing these facts and figures is to show that most of the prosperity that came to the Philippines as a result of free trade with the United States remained in Filipino hands and was not siphoned off into the bank accounts of foreign investors. Absentee ownership, so often complained of in Puerto Rico, prevailed to a relatively small extent in the Philippines. Dwight F. Davis, governor general from 1929 to 1932, estimated that the average standard of living in the Philippines was 300 per cent higher than the standards in neighboring areas of the Far East.[96]

The economic relationship with the Philippines was also, at least to a superficial observer, profitable to the United States. If we may rely upon an estimate as of 1943, American investments in the islands amounted to $167,000,000—22 per cent of American investments in Asia as a whole and slightly over 1 per cent of all United States investments abroad.[97] The investors appeared to be satisfied. From 1925 to 1930 the Philippines bought on the average $78,000,000 worth of goods annually from the United States. They were among the best foreign customers for such articles as cotton manufactures, wheat flour, dairy products, chewing tobacco, cigarettes, automobile tires and tubes, galvanized pipe, nails, and mixed paints. Since a third of the exports to the islands were agricultural products, the American farmer as well as the manufacturer benefited from the connection.[98] Mineral resources, as yet only slightly exploited, that might be of considerable interest to the United States included gold and silver, chromite, manganese, iron ore (in large quantities in Mindanao), and copper.[99]

From an economic standpoint, then, it would seem that the marriage of the United States and the Philippines was a union which, though mildly beneficial to the stronger spouse, was essential to the welfare of the weaker.

The Filipino drive for independence had nothing to do with economics. It was firmly based on the psychology of politics. Whether or not the Filipino masses had any informed interest in independence is a debatable question, but, as was shown in the last chapter, from the election of the first Philippine assembly in 1907 virtually all Filipino politicians took their stand for early independence. This attitude was a perfectly natural one. Government under American tutelage implied an inferiority that Filipino leaders, clever and often well educated politicians, could not admit. They were not unaware of the benefits of American rule in economic prosperity, domestic tranquillity, and protection from foreign aggression, but in the enthusiasm of their desire to be masters in their own household, they minimized these benefits. When they were assailed by misgivings over the perils of independence, as they sometimes were, they could not afford politically to admit their doubts.

The official declarations of Governor General Harrison and President Wilson, in 1920, that the Philippines were ripe for independence gave great impetus to the Filipino campaign. The legislature and municipal councils had already formed the habit of passing annual independence resolutions. Beginning in 1918, the legislature sent annually an official Independence Commission to urge the cause in Washington. In 1920, probably fearing a veto by some future governor general, it made a standing appropriation of $500,000, one half to be used by each house in financing the commission's junket to Washington. When Messrs. Wood and Forbes, in their report of 1921, stated that most Filipinos who desired independence wished at the same time a continuance of American protection, both political parties (the dominant Nationalists and the minority Democrats) adopted as their slogan, "Immediate, absolute, and complete independence." This continued to be the official position. A leading Filipino political scientist, Maximo M. Kalaw, declared in an article published in September, 1931 that the Philippines wanted no protection from the United States, no Platt Amendment granting independence with strings attached. A treaty insuring their neutrality, or a guarantee of their independence by the League of Nations would be acceptable and sufficient. The Philippines had nothing to fear; the day of aggression was past. "Out of some 64 nations in the world today," wrote Kalaw, "there is not a case of invasion at present."[100]

But if, in public, Filipino *politicos* continued to demand "immediate, absolute, and complete independence," privately they confessed that they would be satisfied with less. Governor General Stimson's policy of conceding something approaching parliamentary government to the Filipinos, described in the preceding chapter, not only quieted the independence agitation, it also brought from Manuel Quezon an admission that if he could get a modified form of dominion status with an assurance of continued free trade, he would be willing to drop all agitation for independence for 30 years.[101] This was in 1929. Five years later, after the Philippine legislature had rejected the first independence act (to be noted hereafter), and while further legislation was under consideration by Congress, a commission headed by Quezon visited Washington. At the request of the President a former governor general, Theodore Roosevelt, Jr., conferred with the commission to learn just what they wanted.

> I saw the commission [he relates], and they told me that their desire was to see nothing done at the moment and to plan for a dominion status in the future. They said that if no bill were passed, the Philippine legislature would invite a commission from Congress to visit the islands and pay the cost. Then perhaps some permanent relationship might be arranged. They said, however, that they could not say this publicly for . . . political reasons. . . .[102]

Blessings brighten as they take their flight. Quezon was well aware what loss of the American market would mean to the Philippines. When this conversation occurred, moreover, Japan was on the march in the Far

East and American protection appeared more valuable than before. But it was too late to divert the course of history away from independence. The American Congress had decided.

Neither political party, and no President, in the United States had ever closed the door upon eventual independence for the Philippines, but parties and Presidents had differed widely as to the time and conditions of that eventuality. As a prerequisite for independence, the Democrats had emphasized the existence of a *stable* government, whereas Republicans, curiously enough, had stressed the need of a *democratic* government. Thus President Wilson had suggested that the self-government to be developed in the Philippines should be based on their own "counsel and experience" rather than on American standards. But Mr. Taft, as Secretary of War, had written in 1908:

> What should be emphasized in the statement of our national policy is that we wish to prepare the Filipinos for *popular* self-government. This is plain from Mr. McKinley's [*i.e.* Secretary Root's] letter of instructions and all of his utterances. It was not at all within his purpose or that of Congress which made his letter a part of the law of the land that we were merely to await the organization of a Philippine oligarchy or aristocracy competent to administer the government and then turn the islands over to it.[103]

Wilson was satisfied as to the existence of a *stable* government in 1920. The Republican Presidents who followed him—Harding, Coolidge, and Hoover—were apparently not convinced that *democratic* government had been achieved or that the Filipino masses were safe from exploitation by a native "oligarchy or aristocracy."

Another kind of deterrent to early independence appeared in the middle 1920's in the possibility that the United States might find in the Philippines a source of rubber that would free it from the near-monopoly of that commodity enjoyed by the British Empire. In 1926 Harvey S. Firestone, Jr. visited the Philippines and upon his return conferred with President Coolidge. The President informed a press conference that the government would encourage rubber development in the Philippines and that American capitalists were ready to enlist in such a venture if they could secure from the Philippine legislature an amendment to the land laws to permit the leasing for 75 years of holdings up to 500,000 acres in extent. In his subsequent message to Congress President Coolidge gave formal and official blessing to the project. Large areas in the Philippines, he said, were "adaptable to the production of rubber." Plans for developing these possibilities could be safely made, for

> no one contemplates any time in the future either under the present or a more independent form of Government when we should not assume some responsibility for their [the Philippines'] defense.[104]

Though the plans for rubber-growing were defeated by the refusal of the Filipino lawmakers to grant the concession asked, and Harvey Firestone turned to Liberia instead of the Philippines, an objective observer in the middle 1920's would still have predicted a long postponement of Philippine independence. There were always a few anti-imperialists in Congress, but they were not influential, and their allies in the press were largely confined to such liberal periodicals as *The Nation* and *New Republic*. The revival and final success of the American movement for Philippine independence were results of the depressed state of American agriculture and the demand of suffering agricultural groups and sections to be relieved of the supposed burden of Philippine competition.

As early as 1924 one writer had noted that independence for the Philippines was advocated by certain groups in the United States engaged in the production of beet and cane sugar, tobacco, and vegetable oils because of the competition with their products of duty-free commodities from the Philippines.[105] A proposal to limit importations of duty-free sugar from the Philippines was made in the House of Representatives in February, 1928.[106] With the meeting in 1929 of a special session of Congress called by President Hoover to revise the tariff, the new forces advocating Philippine independence really began to operate. When the tariff bill reached the Senate in September, Senator William H. King of Utah (long an independence advocate) offered as an amendment an article providing for independence for the Philippines. He explained that there was a move on foot to restrict duty-free imports from the Philippines and that a grant of independence would end such importations without injustice to the Filipinos. Another sugar state senator proposed to tax imports from the Philippines at the regular rates. The debate that followed exhibited the urgent demand of the sugar, cotton, and dairy interests for protection against Philippine sugar and coconut oil, as well as the conscientious feeling of many senators that to hold the islands under American rule and at the same time place a tariff on their products would be unjust and immoral. The prevailing sentiment of senators from the farm states was phrased frankly if crudely by Heflin of Alabama. The Philippines, he said,

> are hanging like a millstone about the necks of our cotton producers and the peanut, bean, and corn producers of the United States. Let us give them their independence and get rid of the Philippine Islands now.[107]

The proposed amendments to the tariff bill were voted down, but not until Senator Hiram Bingham, chairman of the Committee on Territories and Insular Possessions, had promised hearings and a vote on Philippine independence in the next session of Congress.[108]

The groups that desired Philippine independence for their own advantage were now mobilizing for the campaign. Their identity was a matter of public record. Senator Harry B. Hawes of Missouri listed them in a speech in the Senate. They included 3 national farm organizations, 2 national dairy organizations, the sugar growers of 27 states (19 beet and 8 cane), American investors in Cuban sugar, the American Federation of Labor, a group fearing that Filipinos would displace Negroes in certain occupations, and another group desiring to exclude Filipinos from the United States for the same reasons that explained the exclusion of Chinese and Japanese.[109] That the A.F. of L. and other opponents of Filipino immigration took a hand in the agitation is evident,[110] but it is equally evident that the farmers and dairymen were spearheading the movement. Eight farm

organizations representing largely sugar, cottonseed, and
dairy interests submitted a brief in favor of independence in December, 1932.[111] Representative of the farm
attitude was the argument of the American Farm Bureau
Federation that free trade with the Philippines was injurious to American farmers because, as it alleged, 95
per cent of imports from the Philippines were products
of agriculture, whereas 80 per cent of exports to the
Philippines were industrial products.[112]

The competition of Philippine sugar with American
and Cuban sugar, and the competition of Philippine
coconut oil with cottonseed oil (in soap) and with butter (in margarine) were the chief injuries that American
producers believed they suffered at the hands of the
Filipinos. The cotton and dairy organizations, it seems
certain, exaggerated the losses and minimized the profits
they realized from free trade with the Philippines.[113] *The
American Chamber of Commerce Journal,* which opposed independence, contended that the cotton and
dairy interests gained more than they lost by this trade
and pointed out also the large stake of fruit, vegetable,
and tobacco growers, and the fishing industry, in the
Philippine market. It charged that the movement to shut
off or restrict imports from the Philippines had been in-
stigated by Cuban sugar interests, which had enlisted
the support of the American farmer by fallacious
arguments.[114]

Another argument for independence often heard in
the debates in Congress was the assertion that the Philippines would be impossible to defend in the event of war
in the Far East. The idea was not new but it had new
force. As far back as 1907 Theodore Roosevelt had re-

garded the Philippines as "our heel of Achilles" and had proposed that we give them independence as soon as possible to "remove a temptation from Japan's way."[115] At the Washington Naval Arms Conference of 1921-1922 the United States had renounced for 15 years the right to strengthen the inadequate defenses in the Philippines and on their approaches in the western Pacific and had accepted such limitation upon its battleship strength as would render hazardous the waging of war against Japan in the Far East. The initiation of Japan's career of conquest in 1931 aroused the fear that the United States, if it retained the Philippines, might be challenged to defend them in a useless and difficult war.

On the whole, by 1932 the impression had become widespread in the United States that the Philippines were an inconvenient appurtenance, a burden rather than a blessing in time of peace, costly if not impossible to defend in time of war.[116] It was in this atmosphere that Congress made its decision. Although President Hoover, Secretary of State Stimson, other members of the Cabinet, and a large majority of American newspapers[117] opposed immediate independence, Congress passed on December 29, 1932 and repassed on January 17, 1933, over the President's vigorous veto, the Hare-Hawes-Cutting Act permitting the Philippines, if they so desired, to attain their independence after a ten-year transition period.[118]

The act was not to take effect until its terms had been accepted either by the Philippine legislature or by a convention called for that purpose. Following such acceptance, the legislature was to provide for the election of a constitutional convention to meet within one year of the passage of the act. The constitution devised by this body must be republican in form, must contain a bill of rights, and must recognize the sovereignty of the United States during the period of transition. When the President of the United States, to whom the constitution was to be submitted, should certify that it met the requirements of the act, it was to be submitted to a plebiscite of the voters of the Philippines. A majority vote in favor of the constitution would be interpreted as a decision in favor of independence, and this decision would be final. An election of officers under the constitution would then be held, whereupon the existing government would terminate and the transition period would begin. On July 4 following the expiration of ten years from the inauguration of the new government, the President of the United States should proclaim the independence of the Philippines. The United States would thereupon cede to the Philippine government all public property in the islands with the exception of such military and naval bases as the President might designate for retention by the United States. The President was directed to invite foreign governments to recognize the independence of the Philippines. He was also requested to open negotiations for an international treaty of neutralization.

During the transition period the sovereignty of the United States would continue. The United States would be represented in the Philippines by a high commissioner and the Philippines would have a resident commissioner in Washington. Amendments to the constitution must be submitted to the President for approval, and the President might suspend any law of the Philippine legislature that in his opinion would impair the obligations of the

Philippines or violate any international engagement of the United States.

Of special interest, in view of the economic motives of the legislation, were its trade provisions. These were hardly generous. Throughout the transition period American products would continue to be admitted free of duty to the Philippines. Philippine imports into the United States, on the other hand, would be subjected to progressive restrictions. During the first five years they would continue to be admitted freely, though within quotas for sugar, coconut oil, and cordage—imports of those commodities in excess of quotas to pay the regular tariff rates. In the sixth year the Philippine government would collect on commodities exported to the United States an export tax equivalent to 5 per cent of the United States tariff, and this tax would be increased gradually to 25 per cent in the tenth year. Proceeds of the export taxes would be placed in a sinking fund to discharge the bonded indebtedness of the Philippine government. After independence the full tariff rates would apply, unless a conference, to be called at least a year before independence, should result in some sort of reciprocal trade agreement.

To satisfy American labor and other elements opposed to Filipino immigration, the act stipulated that from the time when it should go into effect Filipinos should have the status of foreigners and have an immigration quota of 50 annually, though during the transition period the Secretary of the Interior might admit a larger number of laborers to Hawaii. After independence all United States immigration laws would apply, "including all the provisions thereof relating to persons ineligible to citizenship." Like other Orientals, Filipinos would then not be eligible for immigration or naturalization.

The economic clauses of the independence act confronted the Filipinos, in the event of acceptance, with the necessity of making drastic downward adjustments in their economy. Sugar, their foremost industry, faced certain disaster. Philippine sugar was a high-cost product which could compete with the sugar of Cuba and other low-cost areas only because of preference in the American market, which it was now to lose. The imposition of the American tariff would also have ruinous effects upon the Philippine tobacco and cigar industry and upon such minor enterprises as the making of pearl buttons and embroidery. The extraction of coconut oil and the manufacture of rope and cordage could not be expected to continue profitably after loss of the free market for those commodities. Hemp and copra were not dutiable in the United States and would not be affected by the terms of the independence act; but in 1934 Congress imposed an excise tax on imported copra, which, though it gave preferential treatment to the Philippine product, was a warning of possible new impositions to come.[119]

All in all, the economic outlook for an independent Philippines was gloomy enough. Certain features of the act were glaringly unfair. The time allowed for economic readjustment was too short. The free market guaranteed to American products in the Philippines to the end of the transition period would postpone till independence any opportunity for the Philippines to make reciprocal trade arrangements with other countries. The Filipinos must make their final decision for or against independence before experiencing any effect of the cur-

tailment of the American market. The legislature or the
voters might reject the terms of the act, but in the existing mood of Congress, rejection would almost certainly
be followed by the imposition of tariff or quotas or both
on Philippine imports. The Filipinos might reject independence with trade restrictions, but the probable alternative was trade restrictions without independence.
Finally, the offer of independence, such as it was, came
at a time when Japan had started on her career of conquest in the Far East and had already achieved considerable economic penetration of the Philippines. "Freedom" from the United States might be only the prelude
to subjection by a harsher master.[120]

Partly for the reasons here summarized, partly because
of internal political squabbles, the Philippine legislature
rejected the independence offer of 1933. Sergio Osmeña,
Manuel Roxas, and others, who had maintained liaison
with Congress while the act was being written, were
attacked by Manuel Quezon for having made a bad bargain. In a spirited contest, the legislature followed Quezon's lead and in a joint resolution of October 17, 1933
rejected the act, giving as reasons the unfairness of the
provisions on trade and immigration, the indefinite powers of the American high commissioner, and the proposed retention by the United States of military and
naval bases. The retention of such bases on Philippine
soil, it said, would be inconsistent with independence,
would "violate national dignity," and would be "subject
to misunderstanding."[121]

Quezon headed a new mission to Washington. As related above, he and his confrères intimated to an unofficial envoy of the President that they would welcome

postponement of the independence issue with a view to an eventual solution in dominion status. They learned, however, that they could expect nothing better than a very slightly modified version of the act they had just denounced. This they decided to accept. The Tydings-McDuffie Act, signed March 24, 1934, differed from its predecessor in only one significant respect. It refrained from insisting upon retention of military bases and stipulated that the retention of naval bases and fueling stations should be subject to negotiation between the United States and the Philippines.[122] The trade and immigration clauses were unchanged.

Quezon now returned to Manila as the chief defender of the new law and the chief advocate of its acceptance by the Philippines. In May, 1934 the legislature gave its acceptance. A constitutional convention sat from July 30, 1934 to February 8, 1935. The constitution, approved by President Roosevelt, was ratified by an overwhelming vote of the Filipino people on the following May 14, elections were held in September, and the transition government, with Quezon as president and Osmeña as vice president, was inaugurated November 15, 1935. The date for complete independence was therefore July 4, 1946. Much was to happen before that day arrived.

During the transition period the new political entity was known as the Commonwealth of the Philippines. After independence it would be simply The Philippines.

War and conquest forestalled more than a beginning of the application of the economic provisions of the Tydings-McDuffie Act. In the interval the United States made some slight concessions to the Philippines. By an act of August 7, 1939 Congress provided that for cigars,

scrap tobacco, coconut oil, and buttons the export tax
should be waived and instead, beginning in the sixth
transition year, the duty-free quotas of these items should
decrease 5 per cent annually.[123] In the spring of 1941 the
Philippine national assembly petitioned Congress to alter
or suspend certain burdensome economic provisions of
the independence act. Legislation for that purpose was
introduced in June, 1941 but not till after Pearl Harbor,
when such a gesture had become meaningless, did Congress act on it. On December 22, 1941 the President
signed a bill suspending until December 31, 1942 the
imposition of export taxes on Philippine products exported to the United States and further decrease of
quotas on the quota items.[124]

The United States was the first modern power to grant
independence voluntarily to a rich colonial possession.
American public men have frequently pointed to that
act as one of generosity and statesmanship, which other
colonial powers would do well to copy. It is unpleasant
to have to record that the law thrusting independence
upon the Philippines showed little statesmanship and no
generosity. It sacrificed the well-being of the Philippines for the supposed benefit of American farmers and
workers, disguising the injury with the kiss of independence. It was, of course, within the power of Congress
to restrict or tax Philippine imports and yet to refuse
independence. But it is no valid defense of an ungenerous act to say that a still more ungenerous one was
possible.*

---

* For a summary of United States–Philippines relations since World
War II see Appendix I.

CHAPTER EIGHT

The Retreat from Empire ～ ～

WHEN the United States, in 1934, took the decisive step toward "freeing" the Philippines, it was already well along in the process of renouncing its protectorates in the Caribbean and even of repudiating the principle upon which they had been founded. The Roosevelt Corollary of the Monroe Doctrine had been discarded, the right of intervention was being abandoned, the "good neighbor policy" was replacing "Yankee imperialism." The change in policy had had a small beginning in the Harding administration, had languished under Calvin Coolidge, made significant gains under Herbert Hoover, and reached full maturity under Franklin D. Roosevelt.

The change of policy came about by force of circumstances and a slow drift of opinion rather than as a product of any organized movement. The Anti-Imperialist League, formed in 1898 to oppose annexation of the Philippines, continued to exist until the death of its secretary, Erving Winslow, in 1923, but in 1913 Moorfield Storey, its president, confessed that, despite "a very imposing list of vice presidents," the League consisted "substantially" of himself and Winslow. After Winslow's death he wrote that the League

has ceased practically to function. Almost everybody who belonged to it is dead, and the young

311

men do not take up the work. I am still its representative, but I have no followers.[1]

Though the Anti-Imperialist League might be moribund, there was no lack of anti-imperialists. "Liberal" groups and individuals in the United States, former followers of Woodrow Wilson who had broken with him over the alleged imperialistic features of the League of Nations, turned to criticism of imperialism nearer home. Having attacked the League for its supposed endorsement of British, French, and Japanese imperialism in Ireland, India, Africa, and the Far East, they could not consistently refrain from finding fault with some aspects of American policy.[2] Representative of these groups were the two liberal periodicals *The Nation* and *New Republic,* which maintained a fairly consistent opposition to American policy in Haiti, the Dominican Republic, and Nicaragua, favored Philippine independence, and criticized official practices in Puerto Rico and the Virgin Islands. Similar positions were taken by a few senators, notably William H. King of Utah and William E. Borah of Idaho. In the late 1920's and early 1930's a flood of volumes on different aspects of American imperialism issued from the presses of Boston, New York, and Washington. They dealt with American policy in Cuba, the Dominican Republic, Haiti, Nicaragua, Colombia, Puerto Rico, and the Philippines. Nearly all were critical of that policy; most of them attempted to be objective, a few were obviously biased.[3] They had their influence, and they indicated a trend in public opinion.

Such defenders of imperialism as remained had difficulty in finding convincing arguments to support their case. The economic benefits of their policy to the United States and its social and moral benefits to the people of the dependencies had been less impressive than the optimists of 1898 had predicted. The naïve popular enthusiasm that had supported the "large policy" of 1898 had given place to an attitude of disillusionment and skepticism. Even the practical strategic arguments of Mahan had lost much of their force, for World War I, by removing all immediate danger of European intervention in the Caribbean, had also removed the principal excuse for American intervention in that area.

But just as a belief that retention of the Philippines was economically costly to the United States was essential to effectuate Philippine independence, so a realization that intervention in the Caribbean area was injuring the political and economic interests of the United States in all Latin America was a prerequisite to the abandonment of that phase of American imperialism.

The Withdrawal Begins

That President Harding became an anti-imperialist to a very small degree was due to accidents of the presidential campaign of 1920. The Republican platform of that year contained no criticism of Wilson's Caribbean policy, but an indiscreet utterance of the Democratic candidate for vice president invited an attack on that policy. In a speech at Butte, Montana, August 18, 1920, Franklin D. Roosevelt, former Assistant Secretary of the Navy, ridiculed the Republican contention that Great Britain would have six votes in the Assembly of the League of Nations to one vote for the United States.

> It is just the other way [he was quoted as say-
> ing]. As a matter of fact, the United States has
> about twelve votes in the Assembly. Until last
> week I had two of them myself, and now Secretary
> [of the Navy] Daniels has them. You know I have
> had something to do with the running of a couple
> of little republics. The facts are that I wrote Haiti's
> Constitution myself, and, if I do say it, I think it
> a pretty good Constitution.

Haiti, Santo Domingo, Cuba, and other small states to a
total number of at least 12, Roosevelt explained, viewed
the United States as a guardian and would vote with it
in the League Assembly.[4]

These assertions gave Senator Harding, the Republican presidential candidate, an excellent opening for an
attack, and he took advantage of it a few days later. If
elected, he declared,

> I will not empower an Assistant Secretary of the
> Navy to draft a constitution for helpless neighbors
> in the West Indies and jam it down their throats
> at the point of bayonets borne by United States
> marines. . . . Nor will I misuse the power of the
> Executive to cover with a veil of secrecy repeated
> acts of unwarranted interference in domestic affairs
> of the little republics of the Western Hemisphere,
> such as in the last few years have not only made
> enemies of those who should be our friends, but
> have rightfully discredited our country as their
> trusted neighbor.[5]

Such strong words from Candidate Harding implied
deeds from President Harding. The President picked the
sorest spot in the Caribbean, the Dominican Republic,

which the United States Navy had governed with an iron hand, but with some excellent material results, since 1916. The Wilson administration had already proposed a plan of withdrawal with safeguards for vested rights but had failed to reach agreement on its terms with Dominican leaders. Harding's negotiators encountered similar difficulties, but in June, 1922 they agreed with the native politicians upon a plan for terminating the occupation. Under this arrangement a native provisional government replaced the United States naval government; the marines who had policed the republic were withdrawn to a few coastal towns, leaving the preservation of order to the native constabulary; and a new treaty with the United States validated the acts of the military government and extended the receivership of 1907 until the existing bonded indebtedness should have been liquidated. Under this provisional arrangement regular elections were held and the elected government was installed on July 12, 1924. Thereupon the last of the United States marines embarked for other shores, leaving the government of the Dominican Republic in the hands of its own people, except for the continuance of the customs receivership under United States control.[6] Thus the first step in the withdrawal of the United States from its Caribbean protectorates, initiated by President Harding, was completed after his death (August 2, 1923) under his successor, Calvin Coolidge.

The termination of the military government in the Dominican Republic was, however, the only anti-imperialist gesture made by Harding during his brief term in the White House. Puerto Ricans and Filipinos who asked independence or more self-government were lectured upon their good fortune in living under the benevolent rule of the United States. The legation guard of marines remained in Nicaragua. In Haiti the marines continued to maintain order, and the many-sided control machinery that had been established by treaty remained intact, with the difference that in 1922 an American high commissioner was appointed to coordinate the work of the several United States agencies. A Senate committee that investigated the occupation of Haiti acknowledged that mistakes had been made but praised the occupation authorities for their achievements and recommended that the occupation continue.[7] Far from being an anti-imperialist, Harding was reported after his death to have had ambitious plans for expansion in Central America. He had "informed friends privately," a *New York Times* reporter was told,

> that he desired the chief international accomplishment of his Administration to be the bringing of Central American countries under the Stars and Stripes; that is, to have the sovereignty of the United States extended to them with the ultimate object of granting them rights of statehood.[8]

Calvin Coolidge, the businessman's President, was no more anxious than was Warren Harding to preside over the liquidation of the American Empire. At reading moral lectures to complaining colonials—in his view, ungrateful beneficiaries of American prosperity—he was even better than his predecessor,[9] and in asserting the duty of the United States government to follow and protect its citizens and their property wherever found, he perhaps went further than any other President.

> The person and property of a citizen are a part
> of the general domain of the nation, even when
> abroad [he declared in 1927] . . . there is a dis-
> tinct and binding obligation on the part of self-
> respecting Governments to afford protection to the
> persons and property of their citizens, wherever
> they may be.[10]

Such a philosophy contained possibilities of endless interventions in foreign countries. Coolidge did, without
any formal announcement, terminate the meddlesome
interference in Cuban governmental affairs in which the
United States, with the best intentions and supposedly
under authority of the Platt Amendment, had for years
been indulging,[11] and the Cuban government was left
free to develop into the type of corrupt dictatorship that
was seemingly indigenous to the soil. Coolidge's only
other anti-imperialist gesture had unfortunate and unexpected consequences.

Since 1912, it will be recalled, a small legation guard
of United States marines had been stationed at Managua,
the capital of Nicaragua. Their presence had helped to
discourage revolution or other disorder and to keep in
power governments friendly to the United States. All
seemed so tranquil in the little inter-oceanic republic
that in August, 1925, in conformity with a decision of
1923, the marines were withdrawn.

The withdrawal, it turned out, was premature. By a
series of *coups d'état*, October, 1925 to January, 1926,
Emiliano Chamorro, a Conservative, forced the resignation of President Salorzano, a Liberal, and had himself
installed in his place. The United States, which had endorsed the principles of a Central American treaty of

1923 denying recognition to governments that owed their origins to revolution, withheld recognition from Chamorro, as did the other Central American governments. In October, 1926 Chamorro resigned, and in his place the Nicaraguan congress elected Adolfo Diaz, Conservative and old friend of the United States, which promptly recognized him. Sacasa, Liberal vice president under Salorzano, who had been exiled as a part of Chamorro's *coup,* returned to Nicaragua and, with Mexican recognition and support, laid claim to the presidency, now held by Diaz. Faced with rebellion by Sacasa and the Liberals, Diaz asked aid from the United States. Early in 1927 the marines were sent back to Nicaragua to neutralize certain areas and to protect American and other foreign lives and property.[12]

The renewed intervention in Nicaragua provoked widespread criticism in both the United States and Latin America.[13] President Coolidge defended the intervention as warranted by "the proprietary rights of the United States in the Nicaraguan canal route" and "the obligations flowing from the investments of all classes of our citizens in Nicaragua." The United States, he said, could not

> fail to view with deep concern any serious threat to stability and constitutional government in Nicaragua tending toward anarchy and jeopardizing American interests, especially if such a state of affairs is contributed to or brought about by outside influences or by any foreign power.[14]

But when it appeared that President Diaz, even with the advantage of arms supplied by the United States, was unable to suppress his Liberal opponents and that Nicaragua faced the probability of a prolonged civil war, the United States undertook to bring about a compromise settlement. For this purpose Coolidge requested Colonel Henry L. Stimson, who had served as Secretary of War under President Taft, to go to Nicaragua as a special representative of the United States and to confer with the leaders of both factions.

Stimson's mission was extraordinarily successful. In the course of a month in Nicaragua he arranged an agreement—the "peace of Tipitapa"— between Diaz and General Moncada, the principal Liberal leader. Under this agreement, both sides were to be disarmed by the United States forces, and a National Guard (theoretically divorced from politics) was to be trained and temporarily officered by United States marines. Diaz was to continue in office, with Liberals admitted to his cabinet, until the 1928 elections, which were to be supervised and their fairness guaranteed by the United States.[15]

The arrangement, of course, committed the United States to further intervention in Nicaragua. The occupation forces, it turned out, supervised not only the elections of 1928 but those of 1930 and 1932 as well. The fairness of those elections is sufficiently attested by the fact that they were won by the Liberals—traditionally the anti-American party—Moncada being elected to the presidency in 1928 and Sacasa in 1932. One liberal leader, Sandino, had refused to abide by the terms of the peace and carried on for three years a guerrilla warfare against the marines, thus keeping the bloody aspects of intervention steadily before the American public. By February, 1931 peace was so far restored that Mr. Stimson, now Secretary of State, announced that the marines would be gradually withdrawn, leaving the further suppression of guerrillas to the National Guard, and that the intervention would be terminated after the elections of 1932. This decision was not altered when a new outbreak of guerrilla warfare, or "banditry," occurred in the interior in April, 1931.[16] In January, 1933 the last of the marines were withdrawn, leaving as the only element of American control the customs receivership agreed upon in 1911 and modified in 1917.

THE END OF THE ROOSEVELT COROLLARY

The withdrawal of the marines from Nicaragua, and especially the refusal to augment the existing force during the disturbances of 1931, typified the new Hoover-Stimson policy toward Latin America.[17] This "new policy toward Latin American countries" was described in the *New York Times* on "high authority" as representing "a determination on the part of the United States not to intervene in the internal affairs of any of those countries."[18] The policy had been foreshadowed in Mr. Hoover's "good-will tour" of Latin America between his election and inauguration in the winter of 1928-1929, in friendly references to Latin America in his inaugural address, and in a Gridiron Club speech a few weeks later in which he stated:

> I can say at once that it never has been and ought not to be the policy of the United States to intervene by force to secure or maintain contracts between our citizens and foreign States or their citizens.[19]

The policy was exhibited in the prompt abandonment of

the Wilsonian practice of refusing recognition to revolutionary governments—a form of intervention—and a return to the traditional American policy of recognizing any government that was *de facto* in control and able and willing to observe its international obligations.[20] It was supported by the publication in 1930 of a *Memorandum on the Monroe Doctrine*, prepared in 1928 by Under Secretary of State J. Reuben Clark and now made official doctrine. The *Memorandum* was an outright repudiation of the Roosevelt Corollary.

> The [Monroe] doctrine [it declared] states a case of United States *vs.* Europe, not of United States *vs.* Latin-America.
>
> Such arrangements as the United States has made, for example, with Cuba, Santo Domingo, Haiti, and Nicaragua, are not within the Doctrine as it was announced by Monroe.[21]

It is to be noted that the Clark *Memorandum* did not repudiate the right of the United States to intervene in the affairs of neighboring states when its interests were endangered. It merely denied that such right found any basis in the Monroe Doctrine. Arrangements such as those with Cuba and the other states mentioned "may be accounted for as the expression of a national policy which . . . originates in the necessities of security or self-preservation." Here was no admission that the United States had done wrong in intervening in the states of Central America and the Caribbean, no promise that it would not intervene again in the interest of "security or self-preservation." But since virtually all the interventions after 1904 had been given a basis in the

Roosevelt Corollary of the Monroe Doctrine, and since that basis was now discarded, the issuance of the *Memorandum* was an important step in the direction of complete nonintervention. Taken with other features of the Hoover-Stimson Latin American policy, it warrants the assertion that those two statesmen laid the basis of the "good neighbor policy" of the 1930's.[22]

Though it is not possible to speak with too much assurance of the motives of President Hoover's alteration of our Latin American policy, it may be surmised that as a devotee of nineteenth century liberalism he had a basic distaste for imperialism. There is also reason to believe that, as Secretary of Commerce, he had been disturbed at European encroachments upon American trade in Latin America and attributed them in part to hostility toward the United States provoked by American policies in Nicaragua and Haiti.[23] During his pre-inauguration tour of Latin America he sought earnestly to convince the sister republics that the United States had no aggressive purposes and that the interventions in which it had engaged were temporary and motivated only by a desire for peace and order. His words and actions, built upon by the succeeding administration, went far to remove Latin American suspicion of "Yankee imperialism" and had important consequences in improved relations, both economic and political, between the United States and its southern neighbors.

A Policy "Opposed to Armed Intervention"

President Franklin D. Roosevelt's original "good neighbor" declaration had no special reference to Latin America and was quite innocuous in any event.

> In the field of world policy [he announced, March
> 4, 1933] I would dedicate this Nation to the policy
> of the good neighbor—the neighbor who resolutely
> respects himself and, because he does so, respects
> the rights of others.

More significant was his declaration at a Woodrow Wilson Foundation dinner, December 28, 1933, that "the definite policy of the United States from now on is one opposed to armed intervention."[24] This statement, though it went much further than the Clark *Memorandum,* was, like it, unilateral. It did not bind the United States to a policy of nonintervention.

Two days before Roosevelt's speech, however, the United States delegation at the Seventh Inter-American Conference at Montevideo had signed a convention on the rights and duties of states which declared, in Article 8: "No state has the right to intervene in the internal or external affairs of another." Secretary of State Cordell Hull, who headed the American delegation, attempted to reserve to the United States its rights under "the law of nations as generally recognized and understood," and the Senate appended a reservation to that effect in giving its sanction to the treaty; but at a Special Inter-American Conference for the Maintenance of Peace, held at Buenos Aires in 1936, the United States accepted, without reservation, a protocol stating:

> The High Contracting Parties declare inadmissi-
> ble the intervention of any one of them, directly
> or indirectly, and for whatever reason, in the inter-
> nal or external affairs of any other of the Parties.[25]

Thus the United States followed up the setting aside

of the Roosevelt Corollary by a complete renunciation of any right to intervene in the affairs of neighboring states—the right or supposed right under which it had established protectorates in five Caribbean and Central American republics.

Meanwhile Roosevelt and Hull were giving evidence of their sincerity by liquidating what remained of those protectorates. They had inherited from the Hoover administration a piece of unfinished business in Haiti, where student strikes and other demonstrations against American control and the American protégé, President Louis Borno, had led President Hoover in 1930 to send an investigating commission to the island. As a result of the commission's recommendations,[26] President Borno withdrew, elections were held (the first since 1917), and a new legislature and administration were installed. The public works, public health, and agricultural services, which had been under American control, were rapidly Haitianized. A United States minister replaced the high commissioner. In September, 1932 a treaty was negotiated providing for the Haitianization of the *Garde d'Haiti* (the American-officered constabulary) and the withdrawal of the marines, but for the continuance of a limited financial control by the United States until the existing bonded indebtedness, contracted in 1922, should have been discharged. The last point proved objectionable to the Haitian legislature, which on that account rejected the treaty.

Thus matters stood when the Roosevelt administration came in in 1933. What a treaty had failed to accomplish was brought about by an executive agreement of August 7, 1933. Under this arrangement the *Garde* was to be completely Haitianized by October 1, 1934, the marines were to be withdrawn within 30 days thereafter (they were in fact withdrawn as a gesture of good will in July and August, 1934) and a "fiscal representative" nominated by the President of the United States was to replace the financial adviser–general receiver and to retain control of Haitian customs until the 1922 bonds were paid off.[27] Subsequently, in 1941, the National Bank of Haiti, with representatives of both the Haitian government and the bondholders on its board of directors, replaced the fiscal representative as administrator of the customs and the service on the debt.[28] Thus the United States government withdrew from the picture entirely. The Haitian protectorate was liquidated.

The same statement is applicable to the Dominican Republic. By a treaty signed September 24, 1940, and ratified in the following February, the United States relinquished the right to name the general receiver of customs, and the Dominican government in return guaranteed service on its bonds by a lien on its general revenues.[29] Only in Nicaragua did an American collector general of customs continue, with the full approval of the Nicaraguan government, to administer the customs and the service on the national debt.

An area much more vital to the security of the United States than the republics just mentioned was Panama, but even here the good neighbor policy was allowed to prevail. By a treaty signed March 2, 1936, replacing the treaty of 1903, the United States, on the one hand, dropped its guarantee of the independence of Panama and, on the other hand, renounced its right to intervene in Panamanian affairs for the preservation of order and also its right to acquire by eminent domain lands or properties in the Republic of Panama that might be needed for the purposes of the canal. Article 10 of the treaty provided that in the event "of an international conflagration or the existence of any threat of aggression which would endanger the security of the Republic of Panama or the neutrality or security of the Panama Canal," the two governments would take such measures as they deemed necessary "for the protection of their common interests," but that measures deemed necessary by one government that might affect the territory of the other would be "the subject of consultation between the two Governments."

This article, which implied that in an emergency the United States must secure the consent of Panama before taking measures on Panama soil for the protection of the canal, alarmed the United States Senate, and the treaty was not approved until 1939, after an exchange of notes with Panama by which the latter agreed that in an emergency consultation might follow action instead of preceding it.[30] An agreement of March, 1941 permitted the United States, for the duration of the war in Europe, to maintain listening-posts, searchlights, and anti-aircraft batteries in Panamanian territory.[31]

In keeping with the abandonment of the protectorates over Nicaragua and Panama was the conclusion in 1937 of a new treaty with Mexico abrogating Article 8 of the Gadsden Treaty of 1853.[32] This article had guaranteed to the United States the use of a proposed plank-and-rail road across the Isthmus of Tehuantepec for its citizens, its mails, its property, and its troops and had authorized the United States to extend its protection to the route whenever it should feel such protection "sanctioned and warranted by the public or international law." The United States had never availed itself of its privileges under this article, but it was natural that Mexico should feel its terms to be an infringement upon its national independence, and natural too, in the atmosphere of the 1930's, that the United States should accede to its abrogation.

It remains to speak of the relations of the United States with the earliest of all its Caribbean protectorates, the Republic of Cuba. Here, under the Platt Amendment, the United States still possessed a theoretical right of intervention, which it had not exercised, however, since 1923. The elections of 1924 brought to the presidency Gerardo Machado (1924-1933), who at first won considerable acclaim for conducting an honest and efficient government,[33] but who later trod the dictatorial path so common in republics of that area. Dissatisfaction with his one-man rule was intensified after 1929 by the world depression, which was particularly hard on single-crop countries like Cuba. An open rebellion was suppressed in 1931, but underground resistance continued. By the spring of 1933 the universities and colleges were closed, popular liberties were suppressed, and terrorism was the rule on both sides of the struggle.[34]

This distressing situation led the Roosevelt administration into the single serious deviation from its policy of nonintervention, and such intervention as occurred in Cuba was brief and unaccompanied by the landing of armed forces. Mr. Sumner Welles was sent to Cuba as ambassador, ostensibly to mediate between Machado and his enemies; really, there is reason to think, to secure

Machado's resignation. This he obtained in August, 1933, with the aid of pressure from Cuban army officers. In the following months, by withholding recognition from presidents whom it considered incompetent or untrustworthy, the United States succeeded in bringing about the election of its candidate, Carlos Mendieta, in January, 1934. Thereafter it not only ceased interference but in the following May negotiated a new treaty with the Mendieta government by which the Platt Amendment was abrogated, reserving only the right of the United States to use the naval base at Guantanamo Bay until that right should be set aside by mutual consent.[35] Thus the United States surrendered all claim to financial control of Cuba and all right to intervene in its affairs.

The Fruits of Intervention

It would be pleasant to record that the small republics that had experienced American intervention had thereby become habituated to the practice of settling their political contests by fair and free elections, as President Wilson had perhaps hoped.[36] The facts are otherwise. With American controls removed, there was a rapid drift toward dictatorial government. The chief difference from the earlier period was in the fact that the new constabularies, which had been organized and trained by the United States in Nicaragua, Haiti, and the Dominican Republic with the idea that they should be divorced from politics, became, in two instances at least, more efficient instruments of dictatorship than any before known. Rafael Trujillo and Anastasio Somoza, who quickly emerged as the "strong men" of the Dominican

Republic and Nicaragua respectively, rose to power as commanders of the constabulary. In Haiti, the first post-intervention elected president, Stenio Vincent, took the precaution of exiling the commander of the *Garde d'Haiti* lest he follow the example of Trujillo. In Cuba, where there was no exact counterpart of the constabularies of the other republics, a former army sergeant, Fulgencio Batista, made and unmade presidents until 1940, when he took the office himself for a four-year term. In Panama, revolutions and *coups d'état* occurred often enough to lend variety to politics. American intervention had unquestionably strengthened the financial positions of most of the governments concerned. It had made no appreciable change in political attitudes or habits.

CHAPTER NINE

The Quest for Security ~ ~

THE ADOPTION of the good neighbor policy and the decision in favor of Philippine independence appeared to have written *finis* to the story of American territorial expansion. But unexpected events added a new, though brief, chapter to that narrative. The needs of commercial and military aviation and the international disturbances of the 1930's sent the United States in quest of new landing fields for its airplanes. The perils and necessities of World War II brought under its temporary control land, air, and naval bases in the six continents and the seven seas. A postwar flurry of expansionist sentiment, arising from the supposed requirements of national security, called for the retention of many of the bases built or conquered during the war. The more extravagant of such proposals were not pressed. At the end of 1949 the United States had added a few tiny islands to its possessions, held leases for longer or shorter terms to some dozens of widely distributed bases, exercised a United Nations trusteeship over numerous small but strategically important Pacific islands, and still occupied former island possessions of Japan whose ultimate disposition had not been determined. The spots owned or controlled in these various ways were insignificant in area and population and almost certain to be economic liabilities rather than assets. Their sole value was strategic. The United States held them, as it had taken them, in the interests of national security.

PACIFIC STEPPING STONES

In the same decade in which the United States was surrendering its Caribbean protectorates and granting independence to the Philippines, it was asserting long-forgotten claims to a number of tiny Pacific islands that derived new importance from the coming of the airplane. By the middle 1930's the administration in Washington had become very air-conscious, particularly with reference to the Pacific area, and was doing what it could to encourage American companies to develop trans-Pacific traffic. How far the urge for such development was purely commercial, how far it was stimulated by the thought of future military needs, we can only conjecture, but no prophetic gift was needed to foresee possible trouble with Japan.

For air travel across the Pacific to the Philippines and southern China the United States already had well spaced landing points at Hawaii, Midway, Wake, and Guam. Over this route the China Clipper began regular flights in 1935. But for flights to the southwest Pacific—Australia and New Zealand—the United States possessed no comparable stepping stones. At least, it possessed none unless certain old claims could be made good. New England whalers had busily explored the central Pacific in the first 50 years after American independence. The Wilkes exploring expedition of 1838-1842 had surveyed scores of islands in the same area. Searchers for fertilizer under the Guano law of 1856 (see page 11) had acquired for the United States dozens of small "appurtenances" in tropical Pacific waters. There was, indeed, a time when German and British maps had labeled the central Pacific "American Polynesia." But the American government had attached little importance to such islands and generally had made no objection when they were claimed by other powers. Now a study was undertaken by the State and Navy Departments to determine which of these old claims might be usefully and legitimately reasserted, and as a result certain islands strategically located on the route to the southwest were brought under American control.[1]

The first islands acquired as a fruit of the new policy were Baker, Howland, and Jarvis Islands, all lying near the equator, Baker and Howland southwest, Jarvis south, of Honolulu. All had once been claimed by the United States as guano islands, and although they had subsequently been allowed to pass under British control or influence, the British government made no objection when the United States, in 1935 and 1936, reasserted its claim, occupied each of the hitherto uninhabited islets with four young Hawaiian "colonists" from Honolulu, and assigned them to the Division of Territories and Island Possessions for administration. On none of the islands was there a lagoon for seaplanes. They were large enough to permit the construction of landing strips for land planes—such a strip was built on Howland in 1937 as a possible emergency landing field for the ill-fated aviatrix, Amelia Earhart—but their immediate use was as weather stations. The "colonists" were provided with radio equipment for reporting their meteorological observations, but probably the principal reason for their presence was to protect the American title against infringement by British or other rivals.[2]

The next step toward the southwest was more productive of controversy. Three hundred and fifty miles southeast of Baker and Howland, about three degress below the equator, were Canton and Enderbury—the former an atoll enclosing a lagoon nine miles in length, the latter presenting a relatively level surface two and a half miles long by one mile wide. Canton was an ideal spot for seaplane landings, Enderbury was equally suitable for land planes, and both lay almost on a direct line from Honolulu to French New Caledonia, whence an easy flight could reach either Australia or New Zealand. The Phoenix Islands group, of which Canton and Enderbury were part, had been discovered, it was claimed, by American whalers in the early nineteenth century; they had been explored and mapped by the Wilkes expedition. The only obstacle to their use by the United States was the fact that they were claimed by Great Britain.[3]

The Phoenix Islands were in an area of the Pacific that for many years had been controlled by the British High Commissioner for the Western Pacific, but until 1937 they had not been formally annexed. The American occupation of Baker, Howland, and Jarvis Islands stimulated competitive activity on the part of the British. By an order in council of March 18, 1937 the Phoenix Islands, including Canton and Enderbury, were annexed to the Gilbert and Ellice Islands Colony. In May and June, 1937 astronomical expeditions from the United States and from New Zealand visited Canton to observe a solar eclipse, and some friction between the parties was reported. An informal Anglo-American agreement to preserve the *status quo* was apparently violated by the erection of a New Zealand radio station on Canton. Not to be outdone, the United States landed "colonists" from Hawaii on Canton and Enderbury on March 6 and 7, 1938. A few days previously, on March 3, President Roosevelt had ordered that the two islands be "reserved, set aside and placed under the control and jurisdiction of the Secretary of the Interior for administrative purposes."[4] The President's secretary told reporters: "The sole reason for the action is commercial aviation. It has nothing to do with war or war plans." He added that the conflicting claims of the United States and Great Britain would "undoubtedly . . . be adjusted amicably."[5]

The British government preserved a calm demeanor in the face of this rather unceremonious foray into its imperial preserves. Prime Minister Chamberlain assured the House of Commons of the validity of British title to the disputed islands, but added that the government intended to propose a settlement which it hoped would "end the controversy in a manner satisfactory to both sides."[6] A tentative agreement was reached in August, 1938, and by an exchange of notes on April 6, 1939 the two governments agreed upon a system of joint control and administration for a period of 50 years, "without prejudice to their respective claims." The islands were to be available for communications and for use as airports for international aviation, but only civil aviation companies incorporated in the United States or in the British Commonwealth might use them for scheduled air service.[7]

In April, 1939 the Department of the Interior made a

contract (subsequently ratified by the British government) with Pan American Airways, leasing to the company certain areas on Canton Island for a station in its service between California and New Zealand. In the following August the Pan American clipper made its first flight by that route, and by 1940 the company had established on Canton Island facilities for fueling, storage, and accommodation of passengers and was maintaining regular schedules between Honolulu and New Zealand. The presence of numerous employees of the company removed the necessity for keeping an official "colony" on Canton. The "colonists" were accordingly withdrawn, and the airport manager was designated field representative of the Department of the Interior. The British government was represented by a deputy administrator.[8]

The "colonists" on the other Equatorial Islands (Baker, Howland, Jarvis, and Enderbury) led a tranquil existence until the outbreak of war with Japan. Early in 1942 the installations on Baker and Howland Islands were shelled, bombed, and machine-gunned by Japanese. Six survivors of the eight Hawaiians on the two islands were rescued by an American destroyer.[9] The air strip on Howland was destroyed by Japanese action; the installations on Jarvis were rendered useless by an American naval vessel to prevent their possible utilization by enemy forces. As reported by the Secretary of the Interior in 1945:

> The Army moved into Baker in force in 1943 and constructed a Marston Mat air strip. . . . The islands of Canton and Enderbury . . . also played an important part in the war. At Canton the air

facilities were greatly expanded and the island will undoubtedly remain an important link in trans-Pacific air routes.[10]

With the return of peace, the presence of numerous civilian personnel at the Canton airport made necessary some provision for civil government and the administration of justice. The joint occupation agreement of 1939 had left all details of administration to be "determined by the two governments in consultation," but no such consultation had taken place. The Division of Territories and Island Possessions, which was responsible for the administration of Canton and Enderbury in behalf of the United States, was reported in 1948 to be at work on a proposal to be submitted to the British government through the State Department as a basis for negotiations "on the details of administration, the establishment of courts, the provision for appellate review of judgments, the definition of crimes, and the application of tort and other law."[11] Meanwhile, Congress had passed a bill to extend to Canton and Enderbury the jurisdiction of the United States District Court for Hawaii.[12] The situation was faintly reminiscent of that projected by the joint occupation of Oregon more than a century earlier.

DEFENSES FOR AN ISLAND EMPIRE—TOO LITTLE AND TOO LATE

While the United States was appropriating these stray bits of land in the Pacific, it was taking only ineffectual measures for the defense of its older possessions. Pearl Harbor and the neighboring area in the island of Oahu were, it is true, being transformed into a powerful fortress, though experience was to show that this stronghold was inadequately defended against attack from the air. In the Aleutians and in all other American possessions west of Hawaii the Washington naval limitation treaty of 1921 prohibited any strengthening of existing fortifications, and after the treaty expired in 1936, Congress hesitated to provide new defenses for Midway, Wake, Guam, and Samoa on the ground that such action might be offensive to Japan! Not until the spring of 1941 did it appropriate a few million dollars for the fortification of these island outposts.[13]

For the defense of the Philippines the United States was responsible during the Commonwealth period, which was to end in 1946. Looking beyond that date, to a time when the Philippines Republic must defend itself, President Manuel Quezon persuaded General Douglas MacArthur, at the expiration of his term as chief of staff, United States Army, to come to the Philippines as military adviser and take charge of the building of a defense force. A ten-year plan, designed to build a trained reserve of 400,000 men that would make the islands "impregnable," bogged down after the first few years. There was a growing realization that only naval and air power, which the Philippines could not provide, could defend them against attack from a neighbor like Japan. Talk of abandoning the independence program[14] was perhaps not taken seriously, but the United States did take seriously, though tardily, its immediate responsibility for defending the islands. On July 26, 1941 President Roosevelt called the armed forces of the Philippines into the service of the United States and placed both them and American land and air contingents in the islands under the command of General MacArthur.[15] In the four months remaining before the break with Japan, air and ground re-enforcements were sent to the Philippines, but here, as in the case of the minor islands, recognition of the imminence of peril had come too late and the increments of force were too insignificant to be effective.

Inadequate preparation for defense bore fruit in disastrous losses. The Japanese followed their initial success at Pearl Harbor with prompt assaults upon Guam, Wake, and the Philippines. Guam was surrendered at once, Wake and the Philippines after heroic defense. In June, 1942 the Japanese occupied Kiska and Attu near the western end of the Aleutian chain. The United States was pushed back to a line running through Dutch Harbor, Midway, Canton, and Samoa. Fortunately, this line held, and from it began the long and costly campaign for recovery of the lost ground.

ATLANTIC OUTPOSTS

Although, for the United States, war actually began in the Pacific, both government and public had felt deeper alarm at developments in Europe than at those in Asia. Europe was far nearer than China, and the prospect of a Europe and Africa under the control of the Nazi-Fascist alliance contained profound threats to American security. Months before Pearl Harbor the United States responded to the danger with lend-lease and other measures designed to give to England, and later to Russia, "all aid short of war" in their battle against Hitlerism. It responded also by making defense agreements with Canada, by leading the other American republics into a system of joint hemisphere defense, and by strengthening its own Caribbean bases (in the Canal Zone, at Guantanamo, in Puerto Rico and the Virgin Islands) and acquiring others through temporary agreements with friendly powers. It is the acquisition of rights to bases outside American territory that concerns us here.

The downfall of France, Denmark, and the Netherlands in the spring of 1940 presented the possibility of German or Italian occupation of their American colonies —an occupation that would have been perilous to the United States and to other American nations. The Secretary of State and the American Congress reiterated the nontransfer principle that had become associated with the Monroe Doctrine—the United States, that is, would not recognize or acquiesce in any transfer of American territory from one non-American power to another.[16] Meeting at Havana in July, the foreign ministers (or their deputies) of the 21 American republics adopted unanimously the Act of Havana, by Article XX of which they agreed that when any American possession of a European state was in danger of being transferred to another sovereignty, the American nations—or in an emergency any one of them—might set up a "provisional administration" in such possession, with the understanding that when the danger had passed, the area in question should either revert to its former status or become independent. Thus dangerous intrusions of non-American powers would be prevented, and yet no American republic would profit territorially from such an emergency.[17] The unanimous adoption of the Act of Havana was a notable victory for the good neighbor policy.

While the foreign ministers were engaged at the

Havana meeting, negotiations were under way between the United States and Great Britain looking to an exchange of bases on British territory in the western hemisphere for some light naval vessels desperately needed by the British for defense against German invasion and German submarines. President Roosevelt was anxious to make the exchange, both as an aid to Britain and as a security measure for the United States. He had first-hand knowledge of the bases offered; being also familiar with "the penurious condition of the native populations of most of the islands," he had no wish to assume permanent responsibility for their upkeep.[18] He therefore preferred leases rather than cession, and leases of the desirable base areas only, rather than of the entire islands. This was exactly what the British offered. Prime Minister Winston Churchill desired to have the transaction appear in the guise of free gifts on each side. American law, however, would not permit the President to give away naval property. Mr. Churchill's preferences and American legal requirements were both taken care of by describing the leases in Newfoundland and Bermuda as granted "freely and without consideration," and the other leases—in the Bahamas, Jamaica, St. Lucia, Trinidad, Antigua, and British Guiana—as granted in exchange for naval and military equipment—specifically, 50 over-age destroyers of 1917 vintage—to be furnished by the United States. The leases were to run for 99 years (though the United States might surrender them at any time within that period) and were to be free of all rent and other charges except compensation, to be mutually agreed upon, for expropriation of, or damage to, private property. Experts named by the two governments were to determine the exact locations and boundaries of the bases and the methods of adjusting the relationships of the British territorial officers and the American authorities within the base areas.

The agreement was embodied in an exchange of notes between the Secretary of State and the British ambassador, September 2, 1940, and reported by President Roosevelt to Congress on the following day. The President described the transaction as "an epochal and far-reaching act of preparation for continental defense in the face of grave danger" and as "the most important action in the reinforcement of our national defense that has been taken since the Louisiana purchase."

In conformity with the spirit of the Act of Havana, Secretary Hull informed the governments of the other American republics that the facilities of the leased bases would be made available to those republics "on the fullest cooperative basis for the common defense of the hemisphere."

The bases leased from Great Britain were the first of several spots on foreign soil that the United States, prior to its entrance into the war, obtained the right to use for defensive purposes. The subjection of Denmark by the Nazis raised the question of the fate of Greenland, a Danish possession, and Iceland, which, though virtually independent since 1918, still owed allegiance to the Danish crown.[19] Greenland, at least, was regarded as lying in the western hemisphere, but the two islands, should they fall under German control, could be equally troublesome to the United States. Both might be used for points of attack against North America. Short of that, they could serve as bases from which to cut the flow of lend-lease war materials to Great Britain. In British or American possession, on the other hand, they would be valuable for the protection of the northern sea routes.

The United States, resisting suggestions that British or Canadian troops occupy Greenland, bided its time until evidence of German aerial activity along the Greenland coast gave it an excuse for acting. On April 9, 1941 Secretary Hull and Henrik de Kauffmann, Danish minister in Washington, signed an agreement by which the United States undertook the defense of Greenland and received in return the right to construct and operate, in Greenland territory or waters, landing fields, seaplane facilities, meteorological and radio installations, and other things needful for their effective maintenance and use. The United States acknowledged the sovereignty of Denmark over the island and agreed that when "the present dangers to the peace and security of the American Continent" should have passed, it would consult with the government of Denmark in regard to the modification or termination of the arrangement. Thereafter either party might terminate the agreement by giving 12 months' notice.

The Danish government, now under Nazi control, immediately repudiated the agreement and recalled the minister. That was to be expected. The United States, regarding the Danish government as acting under duress, paid no attention to the repudiation and continued to recognize de Kauffmann as the representative of Denmark.[20]

The story of Iceland followed a different pattern. After the German occupation of Denmark, the Icelandic Althing (Parliament), declaring the King no longer able to exercise his functions, assumed all powers of government. The establishment of an independent republic was approved by popular vote in 1944. Meantime, in May, 1940, British troops had occupied the island to prevent its seizure by Germany. The British government gave assurances to the United States that the troops would not interfere with the government of Iceland and would be withdrawn after the war. In June, 1941 both the British and the Icelandic governments invited the United States to send troops to Iceland to supplement and eventually to replace the British occupation force, which was needed elsewhere. The terms of the American occupation were defined in an exchange of messages, July 1, 1941, between the Prime Minister of Iceland and the President of the United States. The United States undertook to provide effective defense for Iceland while recognizing its "absolute independence and sovereignty" and promising "to withdraw all their military forces land, air and sea from Iceland immediately on conclusion of present war." On July 7, 1941 President Roosevelt reported the agreement to Congress, with the further information that United States naval forces had on that day arrived in Iceland and that the navy had been instructed to insure the safety of communications between Iceland and the United States.[21]

The acquisition by lease of base areas in the British possessions and the concession of the privilege of establishing bases in Greenland and Iceland did not, strictly speaking, extend the territorial boundaries of the United States. The agreements with Iceland and with the Danish minister in regard to Greenland were for the emergency only. The 99-year leases in the British possessions might be called quasi-permanent; yet they were only leases—they involved no transfer of sovereignty.[22] The subject has been introduced here because the occupation of these bases and of the far greater number held by the United States during World War II subjected both the good faith of the United States and its newly adopted anti-imperialist policy to a severe test at the close of hostilities. Would the United States willingly surrender all the strategic spots beyond its own boundaries that it had occupied during the war or in anticipation of it? Or would it insist, as victorious powers had often done in the past, upon retaining what its statesmen or strategists thought it needed? There would, of course, be a distinction between bases held with the consent of friendly governments and bases wrested from the enemy.

WARTIME BASES IN FOREIGN LANDS

No attempt will be made here to list the military and naval bases on foreign soil occupied by the United States during World War II. From 1940 to 1945 the United States built, it was reliably reported, 434 war bases, of which the great majority were in foreign countries.[23] They were in Panama, Guatemala, Cuba, Peru, Ecuador, and Brazil, where, under inter-American common defense agreements, the United States could properly expect this kind of assistance. They were, as already noted, in the British islands in the Atlantic and Caribbean and in Greenland and Iceland. They were in the Azores, the British Isles, Continental Europe, North Africa, Egypt, Arabia, and India. In the Pacific they were in the Galapagos Islands (Ecuadorian), the Ellice Islands (British), the New Hebrides (Anglo-French), New Caledonia (French), Admiralties (Australian mandate), Solomons (British, and Australian mandate), Marshalls, Carolines, and Marianas (Japanese mandate), Ryukyus, Bonins, and Volcanoes (Japanese), and of course in Australia, New Zealand, and the Philippines. The sun, in those years, never set upon the Stars and Stripes. Many of these bases had been occupied peacefully with the consent of other United Nations powers. Others—for instance, the Solomons, Admiralties, Philippines, and the islands under Japanese sovereignty or mandate—had been taken only after costly and desperate fighting. But whether the bases had cost much or little, the question was sure to arise: What shall be done with those which may be of future strategic importance to the United States?

The United States, through its President or other officers, had given certain pledges that it would not use the war for selfish ends. President Roosevelt and Prime Minister Churchill had declared in the Atlantic Charter (August, 1941):

> First, their countries seek no aggrandizement, territorial or other; second, they desire to see no territorial changes that do not accord with the freely expressed wishes of the peoples concerned.

The Secretary of State and the President had given pledges to Denmark and Iceland respectively that the Greenland and Iceland bases would be surrendered when the emergency had passed. Acting Secretary of State Sumner Welles had denounced as lying Nazi propaganda reports that the United States was seeking permanent footholds in Latin America and had declared that the government had no intention of holding permanently bases established during the war in the western hemisphere.[24] Messrs. Roosevelt, Churchill, and Stalin, meeting at Yalta in February, 1945, had agreed that there should be an international trusteeship system after the war and that under it should be placed areas formerly under League of Nations mandate and territories taken from the enemy powers in the current war, though they left open for future consultation the question of just what areas and territories in those categories should be placed under trusteeship.[25] President Roosevelt, furthermore, had talked much of the establishment of international military, naval, and air bases, from which a future United Nations police force might patrol the world and preserve the peace. Plainly the principles that the United States had professed during the war were contrary to the appropriation of strategic bases for nationalistic ends.

On the other side of the question were ordinary human emotions, practical considerations, and the arguments of "practical" men. The man in the street reacted negatively to the proposal that the United States surrender to an international trusteeship islands it had taken at the cost of much blood and treasure. Why lower the flag so spectacularly placed on the Iwo Jima mountain top?[26] To a leading American devotee of the science of geopolitics it seemed plain that the United States, in pursuit of its proper policy toward Europe and eastern Asia, should retain naval and air bases in Greenland, Iceland, and Dakar—which he assumed could be accomplished through leases. It should also, he believed,

Reproduced by permission from John C. Campbell *et al., The Unite*
for the Council o

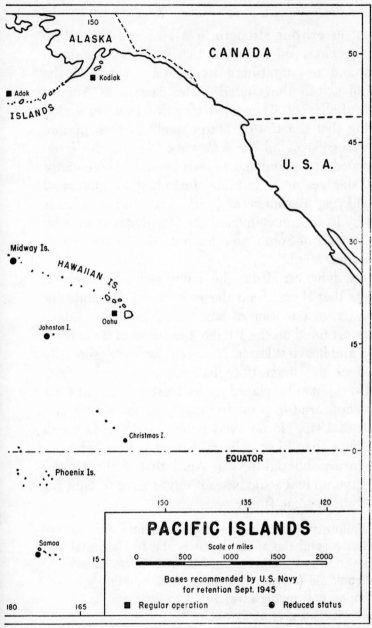

PACIFIC ISLANDS

Scale of miles

0   500   1000   1500   2000

Bases recommended by U.S. Navy
for retention Sept. 1945

■ Regular operation   ● Reduced status

States in World Affairs, 1945-1947 (New York: Harper & Brothers
Foreign Relations, 1947).

augment its existing strength in Alaska and Hawaii by acquiring bases on some of the Japanese mandated islands and re-establishing its military power in the Philippines.[27] In the United States Senate in August, 1944 McKellar of Tennessee introduced a resolution declaring that the United States ought to seek permanent possession of all the following islands: the Japanese-owned and mandated islands between the equator and 30 degrees north latitude, including Formosa and the Ryukyus; Bermuda and all West Indian islands owned by European countries; the Galapagos Islands off the west coast of South America near the Pacific end of the Panama Canal.[28]

It was, however, from the navy and its friends in Congress that there came the most vocal demands for the permanent retention of bases, and the navy's attention was centered on the Pacific, the scene of its hardest fighting and heaviest losses. Naval circles were especially alarmed at the suggestion that the mandated islands taken from Japan be placed under trusteeship, and their protests appeared in print frequently in the spring and summer of 1945. No one was better qualified to speak for the navy than Fleet Admiral Ernest J. King, who declared in a public address in April that if the United States gave up its Pacific bases it might have to fight for them again in some future war.

> Failure to maintain these bases essential for our defense [said the admiral] raises the fundamental question—how long can the United States afford to continue a cycle of fighting and building and winning and giving away, only to fight and build and win and give away again?[29]

Responding to the navy's desires, a subcommittee of the House of Representatives Naval Affairs Committee framed a report, published in August, 1945, recommending that in the interest of its own security, the security of the western hemisphere, and the peace of the Pacific the United States should retain naval bases or anchorages or seaplane bases in the Marshalls, Carolines, Marianas, Ryukyus, Bonins, and Kuriles (all Japanese), in the Philippines, in the Solomons and Admiralties (British, and Australian mandate), in New Caledonia (French), and in the New Hebrides (French and British condominium). Demanding "at least dominant control" of the former Japanese-owned and mandated islands, the subcommittee declared furthermore that the United States should be given "full title" to American bases "constructed on island territories of Allied Nations."

> Those other nations are not capable of defending such islands [said the report]; . . . As these bases are links in our chain of security, and no chain is stronger than its weakest link, we cannot permit any link to be in the hands of those who will not or cannot defend it.[30]

The subcommittee's proposals represented the outside claims in the central and western Pacific. About bases in other directions there was less public discussion but perhaps no less interest in high circles in Washington. A future war with any north European power was visualized as involving long-range bomber attacks across the Arctic wastes or by routes that led over Greenland and Iceland. Bases in those islands and in Canada would be desirable. A landing field in the Azores, put at United

States disposal in 1944, had proved most convenient in the later phases of the war in Europe and might be useful again if it could be kept. At Dhahran on the Persian Gulf, King Ibn Saud of Saudi Arabia had graciously given President Roosevelt permission to establish a major base for long-range bombers. The base was nearing completion when the war ended. It was no longer needed as a way-station for B-29's bound for the Far East, but it was conveniently located in relation to American oil concessions in Saudi Arabia and Kuwait and might be valuable if some future war threatened the Middle East. Nearer home, the installations in the Republic of Panama and the Galapagos Islands were considered vitally important for the defense of the Canal. Those in Cuba, Peru, and Brazil were less highly valued.

Well might the people of the United States, as they contemplated the vast reaches of their power in 1945, have behaved, like Horace Walpole's Englishmen of 1763, "with Roman insolence" or with "more haughtiness than an Asiatic monarch." They might, like Walpole, have threatened to burn their Greek and Latin books (if they had had any!)—"those histories of little people." Never before had one nation developed such enormous power or won so many impressive victories in such widely scattered corners of the globe. Had the United States been sufficiently anxious to retain all the bases that appealed to the eyes of the strategists, it could have done so, at a price, and thus have attained a position of world domination. The price would have been the cost of upkeep of a great military establishment, the violation of pledges and professed principles, and boundless ill will on all sides. The United States would then have deserved the charge of "imperialism," with all the sinister connotations of that term, that the Russians and their satellites were soon to make against it without justification.

The United States had no yearning for world domination. What it wanted was security, and for this it was willing, as a compromise, to trust partly to the United Nations, partly to its own greatly reduced military establishment (plus the atom bomb) and to a system of bases very much below the outside proposals of some admirals, senators, and congressmen. American postwar policy with reference to bases may be summarized thus: where bases in the territory of friendly nations were concerned, to retain nothing that could not be kept with the full consent of the sovereign state, and in practice this meant that little was retained; in the case of former Japanese islands and Japanese mandates that had been conquered and occupied by the United States, to keep whatever was considered necessary for American security. The former Japanese mandates became "strategic trust areas." Other Japanese islands, such as the Ryukyus and Bonins, remained under American military occupation pending a treaty of peace, which would presumably give the United States what it wanted.[31]

The compromise was not wholly satisfactory either to the idealists or to the naval and military strategists. But though, on the one hand, it made the United States the keeper of its own security on the Pacific front, on the other, it violated no specific pledges, and it was debatable whether it infringed even the vague and general principles of the Atlantic Charter. It was not, obviously, compatible with full faith in the United Nations as an organ of collective security.

THE MINIMAL REQUIREMENTS OF SECURITY

The postwar military occupation of Germany and Japan entailed the retention for the period of the occupation not only of bases in the occupied countries but also, in the German case, of air bases or landing fields in Great Britain and France. These had no flavor of permanence, and only Communists showed concern about them. Military air traffic to Germany and to Greece, after the decision in 1947 to give military aid to that country, called for the control of landing fields along the way. The United States retained its naval and air installations in the leased bases in Newfoundland, though when Newfoundland joined Canada in 1949, it was understood that the leases would be subject to renegotiation with the Canadian government. The government of Iceland was unwilling to extend the rights of military occupation beyond 1946, and the airport constructed by the United States at Keflavik was turned over to Iceland in October of that year. Iceland agreed, however, that until the United States should have fulfilled its obligations in Germany it might continue to use the airport for its military planes and to maintain the services, facilities, and personnel necessary to care for such planes, though native personnel were to be trained for this service to the greatest extent possible.[32]

In Greenland small contingents of United States troops continued to occupy a few airfields and weather stations. The postwar Danish government approved the agreement made with Minister de Kauffmann in 1941, and although there were intermittent discussions of terminating that agreement, December, 1948 found American air force groups still stationed at two out of an earlier chain of eight weather and communications stations on the west coast of the island.[33]

Arrangements with both Iceland and Greenland were considered less than satisfactory by the American military strategists. Of all the approaches to the United States, that from the northeast was least adequately protected by bases or by reciprocal defense agreements.[34]

In the Azores a military air base constructed by the United States on Santa Maria Island under a 1944 agreement was turned over to Portugal in June, 1947, but a new agreement permitted American aircraft servicing the occupation troops in Germany and Japan to use the facilities of Lagens Airfield on Terceira Island for three years from December 2, 1947, with the possibility that the privilege might be extended for two additional years.[35]

From the Azores, planes bound for either Europe or the Near or Middle East could hop to Marrakech, French Morocco, and thence, after May, 1948, to Mellaha, ten miles from Tripoli in Libya, where Great Britain, the occupying power in this former Italian colony, permitted the United States to reopen a wartime airfield. Although this agreement was announced in January, 1948, it was not until May that 100 technical troops arrived in Tripoli to open the airfield. Though news dispatches emphasized the strategic significance of the Mellaha location, Secretary of Defense Forrestal stated that the field was not "an air base in the military sense," but merely a "way station on a trunk line to Athens." The United States, he said, had no plan for rebuilding an air base system in Africa.[36]

A wartime airfield in Cairo, Egypt, was surrendered to the Egyptian government late in 1946, and the occupying force and movable supplies were transferred to Dhahran, on the Persian Gulf, described as the most important air base in the Middle East. The relations of the United States with the Middle East during the war could probably come nearer justifying charges of "imperialism" than any other feature of its policy. In this oil-rich area, five of the largest American oil companies had investments estimated at $250,000,000 in value. Most promising of the concessions was that held in Saudi Arabia and on the island of Bahrein by the Arabian-American Oil Company (jointly owned by the Texas Company and Standard Oil of California). Dwindling oil reserves in the United States and the Caribbean magnified the importance of Middle Eastern oil as a factor in the national security. Consequently the government sought to control the richer concessions or to ensure the availability of their product for military purposes.[37] During the war Secretary of the Interior Harold Ickes, as Petroleum Administrator for War, had attempted, first, to purchase for the government all or part of the stock of the Arabian-American Oil Company; when the owners refused to sell, he had sponsored a plan for building, at government expense, a pipeline from the Persian Gulf to the Mediterranean. The second plan was defeated by the opposition of American petroleum interests that would not benefit from the pipeline.[38] Either scheme, if carried out, would have made the United States government itself a heavy investor in Middle Eastern properties and have involved it in their protection whenever necessary.

After the war, although the United States was willing to concede to Great Britain primacy of great-power interest in the Middle East,[39] it was still concerned about the security of the American stake in Middle Eastern oil. Consequently, when the surrender of Japan removed the principal reason that had led to King Ibn Saud's gift of air base rights at Dhahran,[40] the army continued, nevertheless, to develop the field at Dhahran into a first-class air base with facilities for the largest bombing planes. The agreement with Saudi Arabia was not made public, but information divulged through the press indicated that, unless the contract was extended, the base was to be turned over to Saudi Arabia in March, 1949, though with preferential rights for the United States thereafter.[41] Negotiations for a renewal of the agreement or extension of American rights, conducted in the spring of 1949, were shrouded in secrecy. Though it was stated unofficially that the conversations were "going smoothly" and were "virtually completed," no announcement of their completion was issued.[42] The Dhahran question had apparently become snarled in the tangled web of middle eastern politics. As of June, 1950, the United States was still privileged to use the base but without assurance as to how long the privilege might continue.

Any plans that the United States may have had for guarding its northern frontier by means of permanent air bases in Canada encountered Canadian resistance to any measure that might suggest impairment of its sovereignty. The two nations agreed to continue their wartime collaboration "for peacetime joint security purposes" with "mutual and reciprocal availability of military, naval and air facilities" to be agreed upon in specific instances. This principle neither permitted the United States to establish bases in Canada nor obligated the Canadian government to provide such bases as the United States might need. There were, however, joint weather stations and a joint base at Churchill on Hudson's Bay.[43]

To the southward the United States had, by the end of 1946, returned three air bases to Cuba, an air base to Peru, and to Brazil its wartime naval base and its several air bases in that country, including the great airport at Parnamirim which, at the height of its wartime activity, had handled an average of 800 planes a day.[44] Less willingly it had given up bases in the Galapagos Islands and Panama which some military men deemed essential for the defense of the Panama Canal. Negotiations looking to the retention of an army air base on Seymour Island, in the Galapagos, failed to effect their object and on July 1, 1946 the base was returned to Ecuador, though a small group of army technicians remained to help in keeping the base in serviceable condition.[45]

Panama furnished perhaps the most exacting test of the postwar good neighbor policy. There, in the spirit of the Inter-American agreements for common defense and of the 1936 treaty with the United States, Panama had, in May, 1942, made available 134 sites in its territory for the defense of the canal. The United States desired to retain the use of a few of these that were especially well located for canal defense, and after 16 months of negotiation the two governments agreed upon 5-year leases for 13 bases and a 10-year lease for a fourteenth, the heavy bomber base at Rio Hato, 50 miles southwest of Panama City. Denunciations of "Yankee imperialism" and a riotous strike of students of the National University so affected the members of the Panama National Assembly that they voted unanimously for rejection of the agreement. Thus the representatives of some 600,000 Panamanians vetoed a program thought essential to the safety not only of the 140,000,000 people of the United States but of all the American republics, including Panama itself. In an effective refutation of the charge of "Yankee imperialism," the United States government announced that it would take immediate steps for the evacuation of all bases in Panama outside the Canal Zone, adding: "Failure to conclude an agreement will not, of course, affect the normal friendly relations between the two countries."[46]

In the central and western Pacific, meanwhile, the armed services had moderated their demands. A turn toward economy in the United States, a reluctance on the part of other governments to surrender their strategic island possessions, and the prospective development of very long-range aircraft (such as the B-36), combined to persuade the military and naval spokesmen that they could be content with fewer bases than they had at first thought necessary. Outside of territory either American or Japanese (including the mandates), the navy eventually asked for bases only in the Philippines and in the island of Manus.[47]

Manus lies in the Admiralty Islands just north of New Guinea and was included in Australia's New Guinea mandate. Taken by the Japanese early in the war, it was reconquered by the United States and became a major staging base for the campaign against the Philippines. The cost to the United States of building up and equipping the base was put by some accounts as high as $250,000,000,[48] and the navy in particular was loath to give it up after the war. Australia was unwilling to surrender the island to the United States but would not object to sharing the use of the base with the United States navy, provided that British Commonwealth navies might have reciprocal rights to use United States bases in the northern Pacific. Discussions of the Manus question were reported in the press over a period of many months[49] but apparently never resulted in a mutually satisfactory solution. Eventually the base was taken over by Australia, but Prime Minister Evatt informed the Australian parliament that United States naval forces would use it in an emergency "and Australia would use United States bases in the Pacific area."[50]

The Philippine legislature, it will be recalled, had rejected the first independence act passed by Congress because, among other objectionable features, it had reserved to the United States the right of holding military and naval bases in the islands. The act finally accepted had omitted mention of military bases and made retention of naval bases a subject for negotiation between the two governments. The war had brought its lessons to both the United States and the Philippines—to the United States, the importance of the Philippines as its first line of defense in the Pacific; to the Philippines, the inability of a small state to defend itself against a powerful aggressor. Both governments—the Philippines attained in-

dependence, as originally planned, on July 4, 1946[51]—
were ready to adopt cooperative measures for security.
The United States at first asked for 70 land, naval, and
air bases in the Philippines but subsequently reduced

BASES U. S. OBTAINS IN THE PHILIPPINES

Under the 99-year agreement of March 14, 1947,
the army will maintain its principal establishments
at Fort Stotsenberg and Clark Field (A), while the
navy will have operating areas at Subic Bay, Sangley
Point, Guiuan, and Tawi Tawi (B). A portion of the
Manila port area will be available to both army and
navy. Smaller bases will include installations at Baguio and on Palawan (C). Later others will be
developed at Aparri and on Mactan Island (D). *New
York Times,* March 15, 1947 (by permission).

the number to 23. President Roxas of the Philippines was quite willing to lease the necessary bases but insisted on concessions in certain details, especially that the military establishments be remote from centers of population and that extraterritorial rights for Americans be limited to the base areas. These wishes were for the most part met by the United States, and on March 14, 1947 President Roxas and United States Ambassador Paul V. McNutt signed an agreement by which the United States received the right to occupy and use 23 base areas in the Philippines for 99 years. The principal army and air force installation was to be at Fort Stotsenberg and the neighboring Clark Field in central Luzon. The navy retained its old footholds at Sangley Point, Cavite, and at Subic Bay northwest of Manila, but apparently planned its more important installations in the Samar and Leyte area and at Tawi Tawi in the extreme south. Other reservations were at Aparri on the north coast of Luzon, Baguio, Mactan Island between Cebu and Mindanao, and in Palawan in the southwest.

The Philippines retained the right to exercise jurisdiction over all offenses committed outside the base areas "unless in the performance of specific military duty or in cases involving only Americans." Assurances were given that the United States would remove from the Philippines all troops not needed to man the bases and to constitute a small military mission. The agreement provided that in the interest of international security the bases might be made available to the Security Council of the United Nations.[52]

There remained the problem of Japan's former possessions and mandated territories. The surrender terms dictated to Japan from Potsdam had limited her sovereignty to the four principal Japanese islands and such minor islands as the victors might determine. By other declarations and agreements Formosa and Manchuria were to be restored to China, Korea was to be independent, and the Soviet Union was to receive southern Sakhalin and the Kurile Islands. Nothing had been said of the Ryukyus (Okinawa), the Bonins and Volcanoes (Iwo Jima), or the mandated Marshalls, Carolines, and Marianas, all of which United States forces had either wrested from Japan or occupied after Japan's surrender. That these strategically important islands must not be returned to Japan all were agreed, but should they be annexed by the United States or placed under international trusteeship? American naval and military men would certainly have preferred outright annexation—if not of all, at least of those that appeared most suitable for military or naval bases—but the United States and its partners in the United Nations had forsworn territorial aggrandizement as an object of the war, and President Roosevelt and Secretary Hull had committed the government to the support of a system of international trusteeships for former mandated territories and territory conquered from the enemy. The United States could hardly contravene its own declared principles by annexing the mandated islands. It might, however, find a way to adjust the trusteeship arrangement to the demands of its own security.

The formula for international trusteeship was worked out at the San Francisco Conference on International Organization, April 25 to June 26, 1945.[53] It was largely the work of the United States delegation and embodied a compromise between the views of the State Department and those of the army and navy. Ordinary trusteeships, corresponding generally to the League of Nations mandates, were to be under the authority of the General Assembly of the United Nations, but Articles 82 and 83 of the new Charter provided that "strategic areas" might be designated in any trust territory and that all functions of the United Nations relating to such areas should be exercised under the authority of the Security Council. Since each great power had a veto in the Security Council, the United States, if it should become the administering authority in a strategic area trusteeship, could block any move in that body which it thought prejudicial to its security.

The San Francisco Conference, however, dealt only in general principles. It made no attempt to assign trusteeships; and the Charter, though listing the categories of territories which might be placed under the system, stated expressly: "It will be a matter for subsequent agreement as to which territories in the foregoing categories will be brought under the trusteeship system and upon what terms."[54]

From the time of Japan's surrender onward the administration in Washington assumed that it enjoyed the right to determine the disposition of Japanese islands that had come or might come into its hands. When the United States should have received control of the islands, said a seemingly authoritative dispatch from Washington on the eve of the surrender, the administration would "decide whether to place any or all of those islands under the control of the Trusteeship Council of the new United Nations security league."[55] Later President Truman declared the United States would insist on being sole trustee for "islands conquered by our forces and considered vital to this country's future security," whereas other islands not considered vital would be placed under U.N. trusteeship "to be ruled by a group of countries named by the UNO."[56]

The army and navy were still not reconciled to the trusteeship solution, even under the strategic area formula, and in their preference for annexation they had the support of many senators and representatives. On the other hand, men and groups with faith in the United Nations were pressing for a definite acceptance of the trusteeship plan, and American delegates in the U.N. General Assembly, which was debating trusteeship proposals from other powers, complained to Washington that they were embarrassed by the failure of their government to take a stand in the matter.[57]

At length, on November 6, 1946 the President announced that the United States was

> prepared to place under trusteeship, with the United States as the administering authority, the Japanese Mandated Islands and any Japanese Islands for which it assumes responsibilities as a result of the second World War.

Simultaneously the President released a draft trusteeship agreement, said (like the original strategic area formula) to represent a compromise between the State, War, and Navy Departments, for the former Japanese mandated islands. It designated the entire area of the Marianas, Carolines, and Marshalls—some 2,500 miles from east to west and 1,200 miles from north to south—a strategic area over which the United States, as the administering authority, should have "full powers of administration, legislation, and jurisdiction." The United States accepted full responsibility for promoting the welfare of the inhabitants of the islands (about 50,000 persons) and their progress toward self-government, but it reserved the right to establish bases and erect fortifications in the trust territory and to unite it for fiscal, customs, or administrative purposes with other territories under United States jurisdiction. The United States also reserved the right to define the extent to which the Trusteeship Council (acting for the Security Council) might exercise the prerogatives of visit and investigation in "any areas which may from time to time be specified by it [the United States] as closed for security reasons," and it stipulated that the terms of the agreement should "not be altered, amended or terminated without the consent of the administering authority."[58]

The draft agreement was officially presented to the Security Council by Delegate Warren R. Austin on February 26, 1947. In the meantime, John Foster Dulles, American member of the Trusteeship Committee of the General Assembly, had served notice that if the United Nations did not accept the draft agreement, the United States would continue *de facto* control of the islands.[59] In the debate in the Security Council, Mr. Austin let it be known that though he would not veto any proposed amendment to the draft agreement, he would withdraw the agreement if the Council should adopt an amendment objectionable to the United States. With a few unimportant amendments, accepted by the American delegate, the agreement was approved by the Security

Council on April 2, 1947. Upon its approval by Congress on the following July 19, the agreement went into effect, and the United States became the trustee for what was henceforth known as the Trust Territory of the Pacific Islands—the Marshalls, Carolines, and Marianas, with their 50,000 Micronesian inhabitants. Civil government, though for the time being still under the Secretary of the Navy, replaced the military government that had functioned since the beginning of the American occupation.[*] In the words of one authority, "The United Nations had, on paper, a new international trusteeship, and the U. S. Navy had its Pacific islands, to do with as it wished."[60]

Who should receive the Ryukyus, Bonins, and Volcanoes was a question that would have to be answered in the peace treaty with Japan, if one was ever made.[61] In the meantime they too were in the hands of the United States armed forces.

TERRITORIAL BALANCE SHEET, 1950

In outright territorial possessions, the United States had as yet acquired nothing from the war. It might yet acquire full title to certain islands formerly Japanese, and its position in the Trust Territory of the Pacific Islands was in practice the equivalent of possession. Its interest in the islands of Micronesia and in those that might be taken from Japan was the interest of the strategist, faintly tinged with that of the anthropologist and humanitarian. Certainly it was not economic, for the Pacific islands were unlikely to prove much more profitable than the Caribbean Virgins.

---

[*] For the government of the Trust Territory see Appendix II.

Aside from possessions, the United States had 99-year leases to certain military and naval bases in the Philippines and the British islands on its eastern frontier, and it had a few short-run airfield privileges in such places as Greenland, Iceland, the Azores, Tripoli, and Dhahran. Just what it might have in the way of reciprocal rights to the use of bases in Canada, the other American republics, or the nations of the North Atlantic Pact lay in the realm of military secrecy.[62] In any event, such rights were matters of military strategy and policy, not of territorial expansion.

There were, of course, those who lamented that the United States had not exhibited a more "capacious swallow for territory" and who were anxious to repair the omission. There was, for example, Representative Bertrand W. Gearhart of California, who introduced in the House of Representatives a set of resolutions requesting that Denmark be asked to cede Greenland to the United States, that Iceland be invited to become the forty-ninth state, and that negotiations be opened with Great Britain, France, and such other powers as might be involved, for the purchase of all islands off the coasts of the United States, in the Caribbean, and in the Pacific that might be deemed essential to the defense of the United States, the Panama Canal Zone, and the Philippine Islands. His proposal included, he explained, the acquisition without cost to the United States of all islands formerly owned by, or mandated to, Japan that might be deemed essential to the maintenance of peace in the Pacific.[63] The proposals of this latter-day apostle of manifest destiny were referred to committee and not heard of again.

More formidable was an attempt in 1946, during the

debate on a proposed postwar loan of $3,750,000,000 to Great Britain, to require, as a condition of the loan, that Great Britain make permanent the rights to military, air, and naval bases held under 99-year leases, that it consent to the use of these bases for commercial as well as military purposes, and that it secure for the United States the "peacetime commercial use . . . of other bases built by the United States in the British Empire or in areas controlled by Great Britain." The value of properties and rights thus acquired was to be deducted from Great Britain's World War I debt to the United States![64]

This proposal, introduced by Senator E. W. McFarland of Arizona, received some support in the press[65] and was seriously debated in the Senate. It was defeated by the close margin of 45 votes against, 40 in favor. We may conjecture, however, that many of the 40 supporters of the McFarland amendment were more interested in defeating the loan than in acquiring title to the bases.[66] With this amendment's defeat and with Congress's approval the following year of the Pacific trusteeship agreement, the expansionist impulse generated by World War II had apparently spent itself.

United States-Philippines Relations After World War II ~ ~

THE JAPANESE, after completing their conquest of the Philippines in 1942, set up a Philippine government under José P. Laurel as president and on October 15, 1943 inaugurated a so-called Philippines Republic. This collaborationist government collapsed after the return of American forces in the fall of 1944. Meanwhile the American Congress, by a joint resolution of June 29, 1944, had authorized the President to advance the date of Philippine independence to a day prior to July 4, 1946, if he considered it expedient to do so. It had authorized him, by the same resolution, to obtain by negotiation with the president of the Philippines such bases in addition to those provided for by the Tydings-McDuffie Act as he might "deem necessary for the mutual protection of the Philippine Islands and of the United States."[1]

President Manuel Quezon of the Philippine Commonwealth, who had left the Philippines with General Douglas MacArthur, died in the United States in August, 1944, and Vice President Sergio Osmeña became president of the Philippine "government in exile." He returned to the Philippines with General MacArthur and served as president until May 28, 1946, when he was succeeded by Manuel Roxas, his successful rival in the April elections.

President Truman had chosen not to advance the date for independence set by the Tydings-McDuffie Act. Consequently the independence of the Philippines was proclaimed on July 4, 1946, and Roxas thus became the first president of the independent Philippines. In March, 1947 President Roxas signed agreements with the United States by which the latter secured the right for 99 years to maintain bases in the Philippines (see pages 361-362) and promised for 5 years from the date of independence to supply arms, munitions, technical advice, and training for the armed forces of the Philippines.

As important for the Philippines as these military arrangements were two acts passed by the United States Congress and signed by President Truman on April 30, 1946. Known officially as the Philippine Rehabilitation Act of 1946 and the Philippine Trade Act of 1946, they were popularly referred to as the Tydings and Bell Acts, respectively.[2] The Rehabilitation Act provided for rehabilitation and repair of war damage in the Philippines at United States expense to a total amount of $620,000,000—$400,000,000 to be paid for war damage claims of individuals and associations, as determined by a commission created for that purpose; $120,000,000 to be allocated by the President of the United States for the rehabilitation and repair of public property, including buildings, public roads, harbor facilities, means of inter-island navigation, and so on; $100,000,000 in surplus property to be used for similar purposes.

There was, however, one important string attached to these seemingly generous grants. Section 601 of the act stipulated that no payment in excess of $500 should be made to any individual or association until the Presidents of the United States and the Philippines should have entered into an executive agreement defining trade relations between the two countries and until that agreement should have become effective. The nature of this proposed agreement was set forth in the Philippine Trade (Bell) Act.

The terms of the Bell Act were to be put into effect by an executive agreement between the two presidents, supported by necessary legislation by the Philippines congress and by an amendment to the constitution of the Philippines. When thus made effective, the Bell Act would supplant the trade provisions of the Tydings-McDuffie Act of 1934, under which the Philippines was to be treated in every way as a foreign country after July 4, 1946. Under the new legislation there was to be complete free trade between the United States and the Philippines until July 3, 1954, except that reasonably generous quotas were set upon importation from the Philippines of sugar, cordage, rice, cigars, scrap tobacco, coconut oil, and shell or pearl buttons. Over a 20-year period from 1954 to 1974 the duty-free quotas of cigars, tobacco, coconut oil, and buttons were to be reduced 5 per cent annually, reaching zero in 1974. On other commodities, of which sugar was the most important, United States tariff duties would apply, beginning with 5 per cent of the regular rates in 1954 and increasing by 5 per cent annually to reach the full rate in 1974. After 1974 products of the Philippines would be treated like those of any other foreign country.

Thus the Bell Act allowed an adjustment period of 20 years (1954-1974) compared with the 5 years previously allowed by the Tydings-McDuffie Act (see pages 306,

309). Furthermore, whereas the Tydings-McDuffie Act had forbidden the Philippines to levy duties on imports from the United States during the adjustment period, the Bell Act expressly provided that from 1954 to 1974 the Philippines tariff rates should be progressively levied upon imports from the United States, beginning at 5 per cent of the regular rate and rising to the full rate in 1974. The Bell Act, therefore, was less one-sided than its predecessor and placed the Philippines in a better position than formerly to experiment with the stimulation of home industries and to seek out non-American markets for its staple products.

In other respects the act was less than generous to the Philippines. Its trade provisions would take effect only when the two presidents had signed the proposed executive agreement and when the Philippines congress had legislated accordingly. The act specified that the agreement must secure for American citizens and corporations equality with citizens of the Philippines and corporations owned or controlled in the Philippines, in the exploitation of the natural resources of the islands. This stipulation necessitated an amendment of the Philippines constitution, which had expressly reserved the exploitation of natural resources to citizens of the Philippines or to corporations or associations at least 60 per cent of whose capital was owned by such citizens. The Philippines must agree, furthermore, that the value of Philippine currency (the peso) in relation to the dollar would not be changed during the life of the agreement and that no restriction would be placed upon the transfer of funds from the Philippines to the United States, except with the consent of the President of the United

States. The agreement was also to provide that for at least 5 years a specified number of Americans (not less than 1,000) be permitted to enter the Philippines annually without regard to any numerical limitations imposed by law.[3]

Either party might terminate the agreement on five years' notice; if either president determined and proclaimed that acts of the other party nullified the agreement, he might terminate it on six months' notice. The President of the United States might also suspend the agreement if he found, after consultation with the President of the Philippines, that the Philippines or any subdivision thereof was discriminating against United States citizens or business enterprise. In such case the agreement might be restored if the discrimination ceased, or terminated entirely if it did not cease after a reasonable time.

These features of the Bell Act might be characterized as a latter-day manifestation of dollar diplomacy. Their evident intent was to open the Philippines to American capital as a price for the act's relatively liberal trade provisions. Acceptance of the terms of the Trade Act was also a prerequisite to the enjoyment by the Philippines of the full benefits of the Rehabilitation Act. Congress, it seems, was disposed to drive a hard bargain.

The Philippines had little choice but to accept the American terms. The required executive agreement was signed on July 4, 1946, the day of Independence, but was not declared in effect till December 18.[4] The Philippines congress passed the necessary legislation, including the constitutional amendment required to give Americans "parity" with Filipinos in the use and development of insular natural resources. The amendment, though strongly attacked by enemies of President Roxas, was approved by a popular vote of about six to one in a special election in March, 1947.[5] It was appended to the constitution as an ordinance, to be effective during the lifetime of the executive agreement of July 4, 1946, but in no event beyond July 3, 1974.[6]

By accepting the terms of the Trade Act, the Philippines made sure of receiving all the benefits of the Rehabilitation Act. To the payments from this source were added other streams of United States dollars flowing into the Philippines—payments to United States armed forces in the islands; payments of various kinds to loyal Filipino veterans; loans from the Reconstruction Finance Corporation, and so on. United States government expenditures in the islands during 1946, for example, totaled 672,000,000 pesos as compared with proceeds from exports amounting to only 128,000,000 pesos.[7] Such expenditures were expected to continue high through 1950, after which they would rapidly taper off. In the meantime the Philippines differed from other war-devastated countries—in fact, from most of the world outside the United States—in possessing abundant dollar exchange.[8] One serious problem for the Philippines was the use to be made of this temporary wealth in dollars. Only if used to a large extent to finance importation of capital goods could it contribute to a permanent rise in the Philippine standard of living.

To study this and related problems the governments of the United States and the Philippines set up in December, 1946 a Joint Philippine-American Finance Commission. This body found that a very small share of the dollar exchange was being expended for capital goods—60,000,000 out of 680,000,000 pesos in 1946. The commission recommended, among other reforms, restrictions upon the importation of luxuries in order to divert the use of exchange to the purchase of capital goods, and the establishment of a central bank and a managed monetary system.[9]

Acting upon the commission's recommendations, the Philippines government restricted luxury imports through quotas set by an Import Control Board and through new internal taxes on luxuries. It also established a central bank with a capital of 10,000,000 pesos ($5,000,000) whose declared functions were to guard the monetary stability of the Philippines, to preserve the international value of the peso and its convertibility into other currencies, and to promote a rising level of production, employment, and real income.[10]

By the close of 1949 import and exchange controls were arousing some alarm among American firms interested in the Philippines market.[11] It was hoped, in the Philippines, that in the long run these restrictions would stimulate local productivity, help to balance exports against imports as United States government payments dwindled, and ultimately assist the Philippines in adjusting to the gradual loss of the free American market.

In the meantime President Roxas, who had engineered the adoption of the legislation and the constitutional amendment required to implement the Bell Act, had died of a heart attack on April 15, 1948 and had been succeeded by Vice President Elpidio Quirino. Quirino was re-elected in November, 1949 over José P. Laurel, one-time anti-American politician and "puppet" president of the Philippines during the Japanese occupation. Reports of fraud, intimidation, and violence in this election aroused fears that Philippine democracy was destined to follow the Latin American pattern rather than that of the United States.

President Quirino, like his predecessor, faced difficult postwar problems. The progress of rehabilitation had been slow and productivity had by no means attained its prewar level. American capital was shy of making further investments in the Philippines. The temporary affluence resulting from the artificial flood of American dollars was in danger of vanishing without leaving a substantial residue. Agrarian unrest, especially in the provinces of central Luzon, took the form of armed resistance to constituted authority—the Hukbalahap revolt.[12] The revolt, whether Communist-inspired or not, presented a dangerous channel for Communist influence as Communism enveloped more and more of Eastern Asia. Under these circumstances the government of the Philippines necessarily continued to look to the United States for assistance.

The Communist invasion of Southern Korea in June, 1950 brought from President Truman an announcement that the small United States forces in the Philippines would be strengthened and that military assistance to the Philippine government would be accelerated. Two days later (June 29) the President revealed that he was sending an American economic survey mission to the Philippines in response to an earlier invitation from

President Quirino. The 20-man mission, headed by Daniel W. Bell, former Under Secretary of the Treasury, would have as its purpose "to survey the entire Philippine economic situation, to make recommendations on measures of self-help which might be undertaken by the Philippine Government itself, and to make recommendations on ways in which the United States might be helpful."[13]

APPENDIX TWO

Government of the Trust Territory of the Pacific Islands ~ ~

From the termination of Japanese control in the islands of the Trust Territory to July 18, 1947, they were under the military government of the United States Navy. On the date mentioned, which marked the approval of the trusteeship agreement between the United States and the United Nations Security Council, the President delegated to the Secretary of the Navy responsibility for the civil government of the Trust Territory on an interim basis until a civilian department or agency should be designated to exercise permanent supervision. The Trust Territory was placed under a High Commissioner (the Commander-in-Chief of the Pacific Fleet) and a Deputy High Commissioner. The latter had headquarters in Guam, which, though not included in the Trust Territory, served for the time being as the seat of government. The Trust Territory was divided into four sub-areas (Northern Marianas, Western Carolines, Eastern Carolines, and Marshalls), each headed by a governor, and these sub-areas were further divided into seven districts, each under a civil administrator. Naval officers especially trained in island administration and a small staff of civilian experts in such fields as political science, economics, agriculture, and education exercised supervision

over the scattered island population. A system of courts
was created, with a high degree of native participation
at the lower levels. A criminal code and a bill of rights
were promulgated. In the words of the Navy Department's report to the United Nations:

> The administration is based upon the preserva-
> tion of the indigenous governmental systems of
> the inhabitants. Local municipal governments are
> authorized to levy, collect and expend local taxes
> and to make local rules. They assist in the enforce-
> ment of orders from higher authority and are re-
> quired to keep records. . . . It is the expressed
> policy of the Administering Authority to establish
> and foster self-governing communities and to give
> due weight to local customs and traditions in all
> general ordinances and regulations. . . . Where
> the inhabitants have been found to be qualified to
> elect representatives, regularly constituted elections
> have been held. . . . The local inhabitants are
> duly represented by their elected or appointed
> leaders who meet periodically with the Civil Ad-
> ministrators or their representatives to discuss cur-
> rent problems and projected plans, to be instructed
> in the new ordinances and regulations and to be
> delegated definite duties and responsibilities in con-
> nection with the prosecution of the mission of the
> civil administration.[1]

In June, 1947 a committee consisting of the Secretaries of State, War, Navy, and the Interior recommended to the President that the Trust Territory be
transferred to a civilian department at the earliest practicable date. The President transmitted the report to
Congress with the further suggestion that Congress

assure to the inhabitants of the Trust Territory the enjoyment of civil liberties and the largest degree of self-government appropriate to their experience and circumstances. Congress named a joint committee which planned to visit the islands but failed to do so. As of August, 1950 no legislation for the Trust Territory had been enacted. The President, however, had indicated an intention to transfer the Territory to the Department of the Interior within two or three years and had directed the Interior and Navy Departments to prepare for such transfer.[2]

How the Department of the Interior was to provide the necessary transportation and communications for an area covering 5,000,000 square miles of the Pacific Ocean had not been determined. Such services would involve expense that could not possibly be met from the native economy of the islands. Critics of the proposed transfer pointed out that the navy must in any event maintain stations and services in the islands and that assumption of governmental functions by a civilian department would mean a costly duplication of personnel and services.[3]

Citation of Sources and Authorities ~ ~

IN GENERAL, every book referred to is identified bibliographically when first cited in any chapter. The following works, however, are cited so frequently that it seems best to give here the requisite bibliographical data and to cite them by the abbreviated titles indicated wherever they appear in footnotes:

BRIEF CITATION	FULL CITATION
Alaska: Report to U.N. (with year)	*Alaska: Information on the Territory of Alaska Transmitted by the United States to the Secretary-General of the United Nations Pursuant to Article 73 (e) of the Charter.* Prepared by the Department of the Interior in cooperation with the Governor of Alaska (Washington: Department of the Interior, June, 1947: June, 1948; June [?], 1949). Similar reports were submitted by the Department of the Interior for Hawaii, Puerto Rico, and the Virgin Islands of the United States (Washington: Department of the Interior, 1947, 1948, 1949), and by the Navy Department for American Samoa, Guam, and the Trust

BRIEF CITATION	FULL CITATION
	Territory of the Pacific Islands (Washington: Navy Department, 1947, 1948, 1949).
American Samoa: Report to U.N. (with year)	See *Alaska: Report to U.N.*
American Year Book (with year)	*The American Year Book, A Record of Events and Progress* (New York and London: Appleton, Century Co. and Macmillan, annually, 1911——).
Bemis, *Secretaries*	Bemis, Samuel Flagg (ed.), *The American Secretaries of State and Their Diplomacy* (10 vols. New York: Alfred A. Knopf, Inc., 1927-1929).
Cong. Rec. (with number of Congress and session)	United States Congress, *Congressional Record: Containing the Proceedings and Debates of the th Congress, . . .* (Washington: Government Printing Office, 1874——).
For. Rel. (with year and volume)	*Papers Relating to the Foreign Relations of the United States, with the Annual Message of the President to Congress* (Washington: Government Printing Office; annually, 1862 ——).
Guam: Report to U.N. (with year)	See *Alaska: Report to U.N.*

Brief Citation	Full Citation
Hawaii: Report to U.N. (with year)	See *Alaska: Report to U.N.*
19 Howard	See 136 [etc.] U.S.
New International Year Book (with year)	*The New International Year Book: A Compendium of the World's Progress for the Year 1907* (New York: Dodd, Mead & Co., 1908, and annually thereafter).
Puerto Rico: Report to U.N. (with year)	See *Alaska: Report to U.N.*
Richardson, *Messages*	[Richardson, James D. (ed.)], *A Compilation of the Messages and Papers of the Presidents,* . . . (with Additions and Encyclopedic Index by Private Enterprise) (20 vols. New York: Bureau of National Literature, [1917?]).
Stat. at L. (with volume)	*The Statutes at Large of the United States of America from* [the Organization of the government in 1789] *to* ——. *Concurrent Resolutions of the Two Houses of Congress and Recent Treaties, Conventions, and Executive Proclamations* (Boston: Little, Brown & Company, 1845-1873; Washington: Government Printing Office, 1875——).

BRIEF CITATION	FULL CITATION
Statistical Abstract of the United States (with year)	U.S. Bureau of the Census (from 1938; theretofore Bureau of Statistics and Bureau of Foreign and Domestic Commerce), *Statistical Abstract of the United States* (Washington: Government Printing Office, annually, 1875——).
Treaties, Conventions	*Treaties, Conventions, International Acts, Protocols, and Agreements between the United States of America and Other Powers* (Vols. I, II, 1778-1909, edited by W. M. Malloy, Washington: Government Printing Office, 1910; III, 1910-1923, Washington: Government Printing Office, 1923; IV, 1923-1937, Washington: Government Printing Office, 1938).
Trust Territory: Report to U.N. (with year)	See *Alaska: Report to U.N.*
U.S. Code, 1946	*United States Code, 1946 Edition, Containing the General and Permanent Laws of the United States in Force on January 2, 1947* (5 vols. Washington: Government Printing Office, 1947-1948).
136 [etc.] U.S.	*United States Reports: Cases Argued and Adjudged in the Su-*

Brief Citation	Full Citation
	preme Court of the United States (Washington [etc.]: Government Printing Office, [etc.], 1798——).
Virgin Islands: Report to U.N. (with year)	See *Alaska: Report to U.N.*

House and Senate Documents are cited in the usual manner, with number of document, Congress, and session. Annual reports of governors of territories and of the Secretary of the Interior, all published in Washington, are cited by year only.

CHAPTER ONE

1 Alaska is an interesting transitional case, rather hard to classify. It was continental, but it was noncontiguous. Its civilized alien population was inconsiderable, but its remoteness and forbidding climate and topography were obstacles to the flow of population that had Americanized all previously acquired territory. The Alaska purchase treaty, promising citizenship but not incorporation, stood half-way between the earlier treaties, which had promised both, and the treaty of 1898 with Spain, which promised neither. The Supreme Court later held, however, that the purchase treaty plus subsequent legislation had made Alaska an incorporated territory. Statehood was a possibility, as current (1950) agitation assumes. All things considered, Alaska seems to belong on the nonimperialistic side of the fence.

2 Richardson, *Messages*, IX, 3886. Italics inserted.

3 *Congressional Globe*, 41 Cong. 3 Sess., 225; *ibid.*, Appendix, 30.

4 *For. Rel.*, 1894, Appendix II, 144.

5 Richardson, *Messages*, X, 4537-4538.

6 This subject is developed in some detail in Julius W. Pratt, *Expansionists of 1898* (Baltimore: Johns Hopkins Press, 1936), Chap. 1.

7 See Richard Hofstadter, *Social Darwinism in American Thought, 1860-1915* (Philadelphia: University of Pennsylvania Press, 1944).

8 John W. Burgess, *Political Science and Comparative Constitutional Law* (2 vols. Boston: Ginn & Company, 1890), I, 30-39.

9 For Burgess's rejection of his own teaching when it was put into practice by the United States see Pratt, *Expansionists of 1898*, p. 11. Another writer whose ideas likewise pointed to a policy of expansion for civilized states like the United States was the British sociologist, Benjamin Kidd. In his *Social Evolution* (new ed. New York and London: G. P. Putnam's Sons, 1895) he argued that the exigencies of food supply would soon compel the more efficient states (preferably the Anglo-Saxons) to take over and develop the resources of tropical lands.

10 Cf. the following from a speech of Beveridge in the Senate, January 9, 1900: "[God] has made us the master organizers of the world to establish system where chaos reigns. . . . He has made us adepts in government that we may administer government among savage and senile peoples." *Cong. Rec.*, 56 Cong. 1 Sess., 711.

11 Collected in the volume, A. T. Mahan, *The Interest of America*

in Sea Power, Present and Future (Boston: Little, Brown & Company, 1897).

[12] A. T. Mahan, *The Influence of Sea Power upon History, 1660-1783* (Boston: Little, Brown & Company, 1890), p. 83.

[13] A. T. Mahan, *The Interest of America in Sea Power, Present and Future*, pp. 102-103.

[14] H. C. Lodge, "Our Blundering Foreign Policy," *The Forum*, XIX (1895), 8-17.

[15] See Harold and Margaret Sprout, *The Rise of American Naval Power, 1776-1918* (Princeton: Princeton University Press, 1939), Chaps. 12, 13; George T. Davis, *A Navy Second to None* (New York: Harcourt, Brace & Company, 1940), Chaps. 3-6. The new navy had begun with the authorization in 1883 of three steel cruisers and a dispatch boat (the "White Squadron"). From 1883 to 1889 Congress had authorized some 30 additional vessels, including the second-class battleships *Maine* and *Texas*.

[16] Pratt, *Expansionists of 1898*, Chap. 5 and pp. 200-215.

[17] The speeches of Lodge and Draper are printed in *Cong. Rec.*, 53 Cong. 3 Sess., 3082-3084, and 53 Cong. 2 Sess., 1844-1849, respectively.

[18] *Ibid.*, 52 Cong. 2 Sess., 997-999. A cartoonist's contribution to this expansionist campaign appeared in the San Francisco *Call* of January 28, 1893. Captioned "Uncle Sam Catches the Ripe Fruit," it depicted Uncle Sam seated under an apple tree with the Hawaiian apple falling into his hat, while Canada, Mexico, Haiti, Cuba, and Samoa still hung upon the boughs, obviously awaiting a similar fate.

[19] Allan Nevins (ed.), *Letters of Grover Cleveland, 1850-1908* (Boston: Houghton Mifflin Company, 1933), pp. 491-492.

[20] Pratt, *Expansionists of 1898*, p. 204. Among the leading supporters of Cleveland's Hawaiian policy was the independent Republican ("Mugwump") Carl Schurz, who, as a senator, had assailed Grant's Santo Domingo treaty over 20 years earlier. In an article entitled "Manifest Destiny," in *Harper's Magazine* for October, 1893, Schurz took issue with Mahan, denied that Hawaii would have military value for the United States, asserted that it was unfit for statehood and could not be ruled as a dependency without endangering the structure and ideals of American government. He reaffirmed his conviction that democracy could not flourish in the tropics and that expansion in that direction would lead to "a future of turbulence, demoralization, and final decay."

CHAPTER TWO

[1] Herbert Croly, *Marcus Alonzo Hanna, His Life and Work* (New York: The Macmillan Company, 1912), p. 278.

[2] Claude Moore Fuess, *Carl Schurz, Reformer (1829-1906)* (New York: Dodd, Mead & Company, 1932), p. 349; Julius W. Pratt, *Expansionists of 1898* (Baltimore: Johns Hopkins Press, 1936), p. 215.

[3] *Blackwood's Edinburgh Magazine,* CLXIII (April, 1898), 563-565.

[4] Pratt, *Expansionists of 1898,* pp. 252-259.

[5] For details of the annexation of Hawaii under McKinley see *ibid.,* pp. 215-221, 225, 317-326; Lester B. Shippee and Royal B. Way, "William Rufus Day," in Bemis, *Secretaries,* IX, 33-40; Sylvester K. Stevens, *American Expansion in Hawaii, 1842-1898* (Harrisburg: Archives Publishing Company, 1945), Chap. 11.

[6] Curiously enough, Secretary of State Sherman was not informed of the negotiations till they were completed. Entrusted to Assistant Secretary William R. Day, they were actually carried on by John W. Foster, who, as Secretary of State, had negotiated the abortive treaty of 1893. Sherman, who had denied, in good faith, to the Japanese minister that annexation was under consideration, was placed in an embarrassing position. Lorrin A. Thurston, famous for his part in the Revolution of 1893 and one of the treaty commissioners of that year, was again on hand as a member of a three-man Hawaiian commission.

[7] Thomas A. Bailey, "Japan's Protest Against the Annexation of Hawaii," *Journal of Modern History,* III (1931), 46-61.

[8] For the final act in the annexation of Hawaii see pp. 74-76. The war with Spain, which provided the necessary impetus to complete the annexation of Hawaii, defeated a new proposal for purchase of the Danish West Indies. Since March, 1897 Senator Lodge had been urging the purchase of these islands. He had secured the President's approval, and the Danish government had consented to sell them for $5,000,000. The approach of war, however, led that government to withdraw its consent to the transaction, which, under the circumstances, might be considered a "diplomatic discourtesy to Spain." Charles Callan Tansill, *The Purchase of the Danish West Indies* (Baltimore: Johns Hopkins Press, 1932), pp. 209-215.

[9] Elbert J. Benton, *International Law and Diplomacy of the Spanish-American War* (Baltimore: Johns Hopkins Press, 1908), p. 22. From 1891 to 1894 an agreement between the United States and Spain permitted reciprocal concessions in tariff duties on certain goods imported from Cuba into the United States and from the United States into Cuba. H. Parker Willis, "Reciprocity with Cuba," *Annals of the*

American Academy of Political and Social Science, XXII (1903), 129-147.

[10] Horace Edgar Flack, *Spanish-American Diplomatic Relations Preceding the War of 1898* (Baltimore: Johns Hopkins Press, 1906), p. 10.

[11] See Marcus M. Wilkerson, *Public Opinion and the Spanish-American War: A Study in War Propaganda* (Baton Rouge: Lousiana State University Press, 1932); Joseph E. Wisan, *The Cuban Crisis as Reflected in the New York Press (1895-1898)* (New York: Columbia University Press, 1934). United States senators who visited Cuba in March, 1898 (several of them, it is true, on the invitation of Mr. Hearst), declared that there was no exaggeration in the newspaper descriptions of the miseries of the concentration camps. *Cong. Rec.,* 55 Cong. 2 Sess., 3128-3132, 3162-3165, 3280-3284.

[12] The attitude of business and the churches toward intervention in Cuba is elaborated in Pratt, *Expansionists of 1898,* pp. 232-252, 279-289.

[13] See especially *ibid.,* pp. 250-251; Edwin F. Atkins, *Sixty Years in Cuba* (Cambridge: Author, 1926), pp. 209, 212, 274, *et passim.*

[14] Pratt, *Expansionists of 1898,* p. 211; *Cong. Rec.,* 55 Cong. 2 Sess., 2919, 3284, 3295, 3413. At least one senator (Gallinger of New Hampshire), on the other hand, believed annexation preferable to independence (*ibid.,* 3131). In October, 1897 Captain Mahan published in *Harper's Magazine* an article entitled "Strategic Features of the Caribbean Sea and the Gulf of Mexico." Though saying nothing of annexation, he made it plain that Cuba was the strategic "key" to the Caribbean.

[15] Wisan, *The Cuban Crisis,* pp. 449-454.

[16] The story of the diplomatic maneuverings that preceded the Spanish-American War is related in all the diplomatic histories of the United States. An especially good account is found in Bemis, *Secretaries,* in the sketches of Richard Olney by Montgomery Schuyler (Vol. VIII) and William Rufus Day by Lester B. Shippee and Royal B. Way (Vol. IX). See also French Ensor Chadwick, *The Relations of the United States and Spain: Diplomacy* (New York: Scribner's, 1909). The international legal angles are treated in the studies by E. J. Benton and H. E. Flack, previously cited.

[17] Richardson, *Messages,* XIV, 6254-6273.

[18] *Literary Digest,* XVI (1898), 367.

[19] *Cong. Rec.,* 55 Cong. 2 Sess., 2916-2919.

[20] *For. Rel.,* 1898, 711-713.

[21] Shippee and Way in Bemis, *Secretaries,* IX, 89-95; Orestes Ferrara, *The Last Spanish War: Revelations in "Diplomacy"* (New York: The Paisley Press, 1937).

²² *For. Rel.,* 1898, 726-727.

²³ Richardson, *Messages,* XIV, 6281-6292.

²⁴ See especially Flack, *Spanish American Diplomatic Relations;* Benton, *International Law and Diplomacy,* p. 108; James Ford Rhodes, *The McKinley and Roosevelt Administrations, 1897-1909* (New York: The Macmillan Company, 1922), pp. 61-65.

²⁵ See especially speech of Senator Daniel of Virginia, *Cong. Rec.,* 55 Cong. 2 Sess., 3880-3887. The debate on McKinley's message and the Cuban resolutions is found in *ibid.,* 3698-4064.

²⁶ The large minority vote in the Senate is not to be construed as opposition to intervention but as dislike of the form of the resolutions. The Senate had originally passed its own resolutions by a vote of 67 to 21.

²⁷ *Cong. Rec.,* 55 Cong. 2 Sess., 3899, 3988, 4012. Senator Teller's amendment was actually offered in the Senate by Senator C. K. Davis, chairman of the Foreign Relations Committee. That it was introduced at the instance of a representative of the Cuban *junta* in New York is stated in Horatio S. Rubens, *Liberty, the Story of Cuba* (New York: Harcourt, Brace & Company, 1932), pp. 339-341. With the exception of Cuba, Teller favored the acquisition of island possessions.

²⁸ The best account of the war, from the military angle, is still French Ensor Chadwick, *The Relations of the United States and Spain: The Spanish-American War* (2 vols. New York: Scribner's, 1911). Walter Millis, *The Martial Spirit* (Boston: Houghton Mifflin Company, 1931) is a graphically written popular account, which makes the war appear more purposeless and ridiculous than it really was.

²⁹ Leslie W. Walker, "Guam's Seizure by the United States in 1898," *Pacific Historical Review,* XIV (1945), 1-12.

³⁰ The account of the settlement with Spain and the forces that shaped it is based largely on Pratt, *Expansionists of 1898,* pp. 259-278, 289-316, and Chap. 9. See the sources there cited.

³¹ George F. Hoar, *Autobiography of Seventy Years* (2 vols. New York: Scribner's, 1903), II, 308.

³² [Henry Cabot Lodge (ed.)] *Selections from the Correspondence of Theodore Roosevelt and Henry Cabot Lodge, 1884-1918* (2 vols. New York: Scribner's, 1925), I, *passim.*

³³ Allan Nevins, *Henry White, Thirty Years of American Diplomacy* (New York: Harper & Brothers, 1930), p. 136.

³⁴ For detailed treatment of this topic see Pratt, *Expansionists of 1898,* pp. 259-278.

³⁵ This threat came at a time when American exporters were already alarmed at a suggestion thrown out by the Austro-Hungarian foreign minister that the peoples of Europe should combine to resist "de-

structive competition with transoceanic countries" (*ibid.*, pp. 259-260).

[36] Sherman expressed the belief that American trade with China would gain as a result of partition. He rejected a British proposal for joint action to preserve the free Chinese market. Under a subsequent Secretary of State, John Hay, the United States was to initiate, at British suggestion, its well known "open door" policy for China.

[37] Pratt, *Expansionists of 1898*, pp. 290-316. Quakers and Unitarians, who had opposed the war, were skeptical of any benefit accruing from "imperialism." The Catholic Church was excusably dubious about Protestant enthusiasm for missionary work in islands that had for centuries been Catholic under Spanish rule. "The unfortunate people of Manila," said *Ave Maria*, "will remember Dewey's bombardment as a restful holiday compared with the times that will come if the preachers ever invade the Philippines, bringing divorce and sundry other things with them." Other Catholic publications, however, and several members of the Catholic clergy, joined with Protestants in welcoming the opportunity for civilizing work in the islands. They expressed little fear of the results of Protestant competition.

[38] L. A. Coolidge, *An Old-Fashioned Senator, Orville H. Platt of Connecticut* (New York and London: G. P. Putnam's Sons, 1910), pp. 287-288.

[39] Thomas Beer, *Hanna* (New York: Alfred A. Knopf, 1929), p. 211 note; Charles S. Olcott, *The Life of William McKinley* (2 vols. Boston: Houghton Mifflin Company, 1916), II, 109-111.

[40] For the peace negotiations see Pratt, *Expansionists of 1898*, pp. 328-345 and sources there cited.

[41] The old idea that either von Diederichs or his government wished to provoke hostilities with the United States or to seize the Philippines by force has been discredited. See Thomas A. Bailey, "Dewey and the Germans at Manila Bay," *American Historical Review*, XLV (1939), 59-81; Lester Burrell Shippee, "Germany and the Spanish-American War," *ibid.*, XXX (1925), 754-777.

[42] Pratt, *Expansionists of 1898*, pp. 302-304, 340-344; Pearle E. Quinn, "The Diplomatic Struggle for the Carolines, 1898," *Pacific Historical Review*, XIV (1945), 290-302. Aside from the disposition of the Philippines and Carolines, the only serious disagreement between the American and Spanish commissioners at Paris was over the Cuban debt. Spain wished this assumed by either the Cubans or the United States. The United States insisted successfully that responsibility for it be retained by Spain. See Benton, *International Law and Diplomacy of the Spanish-American War*, pp. 236-241.

[43] Strictly speaking, the break had come with the passage of the joint resolution annexing Hawaii in the previous July. See page 76.

Though Hawaii was annexed "as a part of the territory of the United States," there was no promise of United States citizenship or of incorporation. Citizenship was conferred on the Hawaiians by the organic act of 1900.

The treaty with Spain is printed in *Treaties, Conventions*, II, 1690-1695. The "other islands" of Spain in the West Indies were Culebra and other tiny islands off the east end of Puerto Rico and the Isle of Pines south of the west end of Cuba. Long in dispute between Cuba and the United States, title to the Isle of Pines was finally relinquished to Cuba in 1925.

⁴⁴ The debate on the Vest and other resolutions and the proceedings with respect to the treaty are summarized in some detail in Pratt, *Expansionists of 1898*, pp. 345-360. The debates are in *Cong. Rec.*, 55 Cong. 3 Sess., *passim*.

⁴⁵ See pp. 157-164.

⁴⁶ For varying interpretations of Bryan's motives see Paxton Hibben, *The Peerless Leader: William Jennings Bryan* (New York: Farrar & Rinehart, 1929), pp. 220-222; Merle Eugene Curti, *Bryan and World Peace* (*Smith College Studies in History*, XVI, Nos. 3-4, Northampton, 1931), pp. 129-132; George F. Hoar, *Autobiography of Seventy Years*, II, 322-323.

⁴⁷ Pratt, *Expansionists of 1898*, p. 358 and note.

⁴⁸ For details of the passage of the joint resolution annexing Hawaii see *ibid.*, pp. 317-326.

⁴⁹ Opponents of annexing Hawaii argued that the United States already had, at Kiska in the Aleutians, a fine harbor much nearer the great-circle route to the Orient than was Hawaii. The claim was correct as far as it went, but it took no account of climatic and supply difficulties in the Aleutians.

⁵⁰ Thomas A. Bailey, "The United States and Hawaii during the Spanish-American War," *American Historical Review*, XXXVI (1931), 552-560 concludes that if the war and Dewey's victory had not occurred as they did, "Hawaii would not have been annexed for some years to come, if ever."

⁵¹ See especially the speech of Senator A. O. Bacon of Georgia, *Cong. Rec.*, 55 Cong. 2 Sess., 6145-6156.

⁵² See p. 11.

⁵³ *Report of the Secretary of the Navy*, 1900 (House Document 3, 56 Cong. 2 Sess.), 452. The date is erroneously given here as January 17, 1900. Cf. *Report of the Secretary of the Navy*, 1899 (House Document 3, 56 Cong. 1 Sess.), 415. See also David N. Leff, *Uncle Sam's Pacific Islets* (Stanford: Stanford University Press, 1940), pp. 21-22; *U. S. Naval Institute Proceedings*, LXI (1935), 807-808.

⁵⁴ George Herbert Ryden, *The Foreign Policy of the United States*

in Relation to Samoa (New Haven: Yale University Press, 1933), Chap. 15; Joseph Waldo Ellison, "The Partition of Samoa: a Study in Imperialism and Diplomacy," *Pacific Historical Review.* VIII (1939), 259-288; William L. Langer, *The Diplomacy of Imperialism, 1890-1902* (2 vols. New York: Alfred A. Knopf, 1935), II, 619-624.

[55] *Treaties, Conventions,* II, 1595-1597.

[56] *Stat. at L.,* XLV, Part I, 1253; G. H. Blakeslee, "The Future of American Samoa," *Foreign Affairs,* VII (1928), 139-143; *American Samoa, A General Report by the Governor* (Washington: Government Printing Office, 1927), pp. 44-50.

[57] Both party platforms are found in Edward Stanwood, *A History of the Presidency from 1897 to 1916* (new ed. Boston: Houghton Mifflin Company, 1916), pp. 46-51, 58-63.

[58] Fred H. Harrington, "The Anti-Imperialist Movement in the United States, 1898-1900," *Mississippi Valley Historical Review,* XXII (1935), 211-230.

[59] Thomas A. Bailey, "Was the Presidential Election of 1900 a Mandate on Imperialism?" *ibid,* XXIV (1937), 43-52.

CHAPTER THREE

[1] Tyler Dennett, *John Hay: From Poetry to Politics* (New York: Dodd, Mead & Company, 1933), pp. 264-266. Hay's renown as Secretary of State derives primarily from his Far Eastern policy—his "open door" notes of 1899 and his declaration a year later in support of the maintenance of the territorial integrity of China. Not until many years after his death did it become known that, in flagrant contradiction of the spirit of the latter declaration, Hay had sought to secure for the United States a naval base and "sphere of influence" at Samsa Bay on the coast of Fukien province and had been prevented from doing so by the objection of the Japanese government, which already had its eye upon this segment of the Chinese coast. See Charles A. Beard, *The Idea of National Interest; An Analytical Study in American Foreign Policy* (New York: The Macmillan Company, 1934), pp. 83-84; *For. Rel.,* 1915, 113-115, footnotes. Hay realized, apparently, that other governments were paying only lip-service to his policy and hence was willing to violate it himself.

[2] Richardson, *Messages,* XIV, 6327.

[3] The material on the diplomatic negotiations and other matters connected with the acquisition of the Panama Canal Zone is voluminous. The reader is referred especially to Gerstle Mack, *The Land Divided: A History of the Panama Canal and Other Isthmian Canal*

Projects (New York: Alfred A. Knopf, 1944); Dwight Carroll Miner, *The Fight for the Panama Route* (New York: Columbia University Press, 1940); Henry F. Pringle, *Theodore Roosevelt, A Biography* (New York: Harcourt Brace & Company, 1931), Book II, Chaps. 5, 6; Tyler Dennett, *John Hay,* Chaps. 21, 30; Alfred L. P. Dennis, *Adventures in American Diplomacy 1896-1906* (New York: E. P. Dutton & Co., 1928), Chaps. 7, 12; *Theodore Roosevelt: An Autobiography* (New York: Scribner's, 1916), pp. 526-546; Philippe Bunau-Varilla, *Panama: The Creation, Destruction, and Resurrection* (New York: McBride, 1914), Chaps. 16-33. Important collections of documentary material are *Diplomatic History of the Panama Canal.* Senate Document 474, 63 Cong. 2 Sess. (Washington: Government Printing Office, 1914); *The Story of Panama: Hearings on the Rainey Resolution before the Committee on Foreign Affairs of the House of Representatives* (Washington: Government Printing Office, 1913).

[4] The relationship between the Alaskan and Isthmian questions is well developed in Lionel M. Gelber, *The Rise of Anglo-American Friendship: A Study in World Politics, 1898-1906* (New York: Oxford University Press, 1938), *passim.* See also Charles Callan Tansill, *Canadian-American Relations, 1875-1911* (New Haven: Yale University Press, 1943), Chaps. 5-9.

[5] The Alaska boundary dispute was finally settled in favor of the United States by a mixed commission in 1903.

[6] *For. Rel.,* 1901, 241-243.

[7] *Literary Digest,* XX (1900), 202-203.

[8] Dennis, *Adventures in American Diplomacy,* pp. 160-161.

[9] Allan Nevins, *Henry White: Thirty Years of American Diplomacy* (New York: Harper & Brothers, 1930), pp. 154-155.

[10] *For. Rel.,* 1901, 241-243.

[11] Text of treaty in *Treaties, Conventions,* I, 782-784. Source material on the negotiations is printed in Senate Document 456, 63 Cong. 2 Sess., and in *Diplomatic History of the Panama Canal,* previously cited. See the secondary accounts cited above and also Mary Wilhelmine Williams, *Anglo-American Isthmian Diplomacy, 1815-1915* (Washington: American Historical Association, 1916), pp. 300-310.

[12] *Literary Digest,* XXIV (1902), 227-228.

[13] The later controversy with Great Britain over canal tolls, which ended in the abandonment by Congress of its proposal to exempt American coast-wise shipping from the payment of tolls, lies outside the field of this study.

[14] Bunau-Varilla's story, though told with much self-glorification in his *Panama,* is more modest in its claims than Cromwell's account, presented as a brief supporting his claim for a fee of $800.000 for services rendered the New Panama Canal Company. If we take Crom-

well's assertions at face value, we must credit him with guiding Congress toward a choice of the Panama route and the Executive toward a mode of acquiring it. He wrote or inspired (according to his story) the Spooner Amendment, Hanna's report and speech on Panama, and John Hay's notes to Colombia (see pp. 95-101). His brief is printed in *The Story of Panama*, pp. 193-298. See also testimony of H. N. Hall, *ibid.*, pp. 103 ff.

[15] *Stat. at L.*, XXX, 1150.

[16] The Commission's preliminary report is in Senate Document 5, 56 Cong. 2 Sess.; its "final" report in Senate Document 54, 57 Cong. 1 Sess.

[17] Senate Document 123, 57 Cong. 1 Sess.

[18] Senator Morgan's prestige as a canal expert is illustrated by the fact that a Republican Senate had made him, a Democrat, chairman of this important committee.

[19] *Cong. Rec.*, 57 Cong. 1 Sess., 2713. Senate Report 783, Part I, 57 Cong. 1 Sess. This was really the report of a subcommittee on the right of the New Panama Company to dispose of its holdings. The majority of the subcommittee denied, and the minority upheld, that right on legal grounds. The majority's comprehensive report favoring the Nicaragua route had been submitted in the previous December in support of a Nicaraguan Canal bill introduced by Senator Morgan. Senate Report 1, 57 Cong. 1 Sess.

[20] [Henry Cabot Lodge (ed.)] *Selections from the Correspondence of Theodore Roosevelt and Henry Cabot Lodge, 1884-1918* (2 vols. New York: Scribner's, 1925), I, 505.

[21] *Literary Digest*, XXIV (1902), 141.

[22] Senate Report 783, Part II, 57 Cong. 1 Sess. The debate in the Senate is in *Cong. Rec.*, 57 Cong. 1 Sess., 6267-7074, *passim*. For Hanna's part see especially Herbert Croly, *Marcus Alonzo Hanna, His Life and Work* (New York: The Macmillan Company, 1912), pp. 376-385; Thomas Beer, *Hanna* (New York: Alfred A. Knopf, 1929), pp. 261-267. Cromwell, in *Story of Panama, passim*, claims not only to have converted Hanna but to have supplied all his facts and figures. See p. 263 for the statement in regard to the survey of ship captains. H. N. Hall, enlarging upon Cromwell's statement, claims that Cromwell actually wrote Hanna's famous speech of June, 1903 (*ibid.*, p. 180). The statement that a contribution by Cromwell of $60,000 to the Republican national campaign fund of 1900 helped to determine Hanna's position in favor of Panama derives from Hall's testimony. Hall gave Bunau-Varilla as his authority. Bunau-Varilla said categorically "I never thought, and therefore never said, such a thing" (*ibid.*, pp. 71, 158; and cf. *ibid.*, p. 42).

[23] *Literary Digest*, XXIV (1902), 703-704, 858-860.

²⁴ *Ibid.*, 859; *Stat. at L.*, XXXII, 481-484.

²⁵ Miner in *The Fight for the Panama Route*, has given the first adequate account in English of conditions in Colombia at the time of the canal negotiations.

²⁶ Text in Senate Document 456, 63 Cong. 2 Sess., 57-72.

²⁷ *Literary Digest*, XXVI (1903), 746; Miner, *The Fight for the Panama Route*, Chap. 7.

²⁸ Miner, *The Fight for the Panama Route*, Chaps. 8, 9.

²⁹ Roosevelt was probably impressed by the weight of expert engineering opinion favorable to the Panama route. A clear statement of the advantages of Panama and the disadvantages of Nicaragua (among other things, the silting up of the harbor at Greytown and the lower course of the San Juan River) is found in an address by the engineer George S. Morison before the Commercial Club of Chicago, January 25, 1902, published as a pamphlet with title "The Isthmian Canal" (copy in Widener Library). See the same author's "The Panama Canal," American Geographical Society, *Bulletin*, XXXV, No. 1 (1903).

³⁰ *Literary Digest*, XXVII (1903), 246-247, 343-344. On June 14, 1903 the New York *World* had published an article, allegedly inspired by Cromwell, accurately predicting the revolution in Panama, prompt recognition by the United States, and a new treaty. *The Story of Panama*, pp. 344-345.

³¹ Lodge, *Selections from Correspondence*, II, 54; Dennis, *Adventures in American Diplomacy*, p. 322.

³² Moore's memorandum, undated, is printed in Helen Dwight Reid, *International Servitudes in Law and Practice* (Chicago: University of Chicago Press, 1932), pp. 241-246. Independently of Professor Moore, Bunau-Varilla developed a similar thesis in an article in the Paris *Matin*, September 2, 1903, a copy of which he sent to President Roosevelt. Several American newspapers made similar suggestions. See the articles in the *Literary Digest* cited in note 30 above.

³³ *Theodore Roosevelt: An Autobiography*, pp. 536, 544-546. In the draft message Roosevelt wrote that if the course proposed did not meet the approval of Congress, he would "proceed at once with the Nicaragua canal."

³⁴ Of the many accounts of the Panama revolution the most satisfactory is that in Miner, *The Fight for the Panama Route*, Chaps. 10, 11.

³⁵ *Theodore Roosevelt: An Autobiography*, p. 537.

³⁶ Dennis, *Adventures in American Diplomacy*, p. 321.

³⁷ *Ibid.*, p. 330.

³⁸ Miner, *The Fight for the Panama Route*, pp. 371-372.

³⁹ Text in *Treaties, Conventions*, II, 1349-1357.

[40] *Literary Digest*, XXVII (1903), 649-651, 689-692.

[41] Richardson, *Messages*, XV, 6880-6889. For defenses by Hay and Root see William Roscoe Thayer, *Life and Letters of John Hay* (2 vols. Boston: Houghton Mifflin Company, 1915), II, 321-327; Joseph Bucklin Bishop, *Theodore Roosevelt and His Time Shown in His Own Letters* (2 vols. New York: Scribner's, 1920), I, 299; Elihu Root, *Addresses on International Subjects* (Cambridge: Harvard University Press, 1916), pp. 175-306. The official justification of the refusal to permit Colombian troops to land on the Isthmus was that the United States was bound by the treaty of 1846 to prevent fighting that would interfere with peaceful transit between Panama and Colon. What of that other clause of the same treaty by which the United States guaranteed "the rights of sovereignty and property" of Colombia in the Isthmus? This question was answered by Roosevelt in the annual message quoted above by the citation of statements from Secretary of State Seward and Attorney General Speed, both in 1865, denying that the treaty guaranteed Colombian sovereignty against internal insurrection; it was a guarantee against external aggression only.

[42] Pringle, *Theodore Roosevelt, A Biography*, p. 330.

[43] J. Fred Rippy, *The Capitalists and Colombia* (New York: Vanguard Press, 1931), pp. 103-121.

[44] The construction of the canal is concisely described in Mack, *The Land Divided*, Chaps. 40-44.

[45] The entire story of the various American attempts to purchase the islands is told in great detail in Charles Callan Tansill, *The Purchase of the Danish West Indies* (Baltimore: Johns Hopkins Press, 1932).

[46] Tansill, *The Purchase of the Danish West Indies*, especially Chaps. 4, 7. For a naval argument on the danger of foreign ownership see Luther K. Zabriskie, *The Virgin Islands of the United States of America* (New York: G. P. Putnam's Sons, 1918), pp. 247-248. Captain Mahan's views on the strategic importance of the islands are briefly stated in his *The Interest of America in Sea Power, Present and Future* (Boston: Little, Brown & Company, 1897), pp. 297-299; Lodge's are found in Senate Document 284, 57 Cong. 1 Sess., 14-19.

[47] *Treaties, Conventions*, III, 2558-2566; *Papers Relating to the Foreign Relations of the United States: The Lansing Papers, 1914-1920* (2 vols. Washington: Government Printing Office, 1940), II, 501-511. In a declaration accompanying the signing of the treaty, Secretary Lansing stated that the Government of the United States would not object "to the Danish Government extending their political and economic interests to the whole of Greenland." *Treaties, Conventions*, III, 2564.

CHAPTER FOUR

[1] Richardson, *Messages,* XIV, 6377. For excellent summaries of United States relations with Cuba from 1899 to 1902 see Charles E. Chapman, *A History of the Cuban Republic: A Study in Hispanic American Politics* (New York: The Macmillan Company, 1927), Chaps. 5, 6; Russell H. Fitzgibbon, *Cuba and the United States, 1900-1935* (Menasha, Wis.: Banta, 1935), Chaps. 2, 3; Herman Hagedorn, *Leonard Wood, A Biography* (2 vols. New York: Harper & Brothers, 1931), I, Chaps. 13-17.

[2] Text in Elihu Root, *The Military and Colonial Policy of the United States: Addresses and Reports* (Collected and edited by Robert Bacon and James Brown Scott. Cambridge: Harvard University Press, 1916), p. 195.

[3] For Root's authorship of the Platt Amendment see Philip C. Jessup, *Elihu Root* (2 vols. New York: Dodd, Mead & Company, 1938), I, Chap. 15.

[4] *Stat. at L.,* XXXI, 897-898.

[5] Jessup, *Elihu Root,* I, 319. Cf. Dexter Perkins, *The Monroe Doctrine, 1867-1907* (Baltimore: Johns Hopkins Press, 1937), pp. 397-402.

[6] Fitzgibbon, *Cuba and the United States,* gives the best account of United States relations with Cuba under the Platt Amendment. Chapman, *History of the Cuban Republic,* is good to the early 1920's. For the intervention of 1906-1909 the standard account is David A. Lockmiller, *Magoon in Cuba: A History of the Second Intervention, 1906-1909* (Chapel Hill: University of North Carolina Press, 1938). See also Raymond Leslie Buell and others, *Problems of the New Cuba: Report of the Commission on Cuban Affairs* (New York: Foreign Policy Association, 1935); Philip G. Wright, *The Cuban Situation and Our Treaty Relations* (Washington: Brookings Institution, 1931); Leland H. Jenks, *Our Cuban Colony: A Study in Sugar* (New York: Vanguard Press, 1928). By a treaty ratified in 1925 the United States recognized Cuba's sovereignty over the Isle of Pines. Meanwhile Cuba had held *de facto* possession of the island.

[7] *Congressional Globe,* 35 Cong. 1 Sess., 2565. For other appearances of the same idea see J. Fred Rippy, "Antecedents of the Roosevelt Corollary of the Monroe Doctrine," *Pacific Historical Review,* IX (1940), 267-279, or the same material in his *The Caribbean Danger Zone* (New York: G. P. Putnam's Sons, 1940), Chap. 3.

[8] Richardson, *Messages,* XV, 6663 .

[9] Perkins, *The Monroe Doctrine, 1867-1907,* Chap. 5 and pp. 407-411. Of the numerous accounts of the Venezuela episode of 1902-1903

that by Perkins is perhaps the best. See also Henry F. Pringle, *Theodore Roosevelt, A Biography* (New York: Harcourt, Brace & Company, 1931), pp. 279-289.

[10] Richardson, *Messages*, XVI, 7053. In his annual message of December 2, 1902 Roosevelt had spoken with similar condescension of the duties of American nations, but without drawing the conclusion as to the responsibility of the United States (*ibid.*, XV, 6758).

[11] According to Carl Kelsey, "The American Intervention in Haiti and the Dominican Republic," *Annals of the American Academy of Political and Social Science*, C (1922), 109-202, esp. 175, in the 70 years, 1844-1914, the Dominican Republic had 19 constitutions and 53 presidents, of whom only 3 completed the terms of office for which they were elected.

[12] In addition to Kelsey, see Sumner Welles, *Naboth's Vineyard; The Dominican Republic, 1844-1924* (2 vols. New York: Harcourt, Brace & Company, 1928), II, 600-660; Melvin M. Knight, *The Americans in Santo Domingo* (New York: Vanguard Press, 1928); Perkins, *The Monroe Doctrine, 1867-1901*, pp. 412 ff.; W. Stull Holt, *Treaties Defeated by the Senate* (Baltimore: Johns Hopkins Press, 1933), pp. 212-229; two articles by J. Fred Rippy: "The Initiation of the Customs Receivership in the Dominican Republic," *Hispanic American Historical Review*, XVII (1937), 419-457 and "The British Bondholders and the Roosevelt Corollary of the Monroe Doctrine," *Political Science Quarterly*, XLIX (1934), 195-206. The correspondence and official documents are printed in *For. Rel.*, 1905, 298-391.

[13] *For. Rel.*, 1905, 311-312.

[14] *Ibid.*, 317. Cf. pp. 6-7.

[15] *Ibid.*, 342-343.

[16] *Ibid.*, 334.

[17] *Ibid.*, 359-366.

[18] *Treaties, Conventions*, I, 418-420.

[19] See pp. 150-152.

[20] Rippy, *The Caribbean Danger Zone*, Chap. 7. Said Taft in December, 1912, of his diplomatic policy: "It is an effort frankly directed to the increase of American trade upon the axiomatic principle that the Government of the United States shall extend all proper support to every legitimate and beneficial American enterprise abroad." Richardson, *Messages*, XVIII, 8151.

[21] Rippy, *The Caribbean Danger Zone*, Chap. 10, for the attempts in Honduras and Guatemala.

[22] J. Fred Rippy, for example, speaks as follows: ". . . both Knox and the brothers of William Howard Taft *may have* held stock in these companies." "Capitalists of the United States *are said to have* contributed large sums [to finance the revolution]" (*ibid.*, pp. 170, 171).

Cf. Wilfrid Hardy Callcott, *The Caribbean Policy of the United States, 1890-1920* (Baltimore: Johns Hopkins Press, 1942), p. 279: "[Zelaya] *apparently* had antagonized certain foreign interests by attempts to adjust or cancel their contracts and *it is said that* one of these was 'La Luz and Angeles' company in which Philander C. Knox *was reported to be* a heavy stockholder. . . . A revolution *said to have been* financed by the company soon threatened." Italics inserted in all these passages. Such evidence as there is for these assertions comes chiefly from statements made to a Senate committee in hearings held some 18 years after the events reported. See U.S. Senate, Committee on Foreign Relations, *Foreign Loans, Hearings before Subcommittee, 69th Congress, 2d Session, Pursuant to S. Con. Res. 15, Relative to Engaging Responsibility of the Government in Financial Arrangements between its Citizens and Sovereign Foreign Governments* (Washington: Government Printing Office, 1927). Among the best accounts of the intervention in Nicaragua are Isaac Joslin Cox, *Nicaragua and the United States, 1909-1927* (Boston: World Peace Foundation, 1927); Harold Norman Denny, *Dollars for Bullets, The Story of American Rule in Nicaragua* (New York: Dial Press, 1929); Dana G. Munro, *The Five Republics of Central America* (New York: Oxford University Press, 1918), Chap. 11; and Chester Lloyd Jones, *The Caribbean Since 1900* (New York: Prentice-Hall, Inc., 1936), Chaps. 16, 17. Good shorter accounts are found in Rippy, *The Caribbean Danger Zone*, pp. 166-182; S. F. Bemis, *The Latin American Policy of the United States* (New York: Harcourt, Brace & Company, 1943), pp. 161-165; Herbert F. Wright, "Philander C. Knox," in Bemis, *Secretaries*, IX, 335-338. See also Charles A. Beard, *The Idea of National Interest; An Analytical Study in American Foreign Policy* (New York: The Macmillan Company, 1934), pp. 170-182.

[23] Jones, *The Caribbean Since 1900*, pp. 403-404.

[24] *For. Rel.*, 1912, 1092.

[25] It is noteworthy that despite the American majority on the commission, American concession-holders who claimed over $7,500,000 were awarded only about $540,000 and that two-thirds of the awards were for small claims held by natives. Munro, *The Five Republics of Central America*, p. 241.

[26] *For. Rel.*, 1912, 1074-1075. A similar treaty with Honduras was rejected by the Honduran Congress (*ibid.*, 560-562).

[27] Dana G. Munro, *The United States and the Caribbean Area* (Boston: World Peace Foundation, 1934), pp. 236-238.

[28] *For. Rel.*, 1911, 670; 1913, 1021-1022; 1914, 953-954.

[29] Cox, *Nicaragua and the United States*, p. 724; Holt, *Treaties Defeated by the Senate*, pp. 237-243; *Treaties, Conventions*, III, 2740-2743.

[30] Denny, *Dollars for Bullets*, p. 132.

[31] Ray Stannard Baker, *Woodrow Wilson, Life and Letters* (8 vols. Garden City: Doubleday & Company, 1927-1939), IV, 66-68.

[32] *Ibid.*, IV, 289.

[33] The development of Bryan's Caribbean policy is well explored in Selig Adler, "Bryan and Wilsonian Caribbean Penetration," *Hispanic American Historical Review*, XX (1940), 198-226.

[34] Jessup, *Elihu Root*, I, 554-555.

[35] The best recent account of the American intervention in Haiti is Ludwell Lee Montague, *Haiti and the United States, 1714-1938* (Durham: Duke University Press, 1940), Chaps. 11-13. Other good accounts are found in Kelsey, "The American Intervention in Haiti," Part II; H. P. Davis, *Black Democracy: The Story of Haiti* (New York: Dial Press, 1928); Raymond Leslie Buell, "The American Occupation of Haiti," Foreign Policy Association, *Information Service*, V (1929), 327-392; Arthur C. Millspaugh, *Haiti under American Control, 1915-1930* (Boston: World Peace Foundation, 1931); Jones, *The Caribbean Since 1900*, Chaps. 6, 7; Munro, *The United States and the Caribbean Area*, Chap. 4; Rippy, *Caribbean Danger Zone*, pp. 182-193; Callcott, *The Caribbean Policy of the United States*, pp. 404-419. A large amount of testimony in regard to the origin and conduct of the occupation of Haiti was taken by a Senate committee in 1921 and 1922. See *Inquiry into Occupation and Administration of Haiti and Santo Domingo, Hearings before a Select Committee on Haiti and Santo Domingo, U. S. Senate, 67th Congress, 1st and 2d Sessions, Pursuant to S. Res. 112* (2 vols. Washington: Government Printing Office, 1922). Hereafter cited as *Hearings*. The committee's conclusions are stated in Senate Report 794, 67 Cong. 2 Sess.

After the outbreak of war in 1914, Bryan suggested that United States bankers buy out the French. In 1917 the National City Bank of New York bought out other United States banks and about 1920 bought all French assets. *Hearings*, I, 106.

[36] For Lansing's statement see Senate Report 794, 67 Cong. 2 Sess., Appendix B, 34-35. The economic and strategic or political factors in the background of intervention are well analyzed in Montague, *Haiti and the United States*, Chaps. 11, 12.

[37] *Hearings*, I, 313.

[38] *For. Rel.*, 1915, 479; *Hearings*, I, 315; Davis, *Black Democracy*, pp. 161-179.

[39] To what extent there was a definite pre-election bargain with Dartiguenave is in some doubt, but it seems clear that he agreed in general to conform to the wishes of the United States. See Montague, *Haiti and the United States*, p. 214 and note; *Hearings*, I, 317, 325.

[40] *Treaties, Conventions*, III, 2673-2677. The Haitian National

Assembly, in consenting to the treaty, had added an "interpretative commentary," which would have nullified to a considerable degree the supervisory powers of the United States. An unsuccessful attempt to persuade Secretary Lansing to accept this as a valid interpretation of the treaty accounted for the long delay in exchange of ratifications (Montague, *Haiti and the United States*, pp. 222-223).

[41] Welles, *Naboth's Vineyard*, II, 640-680. See *ibid.*, II, 680 ff., for a detailed account of the new American intervention and the conditions leading to it. See also the works by Kelsey and Knight, cited in notes 11 and 12 above, and Rippy, *Caribbean Danger Zone*, pp. 193-201.

[42] *For. Rel.*, 1914, 247-248.

[43] *For. Rel.*, 1916, 240-242.

CHAPTER FIVE

[1] Earl S. Pomeroy, "The American Colonial Office," *Mississippi Valley Historical Review*, XXX (1944), 521-532; W. Cameron Forbes, *The Philippine Islands* (2 vols. Boston: Houghton Mifflin Company, 1928), I, 136-138. The Division of Customs and Insular Affairs also handled matters pertaining to civil affairs in the government of Cuba during the American occupation of 1898-1902.

[2] War Department, *Annual Report*, 1901, Vol. I, Part I, 741-743. The Division of Customs and Insular Affairs had at this date become the Division of Insular Affairs. By Act of Congress of July 1, 1902 it was renamed the Bureau of Insular Affairs.

[3] Seven other Pacific islets, without native population, were from time to time assigned to the navy for administrative purposes. See pp. 417-418.

[4] The Division of Territories and Island Possessions has no statutory basis for its existence or its functions and powers. It was created by executive order of the President, and its functions were enlarged by order of the Secretary of the Interior. Its powers have never been clearly defined. For much valuable information on the organization and functions of the Division the writer is indebted to Professor Rupert Emerson of Harvard University, who was Director of the Division from 1940 to 1941 and was well acquainted with its operation thereafter.

In 1949 the Commission on Organization of the Executive Branch of the Government (Hoover Commission) suggested the creation of a separate administration of Overseas Affairs, under the President, to take over the administration of all territories, dependencies, and trust territories, together with that of occupied areas (Germany and Japan), the European Recovery Program, and certain other overseas agencies. It recommended, however, that Congress provide for a comprehensive study of the entire problem of overseas operation and administration. *The Hoover Commission Report on Organization of the Executive Branch of the Government* (New York: McGraw-Hill Book Company [1949]), pp. 477-487.

⁵ *Dred Scott* v. *Sandford*, 19 Howard 393 (1857), 446-450.

⁶ *Mormon Church* v. *United States*, 136 U.S. 1 (1890), 42, 44. Italics inserted.

⁷ A. Lawrence Lowell, "The Status of Our New Possessions. A Third View," *Harvard Law Review*, XIII (1899), 155-176.

⁸ *Downes* v. *Bidwell*, 182 U.S. 244 (1901).

⁹ *De Lima* v. *Bidwell*, 182 U.S. 1 (1901), 174.

¹⁰ *Downes* v. *Bidwell*, 182 U.S. 244 (1901), 294-295.

¹¹ *Ibid.*, 341-342.

¹² Justice Horace Gray, who joined Brown, White, McKenna, and Shiras in upholding the Puerto Rican tariff, wrote a third opinion, reaching his conclusion by still another process of reasoning (*ibid.*, 344-347).

¹³ *Ibid.*, 282; *Balzac* v. *People of Porto Rico*, 258 U.S. 298 (1922), 312-313.

¹⁴ *Downes* v. *Bidwell*, 182 U.S. 244 (1901); *Dorr* v. *U.S.*, 195 U.S. 138 (1904), 148.

¹⁵ *Rassmussen* v. *U.S.*, 197 U.S. 516 (1905).

¹⁶ *Hawaii* v. *Mankichi*, 190 U.S. 197 (1903). It was held in this case that from annexation in 1898 to passage of the organic act in 1900 Hawaii was unincorporated.

¹⁷ *Dorr* v. *U.S.*, 195 U.S. 138 (1904).

¹⁸ *Balzac* v. *People of Porto Rico*, 258 U.S. 298 (1922).

¹⁹ Luther Harris Evans, *The Virgin Islands: From Naval Base to New Deal* (Ann Arbor: Edwards Brothers, 1945), p. 50.

²⁰ Frederic R. Coudert, "Evolution of the Doctrine of Territorial Incorporation," *American Law Review*, LX (1926), 801-864.

²¹ The evolution of self-government in the individual territories and possessions is treated in detail in the next chapter.

²² Hawaii and Alaska are incorporated territories. Although official usage in designating the others varies, Puerto Rico may best be described as a territory organized but not incorporated. The Virgin Islands are described in their organic act as an insular possession but in reports to the United Nations as "an organized but unincorporated territory." The Philippines were also an insular possession till 1935. Other insular possessions are Samoa, Guam, and minor islands.

²³ Citizens of the unincorporated territories and possessions, whether

citizens of the United States or not, were not "aliens" as that term was defined in the immigration laws. Hence they were free to move into the United States or from one territory or possession to another. Under the same laws, all places under the jurisdiction of the United States, with the exception of the Panama Canal Zone, were regarded as parts thereof and hence were within the barriers raised by United States immigration laws. The Philippines had the right, subject to the approval of the President of the United States, to enact their own immigration laws, but did not do so prior to becoming a Commonwealth in 1935. After the institution of the Commonwealth the Filipinos were legally aliens. U.S. Department of Labor, Bureau of Immigration, *Immigration Laws and Rules of March 1, 1927* (Washington: Government Printing Office, 1927), p. 93.

[24] *For. Rel.*, 1898, 907.

[25] See p. 78. Another very trifling exception should be noted here. Article XIII of the treaty with Spain specified that for a period of ten years "Spanish scientific, literary and artistic works, not subversive of public order," should be admitted free of duty into the islands relinquished by Spain. This provision of the treaty was duly implemented.

[26] There is a useful summary in William Smith Culbertson, *International Economic Policies* (New York: D. Appleton Company, 1925), pp. 246-259. Were the Virgin Islands incorporated, export taxes would be prohibited by the Constitution. The Merchant Marine Act of June 5, 1920 provided for the extension of the coastwise shipping laws of the United States "to the island Territories and possessions . . . not now covered thereby." Application of these laws would have excluded foreign ships from engaging in trade between any two ports under the American flag. The President was empowered, however, to defer the extension to any given possession until it was supplied with adequate steamship service. Extension of the law to the Philippines was deferred until independence rendered it inapplicable. American Samoa was exempted from its operation in 1934, and as of 1946 it had not been extended to the Virgin Islands. *U. S. Code, 1946*, IV, 5141, 5433.

CHAPTER SIX

[1] Jeannette Paddock Nichols, *Alaska* (Cleveland: Arthur H. Clark Company, 1924), p. 38; *Statistical Abstract of the United States, 1929*, p. 6. For later population figures see p. 249. Except as otherwise indicated, the statements in this section are based chiefly on Nichols,

Alaska; Henry W. Clark, *History of Alaska* (New York: The Mac-
millan Company, 1930); Merle Colby, *A Guide to Alaska, Last
American Frontier* (New York: The Macmillan Company, 1939);
George Washington Spicer, *The Constitutional Status and Government
of Alaska* (Baltimore: Johns Hopkins Press, 1927); Ernest P. Walker,
Alaska: America's Continental Frontier Outpost (*War Background
Studies*, No. 13, Washington: Smithsonian Institution, 1943).

[2] *Stat. at L.*, XV, 167, 240.

[3] *Ibid.*, XXIII, 24-28.

[4] *Ibid.*, XXXI, 321 ff.

[5] *Ibid.*, XXXIV, 169-175.

[6] *Ibid.*, XXXVII, 512-518.

[7] *Ibid.*, XLIV, 1392-1394; LVI, 1016-1018.

[8] John W. Foster, *American Diplomacy in the Orient* (Boston:
Houghton Mifflin Company, 1903), p. 382 note. For later figures on
Hawaii's population see pp. 258, 259. Except as otherwise indi-
cated the statements in this section are based principally on the follow-
ing works: William Henry George and Paul S. Bachman, *The
Government of Hawaii: Federal, Territorial and County* (4th ed.
Honolulu: University of Hawaii Press, 1934); Ralph S. Kuykendall
and A. Grove Day, *Hawaii: A History* (New York: Prentice-Hall,
Inc., 1948); Robert M. C. Littler, *The Governance of Hawaii* (Stanford: Stanford University Press, 1929).

[9] See p. 21.

[10] *Stat. at L.*, XXX, 750-751. The resolution also accepted cession to
the United States of all public property including the public and
Crown lands, but with the proviso that the existing public land laws
of the United States should not apply and that revenue from such
lands should be used for the benefit of the inhabitants of the islands.
The resolution further extended the Chinese exclusion laws of the
United States to Hawaii and forbade the entry of Hawaiian Chinese
into the United States.

[11] The Report of the Hawaiian Commission, dated December 2,
1898, is printed as Senate Document 16, 55 Cong. 3 Sess. Members of
the Commission were Senators Shelby M. Cullom (chairman) and
John T. Morgan, Representative Robert R. Hitt, and Messrs. Sanford
B. Dole and Walter F. Frear of the Hawaiian Islands. The organic
act is in *Stat. at L.*, XXXI, 141-162. The act differed from the commission's recommendations chiefly in giving to the President instead
of the governor the appointment of judges of the supreme and circuit
courts, and in doing away with certain proposed property and tax-
paying qualifications for holding office and voting.

[12] Sec. 54; *Stat. at L.*, XXXI, 150. This provision was substantially
identical with Art. 70, Sec. 4, of the Hawaiian Constitution of 1894.

Senate Document 109, 55 Cong. 2 Sess., 44. A similar provision is found in the Japanese Constitution of 1889.

13 The United States district court is a statutory court with the judge (judges) serving for a six-year term, not during good behavior as in a constitutional federal court.

14 Governor of Hawaii, *Annual Report,* 1947, 48.

15 For later figures on Puerto Rico's population see p. 265. "Porto Rico," the Americanized form of the name, was used officially from shortly after the acquisition of the island to 1931, when at the request of the Puerto Rican legislature the Spanish spelling was readopted.

Except as otherwise indicated the statements in this section are based principally upon the following works: Knowlton Mixer, *Porto Rico; History and Conditions Social, Economic and Political* (New York: The Macmillan Company, 1926); Vincenzo Petrullo, *Puerto Rican Paradox* (Philadelphia: University of Pennsylvania Press, 1947); L. S. Rowe, *The United States and Porto Rico* (New York: Longmans, Green Co., 1904); Graham H. Stuart, *Latin America and the United States* (3rd ed. New York: D. Appleton-Century Company, 1938); William Franklin Willoughby, *Territories and Dependencies of the United States, Their Government and Administration* (New York: The Century Company, 1905).

16 *Report of Brig. Gen. Geo. W. Davis, U.S.V., on Civil Affairs of Puerto Rico, 1899* (Washington: Government Printing Office, 1900). The report is dated September 30, 1899.

17 *Stat. at L.,* XXXI, 77-86.

18 *Report of the Chief of the Bureau of Insular Affairs to the Secretary of War, 1909* (Washington: Government Printing Office, 1909), p. 21. The governor, until 1909, reported to the President through the Secretary of State.

19 *Stat. at L.,* XXXI, 716.

20 Willoughby, *Territories and Dependencies of the United States,* pp. 107-112.

21 *Ibid.,* p. 95.

22 The Foraker Act was passed before the Supreme Court had clarified the power of Congress in the new possessions; it was the tariff provision in the law that called forth the decision in *Downes* v. *Bidwell* (see pp. 160-162). It is stated on good authority that in imposing the temporary tariff and in withholding United States citizenship from the Puerto Ricans Congress was moved by a desire to make it clear that it did not regard Puerto Rico (or the Philippines) as an integral part of the United States (Rowe, *The United States and Porto Rico,* pp. 129-130).

Congress evidently regarded the arrangements under the Foraker

Act as temporary. The act directed the President to appoint a commission of three (at least one to be a native citizen of Puerto Rico), which should make a thorough study of the insular and municipal government, the administration of justice, the tax system, the educational needs, and so on, and should recommend within a year whatever changes it considered necessary "to secure and extend the benefits of a republican form of government to all the inhabitants of Porto Rico." The commission made an extensive report in two volumes, dated April 12, 1901, recommending among other changes a grant of full territorial status with United States citizenship, the substitution of a delegate for the resident commissioner, repeal of the 500-acre limitation imposed upon agricultural corporations, and adoption of a provision, like that in the Hawaiian organic act, for the carrying over of appropriations from one year to another in the event of a legislative deadlock. Two of the three commissioners recommended an elective upper house. *Report of the Commission to Revise and Compile the Laws of Porto Rico* (2 vols. Washington: Government Printing Office, 1901). With the exception of the carrying over of appropriations, adopted in 1909 by the "Olmsted Amendment" (*Stat. at L.*, XXXVI, 11), none of these recommendations was followed until 1917, when Congress passed the Jones Act.

[23] Mixer, *Porto Rico*, pp. 85-88.

[24] *Stat. at L.*, XXXIX, 951-968.

[25] In 1931 the department of agriculture and labor was supplanted by two departments: labor; and agriculture and commerce.

[26] Congress in 1927 altered the composition of the public service commission. Thereafter it consisted of one public service commissioner and two associated commissioners, all appointed by the governor (with consent of the senate) for staggered three-year terms (*ibid.*, XLIV, 1420).

[27] The following are the principal sources relied on in the section on the Philippines: David Bernstein, *The Philippine Story* (New York: Farrar Straus & Co., 1947); Charles Burke Elliott, *The Philippines: To the End of the Military Régime* (Indianapolis: Bobbs-Merrill Company, 1917) and *The Philippines: To the End of the Commission Government* (Indianapolis: Bobbs-Merrill Company, 1917); W. Cameron Forbes, *The Philippine Islands* (2 vols. Boston: Houghton Mifflin Company, 1928; a revised and abridged edition, 1 vol., Cambridge: Harvard University Press, 1945, is less useful to the student than the original edition, to which all citations in these pages refer); Joseph Ralston Hayden, *The Philippines: A Study in National Development* (New York: The Macmillan Company, 1942—dealing chiefly with the Commonwealth); A. L. Kroeber, *Peoples of the Philippines* (Handbook Series No. 8, 2d and revised ed. New York: American Museum

of Natural History, 1928); James A. Le Roy, *The Americans in the Philippines* (2 vols. Boston: Houghton Mifflin Company, 1914): Manuel Luis Quezon, *The Good Fight* (New York: D. Appleton-Century Company, 1946); D. R. Williams, *The United States and the Philippines* (Garden City: Doubleday & Company, 1924); Dean C. Worcester, *The Philippines Past and Present* (2 vols. New York: The Macmillan Company, 1914).

28 *Census of the Philippine Islands Taken Under the Direction of the Philippine Commission in the Year 1903* (4 vols. Washington: Government Printing Office, 1905). For later figures on the population of the Philippines see p. 294.

29 The intrusion of the clergy into civil government is described in Forbes, *The Philippine Islands,* II, 53-56, and in *Census of the Philippine Islands . . . 1903,* I, 340-346. The contemptuous treatment of "Indians" by Spaniards, both lay and clerical, is a major theme in the novels of the Filipino patriot, José Rizal. These tales, in their English translations (Manila, 1912), are: *The Reign of Greed (El filibusterismo)* and *The Social Cancer (Noli me tangere).*

30 *Report of the Philippine Commission to the President* (4 vols. Washington: Government Printing Office, 1900-1901). Vol. I contains the preliminary report of November 2, 1899, as "Exhibit I," and the recommendations of the final report, January 31, 1900. The other members of the commission were Rear Admiral George Dewey, Major General Elwell S. Otis, Charles Denby, and Dean C. Worcester.

31 *Public Laws and Resolutions Passed by the United States Philippine Commission* (Washington: Government Printing Office, 1901), I, 5-10. For Root's authorship see Philip C. Jessup, *Elihu Root* (2 vols. New York: Dodd, Mead & Company, 1938), I, 354; Forbes, *The Philippine Islands,* I, 130 note; II, 500. The other members of the commission were Dean C. Worcester (the only member who served on both commissions), Luke E. Wright, Judge Henry C. Ide, and Bernard Moses.

32 *Stat. at L.,* XXXI, 910. This was the "Spooner Amendment" to the Army Appropriation Act.

33 Forbes, *The Philippine Islands,* II, 131. It will be recalled, however, that the first commission had recommended the early creation of an elective lower house as well as a partly elective upper house.

34 Those entitled to vote in municipal elections (by act of the commission, January 31, 1901) were male residents 23 years old or over, not citizens or subjects of a foreign power, who had resided in the municipality for six months immediately preceding the election and who also were comprised within one of the following classes: (*a*) those who had held certain offices under Spanish rule; (*b*) those who owned real property to the value of 500 pesos or paid annual taxes of

30 pesos or more; (c) those who could speak, read, and write English or Spanish. *Public Laws and Resolutions Passed by the United States Philippine Commission*, [I], 135.

[35] *Stat. at L.*, XXXII, 691-712. The act contained no provision for veto by the Civil Governor or the President. By implication, however, the Secretary of War might exercise the veto power. See Forbes, *The Philippine Islands*, I, 130 note. See p. 295, for limits on landholding later fixed by the Philippine legislature.

[36] American achievements in the Philippines are generously summarized in Williams, *The United States and the Philippines*, pp. 121-131. Numerous American Protestant churches established missions, schools, and hospitals in the islands. Their combined membership in 1918 was only 1.3 per cent of the population. The principal defection from the Roman Catholic Church was to the Independent Philippine Church, organized in 1902 with a former Catholic priest, Gregorio Aglipay, as "supreme bishop." Differing from Rome at first in politics rather than theology, the Independent Church later carried on flirtations with the Unitarian and Protestant Episcopal Churches in the United States. See Forbes, *The Philippine Islands*, II, 61-66; Hayden, *The Philippines: A Study in National Development*, pp. 571-574. On the virtues and shortcomings of the educational system see [Paul Monroe], *A Survey of the Educational System of the Philippine Islands by the Board of Educational Survey* . . . (Manila, 1925).

[37] Williams, *The United States and the Philippines*, p. 133.

[38] The chief point of difference concerned the discrepancy in the salaries paid to Americans and Filipinos in comparable positions. The government's policy had been to pay the market price, which was much higher for Americans than for Filipinos.

[39] Forbes, *The Philippine Islands*, II, 217. Harrison was appointed in August, 1913. His initial address to the people of the Philippines, conveying Wilson's message, was delivered October 6, 1913, the day of his arrival in Manila. Forbes, whom Harrison displaced as governor general, is naturally critical of the Wilson-Harrison policy and methods —notably of the selection for the American members of the commission of men with no previous experience in the Philippines and no knowledge of Spanish and of the displacing of three of the four experienced Filipino members of the same body. Harrison's defense of his administration is set forth in Francis Burton Harrison, *The Corner-Stone of Philippine Independence: A Narrative of Seven Years* (New York: The Century Company, 1922).

[40] *Stat. at L.*, XXXIX, 545-556. The sponsor of the organic acts for both Puerto Rico and the Philippines, Representative William A. Jones of Virginia, was chairman of the House Committee on Insular Affairs.

[41] The United States Senate had adopted, but the House of Repre-

sentatives had rejected, an amendment to the Jones law making mandatory a grant of independence within not less than two nor more than four years from the date of the act. Forbes, *The Philippine Islands,* II, 252-256.

⁴² *Report of the Special Mission on Investigation to the Philippine Islands to the Secretary of War* (Washington: Government Printing Office, 1921). The report is dated October 8, 1921.

⁴³ *Conditions in the Philippine Islands,* report by Carmi A. Thompson, December 4, 1926, Senate Document 180, 69 Cong. 2 Sess.

⁴⁴ Henry L. Stimson and McGeorge Bundy, *On Active Service in Peace and War* (New York: Harper & Brothers, 1948), pp. 123-128. Cf. Quezon, *The Good Fight,* pp. 140-147. Stimson's suggestions had been set forth in an article, "Future Philippine Policy under the Jones Act," *Foreign Affairs,* V (1927), 459-471.

⁴⁵ Stimson and Bundy, *On Active Service,* pp. 128-145; Maximo M. Kalaw, "Governor Stimson in the Philippines," *Foreign Affairs,* VII (1929), 372-383. See also Stimson's official account of his administration, Governor General of the Philippine Islands, *Annual Report,* 1928 (House Document 133, 71 Cong. 2 Sess.).

⁴⁶ The governors general following Stimson were Dwight F. Davis, 1929-1932; Theodore Roosevelt, 1932-1933; Frank Murphy, 1933-1935. Murphy became first American high commissioner to the Philippines under the Commonwealth.

⁴⁷ "Happily Columbus was not aware of the latest scholarship which reduces XIM from eleven thousand to eleven martyrs." Robert Morss Lovett, *All Our Years* (New York: The Viking Press, 1948), p. 269.

⁴⁸ For description and early history of the Virgin Islands see Theodoor de Booy and John T. Faris, *The Virgin Islands, Our New Possessions, and the British Islands* (Philadelphia: J. B. Lippincott Company, 1918); Waldemar Westergaard, *The Danish West Indies under Company Rule (1671-1754) with a Supplementary Chapter, 1755-1917* (New York: The Macmillan Company, 1917); Luther K. Zabriskie, *The Virgin Islands of the United States of America* (New York: G. P. Putnam's Sons, 1918). The only scholarly account of the period of American rule is Luther Harris Evans, *The Virgin Islands: From Naval Base to New Deal* (Ann Arbor: Edwards Brothers, 1945). This work is particularly useful as a study of government in the islands; unfortunately the narrative ends in 1935. Other useful factual summaries are *The Virgin Islands of the United States: A General Report by the Governor* (Washington: Government Printing Office, 1928) and *Virgin Islands: Report to U.N.,* 1947, 1948. J. Antonio Jarvis, *The Virgin Islands and Their People* (Philadelphia: Dorrance & Company, 1944), is a popular account by a native. Other popular descriptions

are found in John E. Jennings, Jr., *Our American Tropics* (New York: The Thomas Y. Crowell Company, 1938), and Daisy Reck, *Puerto Rico and the Virgin Islands* (New York: Farrar Straus & Co., 1939).

[49] *Stat. at L.*, XXXIX, 1132-1134.

[50] The Colonial Law is printed in *The Virgin Islands of the United States: A General Report by the Governor*, pp. 36-46.

[51] A person of "unblemished character" was one who had never been convicted of "an act ignominious in the public opinion." A voter must have an annual income of $300 or must own property of an annual rental value of $60 in St. Croix or $150 in St. Thomas.

[52] *Stat. at L.*, XLIV, 1234-1235; XLVII, 336.

[53] Evans, *The Virgin Islands*, pp. 58-59, 217.

[54] *Ibid.*, Chap. 10. See also "Autocracy in the Virgin Islands," *The Nation*, CXXI (1925), 470-473; George Washington Williams, "The Virgin Islands under American Rule," *Current History*, XIX (1924), 827-828.

[55] Evans, *The Virgin Islands*, pp. 275-277, 283; *United States Daily*, March 2, 1931. For Brown's mission and report see p. 286.

[56] Evans, *The Virgin Islands*, Chap. 9.

[57] *Stat. at L.*, XLIX, 1807-1817.

[58] Governor of the Virgin Islands, *Annual Report*, 1938, 8-9; *New International Year Book*, 1937, 771; 1938, 773. The organic act expressly empowered the governor to introduce bills in the municipal councils but contained no corresponding provision with regard to the legislative assembly.

[59] The principal authorities relied upon for the section on Guam and American Samoa are Felix M. Keesing, *Modern Samoa: Its Government and Changing Life* (Stanford: Stanford University Press, 1934); Laura Thompson, *Guam and Its People* (revised 3d ed. Princeton: Princeton University Press, 1947); *American Samoa: A General Report by the Governor* (Washington: Government Printing Office, 1927); *American Samoa: Report to U.N.*, 1948; *Guam: Report to U.N.*, 1948; Roy E. James, "The Guam Congress," *Pacific Affairs*, XIX (1946), 408-413; Earl S. Pomeroy, "The Navy and Colonial Government," *U.S. Naval Institute Proceedings*, LXXI (1945), 291-297.

[60] Laura Thompson, *Guam and Its People*, p. 87.

[61] Keesing, *Modern Samoa*, pp. 199-203; *United States Daily*, October 10, 1930.

[62] Laura Thompson, *Guam and Its People*, p. 70.

[63] *Ibid.*, pp. 71-72; *Cong. Rec.*, 75 Cong. 1 Sess., Index under "Guam"; 76 Cong. 1 Sess., 10,984. Miss Thompson's statement (p. 72) that the Senate passed organic legislation for Guam in 1938 is not supported by the *Record*.

[64] *Stat. at L.*, XLV, 1253. A subsequent resolution added a third Samoan chief.

[65] *American Samoa: Hearings before the Commission Appointed by the President of the United States in accordance with Public Resolution No. 89, 70th Congress . . . and Public Resolution No. 3, 71st Congress* (Washington: Government Printing Office, 1931); Senate Document 249, 71 Cong. 3 Sess.

[66] *United States Daily*, October 25, 1930.

[67] It is interesting to find anthropologists well acquainted with Samoa differing upon the merits of the proposed organic act. Margaret Mead considered it a wise adaptation of American concepts to local conditions. Felix M. Keesing, on the other hand, was skeptical of the capacity of the Samoans to handle practical legislative problems and foresaw trouble growing out of the grant of power to override the governor's veto. Margaret Mead, "Civil Government for Samoa," *The Nation*, CXXXII (1931), 226-228; Keesing, *Modern Samoa*, pp. 209-211.

[68] *New International Year Book*, 1931, 722.

[69] Secretary of the Interior, *Annual Report*, 1947, 359-360; 1948, 411; Rupert Emerson *et al.*, *America's Pacific Dependencies* (New York: Institute of Pacific Relations, 1949), p. 132; *Cong. Rec.*, 80 Cong. 1 Sess., 11,674-11,676; *ibid.*, 80 Cong. 2 Sess., 6228-6229, 7950, 8939-8940.

[70] Letter to the author from Commander W. J. Germershausen, U.S.N., Acting Assistant Chief of Naval Operations (Island Governments), August 4, 1949.

[71] *New York Times*, August 25, 1949, 14; September 27, 1949, 13.

[72] *Guam: Report to U.N.*, 1948, 6. The grant of legislative power was on an interim basis, pending organic legislation by Congress. The Guam legislators were apparently bewildered by the perplexing problems, financial and other, which were dumped in their laps by the governor. See Roy E. James in Rupert Emerson *et al.*, *America's Pacific Dependencies*, pp. 83-85.

[73] *American Samoa: Report to U.N.*, 1948, 5.

[74] George Weller in *Buffalo Evening News*, December 8, 1948; Emerson *et al.*, *America's Pacific Dependencies*, pp. 130-131. Roy E. James, author of this section, surmises that navy propaganda may have had some influence upon the adoption of the resolution quoted.

[75] *American Samoa: Report to U.N.*, 1948, 5; *Guam: Report to U.N.*, 1948, 6-9; Emerson *et al.*, *America's Pacific Dependencies*, pp. 86-87, 104-105.

[76] *New York Times*, June 24, 1950, 5; Public Law 630, 81st Cong. In addition to Guam and American Samoa, the following small

Pacific islands, without native population, have been assigned to the
Navy Department by executive order:

	Date of acquisition	Date assigned to Navy
Johnston Island	1898	Dec. 29, 1934
Kingman Reef	1922	Dec. 29, 1934
Kure Island	1898	Feb. 20, 1936
Midway Island	1867	Jan. 20, 1903
Palmyra Island	1898	Dec. 19, 1940
Sand Islet	1898	Dec. 29, 1934
Wake Island	1899	Dec. 29, 1934

Those acquired in 1898 had been claimed by Hawaii and were
annexed with it. *Report to United Nations on Guam, American Samoa
and Other Island Possessions Administered by the Navy Department*
(OPNAV-P 22-100) July, 1946. Prepared by Assistant Chief of Naval
Operations (Island Government), p. 55. See also David N. Leff,
Uncle Sam's Pacific Islets (Stanford: Stanford University Press, 1940),
passim; R. W. Robson, *The Pacific Islands Handbook* (New York: The
Macmillan Company, 1945), *passim.*

[77] Governor of the Panama Canal, *Annual Report,* 1948, 94-95.

[78] Norman J. Padelford, *The Panama Canal in Peace and War* (New
York: The Macmillan Company, 1942), p. 186. Chapter 5 of this
work is an authoritative account of the government of the Zone. See
also Harry N. Howard, *Military Government in the Panama Canal
Zone* (Norman: University of Oklahoma Press, 1931); Marshall E.
Dimock, *Government-Operated Enterprises in the Panama Canal Zone*
(Chicago: University of Chicago Press, 1934).

[79] *Stat. at L.,* XXXVII, 560-569.

[80] An executive order of September 5, 1939 placed the Panama
Canal and the control and government of the Canal Zone under the
command of the Commanding General, Panama Canal Department,
U.S. Army. Thereafter the governor of the Panama Canal was "subject
to that authority and the orders issued under it." The order was still in
effect June 30, 1948. Governor of the Panama Canal, *Annual Report,*
1940, 1; 1948, 2.

[81] After passage of the act unifying the armed forces (July 26,
1947), the Canal Zone was under the Department of the Army. The
Panama Canal also maintains a Washington Office, through which are
handled the procurement of equipment, supplies, and trained personnel.

[82] *U.S. Code, 1946,* IV, 5406.

[83] Governor of the Panama Canal, *Annual Report,* 1948, 3. Routine
negotiations with the Republic of Panama are also carried on by the

governor. In the cities of Panama and Colon (in conformity with the treaty with Panama of 1903) modern water and sewerage systems were installed by the Canal Zone government and remained the property of the United States until 1942, when they were transferred to the Republic of Panama. The operation of these services, however, the furnishing of filtered water to Panama and Colon, and the maintenance of streets in these two cities continued to be functions of the municipal engineering division of the Canal Zone government. By the 1942 agreement, also, extensive lands in Colon and Panama owned by the Panama Railroad Co., were surrendered to the Republic of Panama (*ibid.*, *1942*, 113-114; *1943*, 103-104; *1948*, 100).

[84] *Stat. at L.*, XLVII, 814.

[85] Dimock, *Government-Operated Enterprises in the Panama Canal Zone*, p. 19. Less easily defensible than the absence of political democracy is the sharp color line that prevails in all activities in the Zone. Paul Blanshard, *Democracy and Empire in the Caribbean* (New York: The Macmillan Company, 1947), pp. 238-244.

[86] *New York Times*, February 2, 1950, 47.

CHAPTER SEVEN

[1] J. A. Hobson, *Imperialism: A Study* (revised ed. New York: The Macmillan Company, 1938).

[2] *American Samoa: Report to U.N.*, 1948, 22; *Guam: Report to U.N.*, 1948, 29.

[3] Senate Document 151, 79 Cong. 3 Sess., 62.

[4] Compiled from *Statistical Abstract of the United States*, 1935. Exports to foreign countries include those from Alaska, Hawaii, and Puerto Rico.

[5] Victor S. Clark and associates, *Porto Rico and Its Problems* (Washington: Brookings Institution, 1930), pp. 586-587.

[6] U.S. Treasury Department, *Census of American-Owned Assets in Foreign Countries* (Washington: Government Printing Office, 1947).

[7] *Ibid.*

[8] For information on Guam and American Samoa see the reports to the United Nations cited in note 2 and also Felix M. Keesing, *Modern Samoa: Its Government and Changing Life* (Stanford: Stanford University Press, 1934); Laura Thompson, *Guam and Its People* (revised 3d ed. Princeton: Princeton University Press, 1947).

[9] Gerstle Mack, *The Land Divided: A History of the Panama Canal*

and Other Isthmian Canal Projects (New York: Alfred A. Knopf, 1944), pp. 544-545.

[10] *Ibid.*; Governor of the Panama Canal, *Annual Report,* 1920, 238; 1922, 46; 1923, 41; 1928, 45; 1929, 54; 1931, 56; 1948, 70, 94-95.

[11] Merle Colby, *A Guide to Alaska, Last American Frontier* (New York: The Macmillan Company, 1939), pp. 59, 65. See also Otis W. Freeman, "Alaska," in William H. Haas (ed.), *The American Empire: A Study of the Outlying Territories of the United States* (Chicago: University of Chicago Press, 1940); *Alaska: Report to U.N.,* 1947, 1948, 1949.

[12] U.S. Department of Commerce, Bureau of the Census, *16th Census of the U.S., 1940. Agriculture: Territories and Possessions* (Washington: Government Printing Office, 1943), p. 13; *Statistical Abstract of the United States, 1947,* p. 58. The estimated population in 1948 was 92,000, about two-thirds white. About 147 of the 623 farms were near Palmer in the Matanuska Valley, where, in 1940, about 4,200 acres had been cleared and planted, chiefly to peas, oats, and hay, though wheat and barley and a wide variety of vegetables were also grown. These farms were the remnant of some 200 that had been started in 1935 to provide for families driven from their farms and homes in the states by the dust storms of that period. Given a start by F.E.R.A. and W.P.A., the farmers were now organized in the Matanuska Valley Farmers Cooperating Association, which operated a creamery, cannery, garage, warehouse, hospital, and powerhouse. The construction of an army air base at nearby Anchorage was destined to improve the market for Matanuska produce. Governor of Alaska, *Annual Report,* 1939, 63; 1940, 60-61.

[13] *Current Opinion,* LXXII (1922), 408-409. Cf. George Washington Spicer, *The Constitutional Status and Government of Alaska* (Baltimore: Johns Hopkins Press, 1927), Chap. 6; Henry W. Clark, *History of Alaska* (New York: The Macmillan Company, 1930), p. 136.

[14] *Stat. at L.,* XLIV, 1068-1069.

[15] Secretary of the Interior, *Annual Report,* 1930, 39; 1932, 32; 1935, 23-24.

[16] Colby, *A Guide to Alaska,* pp. 53-55.

[17] Governor of Alaska, *Annual Report,* 1947, 1-13; Richard L. Neuberger, "The State of Alaska," *Survey Graphic,* XXXVII (1948), 75 ff.

[18] *Cong. Rec.,* 80 Cong. 2 Sess., 6264-6266. *New York Times,* November 23, 1949, 5; March 4, 1950, I, 1; May 7, 1950, I, 1; June 25, 1950, I, 15; June 29, 1950, 8. President Truman's special message on Alaska was the result of a preliminary report of an "Inter-Agency Committee on the Development of Alaska" set up in October, 1947,

with representation of all federal agencies having duties in Alaska. Starting with the assumptions that "(1) an increase in the population of Alaska is essential to the defense of Alaska and the United States, and (2) the development of the resources of Alaska is essential to the economy of this country," the committee was formulating various proposals for achieving these ends, early statehood among them. Most of the committee's proposals would require the expenditure of considerable sums of money.

Congress took one minor step for the assistance of Alaska when it raised the limit on taxation of property by the legislature from 1 to 2 per cent, by municipalities from 2 to 3 per cent. Public Law 593, 80 Cong. 2 Sess., approved June 3, 1948.

[19] John E. Dalton, *Sugar; A Case Study of Government Control* (New York: The Macmillan Company, 1937), p. 123. The following works are particularly useful for the economic and social history of Hawaii in recent times: Joseph Barber, Jr., *Hawaii: Restless Rampart* (Indianapolis: Bobbs-Merrill Company, 1941); T. Blake Clark, *Hawaii, The 49th State* (Garden City: Doubleday & Company, 1947); Alexander MacDonald, *Revolt in Paradise: The Social Revolution in Hawaii after Pearl Harbor* (New York: Stephen Daye, 1944); Helen Gay Pratt, *Hawaii, Off-Shore Territory* (New York: Scribner's, 1944). See also John Wesley Coulter, "The Territory of Hawaii," in William H. Haas (ed.), *The American Empire;* and *Hawaii: Report to U.N.,* 1947, 1948.

[20] *New York Times,* April 12, 1931, X, 7; Coulter, in *The American Empire,* 246-255.

[21] Governor of Hawaii, *Annual Report,* 1940, 4.

[22] Barber, *Hawaii: Restless Rampart,* pp. 226-227. Sugar enthusiasts also pointed out that sugar could be converted into alcohol and thence into both high explosives and motor fuel!

[23] Governor of Hawaii, *Annual Report,* 1943, 2-3.

[24] Senate Document 151, 79 Cong. 3 Sess., 62; Governor of Hawaii, *Annual Reports, passim.*

[25] Barber, *Hawaii: Restless Rampart,* pp. 41-45, 67-80. The five firms were Alexander and Baldwin, Ltd., American Factors, Ltd. (before 1917 a German firm), C. Brewer and Company, Ltd., Castle and Cook, Ltd., and Theo. H. Davies Company, Ltd.

[26] *Ibid.,* 49-54. In 1932 the seven pineapple companies joined to form the Pineapple Producers Co-operative Association with purposes generally similar to those of the H.S.P.A. Coulter, in *The American Empire,* pp. 250, 254.

[27] Barber, *Hawaii: Restless Rampart,* p. 52.

[28] Bruno Lasker, *Filipino Immigration to Continental United States and to Hawaii* (Chicago: University of Chicago Press, 1931), pp.

159-173; Leo L. Partlow, "Hawaiian Sugar Plantations," *Asia*, XXXI (1931), 28 *et seq.*; Lillian Symes, "The Other Side of Paradise," *Harper's Magazine*, CLXVI (1932), 38-47.

[29] See pp. 304-309. The act permitted the Secretary of the Interior to make an exception of Hawaii, continuing to admit Filipino labor if necessary. No such exception was made until the year after the war, when 4,000 male workers and 1,365 women and children were admitted to meet a temporary labor shortage. Governor of Hawaii, *Annual Report*, 1946, 4-6.

[30] Governor of Hawaii, *Annual Report*, 1939, 9. The Hawaiians and part-Hawaiians were, according to this report, divided almost equally between three groups: pure Hawaiian, Caucasian-Hawaiian, Asiatic-Hawaiian. The pure Hawaiians had declined from 134,750 in 1823 to an estimated 21,165 in 1939. In an effort to check the threatened disappearance of this native race, Congress in 1921 set aside certain Hawaiian public lands for homesteads for persons of not less than one-half Hawaiian blood and created a Hawaiian Homes Commission "as an agency to rehabilitate and perpetuate the Hawaiian race by giving the Hawaiians an opportunity to lead healthy and comfortable lives in the open country." Governor of Hawaii, *Annual Report*, 1929, 9. In 1940 only 3,448 people were living on such homesteads (*ibid.,* 1940, 51). The number of pure Hawaiians remained, according to estimates, almost stationary from 1924 to 1940. The census of 1940, however, revealed a sharp drop to 14,375 in that category, indicating that the earlier estimates had been fallacious. The Territorial Board of Health estimated the number of pure Hawaiians on July 1, 1948 at 10,650. Letter to author from George H. McLane, Hawaii Statehood Commission, July 27, 1949.

[31] Barber, *Hawaii: Restless Rampart,* Chap. 5, deals at some length with the question of loyalty as it looked just before Pearl Harbor. For the wartime behavior of Hawaiian Japanese see MacDonald, *Revolt in Paradise,* Chap. 9; Andrew William Lind, *Hawaii's Japanese: An Experiment in Democracy* (Princeton: Princeton University Press, 1946). Robert M. C. Littler, *The Governance of Hawaii* (Stanford: Stanford University Press, 1929), pp. 138-142, discusses the Japanese school question.

[32] Governor of Hawaii, *Annual Report*, 1946, 4-6.

[33] MacDonald, *Revolt in Paradise*, pp. 121-125.

[34] *Monthly Labor Review*, XXXII (1931), 792; MacDonald, *Revolt in Paradise,* Chap. 7.

[35] *Hawaii: Report to U.N.*, 1947, 11. Cf. Partlow, "Hawaiian Sugar Plantations," *Asia*, XXXI (1931), 28 *et seq.*

[36] The prewar statehood movement is well described in Barber, *Hawaii: Restless Rampart,* Chap. 4.

[37] *Ibid.,* p. 116.

[38] Senate Document 151, 79 Cong. 1 Sess., 94-95.

[39] After the end of the war, in a *habeas corpus* case originating in the U.S. District Court for Hawaii, the U.S. Supreme Court held that the provision for martial law in the organic act for Hawaii "was not intended to authorize the supplanting of courts by military tribunals." *Duncan* v. *Kahanamoku, Sheriff,* 327 U.S. 304 (1946).

[40] *New York Times,* January 6, 1946, IV, 8; March 15, 1949, 29.

[41] *Cong. Rec.,* 80 Cong. 1 Sess., 7941.

[42] *Statehood for Hawaii: Communist Penetration of the Hawaiian Islands,* Committee Print, 80 Cong. 2 Sess. (Washington: Government Printing Office, 1949).

[43] *New York Times,* February 5, 1950, I, 13; March 8, 1950, 20; April 5, 1950, 26; April 9, 1950, I, 12; May 2, 1950, 46; May 7, 1950, I, 1; June 29, 1950, 8; July 16, 1950, I, 53.

[44] The following figures showing Puerto Rican birth rate, death rate, and net increase annually per thousand of population are illuminating:

	1900 to 1904	1925 to 1928
Birth rate	28.99	40.55
Death rate	26.39	22.43
Net increase	2.60	18.12

Clark and Associates, *Porto Rico and Its Problems,* p. xxiv. Other works largely relied upon in this section are the following: Bailey W. and Justine Whitfield Diffie, *Porto Rico: A Broken Pledge* (New York: Vanguard Press, 1931), an anti-imperialist tract to be used with caution; Arthur D. Gayer, Paul T. Homan, and Earle K. James, *The Sugar Economy of Puerto Rico* (New York: Columbia University Press, 1938); Knowlton Mixer, *Porto Rico: History and Conditions Social, Economic and Political* (New York: The Macmillan Company, 1926); Harvey S. Perloff, *Puerto Rico's Economic Future, A Study in Planned Development* (Chicago: University of Chicago Press, 1950); Vincenzo Petrullo, *Puerto Rican Paradox* (Philadelphia: University of Pennsylvania Press, 1947); Rafael Picó and William H. Haas, "Puerto Rico," in William H. Haas (ed.), *The American Empire;* Rexford Guy Tugwell, *Changing the Colonial Climate* (San Juan: Bureau of Supplies, Printing, and Transportation, 1942), a collection of messages and addresses: Rexford Tugwell, *The Stricken Land: The Story of Puerto Rico* (Garden City: Doubleday & Company, 1947); Trumbull White, *Puerto Rico and Its People* (New York: Frederick A. Stokes, 1938); *Puerto Rico: A Guide to the Island of Boriquén;* compiled and written by the Puerto Rico Reconstruction Administration in Co-operation with the Writers' Program of the Work Projects

Administration (American Guide Series, New York, 1940); *Puerto Rico: Report to U. N.* 1947, 1948.

[45] Office of Information for Puerto Rico, *Puerto Rico Handbook,* 1947 (New York: The Office, 1947), p. 42.

[46] Figures from Gayer, *The Sugar Economy of Puerto Rico,* pp. 63-65, 112-113, are for 1935. The figures are for all land in cane farms. For lands actually planted in cane the ratios are about the same. Concentration of landholding was not a product of American sovereignty. In 1899, 2.18 per cent of the farms embraced 72 per cent of the acreage. Diffie, *Porto Rico: A Broken Pledge,* pp. 21-22.

[47] Gayer, *The Sugar Economy of Puerto Rico,* Chap. 10.

[48] Diffie, *Porto Rico: A Broken Pledge,* pp. 85-86; Petrullo, *Puerto Rican Paradox,* p. 73. "In 1941, a typical wage earning family of 1.2 wage-earners had less than 350 dollars in yearly cash earnings on which five to six persons depended." *Puerto Rico: Report to the U.N.,* 1948, 97. A sampling of 2,000 wage-earning families in 1947 showed 57.8 per cent of such families receiving annual earnings of less than $300 and 80.9 per cent receiving under $500. Alice C. Hanson and Manuel A. Perez, *Incomes and Expenditures of Wage Earners in Puerto Rico* (Washington: Government Printing Office, 1947), p. 24.

[49] Hanson and Perez, *Incomes and Expenditures of Wage Earners in Puerto Rico,* pp. 34-37. Diffie, *Porto Rico: A Broken Pledge,* pp. 176-179, asserted (1931) that the typical Puerto Rican worker spent 94 per cent of his income for food, as compared with a 30 per cent expenditure by the average American. See Mixer, *Porto Rico,* pp. 217-219, for descriptions of the normal diet and housing of the Puerto Rican worker in the 1920's. Perloff, *Puerto Rico's Economic Future,* p. 80, states that Puerto Rico imports 42 per cent by volume and 54 per cent by value of its food consumption.

[50] A survey in 1941 arrived at the following figures for the annual earnings of different groups of wage-earners:

Sugar	$269
Tobacco	180
Coffee	188
Fruits	352
Building	509
All other	381

Petrullo, *Puerto Rican Paradox.* On comparative standards of living see Paul Blanshard, *Democracy and Empire in the Caribbean* (New York: The Macmillan Company, 1947), pp. 216-217.

[51] Cf. Diffie, *Porto Rico: A Broken Pledge, passim.*

[52] Gayer, *The Sugar Economy of Puerto Rico,* pp. 154, 273-291. In no year from 1941-1942 to 1945-1946 did payments to nonresidents

exceed 2.4 per cent of the total net income produced in Puerto Rico. Perloff, *Puerto Rican Paradox,* p. 113.

53 Gayer, *The Sugar Economy of Puerto Rico,* pp. 292-304.

54 *Ibid.,* Chap. 17; Petrullo, *Puerto Rican Paradox,* p. 112; Secretary of the Interior, *Annual Report,* 1940, 426-427; *New International Year Book,* 1940, 640.

55 Governor of Puerto Rico, *Annual Report,* 1944, 68-70.

56 *Puerto Rico* v. *Rubert Hermanos, Inc.,* 309 U.S. 543 (1940).

57 Petrullo, *Puerto Rican Paradox,* pp. 113-115; Governor of Puerto Rico, *Annual Report,* 1946, 44-45; Perloff, *Puerto Rico's Economic Future,* p. 38 note. The proportional profit farm plan was warmly approved by Governor Tugwell, who was skeptical of the efficiency of the individual small farm. Tugwell, *The Stricken Land,* pp. 20, 87, 665; and *Changing the Colonial Climate,* pp. 28-30, 49-61.

58 Tugwell, *Changing the Colonial Climate,* pp. 69-75.

59 *Ibid.,* pp. 138-142.

60 The abnormally large rum purchases in the United States resulted from the wartime whiskey shortage.

61 Governor of Puerto Rico, *Annual Report,* 1946, 38-40.

62 House Report 497, 79 Cong. 1 Sess.

63 *Business Week,* February 7, 1948; *Catholic World,* April, 1948; *New York Times,* January 3, 1949, 68; October 2, 1949, III, 9; January 3, 1950, 84. Perloff (*Puerto Rico's Economic Future,* pp. 350-352) thought it possible that 1960 might see not 360,000 new jobs, but 169,000—100,000 in service industries, 69,000 in manufacturing and handicrafts. As was to be anticipated, the Puerto Rican industrialization program soon faced charges of unfair competition from industries in the United States. In July and August, 1949, spokesmen for the Buffalo pottery industry were complaining that their business was being ruined by Puerto Rican competition based upon "slave wages" of 30 to 40 cents an hour as compared with a wage of $1.45 an hour in the United States. *New York Times,* August 2, 1949, 32.

64 Tugwell, *The Stricken Land,* p. 36. Perloff, *Puerto Rico's Economic Future,* p. 230, remarks that carrying out a birth control program "is inordinately difficult, but it is *the* alternative to facing constantly the possibility of augmented misery and despair."

65 *Catholic World,* April, 1948, 56; *New York Times,* June 16, 1948, 31; House Report 497, 79 Cong. 1 Sess.

66 The American policy of making all Puerto Ricans proficient in English was a failure. In theory, English was taught in all grades and was the language of instruction in the upper grades. Details of the program changed from time to time. Few teachers had an adequate knowledge of English, and children returning to Spanish-speaking families quickly forgot what little English they had learned. In 1940

only 25 per cent of the population knew English well as against a general literacy (in Spanish) of 68.5 per cent. *Puerto Rico: Report to U.N.*, 1947, 3, 25. Only a presidential veto in 1946 prevented a return to Spanish as the language of instruction throughout the schools, and the change then defeated was accomplished early in 1949. *New York Times*, October 27, 1946, I, 33; July 17, 1949, V, 8.

[67] The difficulties that would result from either independence or statehood are surveyed in U.S. Tariff Commission, *The Economy of Puerto Rico* (Washington: Government Printing Office, 1946).

[68] Tugwell, *The Stricken Land*, pp. 164-165.

[69] Any chances for unfettered independence for Puerto Rico were compromised during the war by the development there of major bases by both the army and the navy. The army had military and air bases at San Juan and at Borinquen Field at the western end of the island. The navy began construction of a major base, "Roosevelt Roads," in the waters inclosed by the eastern end of Puerto Rico and the neighboring small islands of Vieques and Culebra. Puerto Rico became a key point in the Caribbean defense system, and the armed forces were not likely to surrender their positions there, whatever should happen to the island's political status. Incidentally, wartime military and naval construction gave temporary employment to some 100,000 Puerto Ricans, thus easing the economic situation. On the other hand, the diversion of shipping and cargo space to military uses made the early years of the war very difficult in an island that exported its chief crops in order to import food. See Tugwell, *The Stricken Land, passim*.

[70] The Tydings statement is quoted in U.S. Tariff Commission, *The Economy of Puerto Rico*.

[71] *Stat. at L.*, LXI, 770-773. The governor must be a citizen of the United States, 30 years of age, able to read and write English, and must have been a bona fide resident of Puerto Rico during the two years immediately preceding his election. He can be removed only through impeachment by the insular legislature. A clause giving the governor the appointment of supreme court judges was struck out in the Senate on motion of Senator Taft. *Cong. Rec.*, 80 Cong. 1 Sess., 10,644-45 (July 26, 1947). Omitted was a proposal of the President's committee that Congress declare that no change would be made in the status of Puerto Rico without the consent of the people thereof or their representatives. Senate Report 659, 78 Cong. 2 Sess.

[72] Luther Harris Evans, *The Virgin Islands: From Naval Base to New Deal* (Ann Arbor: Edwards Brothers, 1945), pp. 139-140, 151, and tables on pp. 193-202.

[73] Earl B. Shaw, "The Virgin Islands of the United States," in William H. Haas (ed.), *The American Empire*, p. 118. Up to 1945 the United States had spent some $45,000,000 for the islands and for

the relief and welfare of their inhabitants. Blanshard, *Democracy and Empire in the Caribbean,* p. 235.

[74] Donald D. Hoover, "Virgin Islands under American Rule," *Foreign Affairs,* IV (1926), 503-506; Arthur Warner, "Our Neglected Crown Colony," *Forum,* LXXII (1924), 175-182.

[75] Shaw, in *The American Empire,* pp. 99-104; Thomas H. Dickinson, "The Economic Crisis in the Virgin Islands," *Current History,* XXVII (1927), 378-381.

[76] Governor of the Virgin Islands, *Annual Report,* 1931, 3-4.

[77] *The Virgin Islands of the United States: A General Report by the Governor* (Washington: Government Printing Office, 1928), 8-9. From 1919 to 1926, births numbered 5,660, deaths 4,751.

[78] *New York Times,* March 27, 1931, 1, 14.

[79] Governor of the Virgin Islands, *Annual Report,* 1931, 4-5.

[80] *Stat. at L.,* XLVI, 1570-1571.

[81] House Document 701, 79 Cong. 2 Sess. *(Report on Audit of the Virgin Islands Co., 1945)*; Senate Report 777, 80 Cong. 1 Sess.; *Virgin Islands: Report to U.N.,* 1948, 42.

[82] Shaw, in *The American Empire,* pp. 115-118; Governor of the Virgin Islands, *Annual Report,* 1942, 1944; *New International Year Book,* 1944, 703.

[83] *Stat. at L.,* LVIII, 827-830.

[84] Governor of the Virgin Islands, *Annual Report,* 1947, 1-3; Secretary of the Interior, *Annual Report,* 1947, 368.

[85] Public Law 149, 81 Cong. 1 Sess., approved June 30, 1949.

[86] *Virgin Islands: Report to U.N.,* 1948, 23, 25, 43-44. Following the example of Puerto Rico, the municipal governments of St. Thomas and St. John and St. Croix offered to new enterprises eight years of exemption from real estate and certain excise taxes. A hotel, a cement block company, and other enterprises were reported to be taking advantage of these privileges. *New York Times,* January 15, 1950, X, 13.

[87] *New York Times,* March 25, 1950, 2; *Virgin Islands: Report to U.N.,* 1948, 1. It is reported that emigration from the Virgin Islands to the United States was being offset by immigration to the Virgin Islands from crowded Puerto Rico. Blanshard, *Democracy and Empire in the Caribbean,* p. 235. A plebiscite held in November, 1948 showed that a majority of those Virgin Islanders who voted desired representation in Congress through a resident commissioner but opposed making the governor elective. *Virgin Islands: Report to U.N.,* 1949 (Supplementary), 1.

[88] Among the most useful works dealing with the economic development of the Philippines and the independence question are the following: David Bernstein, *The Philippine Story* (New York: Farrar

Straus & Co., 1947); Raymond Leslie Buell, "Philippine Independence," (revised ed., *Foreign Policy Reports,* Special Number, October, 1932); Cornelio C. Cruz, Luis J. Borja, and William H. Haas, "The Commonwealth of the Philippines," in Haas, *The American Empire;* W. C. Forbes, *The Philippine Islands* (Boston: Houghton Mifflin Company, 1928); Harry B. Hawes, *Philippine Uncertainty, an American Problem* (New York: Century Company, 1932); Joseph Ralston Hayden, *The Philippines: A Study in National Development* (New York: The Macmillan Company, 1942); Florence Horn, *Orphans of the Pacific: The Philippines* (New York: Reynal & Hitchcock, 1941); Grayson L. Kirk, *Philippine Independence, Motives, Problems, and Prospects* (New York: Farrar Straus & Co., 1936); George A. Malcolm, *The Commonwealth of the Philippines* (New York: D. Appleton-Century Company, 1936); Catherine Porter, *Crisis in the Philippines* (New York: Alfred A. Knopf, 1942); Nicholas Roosevelt, *The Philippines, a Treasure and a Problem* (New York: J. H. Sears & Co., 1926); Theodore Roosevelt (Jr.), *Colonial Policies of the United States* (Garden City: Doubleday & Company, 1937); Robert Aura Smith, *Our Future in Asia* (New York: The Viking Press, 1940); Henry L. Stimson and McGeorge Bundy, *On Active Service in Peace and War* (New York: Harper & Brothers, 1947, 1948); Dean C. Worcester, *The Philippines Past and Present* (new ed. with four additional chapters by Ralston Hayden. New York: The Macmillan Company, 1930).

[89] Based on figures in *Statistical Abstract of the United States,* 1939, p. 588.

[90] *Ibid.,* p. 697.

[91] *The Port of Manila, Commonwealth of the Philippines, 1939, A Year Book Devoted to Foreign Commerce and Shipping of Manila and the Philippines* (Manila [1939]), pp. 48-51.

[92] Kirk, *Philippine Independence,* pp. 63-69; Smith, *Our Future in Asia,* pp. 97-100.

[93] Porter, *Crisis in the Philippines,* pp. 64, 76-78; Walter Wilgus, "Economic Outlook for the Philippines," *Foreign Policy Reports,* XXI (1945), 202-207, especially 203. According to Porter, about 40 per cent of farm families owned house and land, 43 per cent owned the house only, and 17 per cent owned neither.

[94] Buell, "Philippine Independence," pp. 51-54. The limits given above were fixed by the Philippine legislature in 1919. A citizen might acquire a free homestead of 60 acres.

[95] Kirk, *Philippine Independence,* pp. 63-67; Porter, *Crisis in the Philippines,* pp. 76-78.

[96] Smith, *Our Future in Asia,* p. 97. It is not implied, of course, that there was an equal or equitable distribution of the benefits of

the American market. Filipino landlords were not noted for their liberality, and the small landowners and tenants (*taos*) led a frugal existence.

[97] U.S. Treasury Department, *Census of American-Owned Assets in Foreign Countries.* Some years earlier the U.S. Tariff Commission placed the total of American investments in the Philippines at $200,-000,000 (Porter, *Crisis in the Philippines,* p. 26).

[98] *Commerce Yearbook,* 1928, 1930, 1932; Grayson Kirk, "Philippine-American Relations: Recent Trends," *Political Science Quarterly,* LIV (1939), 321-342, especially 334-335.

[99] Porter, *Crisis in the Philippines,* pp. 70-72.

[100] Maximo M. Kalaw, "The Philippine Question: An Analysis," *Philippine Social Science Review,* III (1931), 305-392, especially 386-392.

[101] Stimson and Bundy, *On Active Service,* p. 147.

[102] Roosevelt, *Colonial Policies of the United States,* p. 181. Manuel Luis Quezon, in *The Good Fight* (New York: D. Appleton-Century Company, 1946), makes no mention of this conversation with Roosevelt.

[103] Ralston Hayden in Worcester, *Philippines Past and Present* (1938 ed.), pp. 727-729.

[104] *New York Times,* August 4, 1926, 4; December 8, 1926, 14. Proposals were occasionally made for detaching Mindanao and the Sulu islands from the remainder of the Philippines and retaining the former if and when the latter became independent. *Cong. Rec.,* 69 Cong. 1 Sess., 8830-8836.

[105] Charles C. Batchelder, "A Philippine Commonwealth," *Asia,* XXIV (1924), 432-435.

[106] *Cong. Rec.,* 70 Cong. 1 Sess., 3490, 5209-5212.

[107] *Ibid.,* 71 Cong. 1 Sess., 3567-3568, 4062-4071, 4369-4426.

[108] *Ibid.,* 4380, 4399, 4401, 4426-4427. Hearings were held at the next session, but a vote in the Senate was not reached until December, 1932.

[109] *Ibid.,* 72 Cong. 1 Sess., 13432-13436.

[110] *Ibid.,* 71 Cong., 1 Sess., 697; 72 Cong. 1 Sess., 6326-6327.

[111] *Ibid.,* 72 Cong. 2 Sess., 387. The signatory organizations were: National Grange, American Farm Bureau Federation, Farmers' Educational and Co-operative Union of America, National Dairy Union, National Beet Grower's Association, Tariff Committee of the Texas and Oklahoma Cottonseed Crushers' Association, American Sugar Cane League, National Co-operative Milk Producers' Federation.

[112] *Ibid.,* 71 Cong. 1 Sess., 4069. More objective calculations put agricultural products at one-third of exports to the Philippines. See p. 296.

[113] It has been contended *(a)* "that no domestic vegetable or animal fat can replace cocoanut oil, or some similar lauric-acid-bearing vegetable oil, in modern soap-making, and *(b)* that the quantity which goes into oleomargarine cannot seriously affect the market price of animal fats for margarine or of butter. It is extremely doubtful if cocoanut oil has had any adverse effect upon American dairy, animal fat or cottonseed oil interests." On the other hand, the Philippines were the best external market for cotton manufactures and dairy products. Kirk, "Philippine-American Relations: Recent Trends," *Political Science Quarterly*, LIV (1939), 321-342, especially 326, 334-335.

[114] Reprinted in *Cong. Rec.*, 72 Cong. 1 Sess., 3646-3650.

[115] Henry F. Pringle, *Theodore Roosevelt, A Biography* (New York: Harcourt, Brace & Company, 1931), pp. 408-409.

[116] Rufus S. Tucker, "A Balance Sheet of the Philippines," *Harvard Business Review*, VIII (1929), 10-23, attempted to assess the profits and losses attendant upon American sovereignty. He concluded that the relationship, though very profitable to the Philippines, was of questionable value to the United States. The reasoning by which he put the annual cost of the Philippines to the American public at $26,000,000 is not entirely convincing, but he correctly pointed out that the Philippines had never become, as was expected in 1898, a distribution center for American goods to the Far East in general.

[117] A study of the attitude of 412 American newspapers in 1932 showed 275 papers (67 per cent) vigorously opposed to independence then or in the near future; 107 (26 per cent) noncommittal and only 30 (7 per cent) in favor of immediate and complete independence. *Cong. Rec.*, 72 Cong. 1 Sess., 6193-6199.

[118] *Stat. at L.*, XLVII, 761-770.

[119] The probable effects of independence on Philippine economy are well analyzed in Kirk, "Philippine-American Relations: Recent Trends"; David H. Popper, "Creating a Philippine Commonwealth," *Foreign Policy Reports*, XII (1936), 233-244. Florence Horn, *Orphans of the Pacific*, pp. 279-280, points out dangers to the long established Philippine hemp (abacá) industry from incipient foreign competition.

[120] The adverse effects upon the Philippines and the resulting damage to American prestige in the Far East were the points emphasized in President Hoover's veto of the Hare-Hawes-Cutting bill and in the letters submitted in support of the veto by the Secretaries of State, War, and Commerce. Secretary of Agriculture Hyde, however, devoted his short statement to a demonstration that the measure would not give the American farmer the immediate protection he needed. Perhaps as a deliberate matter of policy, almost nothing was said about the value of the Philippines to the United States. *New York Times*, January 14, 1933, 6; January 16, 1933, 4.

[121] Malcolm, *The Commonwealth of the Philippines*, p. 124.

[122] *Stat. at L.*, XLVIII, 456-465. The title of the act, unlike that of the earlier one, placed independence first among its purposes and preceded "independence" with "complete."

[123] *Ibid.*, LIII, 1226-1234; Kirk, "Philippine-American Relations: Recent Trends"; Frederick T. Merrill, "The Outlook for Philippine Independence," *Foreign Policy Reports*, XV (1939), 154-164.

[124] *Stat. at L.*, LV, 582; Porter, *Crisis in the Philippines*, pp. 89-90.

[125] For a summary of United States-Philippines relations since World War II see Appendix I.

CHAPTER EIGHT

[1] M. A. de Wolfe Howe, *Portrait of an Independent, Moorfield Storey, 1845-1929* (Boston: Houghton Mifflin Company, 1932), p. 250. In 1928 a leftist group, calling itself the All-America Anti-Imperialist League, conducted propaganda against American intervention in Nicaragua. Over 100 of its members were arrested in April, 1928 for attempting to picket the White House. *New York Times*, February 1, 1928, 5; April 15, 1928, I, 21.

[2] For valuable information on this aspect of anti-imperialism I am indebted to an unpublished study by Dr. Selig Adler of the University of Buffalo. Dr. Adler points out that while so-called Liberals were attacking the League of Nations as imperialistic, American expansionists like former Senator Beveridge were opposing American entry into the League on the ground that it would prevent further acquisitions of territory—in Mexico, for example.

[3] Issued by the Vanguard Press and edited by Harry Elmer Barnes under the general title "Studies in American Imperialism" were Bailey W. and Justine Whitfield Diffie, *Porto Rico: A Broken Pledge* (New York, 1931); Leland Hamilton Jenks, *Our Cuban Colony: A Study in Sugar* (New York, 1928); Melvin M. Knight, *The Americans in Santo Domingo* (New York, 1928); J. Fred Rippy, *The Capitalists and Colombia* (New York, 1931). Studies financed and published by the Brookings Institution were Victor S. Clark and associates, *Porto Rico and Its Problems* (Washington, 1930); Philip G. Wright, *The Cuban Situation and Our Treaty Relations* (Washington, 1931). Other volumes with just claims to objectivity were Emily Greene Balch (ed.), *Occupied Haiti* (New York: Writers Publishing Company, 1927); Isaac Joslin Cox, *Nicaragua and the United States, 1909-1927* (Boston: World Peace Foundation, 1927); H. P. Davis, *Black Democracy, The Story of Haiti* (New York: Dial Press, 1928); Harold Norman Denny,

Dollars for Bullets, The Story of American Rule in Nicaragua (New York: Dial Press, 1929); Arthur C. Millspaugh, *Haiti under American Control, 1915-1930* (Boston: World Peace Foundation, 1931); Sumner Welles, *Naboth's Vineyard; The Dominican Republic, 1844-1924* (2 vols. New York: Harcourt, Brace & Company, 1928). Too strongly biased to be reliable were Scott Nearing and Joseph Freeman, *Dollar Diplomacy, A Study in American Imperialism* (New York: The Viking Press, 1926) and Moorfield Storey and Marcial P. Lichauco, *The Conquest of the Philippines by the United States, 1898-1925* (New York: G. P. Putnam's Sons, 1926).

⁴ *New York Times*, August 19, 1920, 15. Roosevelt later denied having said or meant that the United States would "control" 12 votes in the Assembly; he had meant only that the interests of the 12 states would align them with the United States (*ibid.*, August 23, 1930, 3).

⁵ *Ibid.*, August 29, 1920, I, 12.

⁶ Welles, *Naboth's Vineyard*, II, 818-899; Knight, *The Americans in Santo Domingo*, Chap. 11; *Treaties, Conventions*, IV, 4091-4093.

⁷ Senate Report 794, 67 Cong. 2 Sess.

⁸ *New York Times*, April 27, 1927, 1.

⁹ Cf. *ibid.*, March 6, 1924, 1, 3; March 16, 1928, 1.

¹⁰ *Ibid.*, April 26, 1927, 10.

¹¹ Jenks, *Our Cuban Colony*, p. 265.

¹² See Cox, *Nicaragua and the United States*, and Denny, *Dollars for Bullets*, for good accounts of this intervention. Frank B. Kellogg, Secretary of State under Coolidge, charged that Mexican support of Sacasa was engineered from Moscow. Relations with Mexico were already tense because of Mexican policy toward the Roman Catholic Church, expropriation of American-owned agricultural lands, and restrictions placed upon American-owned oil properties. There was open talk of war. The land and oil disputes were settled for the time being by the adroit and informal diplomacy of Mr. Dwight Morrow. Harold Nicolson, *Dwight Morrow* (New York: Harcourt, Brace & Company, 1935), Chaps. 15, 16. Meanwhile the Senate had passed without a dissenting vote a resolution recommending that if negotiation failed, the pending disputes with Mexico be settled by arbitration. *Cong. Rec.* 69 Cong. 2 Sess., 1843, 2113, 2233.

¹³ *Literary Digest*, XCII (1927), 5-8; *New Republic*, XLIX (1927), 177-178; *Independent*, CXVIII (1927), 257; *Christian Century*, XLIV (1927), 263-264.

¹⁴ *For. Rel.*, 1927, III, 288-298.

¹⁵ Henry L. Stimson, *American Policy in Nicaragua* (New York: Scribner's, 1927); Henry L. Stimson and McGeorge Bundy, *On Active Service in Peace and War* (New York: Harper & Brothers, 1948), pp. 110-116; *For. Rel.*, 1927, III, 339-346.

16 *New York Times,* February 14, 1931, 1; April 16, 1931, 9; April 19, 1931, I, 2; *For. Rel.,* 1931, II, 808.

17 Stimson and Bundy, *On Active Service,* pp. 174-187; William Starr Myers, *The Foreign Policies of Herbert Hoover, 1929-1933* (New York: Scribner's, 1940), pp. 41-53.

18 *New York Times,* April 16, 1931, 9.

19 Myers, *The Foreign Policies of Herbert Hoover,* p. 43.

20 Early occasion for the application of the new policy was afforded by an epidemic of revolutions occurring in 1929-1930—in Argentina, Bolivia, Brazil, Dominican Republic, Panama, Peru. Until 1934, when the five Central American republics terminated the treaty binding them mutually not to recognize revolutionary governments, the United States made for those republics an exception to its general policy of recognizing *de facto* governments. For Secretary Stimson's defense of this feature of his foreign policy see Henry L. Stimson, "The United States and the Other American Republics," *Foreign Affairs,* IX, No. 3, Special Supplement (1931).

21 U.S. Department of State, *Memorandum on the Monroe Doctrine,* prepared by J. Reuben Clark (Washington: Government Printing Office, 1930), p. xix. Secretary of State Hughes had anticipated the Clark interpretation in 1923, declaring that the Monroe Doctrine afforded no support for any idea of superintendence or overlordship in the western hemisphere on the part of the United States. Dexter Perkins, *Hands Off: A History of the Monroe Doctrine* (Boston: Little Brown & Company, 1941), pp. 333-336.

22 Cf. Samuel Flagg Bemis, *The Latin American Policy of the United States* (New York: Harcourt, Brace & Company, 1943), pp. 218-223.

23 For a recent perspicacious estimate of Herbert Hoover see Richard Hofstadter, *The American Political Tradition and the Men Who Made It* (New York: Alfred A. Knopf, 1948), Chap. 11. For economic interpretations of Hoover's pre-inauguration good-will tour of Latin America see *New York Times,* November 25, 1928, XI, 1; November 26, 1928, 3; January 6, 1929, III, 1. Parker T. Moon, "Imperializing the Monroe Doctrine," *Survey,* LVIII (1927), 22-24, had warned that intervention in support of vested interests would in the long run defeat its own ends; that the resulting ill will would adversely affect our trade and imperil our security. Hoover's refusal to strengthen the marine force in Nicaragua in 1931 was ascribed, "according to Senators familiar with recent developments," to "the belief that American trade in Latin America was being injured by the activities of the United States Government in Nicaragua" (*New York Times,* April 19, 1931, I, 2).

24 *New York Times,* December 29, 1933, 2.

25 The Montevideo convention with the reservation is in *Treaties,*

Conventions, IV, 4807-4812; the Buenos Aires protocol is in *ibid.*, 4821-4823.

[26] *For. Rel.*, 1930, III, 217-237. The commission was headed by W. Cameron Forbes, former governor general of the Philippines. See L. L. Montague, *Haiti and the United States, 1714-1938* (Durham: Duke University Press, 1940), Chap. 15.

[27] U.S. Department of State, *Executive Agreements Series*, No. 46.

[28] *New York Times*, May 6, 1941, 6.

[29] U.S. Department of State, *Treaty Series*, No. 965.

[30] U.S. Department of State, *Treaty Series*, No. 945.

[31] *New York Times*, March 6, 1941, 7.

[32] See p. 12. The Treaty of 1937 is found in *Treaties, Conventions*, IV, 4502-4503.

[33] Jenks, *Our Cuban Colony*, pp. 311-312.

[34] R. L. Buell, "The Caribbean Situation: Cuba and Haiti," *Foreign Policy Reports*, IX (1933), 82-92; Russell H. Fitzgibbon, *Cuba and the United States, 1900-1935* (Menasha, Wis.: Banta, 1935), Chap. 7; Hudson Strode, *The Pageant of Cuba* (New York: Random House, 1934), pp. 292-330; Harry F. Guggenheim, *The United States and Cuba: A Study in International Relations* (New York: The Macmillan Company, 1934).

[35] *Treaties, Conventions*, IV, 4054-4055. Signed May 29, 1934, the treaty was approved by the Senate two days later without a dissenting vote. Opponents of Machado had charged that the Platt Amendment, with its threat of American intervention to preserve "order" in Cuba, was a barrier to his removal by revolution.

[36] See pp. 139-141. In reality, there had been little or no effort in Haiti or the Dominican Republic to inculcate democracy by example or precept. In Cuba, on the other hand, American representatives had labored tirelessly to devise sound election laws, and in Nicaragua the three American-supervised elections had been excellent models.

CHAPTER NINE

[1] *New York Times*, March 4, 1938, 1; Benjamin Bock, "Anglo-American Rivalry for Pacific Islands," *International Quarterly*, II (1938), 29-34. See also an article by S. Whittemore Boggs, geographer of the State Department, "American Contributions to Geographical Knowledge of the Central Pacific," *Geographical Review*, XXVIII (1938), 177-192.

[2] David N. Leff, *Uncle Sam's Pacific Islets* (Stanford: Stanford University Press, 1940), pp. 42-50; Secretary of the Interior, *Annual Report*, 1936, 27-28.

[3] For the Canton and Enderbury episode see Leff, *Uncle Sam's Pacific Islets*, pp. 51-63; Bock, "Anglo-American Rivalry for Pacific Islands"; *American Year Book*, 1938, 211-212—an account by R. B. Black of the Interior Department, who carried out the occupation for the United States.

[4] *New York Times*, March 6, 1938, 1. The same news dispatch from Washington that carried this announcement intimated that the United States was prepared to press similar claims to many other Pacific islands under British, French, and Japanese control. It stated also that the United States, through diplomatic correspondence, was laying claim to lands in Antarctica discovered by Rear Admiral Richard E. Byrd and earlier American explorers.

[5] *Ibid.*, March 8, 1938, 20.

[6] *Ibid.*, March 10, 1938, 9.

[7] *Ibid.*, April 7, 1939, 11.

[8] Secretary of the Interior, *Annual Report*, 1939, 345; *American Year Book*, 1940, 239.

[9] *Buffalo Evening News*, February 14, 1942, 2.

[10] Secretary of the Interior, *Annual Report*, 1945, 268.

[11] *Ibid.*, 1948, 412.

[12] Public Law 505, 80 Cong. 2 Sess., approved April 29, 1948.

[13] *Stat. at L.*, LV, 34-42. The act of March 17, 1941 appropriated $4,700,000 for Guam, $8,100,000 for Tutuila, $4,115,000 for Midway. Midway had been given $1,550,000 for defense facilities in the previous year (*ibid.*, LIV, 280). The others had received little more than upkeep.

[14] See, for example, the Town Meeting address of Paul V. McNutt, former High Commissioner to the Philippines, February 5, 1940. *Town Meeting, Bulletin of America's Town Meeting of the Air*, Vol. 5, No. 17 (1940).

[15] *New York Times*, July 27, 1941, 1, 13. The move, following the freezing of Japanese funds in the United States, was a clear indication that war with Japan was considered imminent.

[16] *Documents on American Foreign Relations*, edited by S. S. Jones and D. P. Myers *et al.* (10 vols. to date, vols. I-V, Boston: World Peace Foundation, 1939-1943; vols. VI-X, Princeton: Princeton University Press, 1945-1950), II, 88-90.

[17] *Department of State Bulletin*, III, 127-144. The principles of Article XX of the Act of Havana were put in more lasting form in a convention drawn up at the same meeting and declared in effect in January, 1942, after ratification by 14 of the signatory states (*ibid.*, III, 145-148, VI, 158). The American occupation of Greenland, discussed on p. 343, was effected in conformity with the Act of Havana. So was the joint occupation of Dutch Guiana by the United States an `

Brazil in November, 1941. Samuel Flagg Bemis, *The Latin American Policy of the United States* (New York: Harcourt, Brace & Company, 1943), p. 372.

[18] *The Memoirs of Cordell Hull* (2 vols. New York: The Macmillan Company, 1948), I, 834; Winston S. Churchill, *Their Finest Hour* (*The Second World War*, Vol. II, Boston: Houghton Mifflin Company, 1949), pp. 398-416. The relevant documents are conveniently printed in *Documents on American Foreign Relations*, III, 203-228. See also A. Randle Elliott, "U. S. Strategic Bases in the Atlantic," *Foreign Policy Reports*, XVI (1941), 258-268.

[19] Hans W. Weigert, "Iceland, Greenland and the United States," *Foreign Affairs*, XXIII (1944), 112-122.

[20] *Documents on American Foreign Relations*, III, 228-239; *Memoirs of Cordell Hull*, I, 754-758, II, 935-939. The agreement stipulated that the facilities to be established by the United States in Greenland should be open to the other American nations for purposes of their common defense.

[21] *Documents on American Foreign Relations*, II, 413-415, IV, 453-459; *Memoirs of Cordell Hull*, I, 753-754, II, 946-947.

[22] The United States Supreme Court, in a five-to-four decision in December, 1948, held that for purposes of the application of the Fair Labor Standards Act the base area in Bermuda was a "possession" of the United States, though disclaiming the idea that the lease agreement effected a transfer of sovereignty. The Departments of State and Justice had opposed the contention that the leased area was a "possession." In a dissenting opinion, Justice Robert H. Jackson, supported by the chief justice and two other associate justices, accused the majority of the court of "a flagrant breach of good faith" with Great Britain. "Such a decision by this Court," he declared, "initiates a philosophy of annexation and establishes a psychological accretion to our possessions at the expense of our lessors, not unlikely to be received in more critical quarters abroad as confirmation of the suspicion that commitments made by our Executive are lightly repudiated by another branch of our Government." *Vermilya-Brown Company* v. *Connell*, December 6, 1948, 335 U.S. 377 (1948). The decision seems to have caused less alarm abroad than the dissenters feared. In a subsequent decision, involving the application of a different statute, the Supreme Court held without dissent that the leased base in Newfoundland, and hence the other bases leased from Great Britain, were "foreign country." *United States* v. *Spelar*, 70 *Supreme Court Reporter* 10 (1949).

[23] Hans W. Weigert, "U. S. Strategic Bases and Collective Security," *Foreign Affairs*, XXV (1947), 250-262.

[24] *New York Times*, March 7, 1943, I, 27.

[25] *Documents on American Foreign Relations,* VIII, 920.

[26] A Gallup poll in May, 1944, showed 69 per cent of those queried in favor of keeping the islands conquered from Japan to only 17 per cent opposed. *New York Times,* May 24, 1944, 7.

[27] Nicholas John Spykman, *The Geography of the Peace,* edited by Helen R. Nicholl (New York: Harcourt, Brace & Company, 1944), p. 58. The book was published posthumously. Spykman regarded Germany and China as the powers most likely to dominate Europe and eastern Asia respectively and, hence, as probable future antagonists of the United States. Russia he viewed as a probable ally, Great Britain as a certain one. The early history of the question of postwar bases is rather well covered in John C. Campbell and the research staff of the Council on Foreign Relations, *The United States In World Affairs, 1945-1947* (New York: Harper & Brothers, 1947), pp. 40-46, 81-82, 436-438, 458-460.

[28] *Cong. Rec.,* 78 Cong. 2 Sess., 6931.

[29] *New York Times,* April 5, 1945, 1.

[30] *Study of Pacific Bases: Report by Subcommittee on Pacific Bases of the Committee on Naval Affairs, House of Representatives,* August 6, 1945, 1010-1012. Cf. *New York Times,* August 19, 1945, I, 14. The bases mentioned above were, of course, in addition to bases to be maintained in areas already owned by the United States such as the Aleutians, Hawaii, Midway, Guam, and American Samoa.

[31] The Kurile Islands, which the House subcommittee included among sites for American bases, were assigned to Russia at the Yalta Conference. *Documents on American Foreign Relations,* VIII, 924.

[32] *Department of State Bulletin,* XV, 583-584, 826 (1946).

[33] *New York Times,* December 8, 1945, 2; October 17, 1947, 13; December 29, 1948, 1.

[34] *Ibid.,* September 26, 1948, I, 28.

[35] *Department of State Bulletin,* XVIII (1948), 221, 358-359, 839-840.

[36] *U.S. News-World Report,* January 30, 1948, 14-15; *New York Times,* January 15, 1948, 1-2; May 4, 1948, 4.

[37] Bernard Brodie, "American Security and Foreign Oil," *Foreign Policy Reports,* XXIII (1948), 298-311; E. A. Speiser, *The United States and the Near East* (Cambridge: Harvard University Press, 1947), pp. 125-133.

[38] Herbert Feis, *Seen from E. A.: Three International Episodes* (New York: Alfred A. Knopf, 1947), pp. 93-100; Raymond F. Mikesell and Hollis B. Chenery, *Arabian Oil: America's Stake in the Middle East* (Chapel Hill: University of North Carolina Press, 1949), pp. 90-95.

[39] Campbell, *The United States in World Affairs,* pp. 98-100.

[40] Feis, *Seen from E. A.*, pp. 187-188.

[41] *New York Times*, November 24, 1946, I, 22.

[42] *Ibid.*, March 2, 1949, 1, 20; March 16, 1949, 5; April 1, 1949, 7.

[43] Campbell, *The United States in World Affairs*, p. 460; Brookings Institution, *Major Problems of United States Foreign Policy, 1948-49: A Study Guide* (Washington: The Institution, 1948), p. 129.

[44] *Department of State Bulletin*, XV, 866 (1946); *New York Times*, April 25, 1946, 7; September 25, 1946, 18; October 6, 1946, I, 33; Blair Bolles, "Influence of Armed Forces on United States Foreign Policy," *Foreign Policy Reports*, XXII (1946), 170-179.

[45] *New York Times*, January 14, 1946, 7; April 7, 1946, I, 34; July 2, 1946, 17; July 3, 1946, 5.

[46] *Ibid.*, December 11, 1947, 28; December 24, 1947, 1, 2; December 28, 1947, IV, 4.

[47] In the spring of 1946 the United States indicated to Great Britain that it would like to have full sovereignty over Canton Island and cession of Funafuti in the Ellice group and Christmas Island directly south of Hawaii, on both of which it had established seaplane bases. It did not press these proposals, however (*ibid.*, May 12, 1946, 1).

[48] *Ibid.*, April 7, 1946, I, 14.

[49] For example, *New York Times*, February 5, 16, April 7, 19, May 6, 10, June 27, November 9, 1946; May 29, June 10, 1947.

[50] *Ibid.*, December 2, 1948, 10; February 19, 1949, 5.

[51] Manuel Quezon, president of the Commonwealth of the Philippines, left the islands by submarine with General MacArthur. He died in the United States in 1944. His successor, Sergio Osmeña, was defeated for re-election in the spring of 1946 by Manuel A. Roxas, who thus became the first president of the independent Philippines.

[52] *New York Times*, December 13, 1946, 12; March 15, 1947, 1, 7; March 16, 1947, IV, 8.

[53] *The United States and Non-Self-Governing Territories* (Department of State Publications 2812. Washington: Government Printing Office, 1947), documents and official narrative; Rupert Emerson, "The United States and Trusteeship in the Pacific," in Rupert Emerson *et al.*, *America's Pacific Dependencies* (New York: Institute of Pacific Relations, 1949), pp. 19-27.

[54] Article 77. The categories listed were: "*a.* territories now held under mandate; *b.* territories which may be detached from enemy states as a result of the Second World War; and *c.* territories voluntarily placed under the system by states responsible for their administration."

[55] James B. Reston in *New York Times*, August 11, 1945, 1.

[56] *Ibid.*, January 16, 1946. 1.

[57] *Ibid.*, January 17, 1946, 1; July 29, 1946, 3; October 29, 1946, 5;

Campbell, *The United States in World Affairs,* pp. 81-82; Hans W. Weigert, "U. S. Strategic Bases and Collective Security."

[58] *The United States and Non-Self-Governing Territories,* pp. 30-34, 73-84; Emerson, in *America's Pacific Dependencies,* pp. 19-27; Campbell, *The United States in World Affairs,* pp. 436-438.

[59] *New York Times,* November 8, 1946, 1.

[60] Campbell, *The United States in World Affairs,* p. 438.

[61] The island of Formosa, promised to China during the war, was occupied by Chinese Nationalist troops after Japan's surrender, but until a treaty of peace with Japan could be signed and ratified, China's occupation was *de facto* only. The conquest of most of mainland China in 1949 by Communist armies gave rise to suggestions that the United States should occupy Formosa, with or without an invitation from Chiang Kai-shek, to protect it against Communist invasion. President Truman, however, stated on January 5, 1950 that the United States had "no desire to obtain special rights or privileges or to establish military bases on Formosa at this time," nor "any intention of utilizing its armed forces to interfere in the present situation." *New York Times,* January 6, 1950, 3. The policy of noninterference was reversed in June, 1950. After the outbreak of hostilities in Korea, President Truman announced that the U. S. Seventh Fleet had been ordered to prevent any Communist attack against Formosa or any attack by Nationalist forces in Formosa against the Chinese mainland. "The determination of the future status of Formosa." he added, "must await the restoration of security in the Pacific, a peace settlement with Japan, or consideration by the United Nations." *Ibid.,* June 28, 1950, 1.

[62] The Treaty of Inter-American Defense (signed at Rio de Janeiro August 30, 1947, effective December 3, 1948) and the North Atlantic Treaty (signed at Washington April 4, 1949, effective August 24, 1949) pledge the signatory powers to mutual defense against aggression, leaving the means of cooperation to be otherwise determined.

[63] *Cong. Rec.,* 80 Cong. 1 Sess., 1363, 1410. 1387-1388. The date was February 24, 1947, before the Security Council had approved the Pacific trusteeship agreement. The Iceland minister in Washington was instructed to inform the State Department that the Iceland government considered the Gearhart proposal as to Iceland "improper," and the Iceland press ridiculed the suggestion. *New York Times,* February 28, 1947, 9.

[64] *Cong. Rec.,* 79 Cong. 2 Sess., 4180, 4601.

[65] For example, a Washington *Times-Herald* editorial captioned "We Won Those Bases—Let's Keep Them" (*ibid.,* 4182-4183).

[66] Of the 40 senators who voted for the amendment, 32 voted against the loan, 4 voted for it, and 4 did not vote (*ibid.,* 4806). In

the spring of 1948, 50 senators avowed their willingness to discuss the annexation of Newfoundland with a proposed delegation from that British colony. The delegation did not appear, and in December the voters of Newfoundland expressed their preference for confederation with Canada. Annexation to the United States was not presented as an alternative. Confederation was consummated April 1, 1949. John C. Campbell and the research staff of the Council on Foreign Relations, *The United States in World Affairs, 1948-1949,* (New York: Harper & Brothers, 1949), pp. 349-350.

APPENDIX ONE

[1] *Stat. at L.,* LVIII, 625-626.

[2] *Ibid.,* LX, 128-140, 141-159.

[3] An act of Congress of July 2, 1946 made the Filipinos eligible for naturalization in the United States. Two days later a presidential proclamation fixed their annual quota at 100 (*ibid.,* LX, 416, 1363).

[4] *Department of State Bulletin,* XV, 1190 (December 29, 1946).

[5] *New York Times,* March 12, 1947, 15; Shirley Jenkins, "Great Expectations in the Philippines," *Far Eastern Survey,* XVI (1947), 169-174. There was doubt of the validity of the congressional vote on the amendment. The affirmative votes in each house, though more than two-thirds of the votes cast, lacked a few votes of the two-thirds of the entire membership required by the constitution. Nevertheless, the amendment was officially held to have been approved.

[6] *Constitution of the Philippines as Amended . . .* (Manila, 1948).

[7] *Report and Recommendations of the Joint Philippine-American Finance Commission* (House Document 390, 80 Cong. 1 Sess.), 13.

[8] *Ibid.,* 3.

[9] *Ibid.,* 3-9 *et passim.* See also James J. Halsema, "Philippine Financial Policies," *Far Eastern Survey,* XVIII (1949), 97-102; Salvador Araneta, "Basic Problems of Philippine Economic Development," *Pacific Affairs,* XXI (1948), 280-285; Shirley Jenkins, "Financial and Economic Planning in the Philippines," *ibid.,* XXI (1948), 33-45.

[10] Halsema, "Philippine Financial Policies."

[11] *New York Times,* December 1, 1949, 49; December 10, 1949, 21; December 16, 1949, 49; December 18, 1949, III, 1; December 21, 1949, 47; January 4, 1950, 72.

[12] "Hukbalahap" is derived from the initials of the Tagalog phrase meaning "People's Army against Japan." The "Huks" were originally an anti-Japanese guerrilla force. Many of them were tenantry—"share-

croppers"—and after the expulsion of the Japanese they directed their armed resistance against the landlords and eventually against a government thought to represent the landlord interest. Their principal leader, Luis Taruc, was a Communist. See, among other references, David Bernstein, "Lesson from Luzon," *Yale Review*, XXXVIII (1949), 509-519.

[13] *New York Times*, June 28, 1950, 1; June 30, 1950, 6. Filipino critics of American policy had complained that the United States was not living up to its agreement to furnish military aid; that the military equipment turned over to the Philippines was deficient in quantity and poor in quality; and that the United States was not developing or manning its leased bases to an extent that would enable it to defend the Philippines (*ibid.*, February 10, 1950, 12). The weakness of the American military position in the Philippines was exposed by Hanson W. Baldwin in *ibid.*, January 9, 1950, 5.

APPENDIX TWO

[1] *Trust Territory: Report to U.N.*, 1948, 4-15. See also *Handbook on the Trust Territory of the Pacific Islands*, prepared at the School of Naval Administration, Hoover Institute, Stanford University (Washington: Government Printing Office, 1948); *American Year Book*, 1947, 236-237; Walter Karig, *The Fortunate Islands: A Pacific Interlude* (New York: Rinehart & Co., 1948).

[2] Rupert Emerson *et al.*, *America's Pacific Dependencies* (New York: Institute of Pacific Relations, 1949), pp. 119-126; letter to the author from Commander W. J. Germershausen, U.S.N., Acting Assistant Chief of Naval Operations (Island Governments), August 4, 1949.

[3] Eugene F. Bogan, "Government of the Trust Territory of the Pacific Islands," *Annals of the American Academy of Political and Social Science*, Vol. 267 (January, 1950), 164-174.

Index ～ ～